GLOBAL
MANAGEMENT
ACCOUNTING

GLOBAL MANAGEMENT ACCOUNTING

A Guide for Executives of International Corporations

**James A. Heely
and Roy L. Nersesian**

QUORUM BOOKS
Westport, Connecticut • London

Library of Congress Cataloging-in-Publication Data

Heely, James A.
  Global management accounting : a guide for executives of
international corporations / James A. Heely and Roy L. Nersesian.
    p.   cm.
  Includes bibliographical references and index.
  ISBN 0–89930–747–7 (alk. paper)
    1. Managerial accounting.   2. International business enterprises—
Accounting.   I. Nersesian, Roy L.   II. Title.
HF5657.4.H44   1993
658.15'11—dc20   92–43085

British Library Cataloguing in Publication Data is available.

Library of Congress Catalog Card Number: 92–43085
ISBN: 0–89930–747–7

First published in 1993

Quorum Books, 88 Post Road West, Westport, CT 06881
An imprint of Greenwood Publishing Group, Inc.

Printed in the United States of America

The paper used in this book complies with the
Permanent Paper Standard issued by the National
Information Standards Organization (Z39.48–1984).

10 9 8 7 6 5 4 3 2 1

CONTENTS

PREFACE

The world is rapidly growing smaller and international boundaries are increasingly more transparent to the flow of goods and services. There are few companies of any significance in their scope of business that do not have "foreign" operations. But the word "foreign" now has a foreign ring about it—something that no longer describes "nondomestic" operations. Numerous companies have made the transition from a single foreign operation marketing domestically made goods to a far-flung operation with manufacturing and marketing centers of activity located on every continent. This change in the basic structure of companies and the way they conduct their operations is reflected in business vocabulary. The word "foreign" was replaced by "international," then by "multinational," and soon, if it has not been already, it will be replaced by "global." Many U.S. companies report over half of their profits from overseas operations. Many non-U.S. companies have significant operations within the United States—the Japanese automobile companies come easily to mind. Huge consortia of companies are being formed on a transnational basis, such as is occurring in the computer industry between American, Japanese, and German companies. Many corporations already have over half of their operations outside the borders of their nations of domicile and face the prospect that this trend of greater emphasis on transnational operations will continue. The implications are that the companies are in danger of losing their national identities. At that point, companies become global.

This trend toward globalization has a major impact on how a manager fits into an organization. A rising manager within the domestic operations of a U.S. company, for example, will eventually reach a level where he or she is responsible for an operation where distance makes it impossible for him or her to manage through daily observation. An occasional visit may greatly enhance his or her appreciation of the inner workings of an affiliate that is an ocean away in distance and a world away in culture. But, on a day-to-day basis, the manager must ultimately rely on a comprehensive and sophisticated financial reporting and control system to do the job. This book is intended to be an aid to managers making the transition from managing a domestic operation in person to assuming the responsibility of overseeing diverse operations in different countries in absentia.

If a manager overseeing such operations must rely on financial reporting and control systems, then he or she must have an appreciation of the accounting practices that form the foundation, or basis, of these reports. Helping managers gain this appreciation is one of the purposes of this book. Another purpose is to acquaint a manager with challenges that were not present in managing a domestic operation. The challenges associated with overseas operations include exposure to various currencies, some of which may not be easily convertible to U.S. dollars; setting transfer prices for goods moving between affiliates in different nations; transaction and translation gains and losses; the means to counter potential losses when dealing in multiple currencies; and managerial control of far-flung operations. Moreover, a manager needs to appreciate the ''bottom line'' impact of these issues if he or she is to perform effectively.

Formalized education in international business and in appreciating the international aspects of accounting has been somewhat limited in U.S. business schools. The ''internationalization'' of business school curricula is a fairly recent phenomenon, which can be viewed as somewhat beyond its infancy, but probably not yet at the adolescent stage. The appreciation of accounting beyond U.S. borders can better be described as being in its embryonic stage in U.S. business school curricula.

This book however, is not intended to be a textbook as such, but is rather intended as a guide for managers of multinational companies who wish to better understand the complex workings of a global business. The focus of this book is on the gathering, analysis, and interpretation of financial information used in the management decision-making process. Numerous examples of real-world situations are incorporated into the material, along with step-by-step explanations. A bibliography is provided for readers who wish to pursue particular topics in greater detail. The names and addresses of principal accounting organizations around the world are also furnished to aid readers in investigating the financial implications of a managerial decision within a specific nation.

We wish to acknowledge the contributions of the authors of the periodicals and books listed in the bibliography, because these constitute the invaluable reference material used in writing the book. We also wish to thank our wives, Cathy and Marie, for their understanding and patience; Joann Neminski and Marcy Catelli for their valued assistance in researching material; and the faculty and staff of Monmouth College for their kind support.

GLOBAL MANAGEMENT ACCOUNTING

CHAPTER 1

TREND TOWARD GLOBALIZATION

The United States emerged as the world's most dynamic commercial power after World War II. Winning the war without any battles being fought on its soil, and with much of Europe and Japan lying in ruins, American industrial might was unchallenged for a decade or so after the war. This position of preeminence bred overconfidence. As an example, the term "international business" was parochially understood to mean a U.S. firm opening up a branch office, say, in France, to assist the parent in selling American goods in the European market. As Europe recovered from the devastation of war, the concept of international business expanded from a marketing function of U.S. products sold overseas to a manufacturing function of U.S licensed products made, and sold, overseas. This was an early, generally unrecognized, step in the process of globalization, a word that has only fairly recently entered into the business vocabulary. Globalization of commerce and trade took another step forward when the intent of building a manufacturing plant in Europe was the marketing of the goods not just within Europe but outside Europe, including the United States itself.

This exceeded the boundaries of meaning implied by the phrase "international business." This new variant of international business required a new name: the "multinational corporation." The designation multinational corporation, according to a professor at a prestigious institution, could be achieved if a company was a Fortune 500 company with at least a 25 percent equity investment in manufacturing facilities in at least six different nations. This was still a rather parochial view of international or multinational, because the company must be a U.S. domiciled company numbered among the Fortune 500.

By this definition, the multinational company did not come into existence after World War II, but in the latter half of the nineteenth century. Isaac Singer, the inventor of the sewing machine, was both a mechanical and a marketing genius who first recognized the value of advertising, demonstrations, training, and selling on credit. He created an effective sales force of women trained on Singer sewing machines, who, in turn, created a market for Singer machines by teaching other women how to sew using a Singer machine. Isaac Singer knew that women trained on a Singer sewing machine would be most likely to buy a Singer sewing machine, which goes a long way toward explaining why Apple computers are so often found in elementary schools today.

Most families did not have sufficient cash to purchase a sewing machine outright. Singer responded to this impediment to sales by introducing the hire purchase method of buying a sewing machine. All he required was a small down payment followed by monthly payments thereafter, with ownership transferred to the purchaser with the last payment. This gave birth to buying on credit, an indispensable aspect of modern marketing embodied in credit cards. Singer built the world's largest factory of its time in Elizabeth, New Jersey, for the efficient "assembly" of a half million sewing machines per year. Some have maintained that the Elizabeth factory deserved the appellation of "mass production," which is a term invented later to describe the size of Henry Ford's assembly operations.

Isaac Singer also recognized the potential for marketing sewing machines on a worldwide basis. He opened a large factory in Scotland to sell sewing machines in England and built manufacturing plants on other continents and marketed his sewing machines on a global basis. Virtually no village, no matter how remote from the mainstream of civilization, was without a hand- or foot-powered sewing machine. The Singer sewing machine, prominently displayed in the front window of many a cottage, was the symbol of prosperity—not unlike having a luxury automobile parked in one's driveway today. Isaac Singer achieved multinational status in the nineteenth century. If he had a decentralized operation, his might have been the first global company.

GLOBAL BUSINESS

What is new is not international or multinational business, but global business. Global business implies that the parent, or founding, company has become indistinguishable in relative importance from the other operating affiliates. It means that the dominating culture within a global business enterprise is not necessarily American or French or any other nationality. An imaginary global company may be domiciled in the Netherlands Antilles. The home office may be not much more than a communications center tying the various corporate entities together. The choice of the Netherlands Antilles may be for local reporting requirements (minimal), tax advantages (little or no taxes for activities carried out by the home office), access to the international banking community (easy in this age of instant communications), and access to a recognized legal system for the resolution of corporate matters and disputes and to an accepted set of accounting principles for the issuance of consolidated financial reports (the Dutch legal and accounting systems). The choice of the Netherlands Antilles as the corporate headquarters may also be a way of communicating to the world that no particular nation can lay claim as being the nation of domicile or as being the dominant culture within the corporation.

Below the corporate parent would be divisions representing the interests of the company in broad areas of the world, such as continents. Below these would be another layer of organizations representing the business interests of the global corporation in various countries on the continent. Herein lie the beginnings of complications both in operational, organizational, and marketing matters and in financial reporting. The European organization may be headquartered in Switzerland, which may also handle Swiss sales. The Swiss organization may own 75 percent of the company conducting business in Spain and Portugal. This company may conduct business in Morocco through an operating affiliate that is 50 percent owned by a Moroccan company. The Moroccan affiliate may, in turn, own a partial interest in the organization's activities in France, and the French affiliate, in turn, may end up owning a partial interest in another company in Switzerland, which, in effect, competes with the Swiss corporate entity that is supposed to be running matters in Europe. A common problem for multinational companies conducting business through various operational affiliates is the matter of jurisdiction, the drawing of boundary lines separating the activities of one corporate entity from another.

The nature of the corporate organization may be simple when the parent organization sets up manufacturing and marketing affiliates dedicated to serving the company's interests within the borders of a nation. At other times, it may be more convoluted, not to confuse outsiders but to ensure a degree of ownership and, therefore, active involvement of managers responsible for the corporation's operations in their locality. This, in turn, is usually a consequence of a company expanding into a new area where a corporate beachhead has to be first established. This can be accomplished by forming a new affiliate partly owned by key persons, or a local company, to ensure the success of the new venture.

A truly global company probably does not yet exist. The business that is nearest to being organized in this fashion is shipping. A shipping company may have its headquarters domiciled in Bermuda, its marketing organization in New York, its operational organization in London, its manning of vessels conducted through companies in Italy and Pakistan, and may operate its principal assets, ships, under Panamanian and Liberian companies. The company's business is global, moving goods and commodities from one part of the world to another. The orientation of management is global, with little association with any particular country. Many shipping companies, although not all, exhibit little reluctance to move their operations from one country to another, if local government regulations make it uncomfortable for them to remain. This global attitude toward the organization and the operation of a company exists because the corporate assets float. Most companies have assets solidly fixed to land.

Most companies are understandably organized in a more provincial fashion because their assets are not easily moved from the jurisdiction of one country to that of another. However, there certainly is a tendency for companies to conduct their business on a more global basis. No company is forever fixed to any one nation as long as it enjoys the right to build new factories in whatever nation provides the most attractive and stable environment. Therefore, over a long period of time, a company can, and often will, redeploy its assets from one nation to many nations.

THE PROGRESS OF GLOBALIZATION

To examine the nature of the organization of companies operating on a world-wide basis, and to sense the trend of companies becoming more global in their activities, we reviewed annual reports of two arbitrarily selected American companies. One is a major pharmaceutical company and the other a major oil services and chemical company. The pharmaceutical company has operations within the United States, which are conducted through thirty wholly owned corporate entities. These, in turn, have wholly owned operating affiliates in different countries. For instance, Canada is served by eight wholly owned operating affiliates reporting directly to various wholly owned subsidiaries of the U.S. parent organization. In other words, the operating affiliates in Canada do not report directly to the parent organization but to various corporate entities beneath the parent. Thus, there appears to be no direct corporate link between a non-U.S. operating affiliate and the parent organization.

From one to three wholly owned operating affiliates represent the company's business in manufacturing, marketing, and distribution in each of thirteen Latin American countries. From one to ten operating affiliates do business in each of seventeen European countries including Poland, Hungary, Turkey, and Yugoslavia. Anywhere from one to five operating affiliates are in each of twenty-one nations in Australia, the Far and Middle East, and Africa. Presumably, other nations without operating affiliates within their borders are served by those in nations that do have such representation. Perhaps there is cooperative sharing of the market by different operating affiliates. Perhaps they compete for business as though there were no common ownership of the company's shares. Anything is possible in the operations of a multinational company.

The corporate parent issues one income statement and balance sheet. Yet the company consists, from an operating point of view, of over 170 independent companies listed in the company's annual report. Each of these companies may have its own set of subsidiary companies performing marketing and distribution functions in different locales. Even if there is only an average of three such subsidiaries per listed affiliate, there are over five hundred separate entities whose financial reports have to be consolidated or combined, one way or another, into a single annual report to the shareholders.

In a three-year period, the share of revenues for this company in the United States compared to the total revenues fell from 51 percent to 48 percent. Whereas the share of U.S. operating profit rose during this particular three-year period, the percentage of identifiable assets in the United States fell from 54 percent to 52 percent. Although these are not spectacular changes, the trend, if it continues for a decade or so, will certainly make the company less American and more global.

The second example is an oil service and chemical company. Its chemical division is headquartered in the United States with eleven operating affiliates in Europe. However, these are not all wholly owned. Two are 70 percent owned and another is only 15 percent owned by the American parent. The company's petroleum services business is handled by ten separate American corporations that are wholly owned, plus thirty-five others scattered on every continent of the world. Ownership in these operating affiliates varies from 25 percent to 100 percent. About half of the operating affiliates outside the United States are not wholly owned by the U.S. parent.

Owning less than 100 percent of an operating affiliate casts a different light on the role of management. The parent organization cannot manage a partially owned operating affiliate without taking into consideration the minority or majority shareholders. These minority or majority holdings are there for a reason, usually associated with the founding of the affiliate or the expansion of its sphere of activity. The company's annual report, a single set of figures on its income statement and balance sheet, has to reflect not only the large number of operating affiliates making up the whole company, and their respective subsidiaries, but also the fact that these operating affiliates, through which the company conducts its business, are not wholly owned.

For this particular company, an arbitrarily selected three-year period shows that U.S. revenues remained flat at 57 percent of total revenues and assets in the United States remained flat at 51 percent of all assets. However, nearly all operating profit was made outside of the United States. If this is where the profits lie, then this is where new capital investments will be made. With time, this company, too, will become less American.

In some respects, both of these companies, with about a half share of their assets and revenues in the United States, may be more global than one may surmise. In the past, a U.S. subsidiary on non-U.S. soil was headed by an American corporate management team, with local nationals restricted to manning the lower rungs of the management ladder. Decision making was somewhat centralized, with the parent organization playing a decisive role in the operations of an affiliate. Now a corporate entity at a non-U.S. location is apt to be manned from top to bottom by local nationals. Decision making is far more decentralized, with greater emphasis on financial reporting as the primary control mechanism. Although it is true that the U.S. corporate headquarters retains the right to approve major capital expenditures and top executive positions, day-to-day operational, marketing, and personnel decisions are usually made at the local level.

True globalization of these companies may occur when the U.S. corporate parent becomes the U.S. operating affiliate of a company whose headquarters has been moved to Bermuda. The headquarters itself may be no more than a coordination and financial reporting center. A global company is no longer an American or a French company with a large number of foreign subsidiaries. Rather, it is a collection of corporate entities each concentrating in pursuing the company's business in a geographic area. There is no dominant culture within the company, because there is no dominant national corporate entity within the company.

A manager of any nationality has a chance to achieve the ranks of top management. The role of top management is to guide the overall direction of the company in pursuit of an agreed on set of corporate objectives. The role of top management has not changed—it is just that when they do meet around a table, they may not be all of one nationality. They may not even meet around a table. Teleconferencing can electronically create a conference without the physical presence of the participants. Modern means of communications can tie together the top management team no matter where they are located. The orientation of top management may not be bound by the political or economic considerations of any one nation.

The quintessential American company, Coca-Cola, has banned the words "domestic" and "foreign" from corporate communication. Although Americans are still the largest per capita consumers of Coca-Cola, the United States only has about 5 percent of the world's population. That means that 95 percent of the potential market is outside the United States. The U.S. market, in 1991, represented one third of sales and one fifth of the operating income for Coca-Cola. Not only is four fifths, or 80 percent, of operating income outside the United States, but the non-U.S. share is growing and is expected to reach 90 percent in a few years. Top management is increasingly non-American. This is intentional because Coca-Cola wants to become a global company with global management. Coca-Cola is even thinking of global advertising, one commercial to be aired throughout the world. The excerpts from its 1991 annual report in Table 1.1 show the higher growth rates in Coca-Cola consumption in non-U.S. areas of the world than in the United States. A comparison of the ten-year with the five-year figures indicates that this trend is accelerating. The market highlights reveal the company's orientation to penetrating the global market. Clearly, with the passage of time, Coca-Cola's being American in origin will be an historic footnote.

GLOBALIZATION IN OCEAN AND MONMOUTH COUNTIES

Globalization does not only mean American companies becoming less American. Globalization also means non-American companies becoming more American. Ocean and Monmouth counties are two typical New Jersey counties, as American as apple pie. Yet, many people in these two counties work for corporate entities that are owned by non-U.S. companies. A&P is a food retailer employing one thousand people in the two counties. Once A&P was an all-American institution known as the Great Atlantic and Pacific Tea Company, with retail food

Table 1.1
Summary of Selected Country Results—
Estimated Carbonated Soft Drink Unit Case Sales[1]

	Average Annual Growth				1990 Results			
	10 Years		5 Years		Unit Case Growth		Company	
	Company	Industry	Company	Industry	Company	Industry	Share	Per Capita Consumption
Worldwide[2]	6%	4%	7%	5%	7%	4%	44%	83
United States	5	4	5	4	4	3	41	292
International	6	5	9	5	8	5	46	59
European Community	8	5	11	6	12	9	42	109
Germany	5	4	6	8	14	7	42	149
Great Britain	14	7	23	9	8	6	32	99
France	12	5	16	10	22	12	37	48
Pacific[3]	8	7	9	7	11	9	44	41
Australia	7	5	10	6	9	5	54	224
Japan[3]	6	8	7	7	14	10	33	112
Philippines	13	5	10	7	6	10	71	92
Northeast Europe/Africa	7	6	7	1	8	0	35	26
Norway	11	6	13	5	9	3	55	200
Austria	5	6	9	10	17	12	44	128
Turkey	21	11	27	16	23	14	43	20
Latin America	5	4	8	5	4	3	51	125
Brazil	6	5	14	12	3	0	59	99
Colombia	6	3	4	2	1	1	42	111
Mexico	6	5	6	5	4	5	51	263

[1]*Unit case equals 24 8-ounce drinks* [2]*Excludes Soviet Union and China* [3]*Includes Japanese non-carbonated soft drinks*

Table 1.1 (continued)

Market Highlights

United States
Most developed market, with great opportunity ahead... key bottle/can growth channels: mass merchandisers, drug store chains, petroleum retailers, warehouse clubs... incremental fountain growth through several new major accounts...share gain of 0.6 points to 41 percent and the largest share advantage ever over our main U.S. competitor...one share point is 74 million unit cases

Germany
Focus on Coca-Cola, Coke light, Sprite and Fanta... bottling efficiencies gained through continued system rationalization...64 bottling entities consolidated into 37 in 1990...incremental growth provided by new eastern German market

Great Britain
Coca-Cola & Schweppes Beverages highly successful joint venture...four-year average unit case growth 22 percent...larger PET packages and can multipacks support volume advances...new production plant planned for southern England

France
Company-owned bottler handles 91 percent of volume... production rationalized...reorganized total sales function to provide national account service...16,000 vending machines and 5,000 post-mix dispensers placed in 1990... aggressive merchandising added 20,000 displays, 700 coolers in 5,000 supermarkets

Australia
Highest per capita consumption in Pacific...86 percent share of cola segment...growth forged by aggressive marketing, expanded availability...vending machines to double to 50,000 by end of decade

Japan
Coca-Cola leads cola segment with 80 percent share... Company products lead world's largest non-carbonated segment...world's highest vending machine per capita... more than 750,000 in place

Philippines
San Miguel joint venture global model since 1981 formation...14 percent average annual unit case growth since 1981...new Santa Rosa superplant helped meet Manila demand...significant post-mix opportunity...three-year average post-mix growth of nearly 25 percent

Norway
Fanta mandarin rollout sparked growth...1.5 liter returnable/refillable PET launching extended packaging innovation...12 percent Coke light share is among world's highest

Austria
Value pricing strategy and point-of-sale merchandising generated double-digit unit case growth...Sprite light rollout boosted diet segment sales...returnable/refillable PET packaging introduced

Turkey
Company-owned Ankara bottler set growth pace... larger one-way packages, post-mix development, vending placement should drive continued strong growth

Brazil
Solid growth as prices held firm and costs were contained... merchandising and larger packages emphasized...post-mix currently only 7 percent of total volume, representing significant opportunity

Colombia
Larger packages stimulate growth despite overall higher prices...1.5 liter glass bottle introduced...diet Coke relaunched with 100 percent aspartame

Mexico
Per capita consumption second only to U.S....focus on advancing infrastructure, large-size packaging innovation... more than 30,000 coolers/refrigerators placed in 1990... 25 new warehouses opened...new bottling lines commissioned

⑪

stores stretching from coast to coast. The company was dominant in the national food retail chain store business from the nineteenth century until after World War II. There may be employees at A&P today who think they are working for an American company, but they are not. The majority of shares are owned by German investors.

The one thousand employees at the various franchise outlets of Pearl Vision Centers, Haagen Daas, Bennigan's, Steak & Ale, and Burger King may think they are working for American companies, but they are not. These franchises are owned by Grand Metropolitan, an English firm. Although the 650 workers at Ciba-Geigy and the 370 workers at Nestle Foods are probably aware that they are working for U.S. subsidiaries of Swiss companies, this insight may, or may not, be shared by the 450 workers at Air Cruisers, a manufacturer of inflatable rafts, which is owned by a French company. The 400 workers at Dialight, a maker of electronic parts, may not be aware that they are really working for a Dutch company, and the 900 workers at A&S and Sterns may, or may not, be aware that they are employees of a U.S. subsidiary of a Canadian retailer. The 350 workers at New Jersey Steel or the 90 workers at Container Corporation of America may be misled by the American sounding names of their companies into thinking that they are working for U.S. companies. They are not. They are actually working for subsidiaries of a Swiss and an Irish company, respectively. And the list goes on.

AMERICA NO LONGER THE DRIVING FORCE

As American firms have, at least historically, gobbled up overseas companies, American firms are now free game in the worldwide pursuit of companies desiring to extend their markets by buying companies not located on their native soil, or in building factories on American soil. Indeed, the Japanese have largely taken over the mantle of what was once worn by American corporate raiders: the ugly American is now the ugly Japanese. American managers are being warned about the high probability of having to report to Japanese superiors and of how difficult it will be for Americans to achieve the upper echelons of corporate positions at Japanese owned enterprises. Learning Japanese cultural practices and etiquette, even to the extent of learning the Japanese language, are now viewed as ways for the overachievers to overachieve. A decade or so ago, one merely had to substitute "European" for "American" and "American" for "Japanese" and the statements would have been just as applicable.

The globalization of business may be more rapid than one might imagine. Of the largest one hundred companies in the world, 60 percent were U.S. firms in 1960, 56 percent in 1970, and 44 percent in 1980. In 1990, of the one hundred largest companies in the world, fifty-four were Japanese, thirty-four American, seven British, and the remaining six were scattered among other nations. Where the world's largest companies are domiciled is of interest because the top one

thousand companies produce one quarter of the entire world's economic output
of goods and services.

HISTORIC ROOTS OF GLOBALIZATION

The globalization of the conduct of business is part of the process of globalization of the world political and economic systems. This is not a recent
phenomenon. Globalization of the world's political and economic systems has
a long history; driven by the desire to superimpose the will of one nation over
others by warfare it goes back to the dawn of civilization. The Roman Empire,
although built on military conquest, created a single integrated political and
economic system of government covering much of the then known civilized
world. Political integration was achieved on a personal level, with the emperor
selecting the provincial governors. Like-minded thinking by the provincial governors was encouraged by the presence of units of the Roman army who reported
to, and were controlled by, the emperor, thus establishing *Pax Romana*. The
Roman peace was maintained also by cultural integration with the adoption of
Roman customs, dress, language, and religion by the indigenous peoples.

Economic integration was fostered by building a system of roads that was not
exceeded in length and scope until the construction of the U.S. interstate highway
system after World War II. Accompanying the road system to enhance economic
integration was a common currency, uniform weights and measurements, and a
judicial system for resolving commercial disputes. Traders were able to roam
the entire Roman Empire exchanging goods in one region for those of another
without much in the way of tariffs, customs, border inspections, and other
impediments to free trade such as thieves, marauding bandits, and toll collectors.
The Dark Ages in the western part of the Roman Empire has been described as
a thousand-year depression brought on by the cessation of free trade caused by
thieves, marauding bandits, and toll collectors.

Ultimately, the Roman Empire fell, although it took its time. But the dream
of a universal empire never died. Charlemagne and Napoleon attempted to revive
the dream of a single nation state encompassing all of Europe. The Hapsburg
Empire kept the dream of free trade within the open frontiers of its domain alive.
All of these attempts failed, but the dream did not. Unfortunately, for the first
half of the twentieth century, the dream lived on with Hitler and Mussolini.

Now, during the second half of the twentieth century, the dream of a global
political and economic system may be achieved without military action. In fact,
the idea is advancing faster than any army can march. There are no serious
obstacles facing the advance of globalization. No one seems to object. Unlike
in the past, there appears to be no single charismatic leader. After World War
II, the United States appeared to be leading the process, but it is difficult to say
that a particular American was leading the process. Today, one might argue that
Europe, in forming the European Community and in taking the first steps to

bring eastern Europe into the European Community, has assumed the mantle of leadership. However, as before, there does not seem to be an individual leader.

All the leaders of the industrialized nations are marching to the same drum beat. It might be more accurate to say that any national leader who obstructs the process of globalization will not remain in power for long. The words "new world order" (*Novus Ordo Seclorum*) have been on the back of the U.S. dollar bill for a long time without much public mention. Now the words "new world order," along with "global island" and "global community," are bandied about in such a way that one must conclude that there is no opposition to globalization. This is quite remarkable considering that the supposed benefits of the universal state have often been the excuse to justify military conquest.

GLOBALIZATION AND THE U.S. CONSTITUTION

Military aggression with one nationality dominating others was never a popular means to achieve political and economic integration, except for the winners. The losers were unwilling participants and eventually undid what the winners had achieved. Now a new way has been found. The new world political order is to be based on a relationship similar to that which exists among the fifty individual states making up the United States and the nation called the United States. After the American Revolution, the Articles of Confederation bound the thirteen colonies too loosely, so to speak, for any concerted action to be undertaken by the newly independent nation. One might liken the Articles of Confederation to the League of Nations, which came into being after World War I. Both were ineffectual in binding together sovereign states into a single community of not-so-sovereign states. The Constitution arose from the failure of the Articles of Confederation to weld a single nation from the independent states. This was also the essential reason for abandoning the League of Nations in favor of forming the United Nations after World War II. Unlike the charter of the United Nations, the Constitution contained a mechanism to create a single nation out of thirteen sovereign states, without the use of force or the submergence of individual cultures. The United Nations has not been so successful.

The Constitution is well known for creating a system of checks and balances among the judicial, legislative, and executive branches of government to ensure that no branch of the government and, therefore, no individual would dominate the other branches, or the nation. However, another challenge facing the founders of the United States was dealing with the problem of the sovereignty of the various states. Each state jealously guarded its natural rights as a sovereign state. For example, goods could not cross state borders without paying tariffs and being subject to quotas and other impediments to free trade. Money was defined by each state. Some way had to be found to honor the rights of states while yet binding them into a single nation in order for the Constitution to be ratified by the states. This was achieved in the Tenth Amendment to the Bill of Rights: "The powers not delegated to the United States [i.e., the national government] by the Constitution, nor prohibited by it to the states, are reserved to the states respectively, or to the people.''

The Constitution was ratified on the basis that the states ratifying the Constitution knew exactly what degree of sovereignty was being transferred to the national government, and what acts of sovereignty were prohibited to them. Therefore, any other act of sovereignty not specifically mentioned or prohibited was left in the hands of the state, or its people. This division of sovereign power between national and state governments, and the rights given to the people with respect to speech, press, assembly, and to bear arms, made it difficult for the central government to become too intrusive in the lives of the people. The limits placed on governmental powers encouraged a free exchange of ideas. General prohibitions on the rights of states to interfere with interstate trade and commerce, and subsequent legislation against the formation of trusts, such as the Sherman Anti-Trust Act, fostered a free market economy. Some variant of the principles incorporated in the Constitution, and some variant of the free market economy, is present in every nation in the industrialized world. Moreover, democracy and the free market economy are the goals of those nations who are trying to escape from the inefficiencies, capriciousness, and arbitrariness of overbearing bureaucracies or dictatorships.

The true worth of the Constitution is its capacity to amalgamate a single nation out of a community of nations without resorting to force, or to the submergence of individual cultures to a dominant culture. It is interesting to note that the United Nations, the outgrowth of the League of Nations, is not a primary mover in this amalgamation of sovereign and independent nations into vast economic and political units. Perhaps it is the veto, a definitively nondemocratic concept, that permits the superpowers to maintain their sovereignty in world affairs, that prevents the United Nations from fully playing out its intended role.

Economic amalgamation accompanies political integration, or it may be the other way around. Who knows, for it is often difficult to separate the two. Indeed, one may argue that economic integration seems to precede political amalgamation. The General Agreement on Tariffs and Trade (GATT) talks have been continually held since its founding after World War II. The purpose of GATT is to reduce tariffs and remove trade barriers; that is, to set the stage for the economic integration of its member nations. The organization for promoting economic integration is the OECD, the acronym for the Organization of Economic Cooperation and Development, whose name eloquently describes its purposes. The OECD encompasses much of the industrialized world. In the Far East, its members are Australia, New Zealand, and Japan. In North America, the member nations are Canada and the United States. The European members are Austria, Belgium, Finland, France, Germany, Greece, Iceland, Ireland, Italy, Luxembourg, Netherlands, Norway, Portugal, Spain, Sweden, Switzerland, Turkey, and the United Kingdom.

Despite fits and starts, and occasional breakdowns in talks, the efforts of GATT have resulted in a significant reduction in trade barriers and tariffs among the industrialized nations in the Far East, North America, and Europe. Once trade barriers are removed, nations become interested in avoiding ruinous trade wars. The European Coal and Steel Community was formed to coordinate the activities of the coal and steel industry within the member nations. This led to the formation of the European Economic Community, or Common Market, an effort to coordinate a much wider sphere of economic activity with political implications. The European Economic Community was transformed in 1992 to a single market, the European Community, which performs, or administrates, those economic and political functions that have been given up by the individual nations. The European Community differs from the Common Market in that there is to be total freedom of the movement of goods, services, and people throughout the member states. Border stations within the European Community for customs inspections of goods crossing national borders for compliance with quotas and the payment of tariffs, along with the checking of passports, will eventually be relegated to the dustbin of history. The movement of goods, services, and people between Germany and France will be no different, in principle, than between Massachusetts and Connecticut. Moreover, the European Community has been given broad responsibilities to integrate the communication and transportation systems, organize a common European program on energy and environmental issues, bring about a common currency and a European banking system, and harmonize taxation and financial reporting. Much of this activity is associated with the European Parliament, and its various ministries, in Brussels.

GLOBAL MONEY

Globalization requires a global currency. After World War II, the "global" currency was the U.S. dollar. With the recovery of nations after the war, other currencies transformed themselves from soft to hard; that is, from undesirable to desirable currencies in the conduct of international trade. A desirable, or hard, currency is one that is an acceptable medium of exchange and a storehouse of value, characteristics not found in many currencies.

There has been a relative decline of the United States as a world economic power, caused not so much by its industrial decline as by the industrial emergence of the powerhouses in Germany, Japan, and other nations along the Pacific rim. This has dimmed the former luster of the U.S. greenback. As yet, however, a truly global currency has not taken the place of the U.S. dollar. Special Drawing Rights (SDRs), issued by the International Monetary Fund, represent a basket of currencies of the industrial nations of the world. However, SDRs have not been a practical substitute for the role of the U.S. dollar in settling accounts between nations and as a currency for world trade. But that is not stopping the movement toward a global currency.

In late 1991, the members of the European Community more or less agreed to a common central bank and a single currency by 1997, or possibly, by 1999.

The European Currency Unit, or ECU, is intended to replace all European currencies. If this is approved by the member nations of the European Community, then the sovereign power associated with each nation issuing its own money and determining interest rates will be turned over to a common central bank. European nations that have habitually devalued their currencies to make their products more price competitive will then have to directly address the causes of their noncompetitiveness. The nations of Europe will not have the freedom to generate large budget deficits because they will lose the sovereign power to print money to paper over the deficits. These may be considered the disadvantages of a common currency. The chief advantage is not having to exchange currencies when goods cross a border. Businesses will no longer have to worry about the repercussions of adverse currency exchange rate fluctuations between the time of shipping goods and collecting revenue. Nor are goods crossing borders subject to inspection, tariffs, and quotas. Therefore, the cost of conducting business will fall, and presumably, living standards will rise.

To most Europeans, the advantages seem to outweigh the disadvantages. Efforts are already underway among the European nations to reduce budget deficits to ease the pressure on inflation and interest rates in preparation for the day when a new ECU currency will be exchanged for existing European national currencies. The anticipated timetable will not be long once the Maastricht Treaty is approved by the member nations. The European Monetary Institute is to be organized in 1994 and is anticipated to be transformed into the embryonic European Central Bank by 1996. At that time, national budgets are to be more or less in line with one another, in order to have comparable interest and inflation rates among the European nations. This will allow the establishment of a permanent exchange rate among the various currencies, and hopefully, the ultimate step of permitting the exchange of all the currencies for one single currency, the ECU.

In the meantime, there is close coordination between the various central banks of Europe, Japan, and the United States with regard to controlling the trading range of currency exchange rates. If the trading range between all the hard currencies remains sufficiently narrow, then the major currencies, in the aggregate, can be treated as a global currency. Trading ranges among the hard currencies, however, have fluctuated widely, although not nearly as much as the trading ranges among the soft currencies. This makes the reporting of financial results for companies with operating affiliates located in one hundred different countries more difficult because these operations are conducted in one hundred different currencies. This leads to transaction and translation gains and losses resulting from fluctuating currency exchange rates: a sure sign that there is no global currency at the moment.

SOVEREIGNTY AT BAY

Globalization of the world's political and economic activities has not yet been achieved. In some respects, it is still a dream. On the surface, the world still operates under a system of sovereign nations where "the king can do no wrong." However, its appearance may be more superficial than real. The presidents and prime ministers of states gather frequently and their photographs seem to reveal a gathering of governors of states or mayors of cities rather than sovereign rulers "who can do no wrong." Perhaps no one can better attest to the degree of political integration than Saddam Hussein, who made the sovereign decision that Kuwait should be the nineteenth province of Iraq. Never in modern history has there been an instance of all the nations of the world uniting in a common cause. Although some nations were more active, and others more passive or even resistant, the point was that Saddam Hussein had to face a united world community of nations intent on preserving the independence of oil rich Kuwait. This is something that neither Saddam Hussein nor the leaders of the community of nations, thought possible.

TECHNICAL UNDERPINNINGS OF GLOBALIZATION

There is a technical side to the progress being made in global political and economic integration. Certainly, technical advances in communications have helped to integrate the nations of the world. It took a month for the Duke of Palma in the Netherlands to send a message to his master, Philip II of Spain, asking permission to pursue a course of action against the rebelling people of the Netherlands. It also took a month for Philip to communicate his decision back to the duke. Therefore, two months passed before the duke received, or was denied permission, to act. If the duke did not care for Philip's response, add another two months before a decision could be reached. And two more for another round of letters to be exchanged if the two still did not see eye to eye. Even when agreement was reached, circumstances usually had changed sufficiently to start the process over again.

The same approximate passage of time separated George III of England from his colonial governors in the thirteen colonies. The decisions of both kings were largely irrelevant by the time they were received—events had long since passed them by. Today, a retired person in Illinois can be kept abreast with events of a war in the Middle East just as currently as those at the scene. During the Iraq War, he could share the fear of an approaching Scud missile with the people of Tel Aviv. There were several occasions when representatives of governments, including Saddam Hussein himself, relied on the Cable News Network as a source of current information about what was going on in the Middle East in preference to their own official channels of communication.

A common source of information that is current and shared among the governments of the world tends to coordinate and integrate courses of action to be undertaken by the world community of nations. In a sense, the world's leaders are reacting to a common information base while, more or less, sharing the same economic and political goals. This encourages like decisions being made by like-minded leaders. The sovereignty of nations in terms of "the king can do no wrong" has lost most, if not all, of its meaning in today's world.

Logistical systems have been integrated to permit a low-cost and flexible system of moving goods between, and within, nations. The millions of ubiquitous containers can be as easily transported by truck as by barge, rail, and vessel. For certain high-valued and lightweight cargoes, air can be added to the list. Therefore, as long as a river, road, or railroad track connects a factory with a port terminal, the factory is connected to the world. A container can be loaded at a factory and its doors sealed shut. The container can be lifted onto one mode of transport and shifted to another without the expense of off-loading and on-loading the contents of the container. It is the container itself, with its contents untouched, that is moved from one mode of transport to another. The cost of lifting a container off a truck and loading it on a vessel is minuscule. Therefore, the preferred mode of transport is one of convenience and cost. The contents of a container are not off-loaded until it has arrived at its final destination.

Intermodalism is the realization of the concept of the globalization of the world's logistical systems. A factory in Japan can load a container with its goods on a truck or railway car. The container can be trucked or railed down to a port terminal. It is then loaded on a container vessel and can reach France by a choice of routes. For instance, the container can be shipped to a West Coast U.S. or Canadian port. Special dedicated container trains transverse the North American continent for loading the container on another vessel from an East Coast U.S. or Canadian port for movement to a French port. North America becomes a land bridge connecting the Pacific and Atlantic oceans. The final leg from the French, or any European port, to the container's destination in France can be by truck, rail or barge, or combination thereof.

The concept of North America being a land bridge for the movement of containers is matched by the land bridge system that connects east coast Russian ports with Europe. The Trans-Siberian railroad offers direct service from Vladivostok to Vienna. From Vienna, other railroad lines and trucks, with, perhaps, a side trip on a barge towed up the Danube, can carry the container to its final destination. Naturally, the container loaded on a vessel in Japan can reach Europe without the use of land bridges. But the vessel has a choice of transversing the world either through the Suez or the Panama Canals, or bypassing both by sailing around the southern tip of Africa. The vessel can stop at any European port, not necessarily in France, for off-loading the container on a flatbed truck, railcar, barge, or a smaller container vessel for the final leg of its journey.

Containerized freight using intermodal means of transport provides a globalized transport system whose cost is relatively low compared to the value of a container filled with finished, or semifinished, goods. Containers can be shipped from nearly any point to another point on the globe for a cost that adds anywhere from 2 percent to 5 percent to the value of the goods in a container. This is truly a low shipping cost. This means that any location on the globe that offers 2 percent to 5 percent savings in manufacturing costs, be it in the form of labor, material, or financing, can be considered a potential site for a factory. Small wonder that the Ford Escort is assembled from parts made in forty different nations.

The globalization of logistics would not have been possible without a worldwide telecommunications and dataprocessing system to keep track of the millions of containers. An individual container can be on any railroad car, truck, barge, vessel, and possibly airplane, in any nation, or crossing any ocean. The knowledge of the current location of each individual container, and the identification of the carrier, is a sine qua non condition for the functioning of an intermodal containerized freight system. A worldwide telecommunications system that links computers programmed to handle the necessary "paperwork" is an integral part of the workings of a globalized logistics system.

GLOBAL LANGUAGE AND CULTURE

The global language for communication in world commerce is English, or some might say, American. This is a legacy of the times when Great Britain, as progenitor nation of the industrialized world, ruled a quarter of the world's land surface. Although it might be advantageous for a businessman to understand the native language of another businessman with whom he is negotiating a transaction, it is not necessary. In fact, a company that attempts to transact business on a global scale without the ability to communicate in English would be at a competitive disadvantage. One can also sense the rise of a global culture. With much misgivings among individuals, the global culture appears to be American. American TV shows and movies provide much of the entertainment fare for the world's population. The golden arches of McDonald's can be found in every part of the world along with showings of "Married, With Children" and video tapes of Madonna, which to some is a rather gruesome thought.

GLOBAL FINANCE AND TRADE

Another area of globalization is the world financial system. Precious metals, currencies, and securities are traded on a twenty-four-hour basis. A trader in gold can have his account automatically shifted from Tokyo to Hong Kong to trading centers in Europe and then to the United States, and trade gold twenty-four hours a day without sleeping. Major currency exchange centers coordinate their opening and closing times, permitting currencies to be traded twenty-four hours a day. The world's stock markets are moving in this direction.

Single country mutual funds are being organized so that investors can diversify their holdings in Germany, Spain, Mexico, New Zealand, Singapore, Japan, and other nations to suit their global tastes. This is a modern version of investors once being advised to diversify their holdings in different industries within their nation of domicile; 40 percent in steel and 30 percent in computers may now be 40 percent in Japan in 30 percent in Germany. Other global mutual funds are

Table 1.2
GDP Compared with Merchandise Trade Exports

	GROSS DOMESTIC PRODUCT	MERCHANDISE TRADE EXPORTS	EXPORTS AS PERCENT OF GDP
Singapore	$ 28.4	$ 44.6	157%
Belgium	126.5	100.7	80
Hong Kong	52.5	28.7	55
Netherlands	221.7	107.8	49
Venezuela	43.8	13.0	30
Germany	1189.0	340.6	29
Korea	211.9	62.3	29
Portugal	44.9	12.8	29
Canada	488.6	114.1	23
Israel	46.0	10.7	23
New Zealand	41.4	8.6	21
United Kingdom	717.9	152.4	21
Yugoslavia	71.8	13.3	19
Greece	39.9	7.4	18
France	955.8	172.6	18
South Africa	80.4	13.5	17
Italy	865.7	140.7	16
Australia	281.9	33.2	12
Spain	379.4	44.5	12
Brazil	319.2	34.4	11
Japan	2818.5	275.0	10
Iran	150.3	13.0	9
United States	5156.4	346.9	7

already diversified, with holdings spread over various nations. This represents an enormous shift in portfolio management focus from companies to countries.

One measure of the degree of globalization that has already been achieved is the ratio of a nation's exports in relation to its gross domestic product. In the table, merchandise trade exports are all exports such as food, fuel, commodities, and manufactured goods. The gross domestic product (GDP) is a measure of total commercial activity within a nation. Figures are in billions of dollars for the year 1989 and were taken from the *1991 World Development Report* published by The World Bank.

This list of selected nations shows that many nations have exports that are a significant portion of their total domestic economic output, which is a measure of the extent of globalization of world commerce. The Far Eastern trading nations of Singapore, Hong Kong, and Korea are about where one might expect, because their economies are export oriented. One surprise is Japan, which is actually far down the list of exporting nations with regards to the relationship of its exports to its domestic economy. Japan is certainly a major world exporting nation, but its exports in relation to its domestic economy are about the same as those of the United States. This is indicative of the robustness of the Japanese domestic market and the size and living standards of its population. The issue in the financial press is not the size of Japanese exports as such, because both Germany and the United States exceed the dollar volume of Japanese exports. The issue is the size of the trade surplus, which in 1989, was about $68 billion. For the United States, the discussion is on the ramifications of the nation's trade deficit, which in 1989 was $145 billion. Much of the world trade imbalance is between these two countries.

Moreover, in reviewing the list, one can see the impetus for the economic integration of the European Community. The size of individual European exports and imports to and from other European nations in relation to their domestic economy is probably on the same scale of magnitude as individual states in the United States. In 1992, the European Community consisted of Belgium, Denmark, Germany, France, Greece, Ireland, Italy, Luxembourg, Netherlands, Portugal, Spain, and the United Kingdom. The list of participating countries in the European Community is expected to grow with the possible inclusion of Scandinavian and eastern European nations. If Poland, Czechoslovakia, and Hungary join, the potential of member status being given to the nations making up the former Soviet Union becomes more feasible. This may well lead to the "United States of Europe," which like the United States of America, would stretch from the Atlantic to the Pacific.

President Bush's support of a free trade zone encompassing Canada, the United States, and Mexico may be a precursor to the "United States of North America." The "United States of North America," along with the "United States of Europe," may be the precursor to the "United States of the Northern Hemisphere." Japan and other Far Eastern centers of industry could hardly refrain from joining a market that encompasses so much of the world. As preposterous as all this may sound, it is not nearly as preposterous in 1992 as it was in 1982.

Everything is becoming globalized, homogenized, and pasteurized as a new world system of mutual integration of human activity becomes ever more quickly a reality. There is, however, one remaining activity that has somewhat, but not entirely, escaped the onslaught of sameness. That is accounting and financial reporting.

CHAPTER 2

BACKGROUND TO
ACCOUNTING

Accounting, as the word implies, is a reckoning of the financial results of an enterprise between those who control the employment of capital or assets and those who provide the capital or assets. Accounting responds to the needs of business and follows developments in commercial activity. The earliest records of business transactions, the essence of accounting, are over 5,500 years old. These are Egyptian and Sumarian records on agricultural production and tax collection. Other ancient records include both sides of a trade or barter and the amount of inventory in storehouses. The earliest extant records of depreciation, an expression of the idea of the wasting away of physical assets, go back to the days of the Greek and Roman record keepers. A wall, for example, would be depreciated over a period of eighty years, which one might construe as a measure of its useful life and the efficacy of ancient construction practices.

During the Middle Ages, commerce became more reliant on arithmetic and writing, and on money as a medium of exchange. The advancement of accounting practices was evidenced by the discovery of accounting records in Genoa dating back to 1340. These records were in terms of money, one of the first instances where unlike material items were described in terms of a like medium. In addition to expressing accounts in terms of the common monetary unit of the day, these records made the earliest known distinction between capital and income.

As the Renaissance dawned in Europe, there was a growing social acceptance of an individual accumulating private property and capital as something other than sinful. During this time, private property became sanctioned by society and protected by legal rights. There arose a practice of banking, where money was lent to those in commerce. The practice of lending money necessitated establishing some means of measuring performance—that is, the success or failure of business ventures—and some means of judging the creditworthiness of potential borrowers.

The first bankers were goldsmiths with whom those in commerce entrusted the safe keeping of their gold coins, which signified the rewards of success in commercial ventures. After a while, the goldsmiths began to notice that their depositors, in general, kept a sizable portion of their wealth in their safekeeping without withdrawing the coins. The gold coins lay "sterile" in the goldsmiths' safes. The goldsmiths became bankers once they learned that they could make money by lending out a portion of the deposits entrusted to them to finance commerce and trade. That portion depended on the depositers remaining unconcerned with, or ignorant of, the fact that not all the gold deposited with the goldsmiths was physically in their possession. Such concerns could be allayed by paying the depositors interest as an inducement for them not to withdraw their funds. This permitted the bankers to lend a larger portion of these deposits to those in commerce. The final stage of the transformation from craftsmen to bankers occurred when they gave up making artifacts of gold, and spent their days borrowing from depositors at a lower rate of interest and lending the proceeds to borrowers at a higher rate of interest.

But such a system could only succeed if the bankers could avoid, or minimize, losses. This necessitated the development of some way to measure the financial performance of those in commerce for those who financed commerce. In 1494, in one of the first books printed on the Gutenberg press after the Bible, Luca Pacioli (1445?—1517?), a Franciscan friar, educator, and mathematician living in Venice, wrote *Summa de Arithmetica, Geometria, Proportioni et Proportionalita*. This book on everything about arithmetic, geometry, and proportion was concerned with the application of mathematics to Renaissance society. A portion of the book was dedicated to Venetian accounting practices, in order for Pacioli to tutor the sons of a Venetian merchant. Pacioli did not originate but merely recorded already existing accounting practices.

Venetian accounting involved three sets of books. One was a memorandum book to record detailed entries for all transactions. The second was a journal into which all entries were transferred from the memorandum book, and the third was a ledger where each page represented an account. The journal entry began with the debtor listed on the left along with an explanation of the entry and the appropriate amount. The entry for the creditor was listed on the right along with its explanation and amount. When the books were closed at the end of a business venture, a trial balance was made to generate a final profit and loss account. Pacioli also discussed partnerships, correction of accounting mistakes, record keeping by travelers, and accounting for branch locations.

Double entry accounting provided the means for measuring the financial performance of an individual and the information necessary for the Venetian bankers to judge the creditworthiness of borrowers. Pacioli's system made little distinction between a business entity and an individual, because accounting intermingled business and personal transactions. Nor was there any specific accounting period because the accounting records covered an individual business venture independent of the time element. Consequently, there was no conceptualizing of an ongoing concern and of accruals and deferrals of revenues and expenses. Nevertheless, the *Summa* contains the oldest text on double entry bookkeeping. As commercial activity, supported by bank credit, spread across Europe, so did double entry bookkeeping, as described in the *Summa*. For this, Pacioli earned the title "Father of Accounting."

Accounting for specific periods of time, such as end-of-year closing of the books, began in the 1600s. In 1673, France adopted the first official accounting code, which included the obligation to issue biannual balance sheets. Other practices were standardized in their final form such as debits being listed on the left and the credits on the right. The concept of treating a business entity as an individual for both legal and accounting purposes took hold at this time.

TRUE AND FAIR VIEW

The Industrial Revolution again changed the nature of business activity, which necessitated changes in accounting practices. This time, change was fostered by the need to raise massive amounts of capital for first canal, and then railroad, construction. The accounting profession in the United Kingdom, the nation where the Industrial Revolution began, developed the idea of the purpose of accounting being to present a "true and fair" view of the financial results of the operations of a business entity.

Changes in accounting practices, such as the formalized distinction between income and capital and the definition and accounting treatment of fixed assets, inventory, depreciation, and allocation of overhead had to be agreed on in order to present a true and fair view of the financial results of an operation. The demand for a true and fair view of financial results from the merchant bankers was the incentive for the English and Scottish accounting firms to provide such information. They opened branch offices in the United States to obtain the necessary information. These branch offices became the major American accounting firms, thus forging a close link between accounting practices on both sides of the Atlantic. English and Scottish accounting practices form the foundation of accounting practices in many nations because Great Britain was the capital exporter for the development of industry and trade throughout its empire, upon which the sun never set.

During this time, accounting practices were adapted to conform with the change in business organizations from proprietorships and partnerships to limited liability stock companies. Limited liability stock companies were the legal vehicle selected for raising the enormous quantities of capital required for the building of industries first in England, then in the United States and elsewhere. The concept of limited liability was in response to individuals refusing to expose themselves to a loss that exceeded their investment. Limited liability stock companies contained the magnitude of losses to the amount of funds placed at risk in buying the securities of the companies. The liability associated with the failure of a limited liability stock company does not extend beyond the loss of value of its securities to include the personal wealth and property of the founders, officers, members of the board of directors, and other shareholders.

Continental Europe lagged in the adoption of the Anglo view on accounting because the first steps toward industrialization, the building of the railroads, were financed with government (public) funds, not the private funds of individuals and banks. In England and the United States, first canals and railroads, then steel mills and communication systems, the backbone of an industrialized society, depended primarily on private sources of capital. Government involvement with the building of canals was in granting rights of way. To minimize public expenditures for the building of the railroads, the government made it attractive for private capital to invest in railroad construction by providing generous land grants along the railroad's right of way and lucrative mail contracts.

ORGANIZATION AFFECTS ACCOUNTING

As companies became more complex organizations through the formation of subsidiaries and independent operating units, accounting practices took on a new assignment of being a mechanism for internal reporting and control. Accounting had to respond to the mergers of independent companies that took place late in the nineteenth century to form trusts (e.g., U.S. Steel) and the breakup of the monopolistic trusts under Theodore Roosevelt early in the twentieth century (e.g., the Standard Oil Trust). Later in the twentieth century, accounting had to accommodate the demand for a true and fair measure of the financial performance of companies in diverse fields (conglomerates) and to deal with growing government intervention and regulation of business. In addition, a new speciality, tax accounting, came into being.

CODIFICATION OF ACCOUNTING PRINCIPLES

There are many influences at work that affect the nature of the accounting system. The codification of accounting up to the 1970s occurred exclusively within the borders of a nation. When companies were, for the most part, operating units within a national setting, the application of accounting principles, from the point of view of an individual company, was global—global in the sense that the generally accepted accounting practices were universally applied at each operating location of the company.

The application of accounting principles was global also from the perspective of a nation having colonies overseas. Historically, companies operating within the realm of the British empire consistently applied British accounting standards no matter where their activities were located. The same was true for the colonial empires of France, Germany, Belgium, Spain, Portugal, and other European nations. One problem facing accounting today is the fracturing of the codification

process. Although British accounting standards were universally applied throughout the British Empire, the same cannot be said today regarding the accounting
standards practiced in the ex-British colonies (e.g., the United States) or in the
British Commonwealth of Nations (e.g., Australia, Canada, and New Zealand).
Far from it. The ex-British colonies and commonwealth nations have each
adopted a procedure similar to that originated by the English and Scottish accountants to ensure that there was consistency in the application of accounting
principles within Britain and its former colonial possessions.

Rather than having this procedure used in Britain and having its recommendations applied throughout the British Empire, now each individual nation of
the former British Empire sets its own standards of accounting practices. There
is no longer uniformity in the application of accounting principles within the
former British Empire, or among the nations once part of any other former
colonial power. Every nation has generally agreed to do things differently. The
essential problem with global accounting is that there is no such animal.

THE CACOPHONY OF GENERALLY ACCEPTED PRACTICES

When a company operates only within national borders, the company does
apply accounting principles "globally," but not globally when the company has
operations outside the borders of a single state. This means that the accounting
practices applicable in one location may not be applicable at another location.
What is generally acceptable in one location may not be generally acceptable in
another. Accounting principles appropriate for one location, may in fact be illegal
in another. The more transparent national boundaries are to the movement of
goods, the greater the accounting quandary. A company with offices or branches
in the United States and the United Kingdom must employ two sets of accounting
principles. A company that does business in one hundred nations through an
assortment of operating affiliates, a not unusual happening in today's world, has
to take the financial results of each affiliate and cast them into a set of income
and balance sheet statements in a manner acceptable to that nation. That means
casting the financial results of one hundred different subsidiaries one hundred
different ways. Then the process has to be reversed and the income and balance
sheet statements of one hundred operating affiliates must be recast into a single
set of statements in accordance with the set of accounting principles applicable
for the nation of domicile for presentation to the shareholders.

THE DOUBLE SET OF BOOKS

One main purpose of accounting is to fairly represent the financial results of
an operation to the shareholders, who are the individual owners of a business
enterprise. In a general sense, financial profit or loss is the revenue less the cost
of goods sold less the fixed or overhead costs, less interest, taxes, and an

allowance for depreciation on fixed assets. Depreciation is keyed to a period of time that adequately reflects the useful life of the asset while it is under the stewardship, or control, of management. If an asset under the control of management is expected to have a useful life of ten years, then it is usually written off, or depreciated, at 10 percent per year. Management is judged on its performance to generate a profit on an asset under their control for ten years before it has to be replaced by charging management 10 percent of its value per year.

Because the computation of taxes follows the same general format as reporting profits, some feel that pretax profit indicated in a financial report should be the same as the profits reported to the tax authority. In a few countries, such as Finland, Germany, Italy, Portugal, and Switzerland, this conclusion is correct. In most others, it is not. One reason for this is that the allowance for depreciation for reporting financial results may not be the same as the allowance for depreciation for filing a tax return. Whereas the purpose of financial reporting is to fairly represent the financial results of management's stewardship of the shareholders' assets, the purpose of filing a tax form is to calculate a liability. The depreciation schedule selected for calculating taxes to be paid to a tax authority is the applicable schedule of depreciation decided on by the tax authority. The resulting profit is strictly for the computation of taxes, not to judge the performance of management to generate a profit on assets under their stewardship.

There is, in effect, a double set of books: one for the shareholders and one for the tax authority. The double set of books does not imply duplicity. It is a consequence of the financial results of a company being portrayed differently for two distinct purposes. The double set of books may differ on other points besides depreciation schedules. For instance, if a product is sold on the installment basis, in some countries, the financial report may treat this as a cash sale, assuming that the accountants feel that the party making the installment payments is good for the money. For calculating taxes, however, the revenue may be recognized when the installment payments are received. Another possibility for differing reported profits to shareholders and to the tax authority is the handling of inventory. Different methods of accounting for inventory may be applied for financial reports and for calculating taxes. The former is determined by a body of professional accountants setting financial accounting standards and the latter by tax regulations.

In general, a tax deferral arises when there is a temporary difference in timing between recognizing revenue or expenses for financial reporting purposes and for calculating taxable income. These differences may result in financial income exceeding, or being less than, taxable income. Suppose that a company has $50,000 in pretax financial income for year 1 with a tax rate of 40 percent. Also suppose that the company will depreciate a $10,000 asset for financial reporting purposes in equal amounts of $5,000 in years 2 and 3, but that it is permitted to depreciate the entire amount for tax purposes in year 1. At the end of year 1, the company has two tax liabilities—one actually paid and the other reported on its financial reports.

	Year 1	Year 2	Year 3
Pretax financial income	$50,000	-	-
Temporary difference in depreciation	($10,000)	$5,000	$5,000
Taxable Income	$40,000	$5,000	$5,000
Tax Rate	40%	40%	40%
Reported Tax Liability on Financial Report	$16,000	$2,000	$2,000

If the company is domiciled in the United States, it would be obligated to follow the guidelines required by Financial Accounting Standards Board Statement No. 96 (FASB 96). In accordance with FASB 96, the company would report a net income of $50,000 with an associated income tax expense of $20,000 for year 1 even though the actual payment of taxes is $16,000, with $4,000 of tax liabilities being deferred until years 2 and 3. The difference in timing between taxes actually paid to the government and the amount of taxes reported in the financial statements is strictly one of timing as shown in the table.

```
Year 1 Actual Tax Paid
($50,000-$10,000) X 40%                                    $16,000


Year 1 Income Tax Reported
  on Financial Reports ($50,000 X 40%)                     $20,000


Deferred Tax for Financial Reporting
($10,000 X 40%)                                            $4,000
```

In this simple example, where the tax authority permits a more accelerated schedule of depreciation than the financial reporting authority, there is a satisfactory balancing of the two sets of books between the creation of a deferred liability and the actual payment of taxes with the passage of time. In this example, the tax and financial reports will be identical in year 4.

In the "real" world, however, things are not quite so simple. Companies must continually acquire new assets to survive and remain competitive. Most of these may be depreciated at an accelerated rate for tax purposes. This reduces the near-term tax liability, enhancing the cash flow for the company. This continually adds to the amount of the deferred tax liability. Inflation alone adds to the deferred tax liability because a company replaces its assets at ever higher costs as they wear out or become obsolete without the company undergoing any expansion in productive capacity. In essence, this liability is never satisfied; that is, it is forever deferred. Only in the liquidation of the company will this deferred liability become real. Because most firms are on-going concerns without any intention of being liquidated, many analysts view the deferred tax liability as a form of permanent capitalization.

Nevertheless, a company located in the United States is required to report increases in its deferred tax liability as a current expense for financial reporting purposes. This reduces the reported income of a company to the shareholders without affecting the tax actually paid to the tax authority. In direct contrast, a company in the United Kingdom, following U.K. generally accepted accounting principles, does not report a deferred income tax liability, nor is it required to expense this liability currently. The deferred tax liability is only footnoted in the financial reports.

The net effect of this is that, for a given situation, the reported financial profits will be higher in the United Kingdom than in the United States. Were the difference between the two reported profits small, it would not be worth mentioning. This is hardly the case—the differences in reported profits between two large and similarly sized companies, one domiciled in the United States and the other in the United Kingdom, may be in hundreds of millions of dollars or pounds simply on the basis of the accounting treatment of the deferred tax liability. The consolidation of financial reports for a company with operations in both the United States and the United Kingdom will be dramatically different depending on whether the consolidated report of financial results to the company's shareholders is in accordance with U.S. or U.K. accounting principles.

Naturally, if the United States and the United Kingdom were the only two nations in the world, perhaps some agreement could be reached between the two concerning a consistent approach on the treatment of deferred taxes. Of course, such is not the case. Joining the United States in its general accounting treatment of deferred tax liabilities are Australia, Chile, Colombia, and South Africa, but there are differences in the details of handling deferred tax liabilities among these nations. Joining the United Kingdom in not permitting deferred tax liabilities to be included in the income statement and the balance sheet are Finland, France, Germany, Ireland, Japan, and Switzerland. Belgium, Denmark, Hong Kong, Indonesia, Italy, Malaysia, New Zealand, Portugal, Spain, Thailand, Uruguay, Zambia, and Zimbabwe permit, but do not require, accounting for deferred tax liabilities. And to complete this Tower of Accounting Babel, Argentina, Brazil, Mexico, and the Philippines recommend, but do not require, accounting for deferred taxation.

Were financial reporting between different nations consistent in all respects other than deferred taxation, perhaps the differences would be surmountable. Alas, if this were only true. Commonality of generally accepted principles is uncommon. Assets are valued at historical cost in Canada, Germany, Japan, and the United States. In Australia, France, the Netherlands, Sweden, Switzerland, and the United Kingdom, assets are adjusted for changes in price levels, which in an inflationary climate, increase reported shareholder equity. What is legally required in the United Kingdom with regard to adjusting the value of assets, is illegal in the United States.

In the United States, total pension fund assets and liabilities are generally excluded from a company's financial statements, inasmuch as required contributions have been paid to a trustee. The trustee invests these contributions for future pension payments to employees. These pension assets are not listed on a company's financial statements, but the contributions that create these assets are considered a cost that reduces reported profits. In contrast, German companies generally do not pay contributions to an independent trustee. German companies retain the funds as part of corporate assets, while reflecting the pension liability as a general obligation. If two companies had equal financial results, but one was domiciled in the United States and the other in Germany, then in the area of accounting for pension liabilities, the German company would report greater liquidity than the American company. However, in considering other areas of accounting differences, the net result would probably be that German companies report lower earnings than their American counterparts.

In France, Germany, Japan, the Netherlands, Sweden, and Switzerland, management is permitted to establish "general purpose reserves" that are created during times of high profitability. These purely discretionary reserves are not taxed at the time of their creation. During times of low profitability, these reserves can be drawn down, at which time the companies pay the applicable taxes. The effect of these reserves is to reduce reported earnings to the shareholders during the good times and enhance reported earnings during the bad times. The shareholders see less variation in reported profits than what is being experienced by the company. What is really being reported to the shareholders is average earnings, a smoothed out version of the annual swings in earnings caused by variations in the business cycle and other factors affecting the profitability of the company. This practice, although condoned in some countries, is prohibited in others such as Australia, Canada, the United Kingdom, and the United States.

AN ILLUSTRATION OF ACCOUNTING CACOPHONY

An article in the December 1987 issue of *Management Accounting* magazine took a set of financial results and cast them into an income statement and the balance sheet (equity section only) in accordance with the generally accepted accounting principles of four nations. The nations were the United States, the United Kingdom, Australia, and (then) West Germany. The assumed financial results are listed in Table 2.1.

Admittedly, one might argue that no one company would plausibly have all of these types of financial results in a given year. The counterargument is that there may even be more than these because global companies doing business in a hundred different nations may have to face a large number of differing happenings that influence financial results. These financial results have to be cast

Table 2.1
Assumed Financial Results
Sample Company (Items related to fiscal year ending 3-31-86)

Sales	$3,000,000
Net Operating Income	1,500,000
Goodwill Amortization	(8,000)
Accounting Estimate Change: Intangible Write-Off Period Changed from 10 to 5 years [current year effect on income ($4,000), prior years' effect ($15,000)]	
Interest Charges	(12,000)
Dividend Income (Pretax) on Shares Held (ownership less than 20%)	18,000
Gain (Pretax) from Sale of Investments and Fixed Assets	15,000
Loss (Pretax) from Sale of Investments and Fixed Assets	(25,000)
Foreign Currency Transaction Gain (Loss)	(80,000)
Other Items Not Part of Recurring Operations (Net of 40% Tax): Retroactive effect of change in accounting principle: cost to equity method of accounting for investment income. Change relates to additional acquisitions of stock in 1986 which increased ownership of unconsolidated companies above 20%.	60,000
Operating Loss on Discontinued Business Segment	(300,000)
Loss on Sale of Assets of Discontinued Segment	(200,000)
Retroactive Effect of Depreciation Method Change	(235,000)
Loss from Debt Extinguishment	(100,000)
Retroactive Effect of Accounting Error— Accounting Change from Cash to Accrual Accounting	(20,000)
Major Loss Resulting from Asset Expropriation	(30,000)
Insurance Proceeds in Excess of Asset Book Value (Major Fire)	50,000

into profit and loss statements that are consistent and fair in their respective nations. Unfortunately, from the point of global accounting, the income statement and the equity portion of the balance sheet will differ depending on where the financial results are reported.

The income statement and the equity portion of the balance sheet would appear as in Table 2.2 in the United States. The same assumed financial results, had they occurred in the United Kingdom, would appear as in Table 2.3.

In Australia, the assumed financial results would be cast into the income statement and equity portion of the balance sheet shown in Table 2.4.

And in Germany (West Germany in 1986), the same financial results would appear as shown in Table 2.5 in accordance with German generally accepted accounting principles.

Summing up, the reported net profit and the end-of-year retained earnings, assuming a start-of-year retained earnings of $2 million, varies between these four nations as shown in the table.

	U.S.	U.K.	AUSTRALIA	GERMANY
Reported Profits	$34,600	$260,600	$240,600	$10,402
End of Year Retained Earnings	$2,074,600	$2,065,600	$2,065,600	$2,010,402

Looking at the results, a person familiar with one accounting system might be surprised that the reported profits could vary between $10,000 and $260,000 depending on where the accounting is being done. Yet, in viewing the various accounts, there is a similarity of approach between the results stated in the United Kingdom and Australia. They are similar, but not the same, because as already noted the United Kingdom and Australia differ on handling deferred taxation. The similarity, of course, has to do with the historic relationship between the two nations.

MANAGEMENT ATTITUDES TOWARD ACCOUNTING

Attitudes have an important influence on the nature of a country's accounting principles. Indeed, the words ''generally accepted'' mean a consensus, a general acceptance, of how financial results are to be reported by a company to its shareholders. ''General acceptance,'' unfortunately for the conduct of global business, is dependent on where a company is domiciled. The attitude of management in Belgium, Italy, and Switzerland is generally against disclosure of detailed financial results to the public. Switzerland, in particular, is known for its privacy of financial dealings. At one time, a company domiciled in Switzerland with publicly traded shares was required to report only its financial results with regard to its operations in Switzerland. A publicly traded company doing $1 million in business in Switzerland and $1 billion outside Switzerland was required to report only on its financial results of doing $1 million in business in Switzerland. This hardly provides a true and fair picture of the company's operations to a reader of its financial reports.

The concept of privacy is so pervasive in Switzerland that management may not even know who the shareholders and the bondholders are, because stock and bonds can be issued in bearer form. This means that the individual or firm possessing the shares or bonds is the owner of these securities. Dividends and interest payments are made to the individual who physically presents the shares or bonds for payment. One can appreciate the lack of incentive for disclosure in Switzerland if management itself does not know who the shareholders and bondholders are and the shareholders and bondholders themselves are not anxious to reveal their identities. It has been observed that only those who prepare the published financial statements of companies domiciled in Belgium, Italy, and

Table 2.2
United States

Net Operating Income			$1,500,000
Other Income (Expenses)			
Dividend Income		$ 18,000	
Gain from Sales of Investments and Fixed Assets		15,000	
		$ 33,000	
Interest Charges	$(12,000)		
Foreign Currency Difference Loss	(80,000)		
Loss on Sales of Investments and Fixed Assets	(25,000)	(117,000)	(84,000)
Net Operating Income After Other Income (Expenses)			$1,416,000
Less Corporate Income Taxes (40%)			566,400
Net Income from Continuing Operations			$849,600
Discontinued Operations (Net of Taxes):			
Loss from Operations of Discontinued Segment		$(300,000)	
Loss on Disposal of Business Segment		(200,000)	(500,000)
			$ 349,600
Extraordinary Items (Net of Taxes):			
Insurance Proceeds in Excess of Asset Cost		$ 50,000	
Loss from Asset Expropriation	$(30,000)		
Loss from Debt Extinguishment	(100,000)	(130,000)	(80,000)
			$ 269,600
Cumulative Effect on Prior Years of Changing to Different Depreciation Method (Net of Tax)			(235,000)
Net Income			$ 34,600
Retained Earnings (4-1-85)			$2,000,000
Plus Cumulative Prior Year Effect (Net of Taxes):			
Accounting Error	$(20,000)		
Entity Change	60,000		40,000
Plus Net Income			34,600
Retained Earnings (3-31-86)			$2,074,600

Switzerland have a clear understanding of the actual financial results, not those who read the published reports.

On the other side of the coin, managements in Brazil, Finland, Indonesia, Philippines, South Africa, the United Kingdom, the United States, and Zimbabwe have a more positive attitude toward disclosure. It is more positive in comparison with the managements of companies in Belgium, Italy, and Switzerland—human beings are not prone to admitting to their errors. Managements are proud to boast of their accomplishments, but no management relishes reporting on its failures, or poor performance in the generation of profits. Nevertheless, the attitude of management in the United States, the United Kingdom, and in the other afore-mentioned nations is that it is in their best interests to have the public aware of the company's overall financial state. They feel that this is a positive force in the public's participation in the buying of securities issued by their companies.

Table 2.3
United Kingdom

Gross Operating Profit	$1,500,000
Add: Dividend Income	18,000
	1,518,000
Less: Interest Charges	12,000
Loss from Debt Extinguishment	166,667
Foreign Currency Difference	80,000
Gross Operating Profit Before Taxation	$1,259,333
Taxation	503,733
Gross Operating Profit After Taxation	$ 755,600
Extraordinary Items (Net of Taxation) Note 1	(495,000)
Net Profit	$ 260,600

Profit and Loss Account-Cumulative			2,000,000
Prior Period Items (Net of Tax):			
Entity Changes		$ 60,000	
Accounting Change	$(235,000)		
Prior Period Error	(20,000)	(255,000)	(195,000)
Plus Net Profit for Period			260,600
			$2,065,600

Note 1

Extraordinary Items—Net of Tax:	
Losses on Termination of Business	$ (500,000)
Loss from Sale of Investments and Fixed Assets	(15,000)
Gain from Sale of Investments and Fixed Assets	9,000
Loss from Asset Expropriation	(30,000)
Insurance Proceeds in Excess of Asset Book	
Value from Major Fire	50,000
Intangible Asset Amortization—	
Prior Period Effect of Estimate Change	(9,000)
	$ (495,000)

However, these nations are actually the exceptions to the rule. Although most managements of companies throughout the world may not be so negatively disposed as managements in Belgium, Italy, and Switzerland to public disclosure, most are not as positive in attitude as those in the United States and the United Kingdom. Most managements throughout the world are somewhat reluctant to have the financial results of the companies under their stewardship disclosed for public scrutiny. This attitude influences the development of what is generally accepted as accounting principles.

REGULATION AND SELF-REGULATION

Accounting guidelines, or generally accepted principles, can be dictated by the government or can be the result of a consultative process among professional

Table 2.4
Australia

Gross Operating Profit	$1,512,000 *
Add: Dividend Income	18,000
	$1,530,000
Less: Interest Charges	12,000
Loss from Debt Extinguishment	166,667
Income Tax Expense	540,533
Operating Income (before Extraordinary Items)	$ 810,800
Extraordinary Items (Note 1)	(570,200)
Net Profit for the Year	$ 240,600
Unappropriated Profits (4-1-85)	$2,000,000

Prior Period Items (Net of Tax):

Entity Change	$ 60,000	
Accounting change	(235,000)	(175,000)
Plus Net Profit		240,600
Unappropriated Profits (3-31-86)		$2,065,600

Note 1

Extraordinary Items (Net of Tax):

Losses on Termination of Business	$ (500,000)
Foreign Currency Differences	(48,000)
Loss from Sale of Investments and Fixed Assets	(15,000)
Gain from Sale of Investments and Fixed Assets	9,000
Retroactive Effect of Accounting Error	(20,000)
Goodwill and Intangible Asset Amortization (Inclusive of Prior Period Effect)	(16,200)
Loss from Asset Expropriation	(30,000)
Insurance Proceeds in Excess of Asset Cost	50,000
	$ (570,200)

* Intangible Asset and Goodwill Amortization
is excluded from operating income.

accounting organizations within a nation. Some countries have established their accounting principles relying on strong, professional, self-regulating organizations with relatively little government intervention such as Australia, Hong Kong, Ireland, Mexico, New Zealand, Zambia, and Zimbabwe. Thailand, the United Kingdom, and the United States have a strong reliance on professional self-

Table 2.5
West Germany

Income from Operations	$1,512,000*
Income from Investments	18,000
Income from Sale of Investments and Fixed Assets	15,000
Other Income—Inclusive of Extraordinary Income— Insurance Proceeds in Excess of Asset Book Value (Major Fire)	83,330
	$1,628,330
Loss from Sale of Investments and Fixed Assets ($833,330 + $25,000)	$ 858,330
Interest and Similar Expenses ($166,667 + $12,000)	178,667
Foreign Currency Losses	80,000
Depreciation on Intangible Assets	4,000
Loss from Asset Expropriation	50,000
Additional Depreciation of Fixed Assets to Lower Book Value (Accounting Change)	391,667
Additional Provisions Relating to Prior Period Errors and Estimates ($33,330 + $15,000)	48,330
Taxes (40% rate assumed)	6,934
Net Income for Fiscal Year	$ 10,402
Consolidated Retained Earnings (4/1/85)	$2,000,000
Plus Net Income	10,402
	$2,010,402

*Intangible asset and Goodwill Amortization is excluded from operating income in Germany. Also, Goodwill from consolidation and the equity method of accounting is not reflected on statements. EEC Directive #7, adopted in 1986, will require Goodwill disclosure and Amortization, and the equity method, on statements issued subsequent to 12-31-89.

regulating organizations, but a greater degree of government intervention. Belgium, Germany, and Japan have a high degree of government intervention, but with some participation by professional organizations. Finland, France, and Italy have a near total reliance on government agencies to guide the establishment of accounting principles. There are a few countries in the world, such as Portugal, South Africa, and Switzerland, where accounting principles have been only modestly influenced either by government or by professional organizations. It is interesting to note the varying role of government intervention for those nations where there is a strong bias against public disclosure. In Switzerland, as one might expect, the degree of government intervention in establishing accounting principles is low. However, the opposite is true in Belgium and Italy. Although one may argue over the particular roles of the government and professional societies in the setting of standards, the inescapable fact is that there is enormous variation among the nations of the world as to who is involved, and the respective degree of involvement.

NEED FOR AUDITS

Differences in approaches to outside auditors are also noteworthy. Spain does not require an outside audit of private or public or government owned or controlled corporations. Put another way, Spain does not require outside auditors. On the other hand, France, Italy, Malaysia, New Zealand, the Philippines, South Africa, the United Kingdom, and Zimbabwe require an outside audit of all corporate entities, public, private, or government owned. Brazil, Chile, Japan, Mexico, Portugal, and the United States do not require an outside audit of a private company, but public and government owned companies must be audited. Argentina, Colombia, Denmark, Finland, Hong Kong, Indonesia, Ireland, Switzerland, and Thailand require public and private corporations to be audited, but government owned or controlled companies are exempted from this requirement.

OUTSIDE INFLUENCES

One country's financial reporting practices can be influenced by another. It is not surprising to realize that the accounting practices in Australia, Hong Kong, Ireland, Malaysia, South Africa, Zambia, and Zimbabwe are heavily influenced by accounting practices in the United Kingdom. The United States, as an ex-colony of Great Britain, has historically been under the influence of the United Kingdom, but has long since parted ways. The United States, in turn, has influenced the accounting practices in Brazil, Chile, Colombia, Indonesia, and the Philippines. Australia has practices in common with both the United Kingdom and the United States, because it has modified its original British inspired practices with the adoption of current American practices. Italy, Portugal, and Spain are influenced by French accounting practices. Japan adopted German accounting practices in the late nineteenth century and was forced to adapt to American standards after World War II. The nations that most strongly influence others are the United Kingdom and the United States, which, interestingly, have a strong influence on each other.

IMPACT OF LEGAL SYSTEMS

In reviewing acceptable accounting practices around the world, one can observe that there are other influences that seem to play an important role in determining what is acceptable to a particular nation. One of these is the legal system. There are two principal forms of legal systems. Some nations practice a codification of law, where the written law attempts to cover every continguency. Any dispute can presumably be resolved by referring it the nation's code of law. The French Napoleonic Code epitomizes this approach to law.

The other major approach to law is common or case law. Here, legislation is written in more general language, leaving it to the courts to decide on the application of the law to particular situations. In common law countries, a case is tried by referring both to the law itself and to previous court cases that provide interpretation of the broader clauses and statements contained within the law. The United Kingdom epitomizes a nation that relies on a common body of law. The United States, along with the United Kingdom's other ex-colonies and members of the British Commonwealth, rely on common rather than a codified body of law.

The choice of the way to administer the laws of a nation influences accounting practices. Nations with a codified body of law are more apt to have an accounting system that provides little in the way of interpretation by accounting practitioners. On the other hand, a system of law that is permitted to evolve through a succession of court interpretations is more apt to have an accounting system that is more flexible in the interpretation of its pronouncements and more accommodating to a changing financial environment.

The same can be said of political systems. A political system that calls for a centrally planned economy is more apt to have a less flexible accounting system with little leeway on how various financial results are to be interpreted in the preparation of financial statements. One of the many challenges facing eastern Europe today is developing an approach to accounting that is something more than a measure of satisfying a state inspired quota.

ROLE OF PUBLIC DISCLOSURE

The nature of business ownership also impacts on the role of accounting within a nation. The United States has wide public participation in the ownership of its major companies. A government body has been established, the Securities and Exchange Commission (SEC), to test the adequacy and accuracy of published reports. The SEC is also mandated to ensure adequate and timely disclosure of important matters to shareholders. The United States has an active body of financial analysts that scrutinize the financial reports of companies for the purpose of recommending the sale or purchase of the company's shares. The financial press is aggressive in its approach in analyzing the financial results of a company and reporting on its findings. Certain financial publications seem to take particular glee in seeking out opportunities to disagree with the pronouncements of management. The financial press, including a plethora of stock advisory services, publish reports that often contain a comparative financial analysis of companies within the same industry. In America, there is little escape from public scrutiny of management performance of publicly traded companies.

Public disclosure is important in the United States because public ownership of the stock holdings of companies is pervasive. With so many shareholders wanting to know what is going on in the companies in which they own, or are considering purchasing, stock, there is a market, so to speak, for public disclosure. There is also a market for public criticism of management performance. Public disclosure is quite low on the priority list in France, where private ownership is more common. Disclosure is not very forthcoming in Germany, where major shareholdings are held by banks. The German banks, with direct access to corporate information, do not have to rely on public disclosure by way of financial reports to realize what is going on in a company. The bank's close connection to a company is bonded by owning large blocks of shares in the company and sitting on its board of directors. Share ownership and board representation make bankers more than passive lenders of money. They can, and do, guide the destiny of a company. Being in such a position, the bankers need hardly rely on published financial information.

This kind of relationship between banks and corporate borrowers is not tolerated in the United States. Banks are regulated and, with certain exceptions, prohibited from owning stock in corporations, from having access to privileged information that is not properly disclosed, and from controlling the destiny of companies other than what is included in loan covenants. Banks may exercise control when a loan goes into default, but that is presumably temporary in nature, ceasing when a company has overcome its financial difficulties. Banks are normally required to eventually liquidate what shareholdings they may have received in a workout situation for a defaulted loan. Therefore, U.S. banks are dependent on audited financial reports in assessing whether to lend money to a corporation. The same is true for individuals and financial institutions in assessing whether to buy a new issue of stock or bonds from a corporation. All of this adds to the imperative for public disclosure in the United States and, for that matter, in the United Kingdom, which may be lacking in other nations.

Published financial statements are not as indispensable to the workings of the financial system in Japan as they are in the United States. In the United States, stock ownership is dispersed and companies rely on issuing new stock as a source of capital or obtaining loans from financial institutions, which cannot be done without certified and audited statements. Banks require such statements in making loans. This is not the case in Japan. Public ownership of stock represents a fairly small percentage of the shares of stock outstanding. For most Japanese companies, the majority of the stock is held by associated companies within a "heiretsu," a galaxy of interlocking corporations. This mutual holding of shares both within the heiretsu and among the heiretsu is the bonding agent that keeps the heiretsu together and gives it its monolithic appearance to outsiders. Most of the shares of the heiretsu, and the companies making it up, will never find their way to the Tokyo stock exchange, because their purpose is not for trading or speculation but to maintain the corporate integrity of the heiretsu. With the majority of stock tucked away in safes, never to be removed, it is virtually impossible to have forced mergers and takeovers as is common in the United States and elsewhere in the world.

In the United States, bidding up the price of shares of most public corporations high enough will provide the bidder with the majority of shares as long as he or she has the financial wherewithal to purchase the shares. By obtaining a majority of shares, he or she is in a position to force a merger or a takeover of a company. Unfriendly acts of this type are virtually impossible in Japan, because bidding up the price of the stock does not provide the buyer with a majority of shares.

The principal argument in favor of unfriendly takeovers is to unseat an entrenched, and seemingly irresponsible or incompetent management for the good of the shareholders. In Japan, management is entrenched in the sense that no outsider can buy a sufficient amount of stock to unseat management. Although some may maintain that this gives management the opportunity to become complacent, one can hardly ascribe complacency to Japanese management. Japanese management is kept on its toes by the intense domestic competition for market share among the heiretsu. Moreover, the Japanese system of having the majority of shareholdings safely tucked away frees them from the necessity of having their actions dictated by the next quarter's reported profits. Japanese management can focus on obtaining long-term market share rather than on enhancing short-term reported profits. This is one of the contributing factors to the success of the Japanese in the world of global business.

Within each heiretsu, and indeed forming the central control mechanism, is a bank. The bank's purpose is to facilitate the corporate goals set forth by those running the heiretsu, which is a body made up of senior managers and bankers. Major corporate decisions also involve MITI, the influential Ministry of International Trade and Industry, which acts as a sort of clearinghouse among the leading six heiretsu. These six collectively represent much of Japan's industrial might. Even though they compete vigorously in the domestic market, they do, through the coordinating efforts of MITI and the mutual shareholding among the heiretsu of each other's stock, represent a common front to the world—what is called "Japan, Inc."

Japan, Inc. is a sort of "insider's" world, where public disclosure has little meaning. Relatively little stock is sold for the purposes of raising capital. Most capital is raised in the form of debt by the associated bank within the heiretsu. The bank knows all it has to know because of its active coordinating activities in pursuing the goals of the heiretsu and its meaningful shareholdings and directorships of the hundreds of individual companies, subsidiaries, and associated companies within the heiretsu. Disclosure is made, but on the basis that those who really need to know the information already possess it. Individual Japanese investors appear satisfied with the system as it exists. The imperative, or necessity, to disclose financial information is weak in Japan as compared to the United States.

CHAPTER 3

THE WORLD OF ACCOUNTING

Accounting is more than a way to organize financial figures. The goals of a nation and the aspiration of a people influence the structure of an accounting system. There is divergence and variety in the world's accounting systems because there is divergence and variety in the world's cultures. A manager who fails to appreciate this point may assume that the financial statements of a company operating in another nation are in accordance with the accounting system that he or she is familiar with—a dangerous assumption. Without appreciating these differences, a manager might misinterpret the financial statements, and in so doing, distort his or her evaluation of an overseas operation.

The principal accounting systems found around the world are surveyed here in terms of historic development of companies and accounting systems, qualifications of practitioners, professional societies, procedures for changing accounting standards, major influences on setting accounting guidelines, and publishing financial reports including public attitudes on the role of business in society.

THE UNITED KINGDOM

The United Kingdom was the world's first industrial nation and was the first to apply accounting to the modern manufacturing company. These practices spread throughout the British Empire. The historic role played by the United Kingdom in the development of accounting principles for modern corporations, and the promulgation of these principles throughout much, although not all, of the world, is also the foundation of a global accounting system.

Companies are formed in the United Kingdom under the auspices of various Companies Acts, which deal with the incorporation, management, administration, and dissolution of companies. Although it is possible to organize an unlimited company where the shareholders are personally responsible for the indebtedness of the company, the most common form of business organization in the United Kingdom, and throughout much of the industrialized world, is the limited company. In a limited company, the shareholders' liability is the amount owed on newly issued shares. Because shares are usually fully paid when issued, there is no further liability between a company and its shareholders. The company takes on its own legal personality, separate from that of its shareholders. Accordingly, a limited company can enter into contracts, own property, and sue or be sued in its own name without affecting the rights and obligations of the shareholders. This can be modified whereby a holding company guarantees the debts of a subsidiary or where the directors are providing personal guarantees for a loan. In the United Kingdom, these are known as public limited companies (PLC), and their shares are traded on the stock exchange.

The Companies Acts instill the concept of the stewardship of management in managing the assets entrusted to them by the shareholders. As stewards of the assets of the shareholders, the acts require that management maintain adequate and proper accounting records. Furthermore, the directors of a company must present income statement and balance sheet reports to the shareholders at prescribed intervals. The acts also require that these reports be accompanied by an independent opinion rendered by an outside party called an auditor. The concept of an audit, an external and independent check on the adequacy of financial reports to the shareholders, originates in the United Kingdom.

Although the Companies Acts require the disclosure of financial information and the issuance of financial statements, the details of such reports are not contained within the acts. This gave rise to various accounting societies within the United Kingdom to arrive at a mutual agreement as to what constitutes a "true and fair view" in the presentation of financial results to shareholders.

The United Kingdom, as its name suggests, is a nation consisting of four former countries or national entities each with its unique history and accounting society: England, Scotland, Wales, and Northern Ireland. The regional and independent accounting societies in the United Kingdom are as follows:

Institute of Chartered Accountants in England and Wales

Institute of Chartered Accountants in Scotland

Institute of Chartered Accountants in Ireland

Members of these organizations, along with the Association of Certified Accountants, are permitted to serve as auditors. An auditor from the first three organizations is called a chartered accountant. The duty of an auditor is to report to the shareholders on the accounts of a limited company as to whether they represent a true and fair view of the state of the company and to report whether the financial statements are in compliance with the Companies Acts. An auditor cannot be an agent of the company or its management. His or her responsibility is to the shareholders. To ensure the independence of an auditor, the Companies Acts prohibit an auditor from holding an office in the company or being a partner or an employee of any officer in the company. The professional standards require that an auditor cannot hold shares in the companies that he or she audits.

In addition to the previous four organizations, the Institute of Cost and Management Accountants and the Chartered Institute of Public Finance and Accountancy are part of the overall process of determining generally accepted accounting practices (GAAP) in the United Kingdom. Together, these six independent organizations make up the Accounting Standards Committee that is responsible for issuing Statements of Standard Accounting Practice (SSAPs). SSAPs cannot be promulgated unless there is formal, and unanimous, agreement among the regional accounting societies and the other participating groups. Unanimity of opinion means that changes to SSAPs, and the issuance of new SSAPs, require a long maturation period.

SSAPs provide guidance on financial statements presenting a true and fair view of a company's financial position. Although there is no formal definition of a ''true and fair view,'' it is generally considered that financial accounts should be prepared on the basis of the four fundamental accounting concepts. First, the underlying assumption is that the business entity is a going concern and will remain so for the foreseeable future. Therefore, assets and liabilities do not reflect the effects of a wind-up or liquidation of the business entity. Second, accrual accounting, the recognition of elements of income and expense even though cash has not yet changed hands, is mandatory. Third, financial reports should employ appropriate accounting practices that are consistently applied. Fourth, the concept of prudence or conservatism should prevail. The financial statements should present an overall picture that is not in any way misleading and should disclose all information that is material to the proper understanding of the financial condition of the company. The description of accounts should be unambiguous, striking a balance between the completeness of disclosure and the clarity of summarization.

In addition to the Statements of Standard Accounting Practice, there are Statements of Recommended Accounting Practice (SORPs), which provide guidance on accounting principles and rules that are considered best for a particular industry. Companies must inform the readers of the particular accounting policies or practices that have been applied in the financial statements. The Audit Practices Committee, whose membership is derived from the principal accountancy organizations, provides guidance on the conduct of audits.

Financial reports in the United Kingdom have included, for quite some time, observations concerning socially redeeming activities of a company and the impact of the company on society. Exhibit 3.1 shows a portion of the 1987 annual review of Bass, a company in the hotel, softdrink, wine, and brewery businesses. The exhibit mentions such nonfinancial matters as employee involvement for opening lines of dialogue between the workers and management, an employee program to encourage their becoming shareholders in the company,

Exhibit 3.1
Portion of 1987 Bass Review

Employee involvement
Our policy is that for all employees there will be opportunities for Communication, Consultation and Involvement (CCI), by methods appropriate to the subject matter and to the position of the individual within the organisation.

We believe that the implementation of such a policy leads to increased efficiency and a greater commitment by employees to the affairs of the Company.

Employee share schemes
The eighth annual issue of shares through the Bass Employee Profit Share Scheme took place in March 1987, and 1·2 m Bass ordinary shares were appropriated to 18,734 employees. The scheme was introduced in March 1980, and since then shares to the value of £48·4 m have been issued.

1,683 new savings contracts were signed in March 1987, by employees participating in the Bass Employee Savings Share Scheme. There are now 6,114 savers, with options to purchase 4·5 m Bass ordinary shares.

Options were granted in March 1987 to 17 senior executives of the Company in respect of 79,700 ordinary shares.

In September 1987 options were granted in respect of 227,379 ordinary shares to 12 senior executives of Horizon Travel PLC under the provisions of the Finance Act 1987.

Youth training schemes
The two year Youth Training Scheme is now well established in Bass, and the Company's involvement in giving training and experience to young people will continue.

Bass has been involved in discussions with the Manpower Services Commission regarding the new Job Training Scheme. This is aimed at giving people who have been unemployed for more than six months, a package of training, vocational education and practical experience, designed to help them to re-establish themselves in today's job market.

Equal opportunity
It is the Company's policy that there shall be no discrimination in respect of sex, colour, religion, race, nationality or ethnic origin and that equal opportunity shall be given to all employees.

Disabled persons
The Company continues to assist disabled employees by making every effort to provide appropriate employment and by offering opportunities for training, career development and promotion. In recruitment procedures disabled applicants are given full and fair consideration for suitable vacancies.

Pensions
As a result of legislation included in the Social Security Act 1986, members of the Company Pension Plan will from next April be able to choose on an individual basis whether to remain in the Plan, or instead opt for a Personal Pension or the State Earnings Related Pension Scheme.

Explanatory literature will be distributed and a video presentation will be made available to members to ensure that they understand the consequences of a decision to opt out of the Plan.

Government continues to intervene elsewhere in pension matters and changes and restrictions introduced in this year's Finance Act will add further complication to the administration of the pension arrangements.

During the year approximately 1,000 Britvic employees became members of the Plan, and arrangements are being made for employees of businesses more recently coming under the Company's control, notably the Beecham Soft Drinks business, to be brought into membership.

It has been the policy for some time to review pensions on an annual basis, with the aim of matching two-thirds of the rise in the Retail Price Index. This has now been strengthened by also guaranteeing full RPI increases up to 4% per annum. Pensions, including deferred pensions, were increased by this percentage as from 1st October 1987.

Donations
During the financial year the Group made contributions for charitable purposes of £447,012 including £311,986 to the Bass Charitable Trust which supports a wide range of charitable causes, £38,777 to the Licensed Victuallers National Homes and £29,875 (the last of four payments totalling £119,500) to the Alcohol Education and Research Council. In addition, participation in community-linked activities, such as Enterprise Agencies, Youth Training Schemes and secondments of personnel cost the Group over £200,000. No donations for political purposes were made during the year.

training programs for youth, equal opportunity in employment practices with special consideration given to disabled persons, review of the pension program as to its adequacy, and donations to charitable causes.

Most Chartered Accountants have university degrees, although this is not a requirement. A student may take foundation courses in accountancy at polytechnical schools rather than pursue a university degree program. Either way, an aspiring accountant enters into a "training contract" with an approved employer for either three years for students with university degrees or four years for students without such degrees. The trainee, regardless of his or her educational background, must pass two professional examinations to become a Chartered Accountant.

Until 1991, only licensed chartered accounting firms were authorized to train aspiring professionals. Students can now be accepted under the Training Outside Public Practices (TOPP) program, which is offered by nonpublic accounting entities within commercial businesses, government agencies, and not-for-profit organizations. Although such training is oriented to private accountants who work within commercial and noncommercial organizations, upon passing the requisite examinations, an individual can become a public Chartered Accountant.

Another change taking place in the United Kingdom is the formation of the Accounting Standards Board (ASB), which will supplant the independent regional accounting societies as the standard setting body in the United Kingdom. A standard promulgated by the ASB is called a Financial Reporting Standard (FRS), replacing the Statement of Standard Accounting Practice. In 1991, the ASB was in the process of drafting its statement of principles.

THE UNITED STATES

The British approach to accounting, in that financial reports are to be issued regularly, consistent with the principle of stewardship function of management; that they are to be a true and fair view of the financial results; and that they are to be audited by an outside party, spread throughout the British Empire. As in the United Kingdom, the United States has its corresponding body of law concerning the nature of corporations and the requirements to issue financial statements to their shareholders and disclose pertinent information on a timely basis. As in the United Kingdom, the law generally is silent on the matter of the form and structure of how financial information is to be provided. These matters are decided on by a professional accounting society that is responsible for the detailed promulgation of acceptable standards for uniformity in accounting practices.

Founded in 1959, the American equivalent to the British Accounting Standards Committee was the Accounting Principles Board. It was recognized by the American Institute of Certified Public Accountants (AICPA) as the organization through which standards were to be set in the private sector. The Accounting Principles Board was reorganized into the Financial Accounting Standards Board (FASB) in 1973. FASB standards, once agreed on, are the standards by which financial statements in the United States are prepared. The FASB differs from its British counterpart in that there are no regional accounting societies that have to be in agreement before the parent organization can act. The FASB also is different in that its membership is not restricted to public accountants, but also includes representatives of academia, government, private industry, and investment banking firms. However, public accountants have greater influence than the others. The general procedure for establishing or modifying an accounting standard starts with the assembling of a task force of experts who conduct the underlying research and prepare a public document for discussion purposes. The FASB then holds public meetings, prepares various drafts for comment, and, after exercise of due diligence, issues the final standard.

There is somewhat more government involvement in the setting of accounting standards in the United States than in the United Kingdom. In 1934, the Securities and Exchange Commission (SEC) was established with responsibility to oversee the preparation of financial reports of companies whose stocks are publicly traded on the nation's stock exchanges. The SEC is also concerned with timely disclosure of corporate information to the investing public. The SEC has delegated the authority for setting accounting standards to the practitioners. However, the FASB does have a government representative and works closely with the SEC to ensure that the SEC is in agreement with proposed changes to accounting standards. In addition, the SEC does influence the process because its own Accounting Series Releases establish guidelines and regulations regarding the format of annual and other reports required to satisfy the reporting obligations of publicly traded companies.

The SEC is also concerned with proper disclosure by management of important happenings within their firms. A great deal of importance is attached to timely disclosure of pertinent or material events to the investing public and the financial press that serves the investing public's needs. Insider trading, where investment decisions are made on the basis of privileged information that has not been disseminated to the public, is a forbidden practice throughout the free world. The Securities and Exchange Commission in the United States goes to unusual lengths to ensure that there is proper disclosure of pertinent information including changes in the ownership of stock by those who are considered to be insiders (management, members of the board of directors, and major individual shareowners). Trading activity in stocks is often investigated for hints of impropriety before, during, and after the announcements of major corporate events.

There are philosophic differences in auditing between the United Kingdom and the United States. In the United States, auditors are oriented to the shareholder much as they were intended to be in the United Kingdom's Companies Acts. In the United Kingdom, the nature of who the auditor is reporting to has changed with the years. The auditor's function has come to be seen as an extension of the Inland Revenue, the tax collecting authority in the United Kingdom. Chartered accountants are more proactive on behalf of the tax authority in the United Kingdom than in the United States. Indeed, the auditor in the

United Kingdom submits his or her report to both the Inland Revenue and the shareholders, whereas in the United States, the report is made to the shareholders only.

Another difference between the United Kingdom and the United States is that the Companies Acts apply to all corporations, public or private. All companies above a given size must prepare their financial reports in accordance with SSAPs and be audited. In the United States, the requirement for a company to follow FASB pronouncements on generally accepted accounting principles, issue financial reports, and be audited stems from SEC requirements that apply for companies that desire to have a public issuance of stock or whose stock is publicly traded. Therefore, SEC requirements do not apply to all companies. A private company need not have its financial accounting in accordance with FASB guidelines, nor is it required to be audited. Private companies in the United States may follow U.S. GAAP just in case they wish to become registered with the SEC for public issuance of stock or to be acquired by a publicly traded company. Private companies may follow U.S. GAAP as a requirement of their shareholders, as contained in the articles of incorporation, or of their bankers, as a condition for making loans.

One other difference between financial reports in the United States and in the United Kingdom is that the latter has, for a relatively long time, commented on the social responsibility aspects of a company's activities. Accounting statements and auditors' reports in the United States have made little mention of the impact of the company on society. In recent years, there has been a growing practice for U.S. companies to be more proactive in making such statements.

Exhibit 3.2 shows a special supplement on the employee equal opportunity program in a supplement to the 1990 Exxon annual report. This illustrates the emerging trend in major U.S. corporations to dedicate a portion of their annual financial reports to subjects bearing on corporate social responsibility.

Another area of potential confusion between U.K. and U.S. accounting practices is in language. The U.K. term ''ordinary shares'' is the same as ''common shares'' in the United States. The U.K. term ''stocks'' means ''inventories'' in the U.S. ''Own shares'' in the United Kingdom means ''treasury stock'' in the United States. ''Debtors'' versus ''receivables,'' ''provision for bad debt'' versus ''reserve for doubtful accounts,'' and ''taken to reserves'' versus ''included in equity'' are other differences in terminology between the United Kingdom and the United States. This matter of differences in terminology becomes bothersome for non-English speaking companies that desire to issue an English version of their annual reports. Usually, the purpose of the English version is in preparation for raising funds in the London and/or New York capital markets, or to attract American or English investors. The simple decision to translate a company's financial statements into English is complicated by which form of English is more suitable for presentation purposes.

The accounting profession in the United States is represented by the American Insititute of Certified Public Accountants. Slightly less than half of its mem-

Exhibit 3.2
Supplement to 1990 Exxon Annual Report

EXXONCORPORATION*
EMPLOYMENT IN THE UNITED STATES – 1990

	**Total Employment	Employment of Women		Employment of Minorities	
		Number of Women	*% of Employment*	*Number of Minorities*	*% of Employment*
Officials and Managers	6382	669	10.5%	741	11.6%
Professionals	10642	2305	21.7%	1366	12.8%
Technicians	2749	793	28.8%	650	23.6%
Sales Workers	168	49	29.2%	47	28.0%
Office and Clerical	8797	6454	73.4%	3337	37.9%
Craft (Skilled)	8409	517	6.1%	2078	24.7%
Operatives (Semi-Skilled)	4511	552	12.2%	1508	33.4%
Laborers (Unskilled)	327	31	9.5%	72	22.0%
Service Workers	230	59	25.7%	86	37.4%
Totals	42215	11429	27.1%	9885	23.4%

*The terms "corporation." "company." "Exxon." "our." and "its" refer collectively to all domestic regional and operating organizations affiliated with Exxon Corporation.

**The EEO figures include long-term non-regular employees as mandated by law

**Representation of Women and
Minorities in the U.S. Workforce
1990**

Foremost among the resources of a premier company are the people who strive together in the attainment of its business objectives. Exxon values the diversity and international character of its workforce. We want all employees to succeed, and we devote additional attention to women and minorities to ensure that barriers do not exist to their progress. In 1990, there was continued progress in the representation of women and minorities with an increase in the total number of both minorities and women in the company's U.S. workforce. At year end, women filled 10.5 percent of managerial positions while minorities represented 11.6 percent of the managerial category. In professional assignments, minorities and women were represented in 12.8 percent and

21.7 percent of the positions respectively.

The Corporation's objectives in this area are clear ... continuing and substantial progress is expected in all facets of the employment relationship. Examples of management action start with the continued focus on pre-college and college recruiting through the expanded use of scholarships, our "partnerships" with various school systems, co-op assignments, and summer jobs. College recruiting efforts have been intensified by the addition of a full-time minority coordinator, expanded recruiting at selected schools with strong black and hispanic populations, an increase in the use of internships and additional recruiter training regarding diver-

Exhibit 3.2 (continued)

sity. Following actual employment, continued attention is being devoted to new hire assimilation, mentoring, training of managers and supervisors in effectively managing diversity in the workplace, and in stewarding plans aimed at furthering upward mobility. The bottom line ... our managers and supervisors are aware of their responsibility and accountability for continuing and substantial progress.

Identification and Employment of Women and Minorities

Exxon's U.S. based operations hired 2,317 people during 1990. Women represented 38.8 percent and minorities 23.3 percent of the total hires, which is consistent with recent years.

Professional employments remained relatively flat in 1990 with a total of 695. Minorities constituted 21 percent of those employments and women represented 34 percent. Approximately half of all the professionals hired were recruited during Exxon's 1989-1990 campus recruiting program which included visits to over 100 colleges and universities.

In its efforts to actively identify and recruit talented women and minorities, in 1990 the Company made educational contributions of approximately $920,000 at the pre-college, college, and graduate school levels. A primary focus of these contributions was to promote engineering and science education at the high school and college levels.

Exxon organizations offer summer internship and college scholarship programs for women and minority students interested in Engineering, Earth Science, Accounting, Law, Computer Science, and other related business degrees. The Company views these programs as a means of attracting and developing promising students for regular employment in the professional ranks.

Exxon's Early Minority Identification Program (EMID), the INROADS Program and the high school partnership program, continue to provide mentoring and summer employment opportunities with Exxon for women and minority high school and college students. The Math/Science Achievement Award Program, which was expanded in 1990, recognizes minority students and teachers from metropolitan areas in Texas and Louisiana for outstanding academic achievement and excellence in the classroom.

During the fall of 1990, Exxon initiated a Minority Scholarship Program for students pursuing degrees in math/science based disciplines, particularly engineering and geoscience. Under this program, $100,000 in scholarships were awarded to 15 minority students at ten universities around the country. These scholarships fund the majority of college costs including tuition, books, room and board, and lab fees. Along with the scholarship, the students have the opportunity for summer employment with Exxon in jobs related to their respective fields of study.

Since 1966, Exxon has sponsored fellowships to various graduate business schools to support women and minority graduate students seeking Masters degrees in Business Administration. During 1990, the Company donated $117,000 for this purpose. Scholarships were awarded to twenty-eight fellows chosen by the administrations of their respective universities. Also during 1990, a grant of $135,000 was awarded to Stevens Institute of Technology in New Jersey to provide scholarships, mentoring, tutoring, and other assistance for minority engineering students.

Exxon also provides financial support to organizations such as the American Indian Science and Engineering Society (AISES), the National Society of Black Engineers (NSBE), the Society of Hispanic Professional Engineers (SHPE), the Society of Women Engineers (SWE), the National Black MBA Association and numerous other groups who strive to support and develop academic excellence in female and minority students in the disciplines we recruit.

Exxon Education Foundation Minority-Oriented Grants

Complementing the above efforts, in 1990, the Exxon Education Foundation's minority-oriented grant payments totaled $2,926,000. These payments were made in support of numerous organizations, programs, and projects from elementary school through graduate school.

As has been the case for the past several years, the largest component of the Foundation's minority-oriented expenditures was its Elementary and Secondary School Improvement Program. A total of $1,570,000 was spent in 1990 on initiatives focused on the program's three primary objectives: (1) enhancement of educators' understanding of the changing demographics of the student-age population (the proportion of all children and youth who are minority and/or disadvantaged has continued to grow rapidly); (2) redesign of schools in ways that will enable them to be instructionally more effective, especially for minority and disadvantaged students; and (3) improvement of teacher education programs in ways that will increase the supply of teachers who are well prepared to take full advantage of improvements in instructional opportunities in the schools.

In 1990, the Foundation continued its long-standing effort to increase the supply of minority engineers and scientists. A total of $427,000 was spent in support of programs and projects in this area. In an effort to make programs that receive support more comprehensive, the Foundation made a multiyear grant to the Columbia University School of Engineering to develop a prototype high school curriculum that focuses on verbal reasoning and communication skills in addition to science and mathematics.

A total of $372,000 was spent in minority-oriented projects undertaken through the Foundation's Mathematics Education Program. Most of these grants were made to school dis-

Exhibit 3.2 (continued)

tricts with substantial minority student populations to improve mathematics instruction in the primary grades. The Foundation also provided funding to the Mathematical Association of America for its new initiative, Strengthening Underrepresented Minority Mathematics Achievement.

During 1990, the Foundation made $230,000 in grant payments to historically black colleges and universities and the United Negro College Fund. It also made $137,000 in grant payments to the Hispanic Association of Colleges and Universities (HACU) and its member institutions. The American Indian College Fund received support totaling $42,000.

Minority and Women-Oriented Community Activities

Improvement of the economic and social prospects of women and members of racial minority groups was the focus of corporate grants totalling about $1.0 million in 1990. Grantees included organizations which specifically focus on women and minorities such as Catalyst for Women, National Association for the Advancement of Colored People, National Puerto Rican Forum, and National Council of La Raza. A five-year commitment of $300,000 to the Joint Center for Political and Economic Studies supports research and dissemination of information on public policy issues affecting blacks as well as program expansion related to the economic policy area.

Exxon targets its support to activities which deal with issues such as adult illiteracy, family and child welfare, youth unemployment and revitalization of economically disadvantaged neighborhoods, areas which have substantial impact upon women and racial minorities.

Exxon employees continue to be personally involved in programs designed to support/mentor minorities seeking employment within the corporate environment. For example, many black managers and professionals participate in the National Urban League's Black Executive Exchange Program at the campuses of historically black colleges and universities. By serving as role models and providing practical insights into the demands and expectations of the corporate environment, these employees are helping black students formulate strategies for success.

Another thrust of the contributions program complements Exxon's activity with minority purchasing councils and includes grants to Interracial Council for Business Opportunity and Urban Business Assistance Corporation, organizations involved in providing assistance to women and minorities who own or wish to start their own businesses.

Support of Minority and Women-Owned Business

Exxon recognizes its responsibility to assist in the development of minority/women-owned businesses which can be competitive suppliers of goods and services to the Company.

Consistent with legal and ethical obligations to all suppliers, vendors and contractors, Exxon strives to:

— Seek out minority/women-owned businesses capable of supplying the materials and services it requires.

— Identify and advise qualifiable minority/women vendors so they may become competitive and self-sustaining suppliers of goods and services to Exxon companies.

Exxon Company, U.S.A. is a member of the National Minority Supplier Development Council, Inc., and actively works with regional minority purchasing councils in areas where it operates to develop opportunities for minority business enterprises. In 1990, Exxon USA sponsored a major reception at the NMSDC annual conference in Houston. Exxon managers take active leadership roles in several regional councils and in recent years, Exxon Company, USA has received awards and commendations for its assistance in the development of minority businesses.

During 1990, Exxon organizations purchased $158 million in goods and services from 1,836 minority-owned businesses. This represents a 23 percent increase over the prior year. With regard to non-minority women-owned businesses, during 1990 Exxon's Domestic organizations spent over $92 million with 1,712 such businesses.

Assistance for the Disabled

In 1990, Exxon's corporate contributions program included grants totalling more than $1.1 million to organizations which provide care, research and services in areas related to physical and mental health. Exxon's program of health-related grants emphasizes education and preventive medicine, particularly in the area of substance abuse.

Substance abuse programs are focused on prevention, rather than treatment and rehabilitation, and include support for the Children of Alcoholics Foundation, Inc. which has developed programs to deal with the physical, emotional and psychological needs of children whose homes are disrupted by alcoholic elders. In 1990, Exxon contributed funds towards the expansion of this program to a special "Help for Inner-City Minority Children of Addicted Parents" project. Another grant went to The National Health Center to develop an anti-substance abuse component of its "Living Healthy" educational series. Exxon continues to support the University of Texas, Health Science Center, which trains occupational health professionals providing care for the disabled.

In addition to direct contributions to health-related agencies, community-oriented programs provide additional funds to a variety of organizations, many of them in the health care field. One such program offers cash grants of up to $1,000 each to agencies with which Exxon employees or annuitants are involved as volunteers. Another provides funds for the employment of summer interns by nonprofit organizations.

A detailed listing of the contributions and grants mentioned in this document can be found in *Dimensions*, Exxon's annual report on corporate giving.

bership of approximately 300,000 are in public practice. The remainder fulfill internal accounting needs in private industry, business, government, and other organizations. Each state specifies the educational and experience requirements necessary for certification within that state. In addition, all candidates must pass a nationally administered, professional examination given under the auspices of the AICPA. Although each state has its specific set of rules, the general requirements, in addition to passing the AICPA examination, include an undergraduate degree in accounting and several years of practical experience. Reciprocity among the states is not automatic. Public accountants wishing to practice in another state must submit an application to the proper state authorities. Presently, the AICPA is urging that all states require the equivalent of five years of education at the college or university level for those aspiring to become accountants. In 1991, eighteen states have amended their regulations accordingly, and it is expected that all states will conform to AICPA requirements by the year 2000.

AUSTRALIA

Australia has historically been heavily influenced by British accounting practices. The Companies Act of 1961 contains the concept of the accountability of directors to shareholders, including the stipulation that annual accounts and audits of financial statements must be true and fair. In Australia, the courts frequently decide on what is to be construed as true and fair in accounting practices, not the professional accounting societies. Accountants are represented by either the Australian Society of Certified Public Accountants (CPAs) with over 60,000 members, or the Institute of Chartered Accountants with nearly 22,000 members. These organizations compete for both membership and influence, which complicates the process of arriving at generally accepted accounting principles. These are established by the Australian Accounting Research Foundation, which is jointly sponsored by the two professional accounting organizations. Recent decisions have more or less mirrored changes in accounting practices taking place in the United States, which is why Australian accounting is a mix of U.K. and U.S. accounting practices. Australian annual reports contain a section on social responsibility and Australian companies also publish annual reports for their employees.

The Australian Society of CPAs and the Institute of Chartered Accountants jointly approve academic programs of study that will qualify an applicant for eventual professional recognition. To become a CPA in Australia, a trainee must have an undergraduate degree with a major in accounting and three years of experience under the supervision of a CPA or chartered accountant, or five years unsupervised experience in accounting or finance. A trainee must also complete course work designed by the Australian Society of CPAs in auditing, external reporting, insolvency and reconstruction, management accounting, taxation, and treasury, each with its own examination. The total program for becoming a CPA must be completed within five years of enrollment. If not completed within this time, the trainee must re-enroll starting from the beginning.

CANADA

Canada is a member of the Commonwealth of Nations and its companies are organized under legislation similar to the Companies Acts of Britain. However, corporate legislation emanates from dual levels of government: federal and provincial. Similar to a choice of English or French as an official language, a company has a choice as to which provincial or federal corporate law applies when the company is first incorporated. A company actually has a choice of thirteen sets of law (federal law, or the applicable law in ten provinces and two territories). The choice depends on a number of factors including the scope of operations, nature of the business, disclosure and reporting requirements, the structure of the shareholdings, and the residences of the directors.

Canadian companies can also enter into unusual business arrangements from the perspective of the United States. For instance, corporations can form a general partnership where the participating corporations can avail themselves of the income tax advantages of a partnership while not making the shareholders personally liable. A corporation can also become a general partner of a limited partnership where the limited partners enjoy limited liability if they do not manage the operations of the partnership in any way. The shareholders of a corporation that is a general partner can limit their liability and still retain control of the company. Canadian law permits holding companies to be organized in such a way that dividends can be paid from an operating company to a holding company in a very tax advantageous manner. None of these Canadian business arrangements is legal in the United States.

The Canadian Institute of Chartered Accountants is an umbrella organization governed by representatives of the provincial organizations. The provincial organizations have delegated to the national organization the setting of accounting and auditing standards for the nation. The Canadian Institute of Chartered Accountants speaks for the accounting profession on national issues and settles issues between the provincial organizations. Its declarations are given statutory recognition, that is, are legally binding.

The nature of financial statement reporting and auditing requirements differ among corporations, depending on which of the thirteen sets of legislation apply. Although this sounds confusing, there is apparently little difficulty in the preparation of financial statements. Only certified members of the Canadian Institute of Chartered Accountants can conduct audits. There are other organizations such as the Certified General Accountants Association and the Society of Management Accountants, whose members generally fill industrial or government accounting positions. As one might expect, accounting standards issued by the Canadian Institute of Chartered Accountants are influenced by what occurs south of the border. However, the accounting systems in the United States and Canada are not exact replicas of each another.

In Canada, audited statements are required only for large publicly traded companies, whereas in the United States, all publicly traded companies must be audited. Another difference between Canada and the United States is that a person who becomes a chartered accountant in one province is recognized as such by all the provinces. In the United States, a person who becomes a certified public accountant in one state cannot practice in another state. On the point of reciprocity, the United States is more provincial than Canada.

FRANCE

France is a nation of many small companies. The two ways for a business to incorporate itself are SA (Société Anonyme) or SARL (Société à Responsabilité Limitée), which, without translating, says a great deal about French, and Western, attitudes toward the nature and purpose of corporate entities. However, small companies do not have the depth of operations to support large industrial endeavors that transcend national borders. To compete globally, the French government selects what amounts to a national champion in various industries. These relatively few large companies are given monopolistic rights to certain market segments within France. They may also be subsidized by the government to the extent necessary to ensure their competitiveness in the global market.

Accounting practices are uniform throughout the country. The Plan Comptable is essentially a national cookbook for accounting, with detailed instructions on such matters as valuation methods and procedures, disclosure rules, and the standard forms to be used by accountants. This follows, conceptually, the French practice of codifying its laws (the Napoleonic Code). In France, tax laws have precedence over the concept of a true and fair presentation of financial results. In fact, financial reports are usually the tax returns for a company. Yet, as has already been discussed, there are frequently major differences between book and tax returns in the portrayal of the financial results of a company.

The detailed structure of French accounting goes beyond the needs of the government to collect taxes. The Chart of Accounts is prepared by the Economics Ministry and contains an elaborate internal coding system. A company's bookkeeping must be in strict accordance with the coding system set forth in the Plan Comptable. The financial reports must be supported by substantial disclosures in footnotes that cover a variety of financial and nonfinancial items. Some of the nonfinancial items are the number of employees by type of work, a listing of marketable securities, and corporate activity on a geographic basis.

The corporate accounts, prepared in strict accordance with an accounting chart or plan set forth by a government directive, are submitted annually for incorporation into the national statistical data base. The advantage of such a system from the point of view of government planners is obvious. The annual accounts of every company in the nation follow the same format and numerical coding system. This permits easy recall from a computer data base system by government planners. By referring to a code number, planners have access to the associated corporate accounting item for every major company in France, and for the entire nation by aggregating the data. They can also be confident that the determination of the value associated with each code number is the same because the procedure for determining the value associated with a code number has been standardized. This standardization ensures consistency of application with a minimum of interpretation.

This extremely standardized approach to accounting does lend itself to national planning purposes. Other European nations, such as Belgium, Spain, Italy, and Greece, have adopted standard accounting plans to varying degrees. These accounting plans or charts generally originate from a government body such as the ministry of finance or economics. Germany also has a detailed accounting plan, but the plan originates from statute, not from the promulgation of rules by a government bureaucracy.

In contrast, English speaking nations and the Netherlands have less uniformity and, therefore, more flexibility. The portrayal of financial results follows a general, not a detailed, format. The Dutch and English inspired accounting systems focus on portraying a true and fair view of the financial results for the benefit of the shareholders. The European continental accounting systems are intended for tax collecting and state planning. This is a primary example of how accounting can be formulated to meet the demands of a constituency—in this case, the interests of shareholders versus the interests of national economic planners and government tax collectors.

There are two principal organizations in France serving the accounting profession. One is the Order des Experts Comptables et des Comptables Agrees, which has rigorous entry requirement standards. This organization serves more as business advisors than as accountants. The other organization is the Compagnie Nationale des Commissaires aux Comptes. It is less demanding to qualify for this organization, whose members are responsible for the conduct of the statutory audits.

French law mandates two different statutory audits be performed by French auditing firms. By law, these statutory auditing firms are extremely limited in the number of professional staff members that they may employ. Consequently, there are a large number of firms that can provide the statutory audits. U.S. firms are obliged to use the services of French correspondents in performing statutory audits. Exhibit 3.3 is the auditors report on the consolidated financial statements of Societe Generale, a large French bank.

The French also require that financial reports include information concerned with social consciousness. Accountants routinely prepare statements on the number of workers exposed to excessive noise, toxic substances, and other environmental and social matters for companies with over three hundred employees. Accountants are expected to prepare what amounts to environmental impact statements, which seems to be outside their area of expertise, yet is within their sphere of responsibility.

Exhibit 3.3
Societe Generale 1990 Annual Report

CONSOLIDATED FINANCIAL STATEMENTS

TRANSLATED FROM FRENCH

REPORT OF THE STATUTORY AUDITORS ON THE CONSOLIDATED FINANCIAL STATEMENTS
For the year ended December 31, 1990

Ladies and Gentlemen,

In execution of the assignment that was entrusted to us, we are presenting to you our report on:

– the audit of the attached consolidated financial statements of Société Générale,

– the verification of the management report,

for the fiscal year ended December 31, 1990.

I. OPINION ON THE CONSOLIDATED FINANCIAL STATEMENTS

We have made an audit of the consolidated financial statements by applying the procedures that we have deemed necessary according to the standards of the profession.

In particular, we have verified that the two changes in accounting principles which took place during the year were disclosed in the notes to the consolidated financial statements and in the management report.

We certify that the consolidated financial statements are regular and sincere and give a true view of the result of operations for the fiscal year last ended and of the financial situation and patrimony (assets and liabilities) of Société Générale and its consolidated subsidiaries at the close of that fiscal year.

II. SPECIFIC VERIFICATION

We have also carried out, in accordance with the standards of the profession, the specific verification required by law.

We have no observation to formulate on the sincerity and the conformity with the consolidated financial statements of the information given in the management report.

Neuilly and Paris, April 11, 1991

THE STATUTORY AUDITORS

| KPMG Audit | FRINAULT FIDUCIAIRE |
| Fiduciaire de France | |

| Bernard-Louis BRINGUIER | Philippe |
| Jean-Paul GRIZIAUX | PEUCH-LESTRADE |

THE INDEPENDANT ACCOUNTANTS
Arthur Andersen & Co.
(an Illinois, USA Partnership)

The educational requirements to enter the French accounting profession are among the highest in Europe, with regulations having been revised in 1981 and in 1988. Students are required to take at least seven years of study beyond the "baccalaureat," the final high school examination. In practice, it frequently takes an applicant ten years to fulfill all the requirements to join the ranks of professional accountants. Contained within this ten-year period of becoming a professional accountant is a three-year professional training period. During this period, a trainee is expected to be employed by a professional accounting firm in public practice or in conducting statutory audits. A trainee may be employed in the accounting, finance, or control departments of a company for one of these three years.

GERMANY

Germans have a proclivity for working together for the greater good of the nation and for assiduously following the literal letter of the law. These cultural tendencies have a direct impact on accounting. Accounting in Germany is more akin to bookkeeping, which is defined in detail by the tax law. The German

Commercial Code requires annual taking of inventories and issuance of annual financial statements. The 1965 Stock Corporation Law contains accounting principles that are used in the preparation of financial statements. These financial statements are presented to the tax authority as a tax return. If deviations from the law are noted, a tax examiner in Germany may disregard the accounting reports and assess any tax that appears to be reasonable. All financial accounts are examined by the government. Although one may presume that this would be an enormous national undertaking, in actuality, it is not. The reason for this is that German accountants ensure that the financial statements issued by a corporation are in compliance with the law—the proverbial German attitude toward correctness and compliance.

It is interesting to note the impact of a shift of political power in Germany compared to one in the United States. In the United States, a change in the political party in power often has a direct impact on the tax returns because they are based on regulations and these can be changed frequently. A change in political parties in Germany has no impact on tax returns because they are based on the Stock Corporation Law, which was last changed in 1965.

The law is literally interpreted, leaving little choice of action for the German accounting profession. The German Institute of Accountants addresses the larger issues associated with accounting principles. The institute does not have to take any action regarding the specific application of accounting principles because these have already been codified in the preparation of tax returns. The German Stock Corporation Law requires compulsory audits that are conducted by German CPAs. This group of individuals, who only number five thousand in all of Germany, are the most rigorously trained CPAs in the world. The preparation for the admission examinations is so extensive that a candidate is usually over thirty-five years of age before he or she is ready to take them. Being so few in number, and so extensively prepared, German CPAs are highly regarded by the public. Given their task of auditing all publicly traded companies, and the paucity in numbers, one can begin to appreciate the fixed structure of German accounting practices and the degree of compliance of accounting reports with statutory law.

Auditors in Germany frequently prepare long-form reports, similar to those that fell out of favor in the United States during the 1930s and 1940s. These reports typically address each separate caption of the balance sheet and income statements. Current U.S. financial reports generally do not disclose such a detailed level of information. The long-form report prepared by the auditor is not made available to the public. The report, including a listing of any adverse conditions that would be of keen interest to shareholders, is forwarded to the company and to its bank(s). German banks are often quasi-owners of a business, with stock holdings and representation on the Supervisory Board. Furthermore, the German banks are partial owners of some of the independent accounting firms, although a law passed in 1985 prohibited the banks from making future investments in accounting firms. In this insider's world of controlling a company, the financial statements prepared for public consumption need not be terribly informative. As a consequence, public disclosure by German companies to the investing public is not on a par with disclosure in the United States.

Germany and the Netherlands have an institution called the Supervisory Board. This board oversees the Board of Management, which manages the operations of the company. The Supervisory Board is kept informed regularly on the status and development of a company's business through verbal and written reports from the Board of Management. The Supervisory Board endorses the Auditors' Report and examines the financial statements of the company. Although this may sound similar to the Board of Directors in the United Kingdom or in the United States, it is not. The Supervisory Board does not include management participation. In the United Kingdom and the United States, management is not only represented, but may, although not necessarily, dominate the proceedings of the Board of Directors. The Supervisory Board in Germany is made up of outsiders including representation from senior management of other companies, principal bank, and legal firms, as one might expect to see as outside board members in the United Kingdom and the United States. The difference lies in employee representation. For example, Veba, a large German energy and chemical company, in 1990 had a Supervisory Board with two chemical workers, a commercial employee, a driver, a foreman electrician, and an electric engineer, who, as a group, made up 30 percent of the membership of the Supervisory Board. Exhibit 3.4 contains the makeup of the Supervisory Board, the Board of Management, and the report of the Supervisory Board to the shareholders for Veba.

The concept of a supervisory board is supported by business interests in the Netherlands and Germany and opposed by business interests in the United Kingdom, the United States, and elsewhere. Opposition is based on the traditional interpretation of the role of management to serve, fairly exclusively, the interests of the shareholders by maximization of profits and the traditional interpretation of the role of labor as a commodity that is purchased by the hour for the production of goods and services. The rise of Germany and Japan as industrial powers and the well being of the people of the Netherlands are a direct challenge to the traditional Anglo-American viewpoints on the respective roles of management and labor in the operations of a company.

German financial reports, which are also the tax returns for the companies, may exclude foreign-based subsidiaries if their profits are not taxable in Germany. For large companies such as Veba, consolidated financial reports do include foreign subsidiaries in accordance with changing accounting practices within the European Community. In general, the attitude of the government to business is benign in nature. The government desires a high degree of liquidity within German companies. For instance, a German company can fund employee pension plans within the company's financial structure. This means that the company has the right to borrow the money from the pension plan for corporate uses. The net effect of this is that the pension plan is essentially unfunded—it is a source of free, or very low cost, financing for the corporation.

Exhibit 3.4
Veba 1990 Annual Report—Makeup of Boards and Supervisor Board Report

Honorary Chairman of VEBA AG

Dr.-Ing. E. h. HEINZ P. KEMPER.
Grainau

Supervisory Board

Dipl.-Kfm. GÜNTER VOGELSANG.
Düsseldorf.
Chairman

HERMANN RAPPE.
Chairman of the Industriegewerkschaft
Chemie, Papier, Keramik,
Sarstedt,
Deputy Chairman

Dr. GÜNTHER ALLEKOTTE.
Head of the Legal Department, Hüls AG,
Marl

HANS BERGER.
1st Chairman of the Board of the
Industriegewerkschaft Bergbau und Energie,
Bochum

Dr. MARCUS BIERICH.
Managing Director.
Robert Bosch GmbH,
Stuttgart

ROBERT BRAUN.
Chemical worker,
Gelsenkirchen

HORST BREITFELD.
Chemical worker,
Marl

ROLF DIEL.
Chairman of the Supervisory Board,
Dresdner Bank AG,
Düsseldorf

HELMUT GUTHARDT.
Chairman of the Board of Management,
DG Bank Deutsche Genossenschaftsbank,
Frankfurt am Main

Dr. iur. h. c. HORST K. JANNOTT.
Chairman of the Board of Management,
Münchener Rückversicherungs-Gesellschaft,
Munich

Dr. HORST KLOSE,
Executive Partner of the MERO Group
of Companies, Würzburg,
Vice President of the Deutsche Schutz-
vereinigung für Wertpapierbesitz e. V.,
Düsseldorf

HILMAR KOPPER.
Member of the Board of Management,
Deutsche Bank AG,
Frankfurt am Main (as of July 12, 1990)

WALTER MARTIUS.
Business consultant, Chairman of the
Board of Management of the Schutz-
gemeinschaft der Kleinaktionäre e. V.,
Frankfurt am Main, Wuppertal 11

DAGOBERT MILLINGHAUS.
Commercial employee,
Mülheim/Ruhr

HANS NAGELS.
Driver,
Essen-Steele

DIETER PIECUCH.
Foreman electrician,
Dorsten

Dr. NIKOLAUS SENN.
President of the Administrative Board,
Schweizerische Bankgesellschaft,
Zürich

KLAUS STOLLE.
Electric engineer,
Hanover

HERMANN JOSEF STRENGER.
Chairman of the Board of Management,
Bayer AG,
Leverkusen

Dr. MONIKA WULF-MATHIES,
Chairwoman of the Gewerkschaft
Öffentliche Dienste, Transport
und Verkehr,
Bempflingen

Board of Management

KLAUS PILTZ.
Düsseldorf,
Chairman

Dr. HEINZ ACHE.
Düsseldorf (until March 31, 1990)

ALFRED BERSON,
Düsseldorf

Dr. HANS MICHAEL GAUL.
Hanover

Dr. HEINZ GENTZ,
Düsseldorf

Dr. HANS-DIETER HARIG.
Gelsenkirchen

ULRICH HARTMANN.
Düsseldorf

Dr. HUBERT HENEKA.
Gelsenkirchen

Dr. HANS-JÜRGEN KNAUER.
Mülheim/Ruhr

Dr. HERMANN KRÄMER.
Hanover

Prof. Dr. CARL HEINRICH KRAUCH.
Marl

Fully Authorized Representatives

Dr. WERNER MÜLLER.
Düsseldorf (as of July 11, 1990)

WALTER PLATZEK.
Düsseldorf

During the year under review, the Supervisory Board was informed regularly about
the status and development of the company's
business through verbal and written reports
by the Board of Management and maintained
supervision over the management. All significant business developments were discussed
in detail. In addition, the Chairman of the
Supervisory Board was kept up to date on
major developments.

TREUARBEIT AG, Düsseldorf, the auditors
appointed by the Annual General Meeting,
have examined and given unqualified confirmation to the Financial Statements of VEBA
Aktiengesellschaft as of December 31, 1990,
and to the Review of Operations. The Supervisory Board has endorsed the Auditors'
Report.

Exhibit 3.4 (continued)

The Supervisory Board has examined the Financial Statements, the Review of Operations and the proposal of the Board of Management for the appropriation of the net retained profit and, in accordance with the final result expressed of its examination, has expressed no objections. It has approved the Financial Statements as of December 31, 1990, as prepared by the Board of Management, which are therefore established, and also supports the proposal regarding the appropriation of the net retained profit.

The Supervisory Board has taken note of the Consolidated Financial Statements as of December 31, 1990, and of the Group Review of Operations, which were examined and given unqualified confirmation by TREUARBEIT AG, Düsseldorf, as well as of the Auditors' Report.

On July 12, 1990, the Annual General Meeting elected Mr. Hilmar Kopper, Member of the Board of Management of Deutsche Bank AG, to succeed Mr. Alfred Herrhausen, the member of our Supervisory Board who was victim of an assasination on November 30, 1989.

The Supervisory Board wishes to express its gratitude and appreciation to the Board members, employee representatives as well as all employees of VEBA AG and its affiliated companies for their performance.

Düsseldorf, May 15, 1991
THE SUPERVISORY BOARD

Vogelsang
Chairman

There are differing tax rates on earnings. There is a lower tax rate if earnings are paid out as dividends and a higher tax rate if retained. This is an attempt by the government to reduce the so called "double tax," which results when a company pays tax on its earnings, pays a portion of the remainder as a dividend, and the recipient of the dividend is taxed again on this income. Thus, a company can raise or lower reported net income by its dividend policy. If a company has poor earnings in a given year, it may decide to increase its dividend. This reduces the corporate tax rate, which increases the reported earnings relative to decreasing, or not paying, its dividend. Although it is true that paying an increased dividend during times of poor earnings draws down on the liquidity of the company, this can be restored by other means such as increased borrowing. However, controlling earnings through dividend payout policies does not lend itself to the principle of portraying the true and fair view of the financial results of the operations of a company.

The 1990 annual report for Veba AG contains a section on social responsibility. As seen in Exhibit 3.5, the importance of environmental protection is emphasized along with steps taken to protect the environment by reducing pollution emissions to the atmosphere, waste water treatment, recycling efforts, and noise abatement. Other areas of social interest include product and worker safety, growth in employment and compensation, training, corporate/employee communications, and employees becoming shareholders.

Exhibit 3.5
Social Responsibility Section of Veba Annual Report

High Priority of Environmental Protection

VEBA was prompt in recognizing the necessity of environmental protection and in acting accordingly. An excerpt from our Guideline*: "We see it as an important task to further heighten the awareness for the high priority of environmental protection and the economical treatment of resources in all areas and at all levels within the Group. To this end, our companies are working intensively to find concrete solutions."

One example of the great efforts being made to protect the environment is the cleaning of flue gases from coal-fired power stations, a development which was initiated by VEBA companies decades ago and which culminated for the present in the completion of the systems for reducing emissions of nitrogen oxide. To protect the climate, the German Government resolved at the end of 1990 to cut emissions of carbon dioxide (CO_2) by at least 25% by the year 2005. This launches a demanding program to reduce the pollution of the environment to which VEBA will respond.

In 1990, capital expenditures of DM 497 million were made for environmental protection systems in the Group; expenses relating to environmental protection (operating costs and capital service) amounted to DM 1.54 billion. The following table shows the development over the last five years:

Clean Air – Extensive Program of Environmental Protection Completed

With the completion of nearly all of the systems for reducing nitrogen oxide emissions in the VKR, PREUSSENELEKTRA and HÜLS power stations scheduled for long-term operation, we were able to conclude a comprehensive environmental protection program. The result of the work is environmentally safe power stations whose emissions of sulfur dioxide and nitrogen oxide amount to only about 10% of the original levels (graph 12). Dust emissions, more than 99% of which are already absorbed in electrical precipitators, are being further reduced thanks to the desulfurization system. The flue gas cleaning systems, state-of-the-art in concept, work with a high degree of availability and guarantee the sure maintenance of the maximum permissible emission levels. These measures, implemented on the basis of the Large Furnaces Ordinance, necessitated capital spending at VKR and PREUSSENELEKTRA of DM 3 billion.

In mid-1990, we were able to complete the trial run of the denitrification systems in the coal-fired units 1 and 2 of the Staudinger power station operated by PREUSSENELEKTRA. In unit 3, the denitrification system is installed in the flue gas channel of the boiler; it is due to go into operation in May 1991. At the Farge power station operated by

Expenses for Environmental Protection (DM million)

	1986	1987	1988	1989	1990
Capital spending	619	655	698	638	497
Operating costs and capital services	1,140	1,252	1,554	1,531	1,541

* The full text can be obtained on request from VEBA.

Exhibit 3.5 (continued)

PREUSSENELEKTRA, the system to remove the nitrogen oxide from the flue gases is also nearing completion. The structural steel work has been largely completed as have the electrical and conductor work. During the scheduled inspection in the fall, the system was prepared for the installation in the unit's flue gas channel. The operating permit is being expected.

In the oil refineries in which VEBA OEL has an interest, the emissions from the processing plants were further reduced. At the Gelsenkirchen site, the limitation of sulfur dioxide emissions is achieved through refinery means without the use of a desulfurization system. This is done by burning the non-sulfurous refinery gases and the low-sulfur heating oil in the process furnaces heated from below. The strict requirements for the nitrogen oxide emissions from the existing olefin plant in Gelsenkirchen-Scholven and the plant under construction are being satisfied as part of a compensatory solution.

The gas displacement and vapor recycling systems erected in the roadside loading area of the oil refinery in Neustadt has successfully contributed to a reduction in the emissions of hydrocarbons.

Waste Water Treatment

Emissions of VEBA Group Power Stations (1000 tons)   (12)

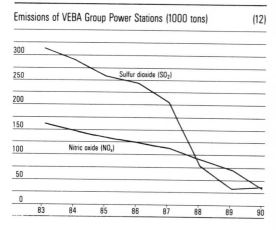

At HÜLS, thanks to the flue gas desulfurization system in power station II in Marl becoming operational, emissions of sulfur dioxide were reduced by 40 % compared with 1988. Thus, both coal-fired power stations now have flue gas desulfurization systems, and the full power station capacity has been equipped with denitrification systems. In other HÜLS locations, too, various waste gas cleaning and incineration systems were put into operation. This means that we are contributing to further reductions in emissions.

As in the past, HÜLS spent the greatest part of its capital spending and high operating costs in the area of environmental protection on measures for the protection of lakes and rivers and the cleaning of waste water. Work on the enlargement of new retainer facilities, on a large number of renovated filling stations for liquid products and on recooling plants is making good progress and is on schedule. In the meantime, 80 % of the plant in the Marl facility is cooled indirectly. A program of action to lessen the burden on the water treatment plants at the Marl facility through cutting down on the amount of production waste water in the manufacturing operations was concluded successfully. Thanks to this package of measures, the total water consumption was reduced by one-third.

Exhibit 3.5 (continued)

Recycling

The environmentally sound disposal of the residual substances occurring during flue gas cleaning was continued with success. VKR has developed recycling concepts in this area with which the residual substances are utilized almost completely in the building industry. In particular, we have been successful in using all of the high-grade gypsum occurring in flue gas desulfurization in the gypsum industry in place of natural gypsum. The gypsum wallboard factory operated by Rigips GmbH, located adjacent to power station in Scholven, alone processes up to 250,000 tons of gypsum annually from VKR facilities.

It is not only public opinion that attaches great importance to the reduction of waste. As part of a program of action, all of the HÜLS sites, starting with the Marl, Herne, Bottrop and Witten locations, were systematically studied to find ways of reducing waste, and appropriate measures were taken. Through increased return of packaging and containers for reconditioning and increased use of reconditioned barrels, in addition to the economic effects, we were able to help reduce waste. The introduction across the board of recycling for used paper, palettes and timber, collecting glass neon tubes, scrap and other material fragments reduced the burden on the sanitation firms.

The HÜLS subsidiary RÖHM achieved a major reduction in the quantities of special waste to be incinerated externally through targeted internal measures to avoid the occurrence of such waste and through the use of drainage containers. Using its own recycling process, RÖHM recovers materials from filter sludge which are then processed directly. In addition, HÜLS has taken a major part in various projects for recycling materials, primarily in the field of plastics.

In the field of glass recycling, RHENUS was able to increase the quantity of used glass sold to the glass factories by over 20 % to approx. 400,000 tons and thus holds an unchanged market share in West Germany of approximately 30 %. The network of collection containers was made even denser with emphasis being placed on the increasing separation of the glass collected by color. The quantities of used paper collected also showed a marked increase.

Noise Protection

In the interest of additional protection of the environment, noise abatement systems were installed at the power stations as part of the retrofitting with flue gas cleaning systems to bring them up to the state of the art. Thus, for example, in the year under review, at VKR a noise abatement wall was completed along the new plant road to the Knepper power station to protect the adjacent residential area from the noise of the trucks going to and coming from the facility. The noise abatement work at older sites concerned roof ventilators, fans, transformers and cooling towers at the power stations in Datteln, Marl and Westerholt.

Product Safety

The amendment of the Dangerous Substances Ordinance and of the Chemicals Act as well as the new Plastics Guidelines issued by the European Community brought with them a whole series of changes in labeling in the registration and stating of new substances and the treatment of old substances. For this purpose, comprehensive studies were taken up, among other things, on the toxicology and ecology and to gain physical and chemical data.

For many years now, the German chemical industry has been systematically examining all used substances relevant because of production volumes or properties on a voluntary basis in cooperation with scientists and public authorities. With the impending Used Substances Ordinance to be issued by the European Community, this examination will now become a legal requirement within the EC. HÜLS is cooperating in the compilation and evaluation of the toxicological, ecological and exposition data, first of all on those substances which are produced in quantities exceeding 1,000 tons per annum.

Exhibit 3.5 (continued)

Personnel Expansion in Many Areas

At the end of 1990, there was a total of 106,877 people employed in the VEBA Group, 12,363 more than in the previous year (graph 13). This means that our workforce experienced a healthy expansion in 1990. This was due, above all, to the inclusion of RÖHM in the chemicals division, and in the trading and services division to the takeover of the co op building markets and of ISTA GmbH. Furthermore, these figures include for the first time the employees of VEBA WOHNEN.

In addition, new employees were taken on through the expansion of activities in the existing business areas. Some 8,000 new employees have been hired by the VEBA companies. Of these, approx. 6,000 came from the labor market and 2,000 from the ranks of our own trainees after successfully completing their training. This was offset by about 6,500

Employees' structure

	Dec. 31.1989	Dec. 31.1990	Change against previous year in %	Share of total workforce in %
Salaried staff	40,369	47,416	+ 17.5	44.4
Wage earners	48,618	53,771	+ 10.6	50.3
Trainees	5,527	5,690	+ 2.9	5.3
Total	**94,514**	**106,877**	**+ 13.1**	**100.0**

people who left the Group's employ so that, on balance, some 1,500 additional jobs were created.

In 1991, the workforce will again be increased through additional acquisitions and our activities in the new Länder.

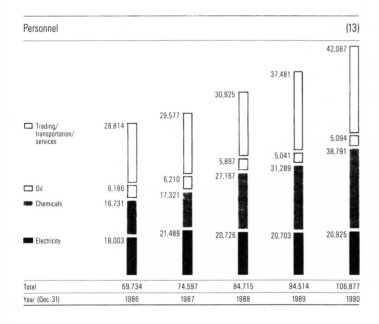

Personnel					(13)

| Total | 69,734 | 74,597 | 84,715 | 94,514 | 106,877 |
| Year (Dec. 31) | 1986 | 1987 | 1988 | 1989 | 1990 |

Legend: Trading/transportation/services; Oil; Chemicals; Electricity

1986: 28,814; 6,186; 16,731; 18,003
1987: 29,577; 6,210; 17,321; 21,489
1988: 30,925; 5,897; 27,167; 20,726
1989: 37,481; 5,041; 31,289; 20,703
1990: 42,067; 5,094; 38,791; 20,925

Exhibit 3.5 (continued)

Personnel and Social Security Expenses

In 1990, the net value-added in the VEBA Group amounted to more than DM 10.7 billion. Of this total, DM 6.1 billion in wages and salaries was paid to employees and DM 1 billion in employer's contributions was remitted for pension, health and unemployment insurance as well as the workmen's compensation insurance fund.

Among the social security benefits, the company pension plan, above all, is increasingly appreciated because, together with the government social security and the necessary individual protection, it contributes to the employees' financial security in retirement. In 1990, the VEBA Group companies spent a total of DM 626 million for company pension plans.

41,001 retirees or their surviving dependants received old-age pension payments. 78,315 employees in the Group have a claim to a company pension after retirement. Despite the reorganization of the pension systems throughout the Group, the company pension plans will remain a major item of expense in the years ahead, also because of the dynamic increases anchored in law.

Employee Qualification

In the area of basic and advanced training, the VEBA companies continued and expanded their activities (graph 14). Following the reorganization in recent years of the training in the industrial trades for electricians', metalworkers' and chemical workers' occupations, the clerical occupations were now updated to bring them in line with technical progress. The Group's companies were quick to equip the training places with modern office communication machines and to adapt the curricula and teaching methods to the heightened requirements.

The introduction of new technologies and the change in operating procedures and organizational structures that goes along with them has also led to new emphases in the area of advanced training. In addition to promoting

the occupational qualifications, the training of management personnel, in particular, was intensified. In this, the VEBA companies are acting in the conviction that cooperative forms of management are best suited to promote the willingness on the part of the employees to perform and to commit themselves. For this reason, enhancing the leadership capabilities of management personnel has become a central element in the management development program throughout the Group.

In East Germany, the VEBA companies have begun a broad spectrum of training measures. Initially, the focus is on the teaching of the basics of business economics and advancing the occupational qualifications so that the people working there will acquire the level of knowledge needed to work to West German standards as quickly as possible.

Trainee Place Initiative for East German School Leavers

At present, getting started in one's chosen field of work in the new Länder is very difficult indeed. Apart from a lack of qualified trainers and suitable training workshops, the situation is characterized by a considerable shortage of trainee places for school leavers.

Motivated by social responsibility as in the early 1980's, VEBA will therefore once again offer initial vocational training in East and West Germany beyond its own requirements so as to ease the situation. The emphasis will be on the new Länder themselves so that as many young people as possible can obtain qualified training near their homes.

The Group companies that already have the entrepreneurial responsibility in East German companies have, moreover, already begun rapidly to modernize the training workshops and to offer what are new training occupations for East Germany, namely in the commercial and services sectors. In addition, as a supplementary measure, we are considering taking part in models of external training.

Exhibit 3.5 (continued)

VEBA and the Labor Market

VEBA has been quick to prepare for the shortage of qualified personnel on the labor market in the old Länder. The first bottlenecks are already occurring in certain skilled occupations, for engineers and qualified management personnel. Even if the influx of Germans from the East does lead to a slight relaxation on the labor market in the coming years, over the medium term a growing shortage of skilled workers and management personnel will remain. Up to now, thanks to their great involvement as trainers and their attractiveness as employers, the VEBA companies have largely been successful in covering their labor requirements.

As a supplementary measure, activities of outward representation aimed primarily at students such as "Open House", corporate presentations and participation in trade shows have proved to be of value throughout the Group. In addition, programs offering short-term practical experience and the employment of working students are increasingly being used to give young people an opportunity to get to know the working world at VEBA.

VEBA Guideline Published

The aim of the VEBA Guideline, which was published at the end of 1990, is to strengthen the understanding for the objectives and the cooperation in the Group and to encourage all of our employees to see the continued development of the Group as a common task.

In line with the decentralized corporate structure, the most important Group companies have also published guidelines that go into their specific structures and tasks. One focus of the guidelines are the jointly developed principles which bring the maxims of management action in the Group into line with one another.

Employee Shares Still in Demand

When in the summer of 1990 employee shares were offered for sale to the VEBA workforce for the 7th time, once again almost half of the entitled employees took up the offer. Despite the turbulence on the stock market, a respectable result was achieved. Almost all of the approximately 43,000 buyers decided to take the maximum of three shares. As part of this attractive form of asset formation, they subscribed for shares with a nominal value of DM 6.3 million. Since 1984, more than 50,000 employees have purchased shares with a nominal value of DM 44.4 million; thus, the employees' share of the VEBA capital stock amounts to 2 %.

Work Safety

The basic requirement for protecting our employees and the environment lies in the safety of the processes and plants and in the responsible handling of dangerous substances. On the basis of this awareness, the VEBA companies have continually strengthened their activities in recent years to train, motivate and inform their employees. The consequence of this is a gratifying trend in the accident statistics in all of our divisions. Compared with the previous year, the number of reportable accidents per 1,000 employees in the manufacturing companies dropped from 31 to 26.

For companies newly integrated into the Group, detailed safety analyses were drawn up and targeted measures to prevent accidents and occupational illnesses initiated so as to bring them up quickly to VEBA's high standards.

Exhibit 3.5 (continued)

In-Company Suggestion System

In the year under review, the VEBA employees in the manufacturing companies submitted numerous suggestions for improvement, thus proving the great interest in solving problems within the company. Of the more than 4,200 suggestions submitted, over 40 % earned awards. In order to utilize the synergy effects, the procedures that in the past were limited to the individual companies will also be linked throughout the Group.

Elections to the Employees' Councils and Spokespersons' Committees

In the first half of 1990, elections were held in the VEBA Group to the Employees' Councils and, for the first time based on law, to the Spokespersons' Committees. At about 75 %, the participation in the Employees' Council elections was about on a par with 1987. Some 2/3 of the council members were re-elected.

JAPAN

Japanese accounting practices originate from two sources. Prior to World War II, the major influence was the German Commercial Code of 1889. Following World War II, the U.S. inspired Securities and Exchange Law became the foundation of how Japanese companies were to report financial results to their shareholders. Both German and American influences can be seen in current Japanese accounting practices. The German influence is seen in the control exerted over accounting practices by government ministries, the lack of public availability of private companies' accounts, uniform formats for published accounts, dominance of tax rules in determining income, and the establishment of legal reserves. There is more emphasis on the form, or layout, of accounts than substance, or depth of meaning, in portraying the financial results of a company. When "form over substance" prevails, the "true and fair view" suffers.

The American influence can be seen in special rules that apply for publicly traded companies that are modeled after SEC rules. These include the requirement for some degree of consolidation by publicly traded companies, adopting the U.S. ordering of items on financial statements, the amortization of goodwill, and the disclosure of earnings per share. However, in reviewing Japanese accounting practices, one must not be too hasty in concluding whether their system is driven by German or American practices. The Japanese borrow from the West, but they adapt to their particular culture. That is, what appears to be American or German on the surface is Japanese underneath.

Not understanding the Japanese adaptation of Western commercial practices can lead to confusion. Some years ago, Western financial analysts scrutinized the financial reports of Japanese companies and came to the conclusion that Japanese companies, in comparison to U.S. companies, were grossly overleveraged. The ratio of debt to equity was extremely high by Western standards. The conclusion of the report was a recommendation to avoid investing in Japan because the companies, by Western standards, were in danger of bankruptcy on the next downward blip in business activity.

What was not understood was the relationship of the bank within the heiretsu to the companies making up the heiretsu. The role of the bank is to facilitate the financing of corporate decisions made by those who manage the heiretsu. Once a decision has been made by the heiretsu that a member company proceed in a certain undertaking, the company need not apply for a loan with the bank that is the focal point of activity within the heiretsu. The financing is forthcoming and the capital infusion is in the form of debt. There is little reason to raise capital in the equity markets because the bank loan takes care of most, if not all, of the financing needs. This, of course, leads to high debt-to-equity ratios.

By Western standards, a company with a high debt-to-equity ratio is generally considered to be closer to bankruptcy for a given level of earnings than one with a low debt-to-equity ratio. In Japan, it is a testimony of the confidence that the bank, as the focal point of a heiretsu, has in a member company when it offers a loan to the company, even though a company may have no immediate use of the proceeds. It is an unforgivable insult for the company to refuse the bank's offer. The company accepts the loan, thereby increasing its debt load, and deposits the proceeds in the same bank, extending the unwanted credit until such time as it is needed. In Japan, a company with a high debt-to-equity ratio has the full backing of a bank. A company with a low debt-to-equity ratio may mean that the bank has lack of confidence in its continued existence. It is considered "risky" in Japan, because no bank is willing to lend money to the company. In the United States and Europe, a low degree of leverage has exactly the opposite meaning.

All Japanese companies are required to publish financial statements. Accounting practices are closely supervised by the Japanese finance ministry. One manifestation of the control over accounting practices by the finance ministry is the observation that the fiscal year for all companies ends 31 March, which is the end of the fiscal year for the government. In addition, the Japanese Securities and Exchange Law requires that the three thousand largest individual corporations be audited. Accounting standards are set by the Business Accounting Deliberation Council, whose members are appointed by the Ministry of Finance. Accounting practices must comply with ministerial orders with regard to the preparation of balance sheets and financial statements—accountants have very little discretion in what they can do. Therefore, the role of the Japanese Institute of Certified Public Accountants is small and the standards for membership in the accounting profession are modest.

There is no need for the accounting profession to go to great lengths to provide a true and fair view of the financial results of a company because Japanese investors' confidence in business is enormous. There is no real demand for greater disclosure or for more financial information than what is currently made available to the public. Auditing is essentially passive or ceremonial in nature. Tax accounting governs financial reporting because auditors are required to issue a clean opinion if the books of the company conform to tax law.

The Japanese government permits, if not encourages, "discretionary reserve accounts," which give management a degree of control over reported profits. Although consolidation of wholly owned subsidiaries is required by the Japanese version of the SEC, there is some leeway in consolidating large shareholdings in associated companies. And large shareholdings is a way of life within a heiretsu. This leaves some managerial control over the nature of reported earnings. The published reason for permitting discretionary reserve accounts and nonconsolidation of financial statements of associated companies is to facilitate expansion plans, whereas the actual reason appears to be income smoothing. By controlling reported profits, the investing public is provided with what amounts to average, not actual, earnings.

Japanese companies wishing to tap Western sources of capital are under pressure to consolidate their various holdings in their financial reports. But Japanese companies operating within Japan that satisfy the demands of the Japanese investors and the desires of the Japanese government need not be too particular in disclosing material details on their financial condition. Japanese investors are not terribly interested and the insiders are already aware of the situation. This is the cultural influence of the Japanese investing public on accounting practices, quite different than the cultural influence prevalent in the United States.

The accounting profession in Japan is relatively young, having come into existence with the enactment of the CPA Law in 1948. In 1987, there were eight thousand CPAs and twenty-one foreign and ninety Japanese auditing firms in Japan. A 1966 amendment to the CPA Law encouraged individual accountants to form corporate entities; partnerships are not permitted. Every Japanese CPA in practice must be a member of the Japanese Institute of Certified Public Accountants. The institute sends representatives to the Business Accounting Deliberation Council, the standard-setting body of the Ministry of Finance. CPA candidates must pass preliminary examinations in order to become junior CPAs and embark on a three-year program of study and practical experience. They become certified by passing both an oral and a written examination.

THE NETHERLANDS

The Netherlands is a small nation whose commerce is largely intertwined with that of its neighboring states. Its government is probusiness in orientation, giving full recognition to the connection between corporate activity and the standard of living of its people. The old American saying "what's good for General Motors is good for the country," no longer subscribed to by the American public, has a surviving counterpart in the Netherlands. The Netherlands Institute of Registered Accountants is an active organization, setting high standards for qualification for its members, reputed to be among the highest in the world. Accounting standards are set by the Act on Annual Accounts of Enterprises, along with requirements on statutory audits.

Accounting principles are closely related to those practiced in the United Kingdom. Dutch accounting principles require that annual financial statements show a true and fair picture of the financial position of the company with all items appropriately grouped and described. Financial statements must be drawn up in accordance with "sound business practice," which is interpreted to mean that accounting principles must be acceptable to the business community. The process of stating assets and liabilities and determining results are to be disclosed. Financial statements are prepared on a consistent basis, with disclosure of material effects of changes in accounting principles. Comparative financial information for the preceding period must be disclosed.

These principles sound much like those espoused in the United Kingdom and the United States, but with one vital difference. In the United Kingdom and the United States, the establishment of accounting principles is the responsibility of the accounting practitioners. The desires of businessmen play a very minor, if any, role in the deliberations of the accounting boards in these nations. The

Netherlands Tripartite Accounting Standards Committee is responsible for the promulgation of accounting standards. This committee is made up of professional accountants and representatives of management, labor unions, and the government. "Sound business practices" have real meaning in determining accounting standards. As an example of the influence of businessmen in the establishment of accounting standards, the Dutch use of replacement cost accounting in determining depreciation for reporting financial results was initiated by the business community representatives on the committee. The Netherlands is also unique in that any interested party, such as a businessman, who is of the opinion that the financial reports of a company do not meet the requirements of commonly accepted accounting principles, can take legal action against the firm. If the suit is successful, then a judicial decision will affect the way a company prepares its accounts. A special court has been established to resolve disputes on accounting matters.

Besides having accounting standards set by business interests along with accounting professionals, Dutch accounting has also been influenced by the international orientation of its business community in the conduct of trade and services within the European Community. This has given an international flavor to Dutch accounting standards. This is also a consequence of two Dutch companies ranking among the world's largest corporations, Royal Dutch Shell and Philips Gloeilampenfabreieken. Their need for capital cannot be satisfied within the Netherlands. As Dutch companies seeking capital from sources outside Netherlands, their financial statements cover three different accounting systems: the Netherlands, the United Kingdom, and the United States.

The Registeraccountants Act of 1962 established the Nederlands Instituut van Registeraccountants (NIVRA). There are no legal or other specifications with respect to practical training. In practice, however, most students are employed in accountancy, either public or private, for the whole period leading up to their NIVRA examination. This period is normally ten or eleven years. As an alternative, students may take a combined course of study at one of five universities. Then, upon completion of a higher degree in economics, they undergo practical training for three years. NIVRA's present membership is about 7,700 professional accountants.

SWEDEN

It has been said that the most socialistic nation in the world is Sweden. With this in mind, it is interesting to note that the government has recently announced that some state-controlled businesses will be privatized. Nevertheless, few countries offer its citizenry such a full range of social benefits. The system has worked fairly well because the Swedish work ethic has surprisingly not been too eroded by the benefits awarded for those not working or by a punitive tax rate for those who do work. In the past, there have been some extreme cases where the incremental tax rate, depending on the nature and the source of the earnings, exceeded 100 percent. That is to say, earning a marginal $100 through a special combination of sources of revenue or earnings meant that the person owed the government $103.

With this keen governmental interest in all aspects of Swedish life, the Swedes have lost some degree of choice, some might say freedom, under a system of such an all-embracing array of social benefits. For instance, certain local government boards select the color of a "privately owned" house. The owner is permitted to select the shade. There should be no surprise in realizing that the Swedish Accounting Standards Board is a government agency where financial reporting is in accordance with governmental desires. Corporate tax rates are high, but the government permits the establishment of reserves, which postpones and reduces the tax liability. Reserves can be set up for inventory valuation purposes, future investment in plants, future increases in pay, and accelerated depreciation of assets, which decrease current taxes. One half of these reserves must be deposited in non-interest-bearing accounts in the Bank of Sweden. Government approval is required for withdrawal and such approval must satisfy the government regulators with regard to the use of the funds.

Setting up special reserve accounts reduces the immediate impact of high taxation. However, in reducing tax expenditures, a company must then follow government dictates on the amount and the purpose for a withdrawal. Consequently, the government can influence the future direction of a company by encouraging the establishment of reserve accounts. The financial inducement for a company to set up a special reserve account is to avoid confiscatory levels of taxation. The consequences of setting up such accounts is that the government approves the use of funds withdrawn from such accounts. This indirect means of government involvement leaves the day-to-day management in the hands of the corporation, but the future direction of the company is affected by government involvement in withdrawals from the special reserve accounts.

One must earn a university degree in economics to become a Swedish authorized public accountant (auktoriserad revisor). In addition, at least five years of working experience in auditing is required of which at least three years must be spent with an authorized public accountant or an authorized auditing firm. The two remaining years can be fulfilled at an accounting firm abroad. During the five-year training period, students take numerous courses in accounting, auditing, tax, and other relevant subjects. These courses can be offered within the accounting firms, which is generally the case for the larger firms, or at the Institute for Professional Education of Accountants. The institute is majority owned and controlled by the Swedish Institute of Authorized Public Accountants (FAR). Until 1991, FAR prepared the tests used by accounting firms to measure the progress of their students. In 1992, these tests will be mandatory for membership in FAR. There are approximately 2,000 authorized public accountants in Sweden of whom about 1,900 are members of FAR.

SWITZERLAND

Switzerland has a five-hundred-year history of being "confidential." This is bound to show up in its accounting practices. There is very little legal guidance in the preparation of financial statements. The Code of Obligations provides only general guidelines that invite broad interpretation of accounting standards. The accounting books must be in accord with the "character and extent" of the business and financial reports should be prepared "completely, clearly and plainly in accordance with recognized commercial principles, so that interested parties may inform themselves as accurately as possible of the economic position of the business." Financial statements are frequently neither consolidated nor audited. Secret reserves are both legal and unlimited in scope. There are one thousand certified public accountants in Switzerland. For private companies, financial statements are made to banks and management, not to the shareholders. For publicly traded Swiss companies, financial reports are made to the share-holders, but in the past, these reports were not consolidated. If not consolidated, one does not obtain the true scope of operations of a company from reading its financial reports. However, in recent years, there has been a trend to begin consolidating financial reports, perhaps reluctantly, as seen in Exhibit 3.6 which is extracted from the 1990 Swissair annual report.

Tax havens are big business in a world where many nations view commerce primarily in terms of a source of tax revenues. There are a number of nations competing for business to be conducted within their domain on the basis of secrecy and freedom from prying government eyes and tax collectors. Vanuatu, located in the far reaches of the South Pacific, promises that non-Vanuatuan banks founded within its jurisdiction need not concern themselves with reserve and minimum capital requirements, publication of accounts, public scrutiny of their records, and so forth. Non-Vanuatuan companies domiciled in this Pacific paradise need not worry about income, corporate, capital gains, withholding, or sales taxes; estate, succession. and gift duties; or financial reports for that matter. One does not have to spend a great deal of time on Vanuatuan GAAP when financial reports are not even required. What does Vanuatu gain by seeing so accommodating? Fees associated with incorporation and mailbox rentals go a long way in balancing the Vanuatuan budget.

EGYPT

Egypt was a monarchy until the 1950s. Agriculture, a key to the Egyptian economy, was controlled by a few families who owned much of the arable land. In contrast, industrial concerns and businesses were owned by individuals. The revolution in the 1950s that brought Nasser to power reversed all this. Land reforms brought landownership to the tenants and businesses were nationalized. A mixed economy resulted, with the government dominating large industrial

Exhibit 3.6
Extract from Swissair 1990 Annual Report

General

In future years, the Swissair Group intends to publish a consolidated set of accounts in accordance with the accounting norms and guidelines of the European Community. In a first step towards this end, the profit and loss account has been consolidated for the Swissair Group. A Group balance sheet, together with the requisite commentary, will be added from next year. We have therefore refrained from publishing individual balance sheet statistics in this year's Review, since these no longer offer any useful basis of comparison.

Principles of consolidation

The consolidated profit and loss account is based on the annual accounts of the companies belonging to the Swissair Group. These accounts have not yet been fully examined by the statutory auditors. All intercompany balances and transactions have been eliminated in the consolidation process. Standardized

principles of valuation and depreciation have been applied for the first time; there are no major deviations from previous-year figures to report. Rates of depreciation are based on business administration principles.

In addition to the results of Swissair Ltd., the consolidated statistics comprise the results of all Swiss and non-Swiss companies in which Swissair possesses, directly or indirectly, a shareholding bestowing more than 50% of voting rights (see "List of subsidiaries and minority holdings", page 20). Figures for these companies are fully consolidated. Excluded from the above are hotels in which a majority holding was acquired in the course of 1990. Both these and Swissôtel were intended to be sold, and are thus not included in the consolidated accounts.

The minor changes made to the group of companies consolidated during the year under review increased total Group turnover by some CHF 30 million.

concerns and with a private sector subordinated to both direct government intervention and to strict government regulation.

In the 1960s, nationalization had proceeded to a point where 80 percent of the nation's economic activity fell under government control or ownership. The government, through the Central Accounting Agency, created a uniform accounting system for all public companies. The head of the Central Accounting Agency reports directly to the president of Egypt. Its function is to audit the final accounts of companies and state enterprises, review the reports of outside auditors of these companies, compare the companies' results to government plans, and report on violations of laws and regulations.

The function of accounting is not to report financial results to private individuals but to provide necessary information to the national planning board to permit the board to exercise planning and control functions over state enterprises. The law establishes numerous and extremely detailed accounting classifications, defines terminology, and sets standards and the details and types of reports.

Egyptian accounting practices are limited to assigning the financial transactions of a company to the applicable accounts.

BRAZIL

Brazil ranks among the world's largest nations in terms of land mass and population. From its beginnings through World War II, Brazil was a commodity-exporting nation. After World War II, Brazil embarked on an industrialization program, becoming the "economic miracle" in the 1970s. Domestic sources of capital were grossly insufficient to finance the building of the Brazilian industrial economy. Much of this economic miracle depended on foreign corporations setting up Brazilian subsidiaries for the importation of both capital and technology. Foreign companies were willing to invest in Brazil because the government, despite frequently being military juntas, was oriented toward a free market economy and welcomed foreign investment.

However, both foreign and domestic direct investment was insufficient for funding the "economic miracle." Important parts of the Brazilian economy such as the utility and extractive industries were government owned and outside the purview of private finance. To finance the building of an industrial infrastructure—utilities, transportation systems, and ports—and to develop its natural resources (such as oil fields and iron ore deposits), Brazil resorted to borrowing from international banks. The upshot of this was that Brazil became the largest debtor nation among the Lesser Developed Countries (LDCs) during the 1980s.

Brazilian accounting practices are driven by the tax law, which is closely related to U.S. tax law. The Corporation Law of 1976 attempted to create financial statements that would be more amenable to the creation of a domestic securities market. Although the intent of the law failed, nevertheless, this law governs financial accounting, including reporting requirements, the nature of consolidated financial statements, statements on the source and use of capital resources, and mandating the equity method of accounting for stock investments in other companies. The Corporation Law of 1976 was unique in introducing the concept of restating financial statements to take into account the inflationary impact of the Brazilian currency.

In addition to Brazil, other Latin American countries, such as Argentina, Bolivia, Chile, and Mexico, have opted for monetary indexing to restate financial reports to reflect changes in general price levels; thus the value of fixed assets, and the amount of depreciation, plus other items on the income statement and balance sheet, changes in relation to the loss of value of the currency. In Brazil, the higher depreciation charges can be used to offset taxes, a somewhat rare event in the world of taxation. Israel has also adopted general price level indexing in its financial reports.

Accounting in Brazil falls under two broad categories. Accounting statements for large, publicly owned companies are audited and considered meaningful. However, for the rest of the companies, financial reporting is not considered reliable and regulation is slight. The accounting profession is represented by the Federal Accounting Council. Accounting professionals are divided into two classes: accounting technicians who require only a secondary school education and accountants who require a university degree.

COLOMBIA

Like Brazil, the Colombian government sets accounting policies. There is no body of generally accepted accounting principles that exists in one publication. The National Institute of Public Accountants has only about 10 percent of the country's five thousand registered public accountants as members. A university degree and one year's experience in accounting is all that is necessary to become a Colombian CPA. Many nations, like Colombia, have few qualified accountants to do all the necessary accounting. When such conditions exist, one should not be surprised to find that accounting procedures are designed for simplicity and straightforwardness of application. Flexibility and freedom of interpretation to present a true and fair view have limited scope in this accounting environment.

OTHER FAR EASTERN NATIONS

In Korea, accounting standards are set by the Ministry of Finance. These standards are both comprehensive and complex. All larger corporations are required to publish annual audited financial statements. Costs and expenses that are not permitted for tax purposes are excluded from financial statements, thus making financial statements closely akin to tax returns. The first CPA law was enacted in 1950. The CPA profession is small with only about two thousand members. The activities of the Korean Institute of CPAs is advisory in nature because the state sets accounting policies.

Unlike most other countries in this region of the world, accounting practices in the Philippines are not heavily influenced by the government. Generally accepted accounting principles are defined by the Philippine Institute of CPAs in conjunction with the Bureau of Internal Revenue, the Securities and Exchange Commission, and other organizations. Larger corporations are required to publish annual audited financial statements, but these statements do not have to be consolidated. The Philippine accounting profession is large and respected with more than seventy thousand members. Accounting standards and procedures are similar to those in the United States.

Quite unlike the Philippines, Taiwan has many laws specifying what is proper accounting. Accounting standards and procedures are dominated by these legal requirements. The Ministry of Finance requires that audited statements be submitted to the tax authorities and the Security and Exchange Commission requires listed companies to publish semiannual audited reports. The Ministry of Finance regulates auditor independence. The accounting profession is small, but is growing in stature. Several organizations of professionals participate with the government in formulating accounting and auditing procedures.

EASTERN EUROPEAN NATIONS

Eastern Europe fell under the yoke of the Soviet Union following World War II. They also fell under the dictums of Lenin concerning accounting in a socialist environment. To Lenin, "the whole society will be a single office and a single factory." Such a system does not demand much from accounting other than being a control mechanism in a highly controlled society. According to Lenin, accounting can be performed by "any literate person with a knowledge of the four rules of arithmetic." Accounting is strictly regulated for uniformity as its mission is to aid in the control of a national economy. Nonmonetary units are often used in the accounting statements, such as units of production or tons of output. Any measure that is useful to the control process is proper for accounting; no attempt is made to have accounting serve the needs of management.

Indeed, it was not possible to have accounting in strictly monetary terms because prices were administered to reflect social policy considerations. Prices were divorced from such considerations as supply and demand, opportunity costs, and the relative scarcity of resources. As a matter of fact, a price placed on goods sold by a company may not even reflect actual costs. If the company ran a deficit, which it often would under such circumstances, the deficit would be covered by the state authorities; that is, it would be subsidized. During the 1950s, all Eastern Bloc countries adopted the Soviet Plan of Accounts.

However, things began to change in eastern Europe in the 1980s. The change began in the Soviet Union when it was widely recognized by both those who rule and those who were ruled that the command driven economy was not working. Indeed, a not-so-secret report by the KGB indicated that the national output of Soviet society would be exceeded by South Korea by the end of the century unless something was done to change the nature of the economic system. The Marxian economic system supposedly dedicated to the material benefit of its people was not working. Seventy years of Leninist history clearly demonstrated that Lenin was wrong. Worse yet, those who gave the commands and those who carried out the commands knew it. The facade could not be maintained. All, except a dogmatic few, gave up hope in communism, and without that hope, the religion of communism died.

The first steps in the demise of the command-oriented society were the advent of glasnost, which was an open discussion on matters that once could not be discussed, and of perestroika, a restructuring of the economy that was once beyond the possibility of being restructured. The planners of the Soviet economy recognized the need for Western assistance to advance the living standards of the Soviet people. Western businessmen viewed a potential market covering one fifth of the world's land mass, encompassing eleven time zones, 400 million people, 150 different nationalities, and seventy different languages, and could hardly restrain themselves from the invitation for assistance. However, these foreign investors wanted financial information that conforms to recognizable accounting standards. Moreover, that financial information had to be made credible by being audited by a recognized accounting firm.

Foreign investments in the postcommunist era were made with accounting standards in a state of flux. Although accounting is moving away from its former mission of determining whether production goals have been satisfied, it is still a long way from being recognizable and acceptable to foreign investors. The accounting for profitability is very important not only for the investors to measure the return on their investment but also for them to measure the benefit of a two-year holiday on paying taxes. The calculation of profit is a real stumbling block for investment in the former Soviet Union. Because foreign investment is deemed necessary by those in power to achieve economic progress, the former Soviet government permitted two American CPA firms (Arthur Anderson and Ernst & Young) to perform audits of a nature acceptable to the former Soviet government. All "Big Six" American accounting firms are expected to open offices in Moscow. American CPAs are teaching accounting in Russian universities, with 170 students having already graduated by 1991.

Foreign investors are not just looking at the former Soviet Union, but also at eastern European nations. Poland is rapidly moving toward a market economy and has joined the International Accounting Standards Committee. Before being occupied by the Soviet Union, Czechoslovakia was the fourteenth most industrialized nation in the world. This is quite an achievement considering the size of this nation. Under Soviet control, it became a third world nation. As an independent nation again, Czechoslovakia desires to rejoin the list of industrialized nations, and in so doing, must conform its accounting to Western standards.

From the point of view of accounting, Hungary is the most advanced country in eastern Europe because of its relatively early reintroduction to a market economy after its takeover by the Soviet Union. Although the Hungarian Revolution was crushed in 1956, the Hungarians did succeed in orienting their economy more to the West than the other eastern European nations. Of course, this is on a relative scale. In absolute terms, the nation had limited exposure to the world market. Nevertheless, the Hungarian revolt resulted in the separation of central planning from economic regulation, the abolition of a central wage system, some introduction of profit motivation and profit sharing, and the abolition of the compulsory delivery of agricultural products to the government authorities. The latter decree created a free market in agricultural products, which coexisted with governmental channels of distribution and sales. The Soviet system of accounting for volume production targets in terms of units or tons gave way to modified five-year plans that were more Western in format. During these years, Hungarian planners sought mathematical models that could substitute for the free market as a measure of the efficient allocation of resources.

Despite these attempts to model the free market, consumer prices were controlled not in economic terms but in political terms to induce cooperation by ordinary people. This led to a situation where consumer prices were considerably below producer costs. In the 1960s, the government ended up funding the resulting deficits, which, in turn, were financed by international borrowing and by planned internal inflation. During the 1970s, gaps between prices and costs were systematically closed.

In the 1980s, Hungarians began to resort to the idea that only those businesses or enterprises that could profitably export their output to the West were to be considered successful. Hungarian industries oriented to the domestic market had their profit margins regulated by the state. Measuring profitability is a function of accounting and the Hungarians were the first eastern Europeans to do so after the Soviet conquest. Even so, the Hungarian financial accounting system was rudimentary when compared to western European standards. The Ministry of Finance obliged firms to show a positive "residual profit." The definition of "residual profit" is more akin to a positive cash flow requirement than a measure of a return on investment.

Until recently, market forces have had little impact on accounting in Hungary. To change the orientation of accounting, the Hungarian government has engaged Price Waterhouse to modernize the nation's accounting system as a prerequisite for the nation's reentry into the European economy. In 1991, Poland, Czechoslovakia, and Hungary applied for associate membership in the European Community. If they become associate members, other eastern European nations may follow suit, necessitating changes to their accounting practices.

SUMMARY

There appear to be two broad classifications for the various accounting systems of the world—whether the accounting system is oriented to commercial or governmental interests. Leaving aside the Soviet model that is being abandoned, the two nations representing the extremes of accounting systems are the Netherlands and Sweden. Joining the Netherlands in having a commerically driven system are the United Kingdom, the United States, and those countries whose accounting practices are modeled after the U.K. or U.S. systems. The Netherlands is different from the United Kingdom and the United States in that businessmen play a prominent role in the setting of accounting standards, whereas accounting professionals are the key players in the United Kingdom and the United States.

Government-oriented accounting systems include much of continental Europe. France, Belgium, Spain, Italy, and other countries have plan-based accounting systems that are set up by government ministries for the purposes of collecting national statistics. The statistics are then used as a source of information in establishing government policies with regard to both society and business, and in monitoring the success or failure of these policies. Germany has a plan-based accounting system, but it is derived from statute rather than from regulatory authorities in the ministries of economics or finance. Japan is a mixture of accounting practices found in Germany and the United States modified to fit the Japanese business culture. The Swedish government plays an important role in setting accounting standards as a means to indirectly control the destiny of Swedish companies.

There are various systems of grouping nations into broad categories that have been proposed by academicians and accounting professionals. Broad categorization of diverse accounting practices, however, is not really the issue. Efforts can be better spent trying to harmonize or standardize accounting practices. This would make corporate financial results, much like goods and services, transparent to national borders.

CHAPTER 4

STANDARDIZATION AND HARMONIZATION

One driving force to develop a global accounting system is the desire to underwrite securities in any, or all, of the world's capital markets using a single set of financial statements. A positive incentive for a capital market to support a global accounting system is the enhancement of its volume of business by being able to participate in underwritings in other capital markets. Reinforcing the positive incentive is the realization that a capital market, which ignores the development of a global accounting system, may find itself with a unique set of accounting standards while the rest of the world relies on a common set of accounting standards. This would lead to an irretrievable loss of business. The desire for potential gain in business by participating, and the fear of a potential loss of business by not participating, encourage support of the concept of a global accounting system regardless of how officials of capital markets may feel about the matter. Opponents to a global accounting system certainly can delay the process, but they may not be able to prevent its eventual success.

The globalization of corporate activity, coupled with economic and political integration of large groupings of nations, are engines of change in accounting practices. Indeed, one might say that change is being pushed on the accounting profession by commercial interests, which find it difficult to accept the necessity of adopting a different set of accounting standards as business activities cross national borders. Two complementary approaches are being taken to tear down the Tower of Babel of Accounting Practices. One is standardization of accounting practices, whereby all nations agree to a common set of standards. The other is harmonization of accounting principles, which attempts to eliminate disparities and narrow differences between accounting systems.

IASC AND IFAC

The first forum for exchanging ideas between accountants of different nations was the First International Congress of Accountants in 1904. No permanent organization existed to provide continuity of purpose between meetings, which were about every five years. The Tenth International Congress of Accountants in 1972 organized two permanent bodies, the International Accounting Standards Committee (IASC) and the International Coordination Committee for the Accounting Profession (ICCAP). In 1976, the latter gave up its charter to permit the formation of the International Federation of Accountants (IFAC), which began operations in 1977. Both IASC, headquartered in London, and IFAC, headquartered in New York, with their permanent staffs, are the principal flag bearers for the standardization of the world's accounting practices.

Both organizations try to avoid duplication of effort and overlapping of activities. The purpose of the IASC is the establishment of a global set of accounting standards, whereas the IFAC focuses on the conduct of accounting and auditing activities, ethical issues, and the education and training of accounting professionals. Since 1984, the professional accounting and auditing members of the IASC have been required to join the IFAC. Dual membership ensures that the complementary purposes of the two organizations are integrated and coordinated. The IASC and the IFAC are private organizations funded by their members. In 1991, the IASC included 107 accounting organizations from seventy-eight nations, representing about half of the world's nations. These organizations, who are also members of IFAC, represent about one million accounting professionals in private and public practice, industry, commerce, education, and government service.

IASC

The overall objectives of the IASC are to formulate and publish International Accounting Standards for preparing financial statements and to promote their worldwide acceptance and observance. In particular, the IASC desires that its International Accounting Standards be acceptable to global capital markets for underwriting securities and to the international business community for making economic decisions based on a uniform approach to the preparation of financial reports. The IASC coordinates its efforts with other private and public organizations in formulating and gaining acceptance of its accounting regulations, standards, and procedures. It seeks compatibility with national accounting organizations to reduce, and preferably remove, existing differences or barriers between national and international accounting standards. In addition, the IASC designs its standards to satisfy the financial reporting needs of developing and newly industrialized nations, including nations that have gained their independence or are emerging from the breakup of the Soviet Union.

The Making of an International Accounting Standard

The IASC board sets up a steering committee to start the process of originating a new International Accounting Standard (IAS) with majority support by the board. The steering committee, headed by a board member, writes a Statement of Intent, which is disseminated to various accounting organizations for comment. After review of the comments and any appropriate revision to the Statement of Intent, it is disseminated again for comment and review. This iterative process continues until closure is reached. The Statement of Intent progresses to the next step of Exposure Draft with two-thirds vote of approval by the board. The iterative process of circulation to interested parties, review of responses, and resubmission of a revised draft continues until the draft is ready for presentation to the board. If approved by a three-quarters vote by the board, the Exposure Draft becomes a new International Accounting Standard.

This process can be seen in greater detail by observing the 1991 status of an important Statement of Intent on the IASC's agenda, the "Comparability of Financial Statements." The board had approved its general objectives by majority vote and a steering committee had discussed its proposed content with other standard-setting bodies, stock exchanges, and business and professional accounting organizations in Australia, Canada, France, Italy, Japan, Korea, the Netherlands, the Philippines, South Africa, Sweden, the United Kingdom, the United States, and Zimbabwe. Moreover, discussions with the European Commission, the OECD Working Group on Accounting Standards, the United Nations Intergovernmental Working Group of Experts on International Standards of Accounting and Reporting, the International Organisation of Financial Executives Institutes, the Council of the International Federation of Accountants, the Federation des Experts Comptables Europeens, and the Interamerican Accounting Association had already taken place. Seven hundred and fifty pages of responses from the consultations with various organizations in over thirty countries, bound in two volumes, had been made available to interested parties. Upon review of these comments, certain issues contained in the Statement of Intent may be changed or deferred for further consideration. After this, the Statement of Intent may become an Exposure Draft with two-thirds majority vote of the board. After a similar process of consultation, review and revision is over, and with approval by three quarters of the members of the board, the Exposure Draft may become a new International Accounting Standard.

International Accounting Standards

When an International Accounting Standard is approved, the individual member organizations of the IASC are bound to introduce the standard in their respective countries. However, the IASC has no powers of enforcement. Therefore, adherence to these standards varies greatly from nation to nation. The first International Accounting Standard, IAS 1, was approved in 1975. The thirty-one standards existing in 1991, whose titles describe the nature of the work of the IASC, are the following:

IAS 1   Disclosure of Accounting Policies

IAS 2   Valuation and Presentation of Inventories in the Context of the Historical Cost System

IAS 3   (Superseded by IAS 27)

IAS 4   Depreciation Accounting

IAS 5   Information to be Disclosed in Financial Statements

IAS 6   (Superseded by IAS 15)

IAS 7   Statement of Changes in Financial Position

IAS 8   Unusual and Prior Period Items and Changes in Accounting Practices

IAS 9   Accounting for Research and Development Activities

IAS 10 Contingencies and Events Occurring After the Balance Sheet Date

IAS 11 Accounting for Construction Contracts

IAS 12 Accounting for Taxes on Income

IAS 13 Presentation of Current Assets and Current Liabilities

IAS 14 Reporting Financial Information by Segment

IAS 15 Information Reflecting the Effects of Changing Prices

IAS 16 Accounting for Property, Plant and Equipment

IAS 17 Accounting for Leases

IAS 18 Revenue Recognition

IAS 19 Accounting for Retirement Benefits in the Financial Statements of Employers

IAS 20 Accounting for Government Grants and Disclosure of Government Assistance

IAS 21 Accounting for the Effects of Changes in Foreign Exchange Rates

IAS 22 Accounting for Business Combinations

IAS 23 Capitalization of Borrowing Costs

IAS 24 Related Party Disclosures

IAS 25 Accounting for Investments

IAS 26 Accounting and Reporting by Retirement Benefit Plans

IAS 27 Consolidated Financial Statements and Accounting for Investments in Subsidiaries

IAS 28 Accounting for Investments in Associates

IAS 29 Financial Reporting in Hyperinflationary Economies

IAS 30 Disclosures in the Financial Statements of Banks and Similar Financial Institutions

IAS 31 Financial Reporting of Interests in Joint Ventures

Exposure Drafts under consideration in 1991 dealt with income taxes, cash flow statements, research and development activities, inventories, capitalization of borrowing costs, and financial instruments. Other Exposure Drafts for changing existing IASs were being considered on construction contracts (IAS 11); property, plant, and equipment (IAS 4 and 16); revenue recognition (IAS 18); effects of changes in currency exchange rates (IAS 21); and business combinations (IAS 22).

Anglo-Dutch Influence in the IASC

The IASC's proposed "Framework for the Preparation and Presentation of Financial Statements" provides an overview of the objectives of financial statements. This framework is the result of examining the guidelines for financial reporting throughout the world. According to the framework, financial statements are to be informative as to the financial position and performance of a company and are to show the results of stewardship of management and the accountability of management for the resources entrusted to it. Given the objectives of the IASC to establish a set of accounting standards to create financial statements amenable to a global capital market and useful in making economic decisions, it should not be surprising to find a strong Anglo-Dutch influence in the proposed framework.

The IASC does not fault small companies for following frameworks modeled after the German Commercial Code, the Swedish Accounting Act, the French General Plan Comptable, or similar accounting coding systems. These "form-over-substance" frameworks may be more desirable, and perhaps more appropriate, for privately held companies than the "substance-over-form" frameworks espoused in the United Kingdom, the United States, and the Netherlands. However, form-over-substance accounting systems do have serious limitations, both in raising capital and in making economic decisions for large publicly traded companies. The IASC framework was developed using published frameworks of accounting organizations in the United States, the United Kingdom, Australia, Canada, the Netherlands, and other nations where the concepts of true and fair view and substance over form prevail. The Dutch view, in IASC's opinion, is closest to the IASC position on the objectives of financial statements. According to the Dutch Civil Code:

The annual accounts shall in accordance with generally accepted accounting principles furnish such insight as to enable a sound judgement to be formed regarding the financial position and results of the legal entity and, to the extent which annual accounts permit, regarding its solvency and liquidity.

United States and United Kingdom Harmonizing with the IASC

In 1991, the U.S. Financial Accounting Standards Board (FASB) announced that it would take a more active role in supporting the activities of the IASC.

The FASB acknowledged the necessity of a common body of international accounting standards to facilitate the flow of capital across national borders. Although the primary mission of FASB remains unchanged in the setting of U.S. accounting standards, the process of setting standards will give greater consideration to international developments in accounting. The FASB also announced its intention to be more active in seeking greater compatibility and conformity between U.S. and international standards, particularly for those international standards that are deemed to be superior to American standards. If the FASB concludes that international standards are inferior to U.S. standards, then the FASB intends to take a more active role in raising international standards to U.S. standards. The twin thrust of the FASB to make U.S. standards more compatable with international standards and/or to influence the development of international standards to make them more compatible with U.S. standards will bring about a greater degree of harmonization.

The United Kingdom's newly organized standard-setting body, the Accounting Standards Board (ASB), also supports the efforts of the IASC. Its proposed draft charter in 1991 stated that future Financial Reporting Standards (FRSs), which are applicable to the accounting profession in the United Kingdom, are to be formulated with due regard to IASC standards. Wherever possible, FRSs are to be fully compatible with the relevant IAS and to harmonize financial reporting with international standards.

IASC Promotion of IASC Standards

The IASC has been successful in having Italy require that all large publicly traded corporations prepare their financial reports in accordance with IASC standards. Emerging industrial nations, which often do not have the resources necessary to develop their own standards, are actively encouraged by the IASC to adopt IASC standards, in part or in full, rather than originate yet another set of standards. By adopting IASC standards, the accounting organizations of these nations become members of the IASC and are, consequently, in a position to influence the future development of IASC standards. The IASC has been successful in having eastern European nations, and the nations within the Commonwealth of Independent States, consider adopting IASC standards. Polish accounting practices are to be based on a blend of European Community Directives, the French Plan Comptable, and IASC standards. The Hungarian Ministry of Finance, the Bulgarian Ministry of Finance, and the accounting standard setting body in Yugoslavia are in the process of establishing IASC standards as the backbone of their national accounting systems. The basic reason for the selection of IASC, or near-IASC, standards is that they provide an accounting system that meets the demands, and bolsters the confidence, of both domestic and foreign investors, who want a true and fair approach to financial reporting. This is a necessary condition before investors provide capital for the industrial and commercial development of these nations.

IFAC

The other organization born of the Tenth International Congress of Accountants is the International Federation of Accountants, whose membership is very similar to that of IASC. Its purpose is described in the following twelve-point program.

1. Develop statements that would serve as guidelines for international auditing practices.
2. Establish a suggested minimum code of ethics to which it is hoped that member bodies would subscribe and that could be further refined as appropriate.
3. Determine the requirements of and develop programs for the professional education and training of accountants.
4. Evaluate, develop, and report on financial management and other management accounting techniques and procedures.
5. Collect, analyze, research, and disseminate information on the management of public accounting practices to assist practioners in conducting their practices more effectively.
6. Undertake other studies of value to accountants such as, possibly, a study of the legal liability of auditors.
7. Foster close relations with users of financial statements, including preparers, trade unions, financial institutions, industry, governments, and others.
8. Maintain close relations with regional bodies as well as assist in their organization and development, as appropriate. Assign appropriate projects to existing regional bodies.
9. Establish regular communications among the members of IFAC and with other interested organizations through the medium of a newsletter.
10. Organize and promote the exchange of technical information, educational materials, professional publications, and other literature emanating from the member bodies.
11. Organize and conduct an international congress of accountants approximately every five years.
12. Seek to expand the membership of the IFAC.

The IFAC operates through standing committees on international accounting and auditing practices; education of the accounting profession; ethical issues associated with accounting, financial, and management accounting; and public sector accounting and internal planning. Under the guidance of the council, the standing committees are responsible for achieving the broad objectives of the IFAC through the issuance of what were originally called guidelines, now called standards. This reflects the growing confidence within the IFAC of its future role in establishing a global approach to the conduct of accounting and auditing. Members of the IFAC are committed to implementing these standards in their respective nations, although like the IASC, there is no way to enforce adoption of IFAC standards.

The International Auditing Practices Committee is responsible for the creation of standards on auditing and reporting practices to improve the degree of uniformity of auditing practices throughout the world. The Education Committee works on establishing a uniform set of education and training standards for professional accountants. The Ethics Committee is concerned with professional ethics, which are fundamental to the accounting profession, and with enhancing the esteem and confidence of the public's perception of accountants. The Financial and Management Accounting Committee deals with accounting concepts, procedures, and techniques that aid in managing and controlling a global organization. The Public Sector Committee is dedicated to accounting functions associated with governments and governmental agencies. The Planning Committee advances IFAC objectives by reviewing its policies and plans and making recommendations for future activities to the council.

As of 1991, the IFAC had issued the following 29 International Standards on Auditing (ISA):

ISA–1   Objective and Basic Principles Governing an Audit

ISA–2   Audit Engagement Letters

ISA–3   (Superseded by ISA-1)

ISA–4   Planning

ISA–5   Using the Work of Another Auditor

ISA–6   Risk Assessment and Internal Control (Addendum 1 includes EDP Characteristics and Considerations)

ISA–7   Control of the Quality of Audit Work

ISA–8   Audit Evidence (Addendum 1 includes Additional Guidance on Observation of Inventory, Confirmation of Accounts Receivable, and Inquiry Regarding Litigation and Claims)

ISA–9   Documentation

ISA–10   Using the Work of an Internal Auditor

ISA–11   Fraud and Error

ISA–12   Analytical Review

ISA–13   The Auditor's Report on Financial Statements

ISA–14   Other Information in Documents Containing Audited Financial Statements

ISA–15   Auditing in an EDP Environment

ISA–16   Computer-Assisted Audit Techniques

ISA–17   Related Parties

ISA–18   Using the Work of an Expert

ISA–19   Audit Sampling

ISA–20   (Superseded by a later revision to ISA-6)

ISA–21   Date of the Auditor's Report; Events After the Balance Sheet Date; Discovery of Facts After the Financial Statements Have Been Issued

ISA–22   Representations by Management

ISA–23   Going Concern

ISA–24   Special Purpose Audit Reports

ISA–25   Materiality and Audit Risk

ISA–26   Audit of Accounting Estimates

ISA–27   The Examination of Prospective Information

ISA–28   First Year Audit Engagements—Opening Balances

ISA–29   (Superseded by a later revision to ISA-6)

In addition to the aforementioned IFAC standards, guidelines and standards have been issued by the IFAC on related services such as principles governing review engagements where an accountant reviews, but does not audit or render an opinion, on financial statements. Guidelines have also been issued for auditing banks and operating in an EDP (electronic data processing) environment.

For the 1990s, the IFAC intends to work closely with the International Organization of Securities Commission (IOSCO), which represents the government regulators of the world's stock exchanges. IOSCO acceptance of IFAC auditing and ethics standards and IASC accounting standards as a basis for international securities offerings would be further steps toward the globalization of the world's capital markets. This would mean that a company might issue securities simultaneously on all the world's stock exchanges and have its securities traded on a global basis with one set of financial statements. Moreover, those involved with making economic decisions could refer to the financial statements of any company in the world and have a better understanding and appreciation of each accounting entity for analytical purposes.

THE UNITED NATIONS

There are several United Nations (UN) organizations involved with global accounting. The Commission on Transnational Corporations has been striving for the establishment of a set of international accounting standards, with emphasis on increasing the degree of disclosure of financial statements for companies that conduct their business on a transnational scale. The Code of Conduct regarding disclosure stipulates that transnational corporations should disclose to the public on an annual basis, in clear terms, in readily accessible reports, full and comprehensible financial and nonfinancial information regarding the structure, policies, activities, and operations of the company as a whole. The financial information would include the balance sheet, income statement with sales and operating results, plus the allocation of net profits within the company, sources and uses of funds, long-term capital investments, and research and development expenses. Nonfinancial information would cover the structure of the transnational company, including its main entities and percentage ownership and shareholdings of all directly and indirectly owned entities, a breakdown of employment, revenue and new investments by geographic region and by lines of business, accounting policies employed in compiling and consolidating financial information, and transfer pricing policies. Notwithstanding the wide sweeping nature of such disclosure, a transnational company would have the right to take into consideration the confidentiality of such information, the effects of releasing such information on its competitive position and the costs involved in gathering the information.

The Organization for Economic Cooperation and Development (OECD) has been given the charge to "achieve the highest sustainable economic growth and employment and a rising standard of living in member countries while maintaining financial stability and, thus, to contribute to the world economy." In 1976, the OECD proposed a code of conduct for multinational enterprises that included, among other matters, financial disclosure. Its guidelines for disclosure are quite similar to those just described for the Commission on Transnational Corporations. They include the publication of financial statements on at least an annual basis, the structure of the enterprise including the nature of direct and indirect ownership of subsidiaries or affiliates, and the description of these operations in both geographic and financial terms. In addition, disclosure would be made for new capital investment by geographical areas and lines of business, sources and uses of funds, number of employees by geographic areas, research and development expenditures, intragroup pricing policies and accounting policies used in preparing financial statements.

Both of these UN organizations have been criticized for being more interested in discovering the inner workings of transnational corporations, for the purpose of attempting to control their activities, than in having corporations disclose their activities for the good of the investing public. Neither of these organizations has exerted the same degree of effort and initiative as the IASC and IFAC in fostering the development of a global accounting system.

EUROPEAN COMMUNITY

The progenitor of the European Community was the European Economic Community (EEC), which was preceded by an organization to coordinate the activities of the European coal and steel industries. The EEC was established by the Treaty of Rome in 1957 to promote full freedom in the movement of goods and labor between member countries. Consequently, the EEC attempted to create a unified business environment including harmonization of company laws, taxation, and capital markets. With regard to this latter activity, the EEC issued directives for the harmonization of accounting standards for its member states.

Representing the accounting profession in the development of these directives is the Federation des Experts Comptables Europeens (FEE), a group of primarily European accounting organizations headquartered in Brussels. The FEE consists of thirty-five member accounting organizations representing 300,000 accountants in twenty-three different nations. Over 90 percent of the accountants belonging to member organizations are within the European Community and 40 percent are in public accounting practice. The FEE works closely with the European Commission, the civil service organization of the European Community, in its efforts to create draft directives for presentation to the European Parliament, an elected assembly with limited powers. Draft directives on accounting issues are also commented on by the Economic and Social Committee, a consultative body of employers and employees.

The final form of a draft directive is presented to the Council of Ministers. If approved by the Council of Ministers, member states of the European Community (EC) are required to introduce applicable national laws within a two-year period to bring their accounting practices into general agreement with the directive. However, EC directives contain discretionary power on how the EC directives are to be incorporated into national law. This permits both delays in adoption and differences in interpretation such that the national laws passed in accordance with an EC directive are not identical among the European nations. Moreover, there is some question as to the effectiveness and willingness of enforcement of these laws among the member nations. Although the directives do not standardize accounting practices in the sense of IASC standards, they do tend to harmonize, that is, eliminate or reduce the scope of disparities of accounting standards. This enhances the compatibility and comparability of accounting practices among the European member nations.

On the positive side, the directives do have the force of law, which promotes compliance, and they do give Europe greater stature in the global forum for discussing accounting issues. The directives stress the importance of the "true and fair" view, and as such, weaken the linkage between tax collection and financial reporting. On the negative side, there still remain substantive issues that have not yet (as of 1991) been addressed, such as deferred taxation, long-term contracts, pensions, and currency translation. Implementation of the directives into national law by the member states is not uniform. Enforcement of compliance varies considerably among the member states. The directive-setting process is slow and may not always take into consideration developments in accounting taking place elsewhere in the world. Despite these drawbacks, and despite the directives being more oriented toward harmonization than toward standardization, the directives must be considered successful in setting up a European accounting system based on substance over form.

First Directive

The First Directive, adopted in 1968, concerns the publishing of accounts, not the nature of the accounts. Publicly traded companies must make their accounting records available to any interested party, who does not have to demonstrate a legitimate interest. This ensures that financial reports are made available to the public at large.

Second Directive

The Second Directive, adopted in 1976, is on the separation of public from private companies, the naming of companies, minimum capital requirements for public companies, and the definition of distributable profits and its impact on paying dividends. The directive is aimed at preserving a company's capital, which may constitute a creditor's security, by prohibiting a wrongful distribution of capital to shareholders and in restricting a company's right to acquire its own shares.

Third and Sixth Directives

The Third Directive, adopted in 1978, and the Sixth Directive, adopted in 1982, deal with mergers. Mergers covered under both directives are only those within a single member state. The type of merger covered in the Third Directive is where an existing company, or a new one formed for this purpose, purchases the assets and liabilities of another. The type of merger covered in the Sixth Directive is where there is a transfer of a part of the assets of one public company to another public company in exchange for shares. The draft Tenth Directive is directed to cross-border mergers of the type dealt with by the Third Directive.

Fourth Directive

The Fourth Directive, adopted in 1978, along with the Seventh Directive, are considered to be the most important and far reaching of all the directives. The fourth concerns the disclosure of financial information by public companies other than banks, insurance companies, and other financial institutions. The objectives of the Fourth Directive are as follows:

1. To coordinate the various national laws dealing with the publication, presentation, and content of financial statements.
2. To establish throughout the EEC minimum requirements for disclosure of financial information by corporations.
3. To establish the underlying principles of a true and fair view of a company's financial condition and the results of its operations.
4. To protect the interests of third parties such as employees, trade unions, governmental agencies, and creditors.

True and fair view remains as it always has been, a concept lacking precise definition. Nevertheless, what has to be disclosed for a financial statement to be considered true and fair can be defined. Required disclosures include a description of corporate accounting policies; listing of affiliates in which a company holds more than a 20 percent share of the stock; description of the type and number of shares outstanding; details on long-term and secured debt; details on commitments, contingencies, and pension obligations; sales by type of product and geographical area as long as this does not seriously prejudice the company's activities; number and type of employees; their aggregate compensation and the compensation, loans, and advances to directors; differences between taxes paid and the amount reflected on the financial statements; and the extent to which operating results have been affected by special tax incentives. The Fourth Directive has specific guidelines on depreciation of fixed assets, writeoff of intangible assets, inventory valuations including noting of material differences between replacement and reported inventory valuations, and guidance on revaluation of tangible fixed assets to take into consideration either inflation or replacement cost.

The Fourth Directive also provides guidance on the types of companies covered by the directive and on the general reporting requirements with regard to the balance sheet; profit and loss statements, and notes pertaining thereto; and the format, content, and publishing requirements of annual reports. The Fourth Directive contains a description of the nature of the national laws that would have to be passed to fulfill its objectives. The requirements of the Fourth Directive are general in nature with allowance for member states to add to disclosure requirements. The true and fair view provisions of the Fourth Directive are contained in the following statements.

1. The annual financial statements shall conform to proper accounting principles. They shall be clear and well set out and give as sure a view of the company's financial position and its operating results as is possible pursuant to the valuation provisions.

2. They shall be drawn up clearly and in accordance with the provisions of this directive.

3. The annual accounts shall give a true and fair view of the company's assets, liabilities, financial position and profit or loss.

4. Where the application of the provisions of this directive would not be sufficient to give a true and fair view within the meaning of paragraph 3 (above), additional information must be given.

5. When in exceptional cases the application of a provision of this directive is incompatible with the obligation laid down in paragraph 3 (above), that provision must be departed from in order to give a true and fair view within the meaning of paragraph 3. Any such departure must be disclosed in the notes on the accounts together with an explanation of the reasons for it and a statement of its effect on the assets, liabilities, financial position and profit or loss. The member states may define the exceptional cases in question and lay down the relevant special rules.

6. The member states may authorise or require the disclosure in the annual accounts of other information as well as that which must be disclosed in accordance with this directive.

The Fourth Directive does not set up standardized accounting practices for the European Community. It aims at comparability and equivalence of the financial information to be published by some 3 million European companies by establishing minimum conditions, while allowing member states to impose additional or more detailed rules. For instance, purchase price or production cost is stipulated for the valuation of assets, but member states may permit alternative methods such as replacement or other means of valuation. Harmonization is achieved by stating the method of valuation, along with the difference between the selected method and the purchase price method, in the notes to the financial statements. Any difference between the two is listed as a revaluation reserve. Valuation methods are in harmony in the sense that there is sufficient disclosure of information to allow the financial statements to be restated to a single valuation method. The Second and Fourth Directives attempt to harmonize the legal foundation of companies and their approach to financial reporting.

It took the entire decade of the 1980s for the various nations in the European Community to implement the Fourth Directive. Although the Fourth Directive contains options that result in differences in the way financial results are measured, presented and published, these differences are not as wide as they once were. In this sense, the overall objectives of harmonization to eliminate disparities and narrow differences have been achieved.

Fifth Directive

The latest draft (1983) of this directive has not yet been adopted. The Fifth Directive focuses on the structure, management, and auditing of companies. This particular directive is strongly opposed by the accounting and the business organizations in the United Kingdom because it would require all public companies to have the functions of management split into a nonexecutive, or supervisory, board and an executive, or management, board, similar to the operation of large companies in Germany and the Netherlands. The supervisory board would appoint the management board and fix their salaries, receive regular reports from the management board, including financial reports, and would be actively involved with important strategic decisions.

U.K. opposition centers mainly on the makeup of the members of the supervisory board, which would include employee representatives. Employees of a company would have the right to appoint between one third and one half of the members of the supervisory board and would have the right of access to company information along with the right of being consulted in major corporate decisions.

The draft Vredeling Directive, named after one of the former EC commissioners, is associated with the Fifth Directive. The draft Vredeling Directive would require businesses to pass information to, and to consult with, their employees. It also calls for annual information to be disseminated from a parent company to its subsidiaries, and from there to employee representatives, on the outlook for investment, sales, and employment. Such information may exclude that which "could substantially damage the undertaking's interests or lead to the failure of its plans." The draft Vredeling Directive is supported by the Netherlands and Germany. The United Kingdom, with its historic antagonism between labor and management, and with its concept of management defined in terms of serving the interests of shareholders, opposes this notion of employee involvement, as do certain multinational companies in the United States and Japan.

The Fifth Directive also requires the preparation of the long-form audit report that would be made available to nonexecutive directors, executive directors, and shareholders. This report would contain a listing of legal infringements by any one associated with the company and explicit observations on any matter that would be adverse to the company's financial position. Auditors in the United Kingdom oppose the long-form audit report from an ethical viewpoint because it provides a forum for special interest groups within a company to "tell tales" and possibly to precipitate a crisis of confidence in the management of a company. There is also the question of the civil liability, which auditors must face from statements or observations that they are obligated to include in the long-form audit report.

Another contentious issue is the establishment of "legal reserves" of undistributed profits, that are common on the European continent. Legal reserves are usually at management's discretion and funds set aside in legal reserves are not reported as profits. Some feel that legal reserves are both proper and a conservative approach to accounting because reported profits are understated with regard to actual profits when funds are placed in legal reserves. Legal reserves are considered to be "creditor-oriented" in that managers can tap these reserves when earnings are not sufficient to satisfy debt obligations. Others consider legal reserves to be at odds with the true and fair view of accounting for the financial results because management has discretion on what portion of earnings is to be reported to the shareholders.

Seventh Directive

The Seventh Directive, adopted in 1983, addresses the issue of consolidations, a subject neglected in the Fourth Directive. Anglo-Dutch accounting professionals are well versed in the necessity and the methodology of consolidations. This is not true in other European nations. For instance, in Germany, non-German subsidiaries are usually not consolidated because financial and tax accounting are one and the same. The Anglo-Dutch view prevails in the Seventh Directive because the Anglo-Dutch view corresponds to the underlying objective of the directives to present a true and fair view.

The Seventh Directive provides details as to which subsidiaries, and subsidiaries of subsidiaries, must be consolidated with a company's financial reports regardless of location. Subsidiaries are defined by such criteria as who holds the majority voting rights, who has the right to appoint a majority of the board members, or who possesses "dominant influence" in the running of a company. The directive requires member states to make consolidation compulsory when a parent company has legal power to control a subsidiary but member states can decide on their own whether consolidation should be compulsory when a parent company has a minority shareholding in a subsidiary.

Financial holding companies that neither manage nor take part in board appointments need not consolidate their financial reports. Exemptions on consolidations are permitted for a variety of reasons such as nonconsolidation of a small subsidiary without listed shares, subsidiaries whose scope of operations is immaterial in relation to the parent, and other reasons that do not thwart the intent of financial statements to present a true and fair view of a company's overall financial results.

The Seventh Directive was adopted into the national law of most of the European Community during the second half of the 1980s. However, requirements concerning consolidation and the definition concerning exemptions, along with the method of consolidation and the selection of valuation methods of assets, vary somewhat among the member nations. Member states can also permit proportional consolidation and the equity method of consolidation. The availibility of choice for member states is part of harmonization where the intent is to eliminate inconsistencies and narrow the differences without forcing all nations to accept one standard. In theory, there is sufficient information provided in the financial reports, and in the notes pertaining thereto, to reconstruct the financial reports according to a single set of accounting principles.

Consolidation in the European context is different than in the United States. In the United States, consolidation implies instruments of legal control of one company over another such as owning a majority of shares. Consolidation under the Seventh Directive is more concerned with actual than legal (de facto over de jure) control. For instance, consolidation is required for enterprises that are under central or unified management, but not necessarily with management representing a controlling degree of ownership in the enterprises. As an example, two companies with no mutual ownership of stock have to be consolidated if they are managed by a single group (unified management). A non-European parent with independent subsidiaries in Europe is required by the Seventh Directive to publish a combined statement of all its subsidiaries, and their associated subsidiaries, within the European Community. For instance, independently operated European subsidiaries of General Motors would have to be consolidated, but without the parent company and its other non-European subsidiaries.

Other articles address the composition of consolidated accounts and the methods and principles of consolidation. These include the valuation of acquired assets at fair market value, consistency of application of accounting principles in preparing accounts and in consolidating reports, and the use of the equity method of accounting for all intercorporate investments where there is significant influence, which is determined by having ownership of more than 20 percent. Other requirements deal with handling positive and negative goodwill, the nature and publication of financial reports, and comparability disclosures with previous consolidated statements and associated footnotes.

Eighth Directive

The Eighth Directive, adopted in 1984, deals with the qualifications of auditors, including a listing of requirements associated with their education, training, experience, and qualifying examinations. The directive deals with the professional independence of the auditor and the nature of professional associations.

Eleventh Directive

The Eleventh Directive, adopted in 1989 but not yet (as of 1991) incorporated in the legislation of the member states, deals with branch accounts for limited liability companies, where the branches are located outside the jurisdiction of the Fourth and Seventh Directives. Disclosure is in accordance with the rules laid down by directives relating to limited liability companies with branches in the European Community. Special provisions are made for branch operations of financial institutions at locations not in the European Community.

Sectoral Directives

Sectoral Directives have been adopted by the Council of Ministers, but not yet incorporated in the legislation of the member states. These deal with certain sectors that are exempt from the Fourth and Seventh Directives such as banks, insurance companies, and other financial institutions. Sectoral Directives make allowances for the special nature of reporting requirements for these institutions in the layout and format of financial reports, special definitions for off-balance-sheet items, breakdown of loans and liabilities with regard to maturity, advances and commitments, management and agency services to third parties, differences between market and face value of securities, the existence of hidden reserves, funds to handle general banking risks, and other matters that pertain to financial institutions.

Other Draft Directives

There are a number of draft documents that have not yet been presented to the Council of Ministers. The draft Ninth Directive is intended to deal with corporate links among groupings of public companies, the Tenth with mergers of public companies domiciled in different member states, the Twelfth with public companies operating within a single member nation, and the Thirteenth with takeovers. Discussions are under way to organize companies under the designation Societas Europea. A company so organized would be subject to EC laws and taxes, not to the laws and taxes of an individual nation. This idea is making little headway, however, because member nations sense a potential loss of corporate tax revenue and national sovereignty.

EEIG

Another idea taking shape is the European Economic Interest Grouping (EEIG), a business arrangement for facilitating joint undertakings. An EEIG is a new legal form for the operation of joint activities of parent corporations from different member states. The EEIG is modeled after the French joint venture scheme called the Groupement d'Interet Economique (GIE), which now numbers in the thousands in France. The EEIG is a non-profit-making legal structure epitomized by the consortia of companies involved in the manufacture of the airbus. Although adopted by the European Council in 1985, the concept of the EEIG is strongly opposed by the United Kingdom because there is no requirement for published accounts or an audit. Participating members of the EEIG do have the right to inspect its books and records. From the point of view of U.K. accountants, EEIGs are not necessary because U.K. companies have entered into partnerships and joint ventures with their EC counterparts without experiencing the difficulties that are supposed to be overcome by the EEIG.

OTHER INTERNATIONAL ORGANIZATIONS

There are many international organizations representing various aspects of the accounting profession, or those affected by accounting, as listed in the accompanying appendix. A sampling of some of these organizations follows.

The African Accounting Council (AAC) represents African countries in their mutual attempts to promote standardized accounting practices in Africa. Members of the AAC must be members of the Organization of African Unity. Accounting practices in African nations are modeled after those of Britain, France, Belgium, and Portugal depending on their colonial history. African nations have not always kept abreast with the development of accounting practices in the colonizing nation after independence. As a result, there is variation in accounting practices among nations with a common colonial history. The objectives of the AAC include standardization of accounting practices, education, research, exchange of information, and contact with other international organizations. Although not much progress has been made, the coordinating activities of the AAC with the IASC may pave the way for international standards to gain a foothold on the African continent.

There are a number of regional accounting organizations serving the interests of the accounting community in Latin and South America (Interamerican Accounting Association), Scandinavia and Finland (Nordic Federation of Accountants), Southeast Asia (Federation of Accountants), West Africa (Association of Accountancy Bodies in West Africa) and Asia (Confederation of Asian and Pacific Accountants).

The membership of the Confederation of Asian and Pacific Accounts (CAPA) includes thirty-one accounting organizations in twenty-two nations including Australia, Bangladesh, Canada, France, Fiji, Hong Kong, India, Indonesia,

Japan, Korea, Malaysia, New Zealand, Pakistan, Papua New Guinea, the Philippines, Singapore, Solomon Islands, Sri Lanka, Taiwan, Thailand, the United States, and Western Samoa. The objectives of CAPA reflect the nature of the objectives of regional accounting organizations in general.

1. The long-term objective of CAPA shall be the development of a coordinated regional accounting profession with harmonized standards. CAPA will give leadership toward the achievement of this objective and in particular will:

    A. Initiate, coordinate, and guide work that has as its goal the achievement of technical, ethical, and educational guidelines for the accountancy profession within the region as well as reciprocal recognition of qualifications, and to work toward this purpose by establishing appropriate committees as well as working through the national organizations for implementation. Where possible, such activities will be coordinated with the work of the International Federation of Accountants.

    B. Encourage and assist the development of national accountancy organizations within the regions with common objectives and formulate guidelines for the structure and constitution of such organization.

    C. Effect changes in CAPA's role, functioning and constitution whenever necessary to achieve its objectives.

2. In furtherance of these objectives, CAPA will arrange regular conferences to bring together the official representatives of professional bodies in the area to discuss ways and develop means for:

    A. Providing services to their own members and their own communities in education for accountancy, including continuing education, accounting research, and ethical conduct.

    B. Promoting the observance of professional standards, practice, and techniques at national level within the framework of national standards.

There are other organizations representing accounting professors and academic institutions. The interests of financial analysts are pursued by the Financial Analysts' Federation, whereas multinational executives are represented by the Financial Executive Institute (FEI). The public and private interests in the world's stock exchanges are served by the International Organization of Securities Commissions and the International Capital Markets Group (ICMG), respectively.

The most prestigious gathering of accountants is the World Congress of Accountants, the new name for the International Congress of Accountants. Meeting every five years, and organized under the auspices of the IFAC, the 1992 Congress is to be held in Washington. Its theme is "The Accountant's Role in a Global Economy," coupled with discussions on global capital markets and privatization issues, reflect the trend toward harmonization and standardization and the trend away from government ownership and control over industry.

COPING WITH CHANGE

Companies are coping with change in the presentation of financial reports. A review of recent European annual reports reveals efforts within the accounting profession to seek commonality in the presentation of financial statements.

SKF

Swedish accounting principles follow the tax and commercial laws, and typically include a number of discretionary items that management is permitted to employ to defer the payment of taxes. These affect net income and distort the true and fair view in presenting the financial statements of a company. SKF is a large Swedish bearing and tool manufacturing company. Table 4.1, excerpted from SKF's 1990 annual report, shows two income figures.

The net income of 1,014 million Swedish kronor represents the income earned by the company under Swedish generally accepted accounting principles (GAAP). The reported income for the year of 509 million kronor represents income as determined under Swedish commercial/tax laws. The various reserves which defer income taxes, and, therefore, reduce reported income, are listed in Exhibit 4.1.

The recasting of the financial reports in accordance with U.S. GAAP is seen in Exhibit 4.2, which describes the different accounting policies between Swedish and U.S. GAAP. The net income is reduced from 1,014 million kronor to 894 million kronor in making the transition from Swedish to U.S. GAAP, a not insignificant reduction in income. This restatement of financial information has not been audited by a U.S. accounting firm and was not covered in the opinion expressed by the Swedish auditors. One apparent purpose is to encourage non-Swedish investors to consider buying the company's shares by restating the financial results in accordance with a set of accounting principles that are more widely accepted outside of Sweden. The company's unrestricted B shares are traded on the Stockholm, London, Paris, Geneva, and Basel stock exchanges, with American Depository Receipts (ADRs) traded on the over the counter (NASDAQ) market. Trading shares on various exchanges expands the potential capital market for a company when it issues shares or bonds. The trading of the company's ADRs in New York probably motivated the company to select U.S., not IASC, standards in restating its financial results.

TELECOM OF NEW ZEALAND

The Telecom Corporation of New Zealand, Ltd., was privatized by the government of New Zealand, but the New Zealand capital market was too thin to accommodate the share offering. The prospectus of the offering was prepared both in accordance with New Zealand (N.Z.) and U.S. GAAP to expand the public offering to include U.S. and Canadian investors. Table 4.2 shows the

Table 4.1
Income Statements of SKF 1990 Annual Report

Consolidated income statements

Millions of Swedish kronor		**1990**	1989	1988
Net sales		**27 766**	25 066	21 248
Other operating income		**164**	305	177
Cost of goods sold		**−19 011**	−16 859	−14 757
Selling, administrative and technical expenses	*note 2*	**− 6 053**	− 5 087	− 4 329
Depreciation according to plan	*note 3*	**− 951**	− 826	− 779
Operating income		**1 915**	2 599	1 560
Financial income and expense – net	*note 4*	**− 165**	− 129	− 41
Income after financial income and expense		**1 750**	2 470	1 519
Taxes on income	*note 5*	**− 719**	− 989	− 543
Equity in loss/income of Associated Companies		**− 133**	78	37
Minority interest in income		**− 26**	− 32	− 34
Income after taxes		**872**	1 527	979
Extraordinary income	*note 6*	**145**	235	–
Extraordinary expense	*note 6*	**− 37**	− 230	–
Taxes on extraordinary income and expense	*note 5*	**34**	− 19	–
Net income		**1 014**	1 513	979
Provisions	*note 22*	**− 843**	− 515	− 82
Reversal of deferred taxes	*note 22*	**327**	181	67
Minority interest in provisions	*note 22*	**11**	− 9	0
Reported income for the year		**509**	1 170	964

Exhibit 4.1
Reserves from SKF 1990 Annual Report

Restricted reserves

In accordance with statutory requirements in Sweden and certain other countries in which the SKF Group operates, the Parent Company and its subsidiaries maintain restricted reserves that are not available for distribution as dividends. Increases or decreases in restricted reserves have no effect on net income.

The Swedish Companies Act requires that 10 percent of net income be transferred to the legal reserve (part of restricted reserves) until the legal reserve amounts to 20 percent of the share capital. Premium paid on newly issued shares must also be transferred to the legal reserve.

In many countries where legal revaluations of assets are made, the revaluation surplus must be transferred to legal reserves.

Unrestricted earnings

The amount includes earnings distributable by the Parent Company and those earnings that may be remitted from subsidiaries to the Parent Company within one year, net of accumulated losses of certain other subsidiaries. In determining the remittable amounts, consideration has been given to exchange and other legal restrictions, but not to the cash position and the financial requirements of the remitting subsidiaries.

Provisions and Special Reserves

General

Tax laws in Sweden and certain other countries permit allocations to reserves that are deductible for tax purposes. To a certain extent, companies can thus allocate income so that it remains in the business without being taxed immediately.

Such allocations from income that have been made to retain funds in the business, are shown in the income statement under Provisions. In the balance sheets the accumulated value of these allocations, less the related deferred tax liabilities, is shown as Special Reserves. Differences between statutory reporting and reporting for consolidation purposes are also treated as Provisions in the income statement and as Special Reserves in the balance sheet.

A description of the major Special Reserves follows:

Inventory reserves

Appropriations related to inventories that are deductible for tax purposes and are in excess of actual requirements.

Investment reserves

Certain countries have tax laws permitting deferral of gains on sales of property, plant and equipment to be used for write-downs of capital assets to be acquired. Further, the tax laws of some countries allow companies to appropriate a portion of their pretax income to an investment reserve to be used for future write-downs of capital assets.

Accelerated depreciation reserves

In certain countries, tax regulations allow depreciation at rates exceeding those applied by the Group.

Other reserves

In general, these reserves represent the aggregated differences between statutory reporting and reporting for Group consolidation purposes.

summary of earnings and shareholders' equity in terms of N.Z. and U.S. GAAP with the principal differences described in note (c), which refers to a difficulty in reconciling N.Z. with U.S. GAAP with regard to obtaining historical cost data on assets acquired from the New Zealand Post Office. This is further described in Exhibit 4.3 along with a listing of significant differences between N.Z. and U.S. GAAP.

Despite this impediment in the recasting of the financial statements of Telecom Corporation of New Zealand, the offering was approved by the U.S. Securities and Exchange Commission. What is noteworthy here is that such an impediment did not prevent the offering of securities, perhaps reflecting a more global outlook on the part of the government regulators of the U.S. capital market.

ROYAL DUTCH/SHELL GROUP

This group of companies is owned 60 percent by Royal Dutch Petroleum Company (the Netherlands) and 40 percent by the Shell Transport and Trading Company (the United Kingdom). The Netherlands' capital market is too small to accommodate the capital needs of one of the world's largest companies. The company's annual reports are available in Dutch, English, French, and German, and the company maintains investor relations offices in the Hague, London, and

Exhibit 4.2

Reconciliation to U.S. GAAP from SKF 1990 Annual Report

U.S. GAAP

Note 26 – Reconciliation to United States Generally Accepted Accounting Principles (U.S. GAAP)

Accounting policies of the SKF Group that differ significantly from U.S. GAAP are as follows:

1. *Deferred income taxes*

U.S. GAAP require deferred tax allocation on all significant timing differences, including the allocations to untaxed reserves. Although there is no requirement for comprehensive recognition of deferred income taxes under Swedish accounting practice, it is the SKF Group's policy that net income and shareholders' equity is determined after consideration of deferred income taxes. Consequently, no adjustment needs to be made for deferred taxes when applying U.S. GAAP.

Adjustments for deferred income taxes in the reconciliation to' U.S. GAAP are attributable to the differences described below.

2. *Revaluation of assets*

In certain countries, assets have been revalued at an amount in excess of cost. U.S. GAAP do not permit the revaluation of assets in the primary financial statements.

3. *Capitalization of interest expense*

In accordance with Swedish GAAP, the SKF Group has not capitalized interest expense incurred in connection with the financing of expenditure for construction of property, plant and equipment. Such interest expense is required to be capitalized in accordance with U.S. GAAP.

4. *Accounting for investments*

Included in investments, are 567 in 1990, 769 in 1989 and 717 in 1988 which relate to Associated Companies. These companies are primarily engaged in bearing and steel activities.

The Associated Companies, which are accounted for in accordance with the equity method, consist primarily of an investment in Ovako AB of 566 (724 for 1989 and 680 for 1988). The Group owns 28 000 000 shares with a nominal value of 280, representing a 50 percent ownership.

Summarized combined financial information for the Associated Companies as a group is as follows:

Balance sheet data

	1990	1989	1988
Current assets	2 853	2 973	2 930
Capital assets	3 270	2 844	2 521
	6 123	5 817	5 451
Current liabilities	2 775	2 043	2 121
Long-term liabilities	2 215	2 327	1 959
Shareholders' equity	1 133	1 447	1 371
The SKF Group's share of shareholders' equity	567	725	682

Income statement data

	1990	1989	1988
Net sales	6 048	6 621	4 972
Operating income	− 30	409	291
Net loss/income	− 265	141	75
The SKF Group's share of net loss/income	− 133	70	37

The above summary of combined financial information approximately represent the SKF Group's share of shareholders' equity and net income in accordance with U.S. GAAP.

5. *Accounting for early termination benefits*

The SKF Group allocates the costs for early termination benefits over years between early and normal retirement for certain Group companies. U.S. GAAP requires costs for early termination benefits to be expensed in the year when the benefits are accepted by the employees.

6. *Gain on sale of real estate*

In 1990, 1989 and 1987, portions of the real estate in Göteborg were sold, with gains of 145, 235 and 244 respectively. The properties are leased back by SKF which also has an option to repurchase them in the future.

Under U.S. GAAP, a sale under these terms shall be accounted for as a financial arrangement where the book value of the property is maintained, and depreciation follows the original plan. The proceeds received are recorded as a liability, and leasing costs paid are regarded as interest and amortization.

7. *Pensions*

Periodic pension cost and the related liability is calculated by the Group according to local laws and accounting principles. Under U.S. GAAP, the periodic pension cost and related liability should be calculated according to the Statement of Financial Accounting Standards No. 87 "Employers' Accounting for Pensions" (FAS 87).

The Group has calculated the approximate impact of and disclosures required under FAS 87 with effect from January 1, 1989 for non-U.S. plans, and from January 1, 1986 for U.S. plans.

The Group sponsors defined benefit plans in several countries, principally Sweden, Germany, France, the United States, and Spain. The Swedish plan supplements statutory pensions where benefits are established by national organizations. The subsidiaries in France sponsor a retirement indemnity plan in accordance with French National Employer/Employee agreements. Plans in Germany, Spain and the United States are designed to supplement these countries' social security pensions. Only the U.S. plans are funded. Benefits are based on a combination of age, salary and service and are available to all employees meeting age, service and other requirements.

The following tables summarize approximate disclosures under FAS 87.

Exhibit 4.2 (continued)

Net periodic pension cost for the plans described above, included in the Group's approximate U.S. GAAP income statement includes the following components:

	1990	1989
Service cost	105	89
Interest cost	378	329
Actual return on assets	-162	-211
Other, net	51	147
Net periodic pension cost	372	354

Pension expense as reported in 1988 for the plans described above, was approximately 283.

Assumptions used in the calculations:

	1990	1989	1988
Discount rates	7–10%	6–9.5%	6–9.5%
Rates of increase in compensation level	2.5–7%	3–7%	3–7%
Investment return	8–11%	11%	11%

The following table sets forth these plans' funded status and amounts recognized in the Group's approximate U.S. GAAP balance sheet:

	1990	1989	1988
Acturial present value of:			
Vested benefit obligation	4 267	3 968	3 711
Accumulated benefit obligation	4 441	4 126	3 826
Projected benefit obligation	4 983	4 552	4 167
Plan assets at fair value	-1 486	-1 248	-1 073
Projected benefit obligation in excess of plan assets	3 497	3 304	3 094
Unrecognized net (gain) or loss	31	142	- 3
Unrecognized net obligation at initial application	- 673	- 723	- 725
Unrecognized prior service cost	- 83	- 89	- 20
Adjustment required to recognize minimum liability	566	539	642
Pension liability	3 338	3 173	2 988

Plan assets are invested primarily in securities and bonds.

8. Foreign operations

Swedish accounting practice does not require disclosure of foreign operations. U.S. GAAP require these disclosures.

Assets of foreign subsidiaries, excluding cash, bank accounts, short-term investments and intercompany receivables and shareholdings, but before consolidation eliminations, amounted at December 31, 1990 to 24 840, 20 866 in 1989 and to 17 929 in 1988. The geographic location of these assets were as follows:

	1990	1989	1988
Europe (excluding Sweden)	16 897	14 737	12 407
United States, Canada and Mexico	4 694	3 072	2 736
Latin America	1 209	1 361	1 250
Africa, Asia, Australia and New Zealand	2 040	1 696	1 536
	24 840	20 866	17 929

Dividends of 1 040 in 1990, 366 in 1989 and 264 in 1988 have been received by the Parent Company from foreign subsidiaries.

9. Statements of Cash Flow

The Group prepares the statements of cash flow in accordance with Swedish GAAP, which require a cash flow statement different from that required by the Statement of Financial Accounting Standards No. 95 "Statement of Cash Flows" (FAS 95) in the U.S. Additional approximate disclosures if the Group were to comply with FAS 95 are as follows:

	1990	1989	1988
Borrowings of long term debt	1 892	440	276
Repayments of long term debt	949	918	503
Additions to debt through acquisitions	979	–	–
Cash interest paid	793	669	659
Cash taxes paid	820	588	418

Significant non-cash transactions are conversion of debentures (see Note 21), deferred tax provisions (see Note 5), provisions for employee indemnities and retirements (see Note 18), extraordinary expense (see Note 6), and equity in Associated Companies and minority interest in income as disclosed in the income statement.

The Group considers current financial assets to be cash and cash equivalents. Refer to Note 7 for a description of current financial assets.

10. Discontinued operations

In 1987, the Board of Directors of AB SKF decided that the SKF Group would gradually withdraw from the field of plasma technology. In 1990, 1989 and 1987, provisions were made for anticipated costs of withdrawal and write-down of part of the Group's investments in ScanDust AB and SwedeChrome AB.

Exhibit 4.2 (continued)

In 1989, a decision was made to shut down the SKF Foundry operations in the U.S. The provision reflects the estimated loss on disposal.

Results. net of taxes, related to the discontinued operations are as follows:

	1990	1989	1988
Discontinuance of SKF Foundry operations in the U.S.		– 17	
Discontinuance of plasma technology operations	19	– 238	
	19	– 255	

11. *Postretirement benefit*

In December. 1990. the U.S. Financial Accounting Standards Board issued the Statement of Financial Accounting Standards No. 106 "Employers' Accounting for Postretirement Benefits Other than Pensions" (FAS 106). Application of FAS 106 is required for U.S. plans beginning in 1993 and in 1995 for non-U.S. plans.

The Group is currently reviewing the provisions of FAS 106 to determine the impact of its implementation upon the financial statements of the Group.

12. *Off balance sheet risk and concentrations of credit risk*

The Group has a firm policy to hedge its exposure to foreign currency exchange rate fluctuations. as well as against unfavourable fluctuations in interest rates. through many different strategies. including the use of various financial instruments such as interest rate caps and floors. foreign currency and interest rate swaps and forward exchange contracts. At year-end the Group had in excess of 8 000 in net forward exchange contracts outstanding. A significant majority of these contracts involve the Swedish krona. German mark. U.S dollar. Italian lira and French franc.

The contracts are placed with several well-established international financial institutions, why management believes credit risk to be very low. The majority of these contracts serve as hedges of net investments in foreign subsidiaries and other commitments. The gains and losses on these contracts would to a great extent be offset by gains and losses resulting from the translation of the foreign subsidiaries' financial statements and on the other foreign currency commitments.

Concentrations of credit risk is limited. primarily because the Group's customer base consists of many geographically and industrially diverse customers.

13. *Summary*

The application of U.S. GAAP would have the following approximate effect on consolidated net income and shareholders' equity.

	1990	1989	1988
Net income as reported in the consolidated income statements	1 014	1 513	979
Items increasing/decreasing net income:			
Deferred income taxes	– 4	17	– 26
Depreciation on revaluation of assets including effect in connection with sale	11	128	36
Capitalization of interest expense	– 12	– 13	– 7
Early termination benefits	– 10	– 2	– 3
Gains on sales of real estate	– 160	– 235	10
Pensions	55	– 9	–
Net increase/decrease in net income	– 120	– 114	10
Approximate net income in accordance with U.S. GAAP	894	1 399	989

	1990	1989	1988
Shareholders' equity as reported in the consolidated balance sheet	12 155	11 444	10 072
Items increasing/decreasing reported equity:			
Deferred income taxes	10	14	– 9
Revaluation of assets	– 233	– 237	– 355
Capitalization of interest expense	80	92	104
Early termination benefits	– 25	– 16	– 13
Gains on sales of real estate	– 629	– 468	– 234
Pensions	44	– 10	–
Net decrease in reported shareholders' equity	– 753	– 625	– 507
Approximate shareholders' equity in accordance with U.S. GAAP	11 402	10 819	9 565

Table 4.2
Summary Financial Information from Telecom Corp. of N.Z. Prospectus

	Summary Financial Information				
	Year ended March 31,				
	1988(a)	1989	1990	1991	1991
	(in millions, except per Share and per ADS amounts)				
STATEMENT OF EARNINGS DATA:					
Amounts in accordance with NZ GAAP:					
Operating revenues	NZ $1,970.2	NZ $2,158.3	NZ $2,292.4	NZ $2,431.8	US $1,426.3
Earnings from operations	286.9	441.2	548.4	634.1	371.9
Net earnings	63.9	235.0	257.4	331.9	194.7
Earnings per Share (b)	.03	.10	.11	.14	.08
Earnings per ADS (b)	.60	2.00	2.20	2.80	1.60
Amounts in accordance with US GAAP (c):					
Net earnings	NZ $53.0	NZ $247.5	NZ $261.0	NZ $348.0	US $204.1
Earnings per Share (b)	.02	.11	.11	.15	.09
Earnings per ADS (b)	.40	2.20	2.20	3.00	1.80
	March 31.				
	1988(a)	1989(a)	1990	1991	1991
	(in millions, except operating data)				
BALANCE SHEET DATA:					
Amounts in accordance with NZ GAAP:					
Fixed assets	NZ $2,961.1	NZ $3,165.3	NZ $3,498.4	NZ $3,767.5	US $2,209.6
Total assets	3,777.4	3,975.9	4,198.7	4,717.6	2,766.9
Debt due within one year	282.3	284.4	344.4	453.7	266.1
Long term debt	569.8	727.6	818.8	1,075.4	630.7
Total liabilities	1,423.0	1,571.0	1,730.1	2,117.1	1,241.7
Total shareholders' equity	2,353.9	2,403.9	2,463.3	2,595.2	1,522.1
Amount in accordance with US GAAP (c):					
Total shareholders' equity	NZ $2,373.0	NZ $2,510.5	NZ $2,601.5	NZ $2,716.5	US $1,593.2
OPERATING DATA:					
Access lines	1,370,000	1,406,000	1,444,000	1,481,000	
Regional operating company employees	N/A	16,595	14,429	12,550	
Access lines per regional operating company employee (d)	N/A	85	100	118	

(a) The Company's balance sheet data as of March 31, 1988 and 1989 and statement of earnings data for the fiscal year ended March 31, 1988 have been extracted from the Company's audited consolidated financial statements for those years after adjustments to ensure that the disclosure and the accounting treatment of certain items are consistent with the 1990 and 1991 balance sheet data and the 1989, 1990 and 1991 statement of earnings data.

(b) Per Share amounts have been calculated on the basis that 2,350,000,000 Shares were outstanding during the periods indicated. Each ADS represents 20 Shares.

(c) The principal differences between the amounts shown in accordance with NZ GAAP and those shown in accordance with US GAAP arise from the treatment of the capitalization of interest costs, the accruals for compensated absences, the write-off of research and development expenditures, the method of providing for deferred income taxes and the timing of reflection of dividends in retained earnings. In estimating the amounts shown in accordance with US GAAP, it has not been possible to quantify the impact on earnings and total shareholders' equity arising as a result of ascribing fair values to the fixed assets acquired by the Company from the Post Office as of April 1, 1987 as required under NZ GAAP rather than using historical book values as required under US GAAP because the Post Office did not maintain a separate fixed asset register or separate historical cost records of all fixed asset additions in respect of the telecommunications business. See Note 19 to Consolidated Financial Statements.

(d) This ratio is commonly used to measure the efficiency of telephone companies. However, because different companies may use somewhat different data in calculating this ratio, comparisons between companies cannot be considered to be precise.

Exhibit 4.3

Note 19 from Telecom Corp. of N.Z. Prospectus

19. SIGNIFICANT DIFFERENCES BETWEEN NEW ZEALAND AND UNITED STATES GENERALLY ACCEPTED ACCOUNTING PRINCIPLES

The consolidated financial statements are prepared in accordance with generally accepted accounting principles ("GAAP") applicable in New Zealand ("NZ") which differ in certain significant respects from those applicable in the United States ("US"). These differences and the approximate effect of the adjustments necessary to restate earnings and shareholders' funds, are detailed below.

(a) Acquisition of the Telecommunications Business of the New Zealand Post Office

As stated in Note 1(a), the telecommunications business of the New Zealand Post Office was acquired by Telecom with effect from April 1, 1987 pursuant to the Sale and Purchase Agreement with the New Zealand government. Under NZ GAAP, the net assets acquired were recorded by Telecom at the amounts contained within the Sale and Purchase Agreement which were considered to be fair values. Since both the New Zealand Post Office and Telecom were under the common control of the Crown at April 1, 1987, US GAAP would require Telecom to record the net assets acquired at the historical book values recorded by the New Zealand Post Office.

Prior to April 1, 1987, the New Zealand Post Office operated three principal lines of business, namely banking, postal and telecommunications. It did not maintain a separate fixed asset register nor separate historical cost records of all fixed asset additions in respect of the telecommunications division. Accordingly, the difference arising as a result of ascribing fair values to fixed assets at April 1, 1987 as required under NZ GAAP rather than historical cost as required under US GAAP cannot be quantified and consequently is not included as a reconciling item in this note. If historical cost records had been maintained, the effect of this difference may have impacted shareholders' equity by the difference between the fair value ascribed to fixed assets and their historical cost. In addition, earnings may have been affected by a difference in the depreciation charge.

Although both Telecom and the New Zealand Post Office were under the common control of the Crown, the Directors of Telecom are satisfied that appropriate fair values have been assigned in respect of the acquisition of the telecommunications business based on the negotiations which occurred to establish the value of the business contained in the Sale and Purchase Agreement and that fixed assets acquired have been appropriately valued on the basis set out in the accounting policies.

(b) Capitalization of Interest Cost Relating to the Construction of Property, Plant and Equipment

In each of the years ended March 31, 1988 and 1989, Telecom did not capitalize interest costs incurred in connection with the financing of expenditures for the construction of telecommunications equipment and other fixed assets. In the year ended March 31, 1990 Telecom changed that policy whereby for each fixed asset project having a cost in excess of $10 million and a construction period of not less than 12 months, interest costs incurred during the period of time that is required to complete and prepare the fixed asset for its intended use is capitalized as part of the total cost.

Under US GAAP, interest cost incurred in connection with the financing of all expenditure for the construction of fixed assets is required to be capitalized during the period of time required to prepare the fixed asset for its intended use. For the purpose of compliance with US GAAP, the estimated amount of interest that would have been capitalized on construction costs incurred on capital projects has been determined and depreciated over the lives of the related assets.

(c) Compensated Absences

Telecom recognizes a liability for compensation for future absences where the obligation relates to rights which have vested. For the purpose of compliance with US GAAP, Telecom has recognized an expense in respect of the estimated liability for compensated absences which relate to rights which will eventually vest but which have not yet been accrued under Telecom's policy.

(d) Research and Development Expenditure

Under NZ GAAP, research and development costs are charged to expense as incurred except where future benefits are expected beyond any reasonable doubt to exceed these costs. Where research and development costs are deferred, they are amortized over future periods on a basis related to future benefit. For the purpose of compliance with US GAAP, all research and development costs have been expensed as incurred.

(e) Short Term Investments

Telecom records short term investments at market values (where available) with the resulting gains or losses taken to earnings. For the purpose of compliance with US GAAP, short term investments should be stated at the lower of cost or market value and unrealized gains due to increases in value

Exhibit 4.3 (continued)

should not be recognized. There is no significant difference between the effect of Telecom's accounting policy and US GAAP.

(f) Deferred Taxation

Telecom uses the partial liability method to account for taxation whereby all items expected to reverse in the foreseeable future are recognized. Under NZ GAAP, deferred tax assets arising from the use of the partial liability method may be recognized to the extent that reasonable certainty of recovery exists. For the purpose of compliance with the US requirements, SFAS 96 ("Accounting for Income Taxes") has been adopted whereby the comprehensive liability method is used to account for taxation. Additionally, under SFAS 96, certain future tax assets are not permitted to be recognized and these have been written off for the purpose of compliance with US GAAP.

(g) Defeasance of Debt

As described in Note 10, Telecom has entered into a financing transaction whereby a portion of the debt has been considered to be defeased in accordance with NZ GAAP. As the in-substance defeasance was instantaneous, US GAAP would require that this transaction be accounted for as a borrowing and investment. Accordingly amounts reported in the balance sheet as of March 31, 1991 as non-current investments and long term debt would both be increased by NZ $266.9 million.

(h) Proposed Final Dividends

Under NZ GAAP, dividends proposed by the Board of Directors after the end of an accounting period, but in respect of that period, are deducted in arriving at retained earnings at the end of that accounting period. Under US GAAP, such dividends are provided in the period in which they are declared by the Board of Directors.

(i) Statement of Cash Flows

Under both NZ GAAP and US GAAP, a Statement of Cash Flows, which discloses cash flows from operating, investing and financing activities, is required to be presented. The components of each of these items differ under NZ GAAP from US GAAP in that under US GAAP interest income and interest expense would be reclassified from investing and financing activities respectively to operating activities. In addition, under US GAAP bank overdrafts would be reclassified as a financing activity rather than a component of cash position. Accordingly, the closing cash position at March 31, 1989, 1990 and 1991 would be NZ $12.5 million, NZ $6.6 million and NZ $6.0 million, respectively.

(j) Financial Instruments

Under SFAS 105 ("Disclosure of Information about Financial Instruments with Off-Balance-Sheet Risk and Financial Instruments with Concentrations of Credit Risk") the following disclosures are required:

Off-Balance-Sheet Risk

Currency and interest rate swaps may be employed to convert foreign currency borrowings into New Zealand dollar liabilities and to manage currency and interest rate exposure. In addition, foreign currency forward exchange contracts and option agreements are used to manage other foreign currency exposure. Fluctuations in foreign currency exchange rates and interest rates give rise to market risk.

Contracts have been entered into with various counterparties having such credit ratings and in accordance with such dollar limits as set forth by the Board of Directors. Telecom does not require collateral or other security to support financial instruments with credit risk. While Telecom may be subject to credit losses up to the notional principal or contract amounts in the event of nonperformance by its counterparties, it does not expect such losses to occur.

The notional principal or contract amounts at March 31, 1991 are as follows (in NZ$ millions):

Currency and interest rate swaps	614.1
Foreign currency forward exchange contracts	311.0
Option agreements	83.0

The cash requirements of these instruments approximates the notional principal or contract amounts, except for interest rate swap contracts (NZ $154 million) and option agreements (NZ $83 million). For interest rate swap contracts the cash requirements are limited to interest payable, which was NZ $5 million. Cash requirements for option agreements occur if such options are exercised. Since virtually all contracts are in a matched position, cash inflows offset these cash requirements.

New York. In Exhibit 4.4, the Report of the Auditors has been issued jointly by three separate accounting firms—one Dutch, one English, and one American.

As noted in Exhibit 4.4, "the financial statements reflect a synthesis of Netherlands, United Kingdom and United States accounting principles." The company notes what it regards as a prudent course of action should there be a conflict between the accounting policies of these countries and provides additional information elsewhere in the report with regard to certain differences between the Netherlands, U.S., and U.K. GAAP. This is an example of the Dutch approach, both practical and business oriented, to harmonizing the accounting principles of three nations.

BASS PLC

Bass is a major British brewer with significant activities in pubs, hotels, and the leisure industry. Its financial statements are presented, and audited, in accordance with U.K. GAAP to "give a true and fair view of the state of affairs of the Company. . . . " In addition, the recasting of the statements in accordance with U.S. GAAP is probably associated with the trading of the company's ADRs in New York. Exhibit 4.5 describes the differences between U.K. and U.S. GAAP. Table 4.3 shows the impact on net income and equity in recasting the financial statements in accordance with U.S. GAAP. Earnings decline from 452 million pounds (U.K. GAAP) to 275 million pounds (U.S. GAAP), and shareholders' equity declines from 3,622 million pounds (U.K. GAAP) to 2,873 million pounds (U.S. GAAP), which are significant differences in both earnings and equity between U.K. and U.S. GAAP.

SKANDIA GROUP

This large Swedish insurance and financial services company notes in its 1990 annual report that the stockholder base has been broadened by having its stock traded on the Oslo and Copenhagen Stock Exchanges, in addition to the Stockholm Stock Exchange. The company's stock also started trading on The International Stock Exchange in London. New EC rules permit a company to use the same prospectus for listing a stock on one EC stock exchange, in this case Copenhagen, to list its stock on another, The International Stock Exchange. Table 4.4 shows the recasting of the company's earnings and shareholders' equity from Swedish to International Accounting Standards. Once again, differences between income and equity based on different accounting principles are significant.

The net income determined by Swedish GAAP of 228 million kroner increases to 292 million kronor, and shareholders' equity decreases from 6,888 million kronor to 6,645 million kroner, when the financial statements are recast in accordance with International Accounting Standards, again, not insignificant changes for the same set of financial results.

These examples show that companies are trying to "internationalize" their

Exhibit 4.4
Portion of Royal Dutch Petroleum Co. 1990 Annual Report

Financial statements

Summary of accounting policies

Principles

The financial statements reflect a synthesis of Netherlands, United Kingdom and United States accounting principles.

In the event of conflict between accounting policies recognized in each of these countries, then, subject to relevant legal requirements, the policy adopted is that considered most appropriate to the circumstances of the Group having regard to the practice of other major international oil companies.

The financial statements on pages 32 to 47 have been prepared under the historical cost convention.

The following summary of policies adopted is provided to assist readers in the interpretation of these financial statements.

Report of the Auditors

To Royal Dutch Petroleum Company and The "Shell" Transport and Trading Company, p.l.c.

We have audited the financial statements appearing on pages 32 to 47 of the Royal Dutch/Shell Group of Companies for the years 1990, 1989 and 1988 in accordance with generally accepted auditing standards.

In our opinion, the financial statements referred to above present fairly the financial position of the Royal Dutch/Shell Group of Companies at December 31, 1990 and 1989, and the results of operations and cash flows for each of the three years in the period ended December 31, 1990, in conformity with the accounting policies described on pages 32 and 33.

KPMG Klynveld, The Hague

Ernst & Young, London

Price Waterhouse, New York

March 14, 1991

The accounting policies followed are consistent in all material respects with generally accepted accounting principles in each of the Netherlands, the United Kingdom and the United States, except for that in use in the United Kingdom in respect of deferred taxation. The effect of this departure is given in Notes 11 and 22.

Additionally, United States accounting principles require the disclosure as supplementary information of a standardized measure of discounted future net cash flows relating to proved oil and gas reserve quantities. This requirement is discussed further on page 48.

Nature of the financial statements

The financial statements take the form of an aggregation in sterling of the accounts of companies in which Royal Dutch Petroleum Company (Royal Dutch) and The "Shell" Transport and Trading Company, p.l.c. (Shell Transport) together, either directly or indirectly, have control either through a majority of the voting rights or the right to exercise a controlling influence. Certain Group companies having a negligible effect on the aggregation are accounted for as associated companies. The accounts of the above two Parent Companies are not included in the financial statements, whose object is to demonstrate the financial position, results of operations and cash flows of a group of undertakings in which each Parent Company has an interest in common whilst maintaining its separate identity.

Investments in companies over which Group companies have significant influence but not control and which are classified as associated companies are accounted for on the equity basis unless immaterial, in which case the investment is accounted for on a cost/dividend basis.

Certain joint ventures are taken up in the financial statements in proportion to the relevant Group interest.

Exhibit 4.5
Portion of Bass PLC 1991 Annual Report

US Accounting Principles

The accounts set out on pages 25-51 are prepared in accordance with accounting principles generally accepted in the United Kingdom (UK GAAP) which differ from those generally accepted in the United States (US GAAP). The significant differences as they apply to the Group are summarised below.

i   Goodwill and other intangibles

In the consolidated financial statements, goodwill, together with the fair value of purchased licences, hotel franchises and management contracts, arising on the acquisition of a subsidiary undertaking, is immediately eliminated against reserves. Under US GAAP such goodwill and other intangibles would be capitalised and amortised to profit and loss account over the estimated useful lives of the assets, not exceeding 40 years.

For the purposes of the reconciliation below, purchased hotel franchises and management contracts are being amortised over 2 to 20 years and goodwill is being amortised over 40 years. On the sale of a business, any unamortised goodwill relating thereto is taken into account in the determination of the surplus/(loss) on sale.

ii   Land and buildings

The Group's properties and related licences are revalued from time to time by the Group's professional staff together with professionally qualified external valuers. Property values are written up in accordance with the valuations; depreciation, where applicable, is based on the revalued amounts. The Group does not depreciate its freehold and leasehold properties with unexpired lease terms in excess of 50 years and related licences. Under US GAAP, revaluations are not permitted and all fixed assets, other than land, must be depreciated over their estimated economic lives.

iii Deferred taxation

The Group provides for deferred taxation using the liability method only where, in the opinon of the Directors, it is probable that the tax liability will crystallise within the foreseeable future. Under US Statement of Financial Accounting Standards (FAS) 96, deferred taxation is fully provided using the liability method. In addition, deferred taxation is also provided under US GAAP on the difference between the accounting and tax bases of assets and liabilities of subsidiary undertakings acquired.

iv   Pension costs

The Group provides for the cost of retirement benefits based upon consistent percentages of employees' pensionable pay as recommended by actuaries. For the purpose of the reconciliation below, the provisions of FAS 87 have been applied with effect from 1 October 1989 in respect of the Group's two principal pension schemes. FAS 87 requires that the projected benefit obligation (pension liability) be matched against the fair value of the schemes' assets and be adjusted to reflect any unrecognised obligations or assets in determining the pension cost or credit for the year.

v   Ordinary dividends

In the consolidated financial statements, final Ordinary dividends are provided for in the year in respect of which they are recommended by the Board of Directors for approval by the shareholders. Under US GAAP, dividends are not provided for until declared.

vi   Foreign exchange hedging arrangements

The Group enters into foreign exchange hedging arrangements. Under US GAAP, certain of these arrangements are not regarded as hedges and the notional profits or losses thereon at the balance sheet date are charged to the profit and loss account. Such amounts were not significant in 1991. Foreign exchange hedging arrangements entered into in 1989 in connection with the proposed acquisition of the Holiday Inn business in North America and the resulting exchange losses were dealt with as part of the purchase consideration. Under US GAAP, these costs and exchange losses would have been charged to the profit and loss account.

vii Acquisition provisions

Included in the provisions relating to the acquisition of Granada Leisure Ltd and the Holiday Inn business in North America are amounts which relate to the rationalisation and reorganisation of certain of the Group's existing bingo club and hotel operations respectively as a consequence of the acquisitions. Under US GAAP, such expenditure would be charged to the profit and loss account as incurred.

viii Extraordinary items and discontinued operations

The items reported as extraordinary under UK GAAP, other than those relating to compliance with the DTI Orders would not be so reported under US GAAP. Such items would be reported in profit before extraordinary items with no change to earnings available for Ordinary shareholders. The Group's share of the results of Delta Biotechnology Limited, sold in November 1991, are shown as arising from discontinued operations under US GAAP.

BASS PLC

Table 4.3
Net Income and Shareholders' Equity from Bass PLC 1991 Annual Report

Net Income under US GAAP

The following is a summary of the estimated material adjustments to earnings available for Ordinary shareholders which would be required if US GAAP were to be applied instead of UK GAAP.

	Group			
For the year ended 30 September 1991	1991 £m	1990 £m	1991 $m	1990 $m
Earnings available for Ordinary shareholders				
as reported in the Group profit and loss account	**452**	470	**808**	808
Estimated adjustments:				
Pension costs	**15**	27	**27**	46
Depreciation and amortisation	**(67)**	(51)	**(120)**	(88)
Acquisition provisions	**(29)**	–	**(52)**	–
Surplus on disposal of fixed assets	**(73)**	21	**(130)**	37
Exchange losses	–	(31)	–	(53)
Deferred taxation	**(24)**	–	**(43)**	–
	(178)	(34)	**(318)**	(58)
Minority share	**1**	3	**2**	5
	(177)	(31)	**(316)**	(53)
Estimated net income as adjusted to accord				
with US GAAP	**275**	439	**492**	755
Arising from:				
Continuing operations	**194**	531	**347**	913
Discontinued operations	**(5)**	(4)	**(9)**	(7)
Estimated income before extraordinary items	**189**	527	**338**	906
Extraordinary items – surplus/(costs) arising from				
compliance with DTI Orders less tax thereon	**86**	(88)	**154**	(151)
Estimated net income	**275**	439	**492**	755

	1991 Pence	1990 Pence	1991 Cents	1990 Cents
Per Ordinary share and per American Depositary				
share as so adjusted				
Income before extraordinary items:				
Continuing operations	**48.9**	147.9	**87.4**	254.3
Discontinued operations	**(1.3)**	(1.1)	**(2.3)**	(1.9)
Extraordinary items	**21.7**	(24.5)	**38.8**	(42.1)
Net income	**69.3**	122.3	**123.9**	210.3

Translation rate £1 = $1.79 (1990 £1 = $1.72)

Table 4.3 (continued)

Shareholders' Equity under US GAAP

The following is a summary of the estimated material adjustments to shareholders' funds which would be required if US GAAP were to be applied instead of UK GAAP.

	Group			
30 September 1991	1991 £m	1990 £m	1991 $m	1990 $m
Capital and reserves as reported in the				
Group balance sheet	**3,622**	2,935	**6,342**	5,486
Estimated adjustments:				
Intangible fixed assets	**1,196**	1,238	**2,094**	2,314
Tangible fixed assets	**(1,855)**	(1,963)	**(3,248)**	(3,669)
Pension costs	**42**	27	**74**	50
Proposed dividend	**111**	83	**194**	155
Acquisition provisions	**–**	18	**–**	34
Deferred taxation	**(218)**	(190)	**(382)**	(355)
	(724)	(787)	**(1,268)**	(1,471)
Minority share	**(25)**	(31)	**(44)**	(58)
	(749)	(818)	**(1,312)**	(1,529)
Estimated shareholders' equity as adjusted				
to accord with US GAAP	**2,873**	2,117	**5,030**	3,957

Translation rate £1 = $1.75 (1990 £1 = $1.87)

financial reports by referring to a variety of standards associated with the IASC, the European Community, and various national accounting bodies. It is also apparent that the final selection is related to the trading of the shares and the company's need to raise capital. More widespread trading of a company's stock enhances public participation and the number of potential capital markets. This is apparently a key determinant in these companies selecting U.S., or IASC, GAAP in recasting their financial statements.

Table 4.4
Portion of Skandia Group 1990 Annual Report

International Accounting Standards

The adjustments required to restate the Group's consolidated profit and shareholders' equity for differences between the Group's accounting principles and International Accounting Standards (IAS) are shown below.

MSEK	NOTE	1990	1989
Consolidated profit			
Net profit for the year after taxes reported in accordance			
with Swedish generally accepted accounting principles		228	1,205
Adjustments			
Share of income in affiliated companies accounted			
for using the equity method	(a)	51	116
Amortization of goodwill	(b)	13	12
Deferred tax liability	(c)	—	813
Net profit for the year after taxes in accordance with IAS		292	2,146
Dividends proposed	(d)	-307	-307
Net profit for the year after taxes and proposed dividend			
in accordance with IAS		-15	1,839
Consolidated shareholders' equity			
Shareholders' equity reported in accordance with Swedish			
generally accepted accounting principles		6,888	6,947
Adjustments			
Affiliated company investments accounted for using the equity method	(a)	290	241
Goodwill	(b)	-226	-239
Dividends proposed	(d)	-307	-307
Shareholders' equity in accordance with IAS		6,645	6,642

NOTES

(a)

Swedish insurance companies generally value investments in affiliated companies at cost less a provision for any permanent decrease in the value of the investment. IAS 28 requires that such investments should be accounted for by the investor using the equity method.

(b)

As a consequence of applying the equity method, goodwill received when affiliated companies became subsidiaries in 1989 has been revalued.

(c)

In 1989 the Group's principles regarding reporting of taxes were changed.

In addition to paid taxes, provisions are made for deferred taxes on income statement items that affect both profit for the year and taxable income, but in different accounting periods (timing differences).

According to IAS 12, the tax rate used in calculating deferred taxes should be the one expected to apply when the timing differences are

expected to reverse. The rate that was expected at the time of preparing the 1988 financial statements was 50 per cent, whereas a rate of approximately 30 per cent (as a result of the Swedish tax reform) was applied in calculating the deferred tax liability for 1988.

In accordance with Swedish generally accepted accounting principles, the effect of the deferred tax provision resulting from the changed tax rate was treated as a movement in reserves in 1988. IAS 12 requires that the effect of the changed rate be included in determining the net profit for the year 1989, when the change was made.

(d)

In accordance with Swedish generally accepted accounting principles, proposed dividends for the year are not incorporated in the Balance Sheet in respect of the year to which they relate, but in the year in which the Annual General Meeting approves the dividends (normally the following year). IAS 10 requires that such dividends be either adjusted or disclosed.

CHAPTER 5

THE CONSOLIDATION PROCESS

The crown of success in management is worn by those who have achieved significant growth in profits. Profitability, of course, depends on profit margins and sales volume. The margin of profit is very attractive when a new product is successfully launched, but a high profit margin attracts competitors. The first casualty in a competitive shuffle is the profit margin. As a product enters its maturity stage, the presence of a few major competitors is sufficient to drive the profit margin to a relatively thin net after tax profit of 5 percent, or less, of revenues. Those seeking the crown of success must look elsewhere to achieve their laurels. Market share is all that is left.

In today's global economy, managers are encouraged by their shareholders, and by their governments, to view the earth as their marketplace. However, whether a New York company is selling its wares in California or in Germany, the parent organization needs some type of local presence. Frequently, the first step in establishing a local presence is for the home office to set up a branch operation to handle the marketing and distribution of its product line. A branch operation requires its own set of books for both reporting and control purposes, and to establish a measure of its financial performance. Branch financial reports must be combined with the parent's in order for the financial performance of the parent to be fairly portrayed to its shareholders.

As business grows, the next step in pursuing continual growth in profits, or market share, is usually establishing operating affiliates. Whereas a branch may be an integral part of the parent organization, an operating affiliate may be an independent entity whose stock is owned by the parent company. Its purpose may go beyond marketing and distribution, to include producing goods to be sold in the local market or to be exported to other markets. Once again, the financial reports of operating affiliates have to be consolidated for a true and fair view of the parent's operations.

Growth can also be achieved by acquiring other companies. One way to expand market share and lessen competitive pressure is horizontal acquisitions, where competitive firms are gobbled up and integrated into the operations of the acquiring company. Vertical acquisitions integrate independent suppliers and distributors under one corporate umbrella. Horizontal and vertical integrations increase the share of the market resulting in a greater volume of production. The economy of large-scale production lowers the unit cost of production, and eliminating duplicated corporate overhead functions as two firms merge into one reduces fixed costs. Savings in variable and fixed costs makes a company more competitive. Fewer competitors allow, presumably, more control over pricing and expansion of capacity. Fewer players mean more profits. It is no accident that most mature industries are dominated by a relatively small number of major corporations.

Managers seeking the brass ring of growth sometimes acquire companies in different businesses to form a conglomerate, where a cash cow supplies sustenance to nurture an emerging business. All of this corporate activity in opening branches; organizing operating affiliates; and acquiring companies horizontally, vertically, or any which way as in a conglomerate require consolidation of financial reports.

Consolidation breeds a host of accounting issues, which may not always be consistently addressed because there are a number of reasonable responses. In branch accounting, there are questions whether the start-up costs of a branch should be capitalized or expensed. If capitalized, how much should be written off over what period of time? How should expenses borne by the home office on behalf of all the branches be allocated to an individual branch? By what means should they be paid—in cash or by an increase in the investment in the branch? When a branch acquires an asset, should the asset be on the books of the branch or the home office? What price should be placed on goods sent from the home office to a branch—cost or a markup above cost?

If there is a markup above cost, the transfer of goods from the home office to the branch creates an element of "profit." A markup in the price of goods transferred from the home office and stored in a warehouse of a branch office cannot be reported to the shareholders of the parent company as a realized profit. The consolidation process of the financial reports of the home office and the branch office must eliminate any profit that has not been realized by sales to third parties. Part of the consolidation process is the elimination of these and other intercompany transactions.

Accounting issues associated with acquisitions are not always easily addressed. During the 1950s and 1960s, managers could create "instant" growth in earnings per share by entering into mergers and consolidating the financial results of both companies using the pooling-of-interests method. As long as the acquiring company had a higher price-to-earnings ratio than the acquired company, pooling-of-interest accounting would create the illusion of growth of earnings per share of the merged company without necessarily increasing the overall earnings of either the acquired or the acquiring company. Financial whiz kids running conglomerates became Wall Street heroes without lifting a finger to improve the operating efficiency or to expand the market or doing anything else that required real effort other than seeking out potential acquisitions whose shares were selling at a low price-to-earnings multiple. The high multiples of conglomerate shares permitted an endless series of acquisitions. The system fed on itself, until, like all speculative bubbles, it burst.

This abuse of accounting practices inherent in the pooling-of-interests method of consolidation was rectified by the accounting profession. The Accounting Principles Board (APB), the predecessor of the Financial Accounting Standards Board (FASB), substantially tightened the rules on pooling in APB Opinion No. 16. Twelve conditions had to be satisfied before the pooling-of-interest method of consolidation could be used. Pooling-of-interests method of consolidation is rarely seen today because very few acquisitions satisfy all the conditions.

Abandoning pooling of interest in favor of purchase accounting gave rise to goodwill for that portion of the purchase of a company that exceeds its fair market value. There is also the possibility of creating negative goodwill, or "ill will," when a company is acquired for less than its fair market value. There are substantive accounting issues associated with goodwill regarding how it is treated on the balance sheet and the income statement, which also affects the consolidation process. For instance, under U.S. generally accepted accounting principles (GAAP), goodwill is written off in 40 years and charged to income. Under U.K. GAAP, goodwill is written off in five years and charged to equity. Consolidation is performed in accordance with the GAAP of the parent organization. If the parent company is a U.K. company, then the consolidation process of including the financial results of a U.S. subsidiary would require the recasting of goodwill on the U.S. subsidiary's financial statements in accordance with U.K. GAAP.

Cap Gemini Sogeti, a French company, is a major supplier of information technology, computer services, and consulting with worldwide operations. Its consolidated financial statements are prepared in accordance with International Accounting Standards and French law. Goodwill is amortized over a maximum of 40 years. But, in 1990, over half of what might be construed as goodwill was set up as a separate account called "Market Shares" as described in Exhibit 5.1.

As noted elsewhere in the Cap Gemini Sogeti Report, the carrying amount of "Market Shares" is $458.3 million. It is not the intent here to perform a critical analysis of the difference between "Market Shares" and "Goodwill," but to illustrate that not only is the accounting treatment different in the United States and the United Kingdom, but that it is handled uniquely by Cap Gemini Sogeti in France. Were this company an operating affiliate of either a U.S. or U.K. company, the consolidation process would probably require a recasting of what is to be included as goodwill.

Exhibit 5.1
Note D from Cap Gemini Sogeti 1990 Financial Statement

d) Market shares

When the acquisition of companies allows the group to obtain significant market share in specific areas, the excess of purchase cost over the fair values of assets acquired is allocated to the market shares acquired.

These market shares are valued at the date of acquisition in relation to objective economic data with reference to activity and profitability indicators.

In view of their nature, these market shares are not amortized. However, at each year end, they are revalued on the same basis as that used when they were acquired. In the event of a diminution in value, a provision is made in the financial statements.

Consolidation of subsidiaries must follow the accounting principles of the nation of domicile. Veba, a large German energy and chemical company, prepares its consolidated financial statements in accordance with German legal provisions as seen in Exhibit 5.2. Note that the auditors' report is signed both by the public and the tax accountants.

TO COMBINE OR TO CONSOLIDATE

If a single legal entity conducts business at multiple locations, such as branch offices for the marketing and distribution of goods, the financial statements of each location are combined into a single financial statement. If a single legal entity conducts business through subsidiaries where the relationship is one of majority ownership of the shares of the subsidiaries, the financial statements of each location are consolidated into a single financial statement. Whether one combines or consolidates depends on the nature of ownership of a branch or subsidiary.

COMBINING BRANCH OPERATIONS (MERCHANDISE BILLED AT COST)

Separate accounting records are maintained when a business is conducted at more than one location in order to monitor operations, measure management performance, and possibly to form the basis for separate tax returns. A true and fair view of the results of a company's operation necessitates the combining or consolidating of financial results from all its locations.

To start with a simple (two location) example, suppose that the home office of Global, Inc., bills merchandise to Branch B at cost and that Branch B maintains complete accounting records and prepares its own financial statements. Trans-

Exhibit 5.2
Portion of Veba 1990 Annual Report

"According to our audit, made in conformity with our professional standards, the Consolidated Financial Statements comply with German legal provisions. The Consolidated Financial Statements, drawn up in accordance with the principles of proper accounting, provide an accurate picture of the current position of the Group with regard to assets, liabilities, finance, and earnings. The Group Review of Operations corresponds to the Consolidated Financial Statements." **Auditors' Report**

Düsseldorf, April 23, 1991

TREUARBEIT
Aktiengesellschaft
Certified Public Accountants
Tax Consultants

Prof. Dr. Dr. h.c. Forster   Siepe
Certified Public Accountant   Certified Public Accountant

actions and events during the first year of operations of Branch B are summarized as follows:

1. The home office forwarded $5,000 in cash to Branch B.
2. The home office shipped merchandise costing $50,000 to Branch B.
3. Branch B sold $75,000 of merchandise on credit, whose cost was $38,000.
4. Branch B collected $49,000 on its accounts receivable.
5. Branch B paid out $17,000 in operating expenses.
6. Branch B acquired $1,200 in equipment to be carried in the home office accounting records.
7. Branch B remitted $25,000 in cash to the home office.
8. The home office incurred operating expenses of $5,000 on behalf of Branch B that were charged to Branch B.

Every transaction affecting both the home office and the branch must be simultaneously recorded on both sets of books.

1. The Home Office Forwards $5,000 in Cash to Branch B.

HOME OFFICE ACCOUNTING RECORDS JOURNAL ENTRIES			BRANCH ACCOUNTING RECORDS JOURNAL ENTRIES		
	DEBIT	CREDIT		DEBIT	CREDIT
Investment in Branch B	$5000		Cash	$5000	
Cash		$5000	Home Office		$5000

The initial investment of $5,000 in cash reduces the cash balance in the home office and creates an opening cash balance in the branch. The home office records an investment in Branch B of $5,000, and the branch reflects a liability to the home office of $5,000.

2. The Home Office Ships Merchandise Costing $50,000 to Branch B.

Investment in Branch B	50000		Inventories	50000	
Inventories		50000	Home Office		50000

The parent or home office ships merchandise to the branch at cost, in other words, without marking up the goods to create a "profit." When the merchandise leaves the home office, its inventory account is reduced, and the home office investment in Branch B is increased by $50,000. Simultaneously, the branch records an increase in its inventory, along with an increase in its liability to the home office of $50,000.

3. Branch B Sells $75,000 of Merchandise on Credit, Whose Cost Was $38,000.

None		Accounts Receivable	75000	
		Cost of Goods Sold	38000	
		Sales		75000
		Inventories		38000

In the ordinary course of business, the branch sells merchandise for $75,000 on credit. The merchandise has an original cost of $38,000, and inventories are reduced by $38,000 reflecting the sale. This transaction has no effect on the home office and, consequently, no entry is made on the home office books.

4. Branch B Collects $49,000 on Its Accounts Receivable.

None		Cash	49000	
		Accounts Receivable		49000

After making the original sales on credit and creating the related accounts receivable, $49,000 of the receivables are collected. The cash account at the branch is increased and accounts receivable are decreased by $49,000. Once again, this transaction is recorded only on the branch records.

5. Branch B Pays out $17,000 in Operating Expenses.

```
None                                    Operating
                                          Expenses      17000
                                            Cash                   17000
```

Operating expenses totaling $17,000 are incurred and paid by the branch office.

6. Branch B Acquires $1,200 in Equipment to Be Carried in the Home Office Accounting Records.

```
Equipment                               Home Office      1200
   Branch B             1200               Cash                    1200

      Investment in
         Branch B       1200
```

Companies can account for the acquisition of property, plant, and equipment (PP&E) in different ways. In this example, equipment acquired and paid for by the branch is carried as an asset on the home office accounting records. Many companies prefer to record PP&E centrally, to simplify the calculations required for depreciation, or gains and losses on sales, or other means of disposing of assets. Tax considerations play an important role in how companies treat PP&E.

The transaction of acquiring an asset for $1,200 originates in the branch, which reduces the local cash balance by $1,200. Rather than record this disbursement as an acquisition of an asset, the $1,200 is treated as a reduction of the liability to the home office. On the books of the home office, the equipment is recorded as an asset and the investment in the branch is reduced accordingly.

7. Branch B Remits $25,000 in Cash to the Home Office.

```
Cash              25000                  Home Office     25000
   Investment in                            Cash                   25000
      Branch B               25000
```

Surplus cash accumulates at the branch with the collection of a portion of the receivables. The home office instructs that $25,000 be transferred to the home office. The cash account in the home office is increased and the investment in the branch is decreased by $25,000. On the branch books, the liability to the home office is decreased along with the cash account by $25,000.

8. The Home Office Incurs Operating Expenses of $5,000 on Behalf of Branch B that are Charged to Branch B.

```
Investment in                            Operating
   Branch B         5000                    Expenses      5000
      Operating                               Home Office           5000
         Expenses            5000
```

Certain expenses incurred by the home office are chargeable to the branch, such as overhead, research and development, advertising, legal, and other expenses incurred at the home office for the benefit of the branches. The home office expects the branch to eventually reimburse it for such expenses. The branch records operating expenses of $5,000 and increases its liability to the home office by a corresponding amount. The home office reduces its operating expenses by $5,000 and increases its investment in the branch by $5,000. In this case, no funds are transferred from the branch to the home office.

Alternatively, cash could be exchanged between the branch and the home office. Obviously, there is a fair degree of discretion in determining the extent of such expenses, the allocation process of these expenses to the various branches, and the means by which these expenses are handled. Billing and collecting for general overhead items is a technique commonly employed by multinational companies to enhance the cash flow from operating affiliates located in nations where there are currency exchange restrictions and limitations on the remittance of profits or on the capital investment in a branch or an operating affiliate.

Table 5.1
Investment in Branch B—Year 1

ITEM	DEBIT	CREDIT	BALANCE
Cash sent to branch	$5000		$5000 dr
Merchandise billed to branch at cost	50000		55000 dr
Equipment acquired by branch, carried in home office accounting records		$1200	53800 dr
Cash received from branch		25000	28800 dr
Operating expenses billed to branch	5000		33800 dr

Table 5.1 shows the home office ledger account for its investment in Branch B, which now has a debit balance of $33,800. Cash and merchandise totaling $55,000 were sent from the home office to the branch. These appear as debits on the home office books, creating an investment in Branch B of $55,000. Although the branch acquired $1,200 in PP&E with its own funds, the PP&E is recorded by the home office by reducing the investment in the branch by the cost of the PP&E. The branch also remitted $25,000 to the home office, reducing the home office investment in the branch to $28,800. Then $5,000 in operating expenses at the home office was charged to the branch, increasing the home office investment in the branch because the branch did not remit $5,000 to the home office.

The ledger account at Branch B in Table 5.2 shows a credit balance of $33,800 in favor of the home office, representing a net liability to the home office.

Table 5.2
Home Office—Year 1

ITEM	DEBIT	CREDIT	BALANCE
Cash received from home office		$5000	$5000 cr
Merchandise received from home office		50000	55000 cr
Equipment acquired	$1200		53800 cr
Cash sent to home office	25000		28800 cr
Operating expenses billed by home office		5000	33800 cr

The income and expense accounts of the branch are "closed out" and the net profit or loss is transferred to the home office at the end of the accounting period.

```
HOME OFFICE ACCOUNTING RECORDS        BRANCH ACCOUNTING RECORDS
      JOURNAL ENTRIES                     JOURNAL ENTRIES

        None                          Sales        $75000
                                        Cost of
                                        Goods Sold      $38000
                                        Operating
                                        Expenses        22000
                                        Income Summary  15000
```

First, the branch reverses (or closes out) the sales account, the cost of goods sold account and the operating expense account. The operating expense account of $22,000 consists of $17,000 of locally incurred expenses and $5,000 charged by the home office. The net operating profit, determined by taking the difference between revenue and expense accounts, is $15,000.

```
Investment in                     Income
  Branch B      $15000              Summary     $15000
  Income                            Home Office       $15000
    Branch B          $15000
```

The branch closes out the $15,000 of income by increasing its liability to the home office. No cash has changed hands. The home office records the fact that the branch has earned $15,000 of income by increasing its investment in the branch correspondingly.

```
Income Branch B    $15000
  Income Summary        $15000
```

The home office now merges the income earned by Branch B with its other sources of income.

Closing the Books

An accountant first prepares a working paper, combining the financial statements of the home office and the branch. The working paper combines similar

asset, liability, revenue, and expense accounts. The working paper also eliminates any intracompany profits or losses and any so-called reciprocal accounts
between the home office and the branch. In closing the books for an accounting
period, certain year-end adjusting entries may have to be made, such as the
shipment of goods to a branch prior to the closing of the books with the receipt
for the goods at the branch occurring after the closing of the books. Other
corrections are associated with the timing of the transfer of cash and the acquisition of equipment or other assets.

The working paper starts with the adjusted trial balances of the home office
and Branch B. Taxes are ignored in this example. Note that home office entries
in Table 5.3 include activities not related to the branch.

Table 5.3
**Global Inc.—Working Paper for Combined Financial Statements of Home Office
and Branch B at End of Year 1**

	ADJUSTED TRIAL BALANCES			
	HOME OFFICE	BRANCH	ELIMINATION	COMBINED
INCOME STATEMENT				
Sales	($510000)	($75000)		($585000)
Cost of goods sold	300000	38000		338000
Operating expenses	121000	22000		143000
Net income	89000	15000		104000
Totals	0	0		0

The home office had sales of $510,000, and the branch had sales of $75,000,
for combined sales of $585,000. The home office did not record the transfer of
merchandise to the branch as a sale. The $22,000 of branch expenses includes
both $17,000 incurred locally and $5,000 incurred by the home office and charged to the branch. Net income is then transferred to retained earnings as
follows.

STATEMENT OF RETAINED EARNINGS				
Retained earnings start of year	($90000)			($90000)
Net (income) for year	(89000)	($15000)		(104000)
Dividends	30000			30000
Retained earnings end of year				164000
Totals				0

The beginning-of-year retained earnings of $90,000 is a credit balance. During
the year, the home office earned $89,000 and the branch earned $15,000 for a

combined total of $104,000, raising combined retained earnings to $194,000 before dividends. The $30,000 in dividend payments reduce end-of-year retained earnings to $164,000, which are then transferred to the balance sheet.

BALANCE SHEET				
Cash	$31000	$10800		$41800
Accounts receivable	73000	26000		99000
Inventories	41200	12000		53200
Investment Branch B	33800		($33800)	
Equipment	230000			230000
Accumulated depreciation	(90000)			(90000)
Accounts payable	(40000)			(40000)
Home office		(33800)	33800	
Common stock	(130000)			(130000)
Retained earnings				(164000)
Totals	0	0	0	0

At the end of the accounting period, the home office has cash of $31,000 and the branch has cash of $10,800. These are combined for the company as a whole, as are accounts receivable, inventory, equipment, accumulated depreciation, and accounts payable. The reciprocal accounts representing the home office investment in the branch and the branch liability account to the home office are eliminated before determining the combined assets and liabilities.

Company assets and liabilities would each be overstated by $33,800 without this elimination. This balance of $33,800 is intercompany business and represents neither an asset nor a liability related to a third party. The combined financial statements shown in Exhibit 5.3 are obtained from the completed worksheet.

COMBINING BRANCH OPERATIONS (MERCHANDISE BILLED ABOVE COST)

More typically, companies do not transfer merchandise to a branch, or a subsidiary, at cost. There is usually an element of intercompany profit, where goods are "sold" to a branch at a "profit." Many theoretical considerations support the inclusion of a profit in the transfer price. The most common justification is that the higher price approximates that which the branch would pay to acquire similar goods from a nonrelated source. The evaluation of profitability at a branch is more relevant when the branch is charged a price nearer to that which would be charged by a third party. Since this profit is not realized until the goods are sold by the branch, it must be eliminated in the consolidation process.

The appropriate adjustments to the previous journal entries for a company that bills merchandise sold to a branch at cost plus a 20 percent markup follow.

Exhibit 5.3
Global Inc.

```
                        GLOBAL INC.
                     INCOME STATEMENT
                         YEAR 1

        Sales                                $585000
        Cost of goods sold                    338000

        Gross profit on sales                 247000
        Operating expenses                    143000

        Net income                           $104000
```

```
                       GLOBAL, INC.
              STATEMENT OF RETAINED EARNINGS
                      END OF YEAR 1

        Retained earnings start of year     $ 90000
        Add: Net income                       104000

         Subtotal                             194000
        Less Dividends                         30000

        Retained earnings end of year       $164000
```

```
                      GLOBAL COMPANY
                      BALANCE SHEET
                      END OF YEAR 1

        Cash                                 $ 41800
        Accounts receivable                    99000
        Inventories                            53200
        Equipment                  $230000
        Less: accumulated
                depreciation         90000    140000

        Total assets                         $334000


            LIABILITIES AND SHAREHOLDERS' EQUITY

        Liabilities
         Accounts payable                    $ 40000
        Stockholders' equity
         Common stock ($5 par, 26,000
          shares issued and
          outstanding               $130000
         Retained earnings           164000    294000

        Total liabilities and
         shareholders' equity                $334000
```

Goods costing the home office $50,000 are transferred to the branch at a price of $60,000. The branch may not know that the home office has included a 20 percent markup in the price of the merchandise to the branch. The branch records the cost of its inventories at the price charged by the home office ($60,000) with a corresponding increase in the liability to the home office account. On the books of the home office, the reciprocal account called "Investment in Branch B" is increased by $60,000, but inventories are reduced by their actual cost, or $50,000. The difference of $10,000 represents the profit charged by the home office to the branch. It is recorded in a separate account called "Allowance for Overvaluation of Inventories." Table 5.4 shows the home office ledger account for the investment in Branch B prior to the closing entries of the accounting period.

Table 5.4

INVESTMENT IN BRANCH B			
ITEM	DEBIT	CREDIT	BALANCE
Cash sent to branch	$5000		$5000 dr
Merchandise billed to branch with markup of 20% over cost	60000		65000 dr
Equipment acquired by branch, carried in home office accounting records		$1200	63800 dr
Cash received from branch		25000	38800 dr
Operating expenses billed to branch	5000		43800 dr

The difference between the balance of $43,800 in Table 5.4 and the balance of $33,800 shown in Table 5.1 is the intercompany profit of $10,000. Table 5.5 shows the corresponding account with the home office on the books of the branch.

Table 5.5

HOME OFFICE			
ITEM	DEBIT	CREDIT	BALANCE
Cash received from home office		$5000	$5000 cr
Merchandise received from home office		60000	65000 cr
Equipment acquired	$1200		63800 cr
Cash sent to home office	25000		38800 cr
Operating expenses billed by home office		5000	43800 cr

HOME OFFICE ACCOUNTING RECORDS
JOURNAL ENTRIES

```
Investment in
  Branch B        $60000
    Inventories            $50000
    Allowance for
    overvaluation of
    inventories             10000
```

BRANCH ACCOUNTING RECORDS
JOURNAL ENTRIES

```
Inventories   $60000
  Home Office          $60000
```

Once again, the balance in this account of $43,800 credit is greater than the $33,800 shown in Table 5.2, with the difference being the branch "buying" goods from the home office at a price including an intercompany profit of $10,000. This profit is artificial and is not realized by the company until the goods are sold to a third party. When the branch sells these goods, it records the inflated cost of goods sold in its accounts. Any unsold goods at the end of the accounting period are recorded on the branch records at a value that includes the 20 percent markup.

Suppose that the inventory on hand at the end of the year was $14,400. By taking the difference between the $60,000 billed to the branch and its end of year inventory, the branch calculates that the cost of its goods sold is $45,600. The branch reports this information to the home office, which is then in a position to prepare the analysis in Table 5.6.

Table 5.6

	COST	MARKUP (20% OF COST)	BILLED PRICE
GLOBAL INC. MERCHANDISE ANALYSIS FOR BRANCH B YEAR 1			
Beginning inventories	0	0	0
Add shipments from home office	$50000	$10000	$60000
Available for sale	50000	10000	60000
Less ending inventories	12000	2400	14400
Cost of goods sold	38000	7600	45600

The home office calculates that the ending inventory reported by the branch is overstated by $2,400, which represents the intercompany markup. The home office also calculates that the cost of goods sold reported by the branch of $45,600 is overstated by $7,600. In Table 5.3, the branch reported a profit of $15,000. Selling goods to the branch at a profit results in less profit being reported by the branch. In Table 5.6, it has been determined that the total cost of goods sold reported by the branch is overstated by $7,600, reducing the reported branch profit to $7,400 ($15,000 − $7,600). The following journal entries are made on the books of the home office.

| Investment in Branch B | $7,400 | |
| Income: Branch B | | $7,400 |

This entry records the profit as reported by Branch B.

| Allowance for overvaluation of inventories Branch B | $7,600 | |
| Income: Branch B | | $7,600 |

The reported income of Branch B is increased and the allowance for over-valuation of inventories is reduced by the amount of intercompany profit associated with goods sold. These entries adjust the profit reported by Branch B to its true value of $15,000.

Income: Branch B	$15,000
Income Summary	$15,000

The Income Summary closes out the adjusted net income reported by the branch. The adjusted amount of profit reported by the branch of $15,000 is the same as in Table 5.3. Table 5.7 shows the ledger accounts after these journal entries have been posted to the home office books.

Table 5.7

INVESTMENT IN BRANCH B			
ITEM	DEBIT	CREDIT	BALANCE
Cash sent to branch	$5000		$5000 dr
Merchandise billed to branch at markup of 20% above cost	60000		65000 dr
Equipment acquired by branch, carried in home office accounting records		$1200	63800 dr
Cash received from branch		25000	38800 dr
Operating expenses billed to branch	5000		43800 dr
Net profit for year as reported by branch	7400		51200 dr

The debit balance of $43,800 is also seen in Table 5.4. The final entry in Table 5.7 records the branch income for the year, which increases the home office investment in Branch B.

Table 5.8

ALLOWANCE FOR OVERVALUATION OF INVENTORIES: BRANCH B			
ITEM	DEBIT	CREDIT	BALANCE
Markup of merchandise shipped to branch during year		$10000	$10000 cr
Realization of 20% markup on merchandise sold by branch	$7600		2400 cr

When goods were sold to the branch, a markup of $10,000 was added to the price charged to Branch B. The Allowance for Overvaluation of Inventories account (Table 5.8) was credited with $10,000 to offset the "overstatement" of inventory. As goods are sold by the branch, the amount by which inventory is overstated and this account are correspondingly reduced. Table 5.9 is the home office ledger account for Branch B income.

Table 5.9

```
                        INCOME:  BRANCH B

          ITEM                        DEBIT    CREDIT    BALANCE

Net profit for year as reported
   by branch                                   $7400    $7400 cr
Realization of 20% markup on
   merchandise sold by branch                   7600    15000 cr
Net income of branch (as adjusted)
   closed to Income Summary account   $15000                 0
```

Closing entries on Branch B accounting records are as follows:

Sales		$75,000
Cost of goods sold		$45,600
Operating expenses		22,000
Income Summary		7,400
Income Summary	7,400	
Home Office		7,400

Table 5.10 is the Home Office account on the books of Branch B.

Table 5.10

```
                        HOME OFFICE

          ITEM                        DEBIT    CREDIT    BALANCE

Cash received from home office                 $5000    $5000 cr
Merchandise received from home office          60000    65000 cr
Equipment acquired                    $1200             63800 cr
Cash sent to home office              25000             38800 cr
Operating expenses billed by home office        5000    43800 cr
Net income for year                             7400    51200 cr
```

Table 5.11 shows the working paper for the combined financial statements of the home office and the branch at the end of the first year. Note that the retained earnings are transferred to the balance sheet section of the worksheet.

The combined amounts on this worksheet are the same as in Table 5.3, which accounted for the merchandise sold to the branch at cost. Both published financial statements for goods sold at cost, and with a markup, are the same.

It is sometimes necessary to transfer merchandise between branches for companies with multibranch locations. The cost of these goods should not be further increased other than for the incremental freight expenses. Normally, branches do not have reciprocal accounts with each other and record all intercompany business as being done with the home office. Suppose, for example, that the shipping cost from the home office to Branch A is $100, the shipping cost from the home office to Branch B is $125, and that the shipping cost from Branch A to Branch B is $60. If a unit of goods is shipped from Branch A to Branch B,

Table 5.11
Global, Inc.

	HOME OFFICE	BRANCH	ELIMINATION	COMBINED
		ADJUSTED TRIAL BALANCES		
INCOME STATEMENT				
Sales	($510000)	($75000)		($585000)
Cost of goods sold	300000	45600	(7600)(1)	338000
Operating expenses	121000	22000		143000
Net income	89000	7400	7600 (2)	104000
Totals	0	0		0
STATEMENT OF RETAINED EARNINGS				
Retained earnings start of year	($90000)			($90000)
Net (income) for year	(89000)	($7400)	($7600)(2)	(104000)
Dividends	30000			30000
Retained earnings end of year				164000
Totals				0
BALANCE SHEET				
Cash	$31000	$10800		$41800
Accounts receivable	73000	26000		99000
Inventories	41200	14400	($2400)(1)	53200
Investment Branch B	43800		(43800)(3)	
Allowance for overvaluation of inventories Branch B	(10000)		10000 (1)	
Equipment	230000			230000
Accumulated depreciation	(90000)			(90000)
Accounts payable	(40000)			(40000)
Home office		(43800)	43800 (3)	
Common stock	(130000)			(130000)
Retained earnings				(164000)
Totals	0	0	0	0

(1) To reduce ending inventories and cost of goods sold of branch to cost, and to eliminate balance of Allowance for Overvaluation of Inventories Branch B.

(2) To increase net income of branch by portion of intercompany profit realized when merchandise was sold.

(3) To eliminate reciprocal ledger accounts.

Branch B would record inventory value as the value of the goods plus a shipping cost of $125, with the "excess" freight of $35 ($100 plus $60 less $125) expensed immediately. The intent is to ensure that the carrying value of the inventory at Branch B does not exceed what it would have been had the goods been shipped directly from the home office.

CONSOLIDATING SUBSIDIARIES

The foregoing illustration deals with a branch location, which is an integral part of the parent company, not a separate legal entity. In addition to a branch operation, a company may act through a subsidiary or operating affiliate as a separate legal entity, where the parent owns some or all of its common stock. Legally, the parent does not own the individual assets of the subsidiary nor is it responsible for the liabilities of the subsidiary, unless the parent specifically agrees to guarantee the subsidiary's obligations. Notwithstanding the subsidiary being a separate legal entity, generally accepted accounting principles may require that the financial statements of the subsidiary be consolidated with those of the parent. The basic premise is that if the parent has a significant measure of operating control over a subsidiary, then fairness of presentation requires the consolidation of both the parent and the subsidiary.

In a manner very similar to branch accounting, accounting for a consolidated subsidiary combines the assets, liabilities, revenue, and expenses of the subsidiary with those of the parent. Real-life applications of consolidation practices are very complex, with entire books dedicated to the subject. Examples contained herein have been simplified for purposes of illustration.

A parent company may account for an investment in a subsidiary in either of three ways:

1. Full consolidation
2. Equity method
3. Cost method

In general, the percentage of ownership dictates which method should be used. For example, in the United States, full consolidation is required if ownership is between 50 percent and 100 percent of the common stock of a subsidiary or operating affiliate. There are some rare exceptions to this rule. The equity method usually applies when a parent company's investment in a subsidiary ranges between 20 percent and 50 percent of the common stock. Finally, the cost method normally applies when ownership is less than 20 percent.

If the parent company P owns 20 percent to 50 percent of the voting stock of a subsidiary company S, the equity method usually applies because of the presumption that P can exercise "significant control" over the operations of S. If P owns less than 20 percent of S, the presumption is that P cannot exercise significant control over S, and therefore, the equity method cannot be applied.

These presumptions need to be examined in each individual case. The main point is that a company that can exercise significant control over a subsidiary should use the equity method of consolidation regardless of the percentage of ownership. The 20 percent ownership test is just an attempt to quantify the notion of significant influence and is not a hard and fast rule.

Solvay is a large Belgian chemical and plastics company with worldwide operations. Its principles of consolidation, shown in Exhibit 5.4, note that its decision on whether to fully consolidate or use the equity method of consolidation is not based strictly on the degree of ownership, but includes a measure of the degree of management control. Note the reference to legislation—a characteristic of continental European (excluding the Netherlands) accounting systems.

Exhibit 5.4
Excerpt from Solvay 1990 Annual Report

NOTES TO FINANCIAL STATEMENTS

1. PRINCIPLES OF CONSOLIDATION

(art.9. par.1.1 of the Royal Decree of September 1. 1986)

A. Consolidation Criteria

The consolidated statements include all the companies meeting the two criteria of control and size.

Control

They integrate the statements of all the subsidiaries in which Solvay & Cie S.A. directly or indirectly owns more than 50% of the capital. In addition, the companies in which the Group's holding does not exceed this threshold are also consolidated if the Group plays a major role in their management.

Size

To be consolidated, companies also have to be of significance compared to the Group as a whole, i.e., fulfill at least one of the three following conditions:
• sales of BEF 400 million (ca.Ecu 10 million) or higher;
• total assets of BEF 200 million (ca.Ecu 5 million) or higher;
• work force of 150 people at least.

However, subsidiaries meeting the above criteria but of which the Group wishes to divest itself are valued according to the equity method described under item 4. IV b, pursuant to customary principles of the standard governing the consolidation of yearly accounts to be certified by a business auditor.

The investments in subsidiaries that do not meet the size criteria are carried at their asset value under "Other investments".

B. Equity method criteria

Companies in which the Group holds 20 to 50% of the capital and plays a significant role are valued according to the equity method, as long as they meet the size criteria mentioned under A.

When they do not meet such criteria, they are carried at their asset value under "Other investments".

U.S. accounting principles (Financial Accounting Standards Board Statement No. 94) require that all majority owned subsidiaries be fully consolidated, except where control of the subsidiary is likely to be temporary or where control of the subsidiary does not rest with the majority shareholder. This applies regardless of the location of the subsidiary.

CONSOLIDATION METHOD—100 PERCENT OWNERSHIP

Table 5.12 shows the consolidated balance sheet worksheet on the day of acquisition of 100 percent of the stock in Company S. At this time, S owed P $6,000.

Table 5.12

			ADJUSTMENTS	CON-
	COMPANY P	COMPANY S	AND ELIMINATIONS	SOLI-DATED

P COMPANY
CONSOLIDATED BALANCE SHEET WORKSHEET
ON DATE OF ACQUISITION

	COMPANY P	COMPANY S	ADJUSTMENTS AND ELIMINATIONS	CON-SOLI-DATED
ASSETS				
Cash	$25000	$5000		$30000
Accounts				
Receivable	70000	25000	($6000)(1)	89000
Inventories	100000	50000		150000
Fixed Assets	200000	29000		229000
Investment in S:				
Fair Value at				
Acquisition	92000		(92000)(2)	
Goodwill	13000			13000
Total Assets	500000	109000		511000
LIABILITIES & EQUITY				
Accounts				
Payable	68000	17000	6000(1)	79000
Capital Stock				
P Company	264000			264000
S Company		50000	50000(2)	
Retained Earnings				
P Company	168000			168000
S Company		42000	42000(2)	
Total Liabilities				
& Equity	500000	109000		511000

In this example, Company P (P) has acquired 100 percent of the common stock of Company S (S) for $105,000. The assets and liabilities of S are already stated at fair market value at the date of acquisition, resulting in $92,000 equity in S. Thus, P has paid a premium, or a difference between the purchase price and net asset value, of $13,000. This amount is reflected as goodwill in the consolidation process.

Entry (1) in Table 5.12 eliminates the intercompany balance of S owing P $6,000 at the date of acquisition. Similarly, entry (2) eliminates P's investment in S of $92,000 against the equity of S. When the intercompany transactions are eliminated, only assets and liabilities external to the company remain. The equity section (capital stock and retained earnings) contains the capital stock and the retained earnings of P only.

MINORITY INTEREST

Suppose the same facts except that P purchased 80 percent of S for a price
of $84,000. The underlying equity of S was $92,000, with P acquiring 80
percent thereof, or $73,600. Goodwill is now $84,000 less $73,600 or $10,400.
In addition, P must recognize that 20 percent of the equity of S is owned by
others, and will create a new account called Minority Interest. At the date of
acquisition, the equity of S owned by others is $18,400 (20 percent of $92,000),
which is shown separately on the consolidated financial statement of P. In the
future, 20 percent of profits or losses of S will also be attributable to outside
shareholders and will not be reflected in the consolidated income statement of
P. Table 5.13 shows the consolidated balance sheet worksheet on the day of
acquisition.

Table 5.13

P COMPANY CONSOLIDATED BALANCE SHEET WORKSHEET ON DATE OF ACQUISITION					
	COMPANY P	COMPANY S	ADJUSTMENTS AND ELIMINATIONS	MINORITY INTEREST	CON- SOLI- DATED
ASSETS					
Cash	$46000	$5000			$51000
Accounts Receivable	70000	25000	($6000)(1)		89000
Inventories	100000	50000			150000
Fixed Assets	200000	29000			229000
Investment in S: Fair Value at Acquisition	73600		(73600)(2)		
Goodwill	10400				10400
Total Assets	500000	109000			529400
LIABILITIES & EQUITY					
Accounts Payable	68000	17000	6000(1)		79000
Capital Stock P Company	264000				264000
S Company		50000	40000(2)	$10000	
Retained Earnings P Company	168000				168000
S Company		42000	33600(2)	8400	
Minority Interest					18400
Total Liabilities & Equity	500000	109000			529400

The minority interest of $18,400 represents 20 percent of capital stock of S and 20 percent of retained earnings of S. All nonintercompany assets and liabilities are reported in the consolidated balance sheet at 100 percent of their value. For instance, cash of P and cash of S are added and reported as $51,000. It initially appears that P enjoys full ownership of all these assets and liabilities of S. This is compensated by reporting that the minority shareholders have a net claim of $18,400 on the equity of S. The minority interest rises and falls thereafter with the equity value of S.

The accounting practices in some countries, such as the United Kingdom, may permit, depending on the circumstances, ''proportional'' consolidation. In proportional consolidation, 80 percent of each asset and liability would be reported in the consolidated financial statements as shown in Table 5.14.

Table 5.14

P COMPANY CONSOLIDATED BALANCE SHEET WORKSHEET ON DATE OF ACQUISITION				
	COMPANY P	COMPANY S	ADJUSTMENTS AND ELIMINATIONS	CON-SOLI-DATED
ASSETS				
Cash	$46000	$5000	($1000)(2)	$50000
Accounts				
Receivable	70000	25000	(5000)(2)	90000
Inventories	100000	50000	(10000)(2)	140000
Fixed Assets	200000	29000	(5800)(2)	223200
Investment in S:				
Fair Value at				
Acquisition	73600		(73600)(1)	
Goodwill	10400			10400
Total Assets	500000	109000		513600
LIABILITIES & EQUITY				
Accounts				
Payable	68000	17000	3400(2)	81600
Capital Stock				
P Company	264000			264000
S Company		50000	40000(1) 10000(2)	
Retained Earnings				
P Company	168000			168000
S Company		42000	33600(1) 8400(2)	
Total Liabilities & Equity	500000	109000		513600

The consolidation process in this case does not show a minority interest. The equity of P remains unchanged, and 80 percent of each asset and liability account of S is included in the consolidation. For example, the consolidated cash balance of $50,000 includes 100 percent of P ($46,000) plus 80 percent of S ($4,000). Entry (1) eliminates that portion of P's original investment equal to the fair value of S that was acquired and eliminates the related capital stock and retained earnings of S. Entry (2) reduces all assets and liabilities of S by the proportion of minority ownership, in this case, 20 percent. Tables 5.13 and 5.14 demonstrate just one of the many possible divergences in the consolidation process of various nations. International Accounting Standards Committee (IASC) rules on consolidation permit proportional consolidation, with appropriate footnote disclosure.

EQUITY METHOD

Acquiring 20 percent to 50 percent interest in another company generally requires the use of the equity method of consolidating financial results. For illustrative purposes, assume that P acquires 30 percent of the common stock of S for $150,000, at a time when the net equity and fair market value of S was $400,000. During the following year, S earns $60,000 and pays $30,000 in dividends.

In this case, P uses the equity method of accounting. The main difference between this method, illustrated in Table 5.15, and the full consolidation in

Table 5.15
Equity Method of Accounting

EQUITY METHOD OF ACCOUNTING		
	INVESTMENT	INCOME (LOSS)
Acquisition Price	$150000	
Earnings for year	18000 (1)	$18000
Amortization of Goodwill	(750)(2)	(750)
Dividends	(9000)(3)	
Earnings pickup for year		$17250
Investment at end of year	$158250	

(1) 30 percent of $60,000

(2) Cost of 30 percent investment in S $150,000
    30 percent of fair market value of S 120,000
    Goodwill 30,000
    Amortization over forty years 750

(3) Thirty percent of $30,000

Table 5.13, lies in the details reported in the consolidated financial statements. Under the equity method, the parent company, P, reports its share of S income as a single amount, which is frequently referred to as a "one line" consolidation, and reports its net investment in S as a single item.

The original investment of $150,000 is increased by P's share of S's earnings for the year and is decreased by P's amortization of goodwill and P's receipt of its share of dividends. Thus, P's investment in S at the end of the year is $158,250. On the income statement, P reports 30 percent of S income ($60,000), reduced by amortization of goodwill ($750), or $17,250.

COST METHOD

The cost method generally applies when P acquires not more than 20 percent of the equity of S. Suppose that P acquires 15 percent of S for $75,000. At the date of acquisition, the net assets and fair market value of S are $400,000. During the year, S earns $60,000 and pays dividends of $30,000. Under the cost method, P records income only when dividends are received, as shown in Table 5.16.

Table 5.16
Cost Method of Accounting

COST METHOD OF ACCOUNTING		
	INVESTMENT	INCOME (LOSS)
Acquisition Price	$75000	
Earnings for year		
Amortization of Goodwill(2)		
Dividends		$4500(1)
Earnings pickup for year		$4500
Investment at end of year	$75000	

(1) Fifteen percent of $30,000

(2) Depending on circumstances, goodwill may also be amortized under the cost method and declines in investment value, whether temporary or permanent, may also have to be recognized.

The effect of owning 30 percent of S under the equity method versus owning 15 percent of S under the cost method is not proportional because 30 percent ownership resulted in reported income of $17,250, whereas 15 percent ownership resulted in reported income of $4,500. Ownership has been reduced by half and reported net income is, in this case, substantially less than half. It is possible that, depending on the amount of dividends, higher reported income may be associated with lesser degree of ownership.

ISSUES THAT COMPLICATE THE CONSOLIDATION PROCESS

1. Is the cost method appropriate inasmuch as dividends received rather than income earned are the basis on which a parent company recognizes its share of earnings of the subsidiary? Obviously, this could lead to distortions because the timing and magnitude of dividend payments can be managed. This is an ethical consideration in accounting in that a company with a loss for the year, but with cash surpluses, can declare a dividend, which is reported by the parent as income. However, the fact that S is losing money, while paying a dividend, might require a write-down of the investment.

2. Is it appropriate to include assets and earnings of subsidiaries located in countries that have controls on remittances or other payments to the parent? For instance, suppose that a factory is built in a nation that, subsequent to the building of the factory, prohibits the repatriation of more than, say, 15 percent of profits per year. Is it appropriate for the parent to report 100 percent of subsidiary profits each year, realizing that these amounts cannot be remitted to the parent?

3. Consolidated financial statements of a parent are presented in one currency, say, the U.S. dollar. Suppose that the parent company does very little business in the United States and its U.S. dollar assets and liabilities are negligible. Is it appropriate for its consolidated financial statement to be expressed in U.S. dollars?

4. Subsidiaries in poor financial health are consolidated with financially healthy companies, possibly obscuring financial difficulties in some of the subsidiaries. For instance, a subsidiary of a parent can be at the point of insolvency, or bankruptcy, and this situation cannot be detected in reviewing the consolidated statement of the parent. Under these circumstances, are the consolidated financial statements presenting a true and fair view of the company?

5. Different companies within a consolidated group may use different accounting principles to measure revenue, value assets, and determine income. Is the true and fair view preserved when this potpourri of accounting principles, lacking comparability, are recast to a single set of accounting principles in preparation for consolidation into a single financial statement?

Despite these caveats, it is generally recognized that consolidated financial statements are more meaningful than separate company financial statements and are essential to a fair presentation of a company's results of operation and financial condition. In almost all cases, the reporting company spells out the basis on which the financial statements are prepared. This is frequently done in the first footnote to the financial statements.

CHAPTER 6

TRANSACTIONS AND TRANSLATIONS

A company with operating affiliates in a hundred nations must deal with a hundred sets of generally accepted accounting principles in the consolidation process. The operations of the company must also deal with business transactions and financial reports denominated in a hundred different currencies. A financial reporting and control system, the mechanism by which a global business is managed, must include in its design a means for handling both multiple currency transactions and currency translations of operating affiliate financial results.

GOLD AS A GLOBAL CURRENCY

Dealing in foreign currencies has not always been a major problem in international trade and commerce. Historically, the most common international currency was gold, followed by silver, or a combination of the two. Gold, in particular, has been universally accepted as a monetary means of exchange and a storehouse of value. The purchasing power of an ounce of gold has remained throughout the ages, whereas the purchasing power of paper currencies has eroded with time. One of the few times when gold lost purchasing power was in the sixteenth century when Spain was inundated with gold from the conquest of the Aztec and Inca empires. This loss of purchasing power is in line with the Webster dictionary definition of inflation as ''an increase in the amount of currency in circulation resulting in a relatively sharp and sudden fall in its value and rise in prices; it may be caused by an increase in the volume of paper money issued or of gold mined, or a relative increase in expenditures, as when the supply of goods fails to meet demand.''

Gold is associated with times of political and economic stability. During times of upheaval (war, civil unrest, economic turmoil), coins were progressively debased until they contained only common metals. Later, when nations learned to substitute paper that was convertible into gold, instability or turmoil would bring about paper currency that lacked convertibility such as the "greenbacks" during the U.S. Civil War. A sign of the restoration of stability would be the reinstatement of the gold standard and the buying back of "greenbacks" with convertible paper money.

Prior to World War I, major currencies were convertible into gold. The relationship between one currency and another was simply their respective conversion rate to gold. If one unit of currency X was convertible into one gram of gold and one unit of currency Y was convertible into two grams of gold, then the exchange rate between currency X and Y was 2 units of X for 1 unit of Y. The exchange rate was fixed. Indeed, it could not fluctuate.

Suppose, however, that the market rate for currency Y became 3 units of X under a gold standard where Y can be exchanged for 2 units of X in terms of gold. An individual holding a unit of currency Y could exchange it in the currency market for 3 units of currency X. He or she could take the 3 units of currency X to the central bank for currency X and obtain three grams of gold. Then he or she could saunter over to the central bank for currency Y and obtain 1.5 units of currency Y. Now he or she has 50 percent more of currency Y than what he or she began with—not a bad return for visiting one currency market and two banks. Obviously, an anomaly between currency exchange rates and their respective conversion rates into gold could not exist. The principal advantage of the gold standard is a fixed exchange rate between currencies based on their respective conversion rates to gold. International business is conducted as though there is a single, or global, currency. A global currency, or world currencies whose respective exchange rates are fixed and unchanging, reduces the complexity of both conducting international business and consolidating financial reports denominated in different currencies.

However, the gold standard had its reputed disadvantages. First of all, the expansion of the monetary supply of gold was limited to the amount of new gold mined, which was grossly inadequate when measured against the growth of international trade. Presumably, the benefits of international trade in raising living standards by the exchange of goods between different parts of the world would be difficult to achieve with trade growing at 10 percent per year and the gold supply expanding by 2 percent per year. In time, and in theory, there would be inadequate monetary reserves to support the volume of international trade. One argument against gold as a medium of exchange is the potential of an inadequate supply of gold inhibiting commerce.

Under the gold standard, trade imbalances between two nations eventually required a movement of gold between two nations. As a consequence of World War II, much of the world's gold ended up in U.S. bank vaults for safekeeping. Following the war, transfers of gold between nations were accomplished by moving gold from one location in a bank vault to another, signifying the settling of trade imbalances between nations. Photographs of these quaint scenes supposedly showed the apolitical disciplinarian nature of the gold standard: a nation with a trade deficit better have some gold in its corner of the vault.

In theory, under the gold standard, nations with chronic balance of payment deficits in international trade could not paper over their economic difficulties by turning on the monetary printing press. Continuing deficits in trade would result in a loss of gold reserves. A nation whose paper currency was convertible into gold would suffer a loss of its money supply. Less money in circulation would induce a recession. Loss of jobs would cut demand for goods and reduced demand would cause prices to fall. The contraction of business activity would last until prices had fallen to the point where the nation's products became competitive in the world market. More competitive prices enhanced exports and the pickup in the volume of goods sold to overseas markets created job opportunities for the factory workers. Gold would flow into the nation as its trade balance turned positive, increasing the nation's money supply and fueling the continued expansion of the economy. Unfortunately, an expanding economy fostered higher wages and prices. When wages and prices once again became out of line with the world market, product exports would shrink, imports would grow, the trade surplus would be transformed to a trade deficit, setting the stage for a repeat of the cycle.

Another argument against gold is that the gold standard induces cyclicality in business activity through the self-correcting mechanism of an endless series of contractions and expansions accompanying the tidal movement of gold in and out of the central bank's vault. Although the expansion phase of a business cycle is enjoyed by labor and capital alike, the contraction phase is not—thus, the battle cry of those against the gold standard of "mankind being crucified on a cross of gold."

Lastly, no nation is eager to be bled of its gold reserves. This goes beyond the consequences of a loss of money supply. It is a point of national pride to have an increasingly larger pile of gold bars in the central bank's vault and a matter of national concern when the golden security blanket is threatened. Having gold as a medium for settling accounts between nations has a tendency to induce government officials and rulers to favor a trade policy that results in an ever growing stack of gold bars in the central bank's vault. Consequently, they are motivated to take whatever actions are necessary to enhance the inflow, and restrict the outflow, of gold, the success of which can be easily measured by counting the gold bars. Adam Smith called this economic practice, or behavior pattern, mercantilism.

Mercantilism declared that the winner in international trade was the nation with the largest hoard of gold. Adam Smith realized that an economic system in which every nation is trying to maximize the inflow and minimize the outflow of gold is not conducive to international trade. Such conduct leads to encouraging exports, which adds to the stack of gold, and discouraging imports, which reduces the stack of gold. This contradictory behavior pattern results in the erection of trade barriers and the contraction of international trade.

Adam Smith believed that the material welfare of the people is enhanced if every community, and every nation, specializes in what it does best and relies on domestic and international trade to satisfy its other needs. Anything that inhibits trade eventually lowers the living standards of the people. The last argument against the gold standard is that it encourages rulers and governments to maximize their gold reserves by erecting trade barriers against imports, which impede international trade and lower living standards.

Some say that this lesson taught by Adam Smith over two hundred years ago has yet to be learned by Japan. Japan has been criticized as the world's greatest mercantilist nation by its insistence in accumulating the world's largest hoard, not of gold, but of U.S. dollars. This is done by pushing its export industries while at the same time making it difficult for imported finished products to reach Japanese consumers. Accumulating a hoard of U.S. dollars may be of comfort to the Japanese government, but it is having a deleterious impact on the U.S. economy. This condition cannot continue indefinitely because the ultimate outcome is a "rustbelt" of unacceptable and unparalleled proportions.

In fairness, Japan has reinvested a large portion of its surplus in direct investments in the United States, totaling $104 billion at the end of 1989. These included the building of transplant factories and the acquisition of real estate properties plus investments in Treasury securities. Japan is under intense pressure to open its markets to non-Japanese-made products, and has done so in a limited way. Interestingly, although most associate Japan with having the largest hoard of monetary reserves, in 1990, Taiwan actually held the honor, followed closely by Japan.

U.S. DOLLAR AS A GLOBAL CURRENCY

The twentieth century was a tough time for the gold standard. World War I, the Great Depression, and World War II forced nations off the gold standard. Being off the gold standard did not necessarily save mankind from being crucified on a cross of gold, a cross of paper could do the job just as nicely. The inflation of the German mark during the Weimar Republic destroyed the savings of the German people, caused the economy to collapse, and paved the way for Hitler. In 1944, the principal nations of the world met at Bretton Woods, New Hampshire, to hammer out a new international monetary system. The Bretton Woods Agreement created the International Monetary Fund (IMF), whose purpose was to promote international monetary cooperation among the member nations, to encourage growth in international trade, and to promote stable currency exchange rates between various nations.

The system envisioned fixed exchange rates between various currencies and the U.S. dollar, with the dollar alone being convertible to gold. This made good sense in that the United States, as a result of the war, was the holder of much of the world's gold. The Bretton Woods Agreement provided the essence of the gold standard in that the exchange rates between the primary world currencies and the U.S. dollar were fixed. Therefore, each unit of currency was convertible into a known quantity of dollars, and dollars could be converted into gold at $35 per ounce. Again, international trade could be conducted in what amounted to a global currency as long as the exchange rate between a currency and the dollar was constrained to trade in a narrow range about a fixed exchange rate.

However, the amount of currency in circulation was not fixed by the Bretton Woods Agreement. Individual nations, not the IMF, controlled the speed of the monetary printing presses, and therefore, the amount of money in circulation. It was also the responsibility of each nation, not the IMF, to maintain its currency exchange rate within plus or minus 1 percent of the official exchange rate with the dollar. If the lower limit of the allowable band was about to be pierced, the central bank was expected to purchase its own currency to increase its value. If the currency exchange rate was bumping against its upper limit, the central bank was expected to sell its currency to decrease its value.

As attractive as this may sound, two problems immediately arose. The lesser problem was exceeding the upper limit of a permissible trading band. A nation was expected to sell its currency to depress its value. Ultimately, this meant turning on the printing press to create a sufficient quantity of currency to suppress its exchange rate with the dollar. But a national government might not be eager to do this if it had concerns about the inflationary consequences. Following the war, the West German mark strengthened with the reestablishment of the nation's industrial base and the mark began bumping against its upper limit with respect to the dollar. Remembering the inflation during the Weimar Republic, the West German central bankers and political leaders were reluctant to print marks to depress its value. The mark began to trade above its upper limit.

A potentially knottier problem was dealing with a currency trading near its lower limit. This meant that a nation must buy its currency to enhance its value with relation to the dollar. A nation cannot purchase its currency with its own currency. The Italian central bankers cannot purchase lira with lira to bolster its value. A nation must use its gold or foreign currency reserves to purchase its currency. Without these, a nation cannot offer anything in exchange for its currency. With nothing to offer in exchange for their currencies, both the Italian and British bankers could not prevent their currencies from falling below their lower trading limits.

Therefore, the IMF permitted, with proper consultation, a nation to change the exchange rate of its currency with respect to the dollar. A lowering of the exchange rate was called a devaluation and a raising of the exchange rate was called a revaluation. As long as devaluations and revaluations were not common occurrences, the Bretton Woods system functioned reasonably well, which it did for a quarter of a century as a substitute for the gold standard.

The undoing of the Bretton Woods system was not caused by the disruptions occasioned by devaluations and revaluations, but the growing number of dollars in circulation. It was the U.S. printing presses that were running full tilt to paper over its chronic balance of payments deficits with other industrialized nations that provoked an international financial crisis. These vast holdings of U.S. dollars were partly the result of the outflow of dollars to support the rebuilding of war ravaged Europe and Japan (the Marshall Plan). But much of the dollar overhang was a consequence of a chronic U.S. trade deficit caused by Americans buying more products made overseas than American made products were being sold overseas.

By 1969, it was readily apparent that the holdings of dollars in foreign hands, that is U.S. dollar deposits in non-U.S. banks, far exceeded the amount of gold in Fort Knox. The first patch sewed on to the tearing fabric of international finance was the creation of Special Drawing Rights (SDRs), or paper gold. SDRs were to be a substitute for gold. A nation could cash in excess dollars and supposedly be indifferent whether it received an ounce of gold or a slip of paper declaring itself to be equivalent to an ounce of gold. In fact, SDRs were not even a slip of paper, but an entry in a computer data base. Proponents of SDRs desired such a system to show once and for all that mankind no longer had to resort to that "barbaric relic," gold, as a means of settlement between nations.

Apparently, it did make a difference. One ounce of gold did carry more weight than an entry in a computer data bank declaring itself to be an ounce of gold. This forced President Nixon, in 1971, to "close the gold window." No one could turn in dollars to the U.S. government and expect to receive a specified amount of gold. Although holders of U.S. dollars could buy gold in the open market, the price paid for the gold would be determined by the laws of supply and demand, not by government fiat backed up by gold reserves. This undid the Bretton Woods Agreement. During the crisis, the monetary authorities of the industrialized nations hammered out the Smithsonian Agreement. The Smithsonian Agreement turned out to be a short-lived stopgap agreement that, by 1973, gave way to a totally free floating currency exchange system.

LIVING WITHOUT A GLOBAL CURRENCY

In a floating currency exchange system, only the central bank knows a nation's target exchange rate with other nations and the band in which it is permitted to float without intervention by the central bank. Those in commerce may guess at what this target exchange rate and its associated trading band are, and even if they are good at second guessing, they still cannot conduct international trade with confidence. The central bank may change its mind on the target exchange rate, or may choose not to intervene in the currency exchange market to keep its currency exchange rate within some prescribed trading band.

A "clean" float exists when a country permits the forces of supply and demand to determine its exchange rate with other currencies. A "dirty" float implies government intervention to maintain some control over the exchange rate of its currency with other currencies. Most exchange rates between major currencies are managed, in that central bankers intervene in the currency exchange market to keep their currencies within certain desired limits. Intervention is forced on the central bankers because currency exchange rates have a major impact on the volume of international trade, the monetary balance between imports and exports and the health of the domestic economy.

Suppose that one unit of currency X is fixed at 2 units of currency Y. Two manufacturers make widgets, one in the nation whose currency is X and the other in a nation whose currency is Y. Widgets are a common industrial item, a mature product where manufacturers' profit margins are about 5 percent of sales. In the respective countries, widgets sell for 10 X's and 20 Y's, and the manufacturers' profits are 0.5 X and 1 Y. From the point of view of the manufacturer in the nation whose currency is X, he can sell widgets in the domestic market and receive 10 X, or he can export and receive 20 Y. Upon receiving 20 Y, he exchanges the proceeds for 10 X, pays out his total costs of 9.5 X and nets 0.5 X just as if he had sold the goods in his own nation (assuming for now that transportation costs are the same for both the domestic and international markets, and ignoring taxes).

Now suppose that the market price and the cost of manufacture do not change, but that a floating exchange rate system comes into being. After some period of time, the exchange rate is floating at 1 X to 1.5 Y. The same manufacturer can still receive 10 X in the domestic market or 20 Y in the foreign market. However, when he sells in the foreign market, the 20 Y can now be exchanged for 13.3 X—13.3 X less 9.5 X in manufacturing costs is 3.8 X in profits as compared to making 0.5 X in the domestic market. It is much more profitable to sell in the foreign market. His predictable behavior pattern is to increase production to the greatest possible extent and dump his "excess" production into the Y market.

Assuming efficient production where there is little leeway to cut costs, the only way for the manufacturer in the nation whose currency is Y to respond to this flood of imports is to cut his price. But he can only cut his price to the point of covering costs. This is 19 Y. This price cut can be matched by the exporter. Now he receives 19 Y, which when exchanged for X at the rate of 1 X for 1.5 Y, nets him 12.7 X. His cost is still 9.5 X, so his profit selling in the foreign market is 3.2 X versus 0.5 X in the domestic market. Thus, he continues to flood the Y market by operating his plant at maximum capacity and by building new plants to take advantage of this favorable situation. As long as he can convert his foreign sales to an equivalent of something more than 10 X, he is making more profits in the export market. The manufacturer, as a profit maximizer, would expand his productive capacity until the price for a widget is depressed to 15 Y, which nets him 10 X, the same as selling in the domestic market. In so doing, he will be a hero to his workers as their numbers expand. He will be a hero to the municipal government for the benefits that accrue to the local economy in building new factories and hiring more workers. He will be a hero to the national government for expanding foreign sales. He will be a hero to the shareholders for enhancing the profitability of the company.

Meanwhile, the manufacturer in the nation whose currency is Y is selling in a market where the price is 15 Y and where his manufacturing costs are 19 Y.

He will appeal to the national government for subsidies, trade restrictions, and anything else that may save him and the jobs of his workers. In a world more or less committed to free trade, subsidies and trade restrictions may be difficult to obtain. If this is the case, and if he cannot cut his costs, then the most probable outcome is that the manufacturer, and the entire widget industry in the Y currency nation, will go out of business.

Of course, if the floating rate moved in the opposite direction, the cast of characters would be reversed. The manufacturer whose costs are denominated in currency Y would wipe out the manufacturer whose costs are denominated in currency X. As the floating exchange rate moves up and down much as waves on the open sea, manufacturers in different nations can take turns bludgeoning one another. Floating currency exchange rates open up a whole new dimension of risk that was not present under a fixed currency exchange rate system. In a world of global commerce, an adverse change in the floating exchange rate means a loss of both domestic and international sales. A company whose market is located within walking distance of its factory can lose it to a company located on the other side of the world by an adverse change in currency exchange rates. Alternatively, its market may explode through no effort of its own because of a favorable change in the floating exchange rate. A meaningful change in the exchange rates between two nations is apt to be a bonanza for one set of manufacturers and a disaster for the other. And a floating exchange rate system means that change in currency exchange rates occurs continually.

Consequently, there is a real incentive for national governments to stabilize their currency exchange rates with other nations, particularly those nations that figure prominently in their international trade. The European Joint Float was established in 1972 by France, West Germany, Italy, the Netherlands, Belgium, Luxembourg, the United Kingdom, and Denmark to maintain their currencies within a narrow band, which, at that time, was called a "snake." They also agreed that the snake could wiggle with a greater degree of freedom with respect to other currencies—dubbed the "tunnel." The idea of the snake was to ensure that trade among the European nations would not be severely impacted by wide swings in the floating exchange rates among the European currencies. The snake wiggling in a tunnel permitted the European currencies, as a group, to fluctuate more widely with respect to the currencies of the rest of the industrialized world, which would not have such a severe impact on the European economies.

A snake wiggling in a tunnel was the progenitor of the European Currency Unit (ECU). The ECU is a "basket" currency made up of European Community currencies weighted in relation to the size of their economies. The ECU tends to be more stable than any of its individual currencies, making it a desirable currency for conducting business and financing companies. It is possible that the ECU might become the only currency in Europe, with the full implementation of the European Monetary System (EMS) later in the 1990s, if the Maastricht Treaty is approved by the member nations. The progression of the snake wiggling in a tunnel leading to the ECU as a single currency under the auspices of the

EMS manifests the desire of national governments to stabilize currency exchange rates with their major trading partners.

Whatever benefits accrue from stable currency exchange rates, the plain fact of the matter is that currency exchange rates have been anything but stable. Table 6.1, showing the highest exchange rate for the indicated year between a

Table 6.1
Highest Exchange Rate—U.S. Cents per Unit Foreign Currency

	AUSTRALIAN DOLLAR	CANADIAN DOLLAR	BRITISH POUND	FRENCH FRANC
1989	87.1	86.1	177.4	16.8
1985	81.5	75.5	144.5	13.0
1980	117.4	86.8	241.6	24.8
1975	135.9	100.5	241.8	25.0
1970	111.8	98.4	240.6	18.1

	SWISS FRANC	GERMAN MARK	JAPANESE YEN	S.AFRICA RAND
1989	64.0	57.5	0.79	49.9
1985	47.5	39.8	0.49	51.5
1980	62.7	58.0	0.48	133.2
1975	40.5	43.1	0.35	148.7
1970	23.3	27.5	0.28	139.8

currency and the U.S. dollar, was taken from the U.S. Statistical Abstract.

Interestingly, an adverse change in currency exchange rates need not be accompanied by an industrial retreat. The Midwest "rustbelt" in the United States was not caused by an adverse currency exchange rate change between the dollar and the yen. Quite the reverse, the Japanese yen appreciated with respect to the U.S. dollar. This means that U.S. firms had a clear pricing advantage in selling their goods in Japan. The aforementioned economic model would suggest that U.S. firms should have transformed Japan into a "rustbelt" if changing currency exchange rates were entirely responsible for shifts in the competitive position between nations.

However, the economic model did not include an effective ban of U.S. and other nation's manufactured goods in Japan, which may not have been purchased by Japanese consumers even if they were available. Another assumption violated in the model was the ability of Japanese manufacturers to improve their productivity, which reduced the cost of production, partly compensating for the appreciating yen. The model did not take into consideration the possibility of the Japanese being able to raise prices in terms of U.S. dollars and still gain market share because of a marked preference by U.S. consumers for higher quality Japanese goods.

QUOTING RATES

An American watching the financial news on television sees currencies reported as follows:

British pound	1.77
French franc	5.53
German mark	1.62
Japanese yen	127.70
Canadian dollar	0.84

This presentation of various currencies mixes two ways of quoting rates. A direct quote is made in terms of the number of domestic units for a foreign unit. An indirect quote is made in terms of the number of foreign units for a domestic unit. In the preceding example, the British pound and the Canadian dollar are direct quotes, where 1.77 U.S. dollars purchase 1 British pound and 0.84 U.S. dollars purchase 1 Canadian dollar. The French franc, German mark, and Japanese yen are indirect quotes, where 5.53 French francs, or 1.62 German marks, or 127.70 Japanese yen purchase 1 U.S. dollar. Currency exchange rates published in the *Wall Street Journal*, shown in Exhibit 6.1, are in terms of both direct (U.S. $ equivalent) and indirect (currency per U.S. dollar) quotes.

The South African rand has two quotes: a commercial and a financial rate. The central bank of South Africa examines requests for conversion of the South African rand into other currencies and divides these requests into three categories: commercial, financial, and all others. If a transaction is deemed commercial, the bank exchanges the South African rands at a rate of 2.8098 rands per U.S. dollar. If the transaction is deemed financial, the central bank of South Africa exchanges rands at a rate of 3.62 rands per U.S. dollar. Obviously, it is very important for a holder of South African rands to have a currency exchange transaction deemed commercial rather than financial because more U.S. dollars are received with the former classification than with the latter. If the transaction does not fall into either classification, the central bank of South Africa may not convert the currency. The holder of the currency has to exchange it by some other means. How he does it and what he receives for the rand is no longer a central bank, or official, transaction.

Multiple currency exchange rates are not unusual. In 1983, Venezuela had three official rates—4.3 bolivars per U.S. dollar for essential imports, 6 bolivars for nonessential imports, and 7 bolivars for other purposes. Multiple exchange rates open the door for corruption, as government officials are enticed to declare

Exhibit 6.1
Wall Street Journal Currency Trading Table

CURRENCY TRADING

EXCHANGE RATES

Thursday, February 13, 1992

The New York foreign exchange selling rates below apply to trading among banks in amounts of $1 million and more, as quoted at 3 p.m. Eastern time by Bankers Trust Co., Telerate Systems Inc. and other sources. Retail transactions provide fewer units of foreign currency per dollar.

Country	U.S. $ equiv. Thurs.	U.S. $ equiv. Wed.	Currency per U.S. $ Thurs.	Currency per U.S. $ Wed.
Argentina (Peso)	1.03	1.02	.97	.98
Australia (Dollar)	.7550	.7520	1.3245	1.3298
Austria (Schilling)	.08756	.08834	11.42	11.32
Bahrain (Dinar)	2.6525	2.6525	.3770	.3770
Belgium (Franc)	.02992	.03020	33.42	33.11
Brazil (Cruzeiro)	.00072	.00073	1392.44	1377.40
Britain (Pound)	1.7725	1.7875	.5642	.5594
30-Day Forward	1.7634	1.7777	.5671	.5625
90-Day Forward	1.7456	1.7602	.5729	.5681
180-Day Forward	1.7216	1.7350	.5809	.5764
Canada (Dollar)	.8432	.8464	1.1860	1.1815
30-Day Forward	.8408	.8442	1.1893	1.1846
90-Day Forward	.8366	.8398	1.1953	1.1907
180-Day Forward	.8306	.8339	1.2040	1.1993
Czechoslovakia (Koruna)				
Commercial rate	.0358295	.0359324	27.9100	27.8300
Chile (Peso)	.002970	.002965	336.73	337.22
China (Renminbi)	.183486	.183486	5.4500	5.4500
Colombia (Peso)	.001731	.001745	577.78	573.00
Denmark (Krone)	.1590	.1604	6.2875	6.2350
Ecuador (Sucre)				
Floating rate	.000763	.000763	1310.02	1310.02
Finland (Markka)	.22590	.22805	4.4267	4.3850
France (Franc)	.18093	.18259	5.5270	5.4768
30-Day Forward	.18006	.18164	5.5536	5.5053
90-Day Forward	.17829	.17990	5.6087	5.5587
180-Day Forward	.17591	.17742	5.6848	5.6363
Germany (Mark)	.6161	.6219	1.6230	1.6080
30-Day Forward	.6134	.6192	1.6302	1.6150
90-Day Forward	.6078	.6135	1.6452	1.6300
180-Day Forward	.6003	.6057	1.6659	1.6510
Greece (Drachma)	.005328	.005415	187.70	184.68
Hong Kong (Dollar) ...	.12894	.12894	7.7555	7.7555
Hungary (Forint)	.0131614	.0131614	75.9800	75.9800
India (Rupee)	.03874	.03874	25.81	25.81
Indonesia (Rupiah)	.0004995	.0004995	2002.00	2002.00
Ireland (Punt)	1.6433	1.6650	.6085	.6006

	Feb Thurs.	Mar Wed.	Jun Thurs.	Feb Thurs.	Mar Wed.	Jun
Israel (Shekel)	.4428	.4470		2.2583	2.2373	
Italy (Lira)	.0008201	.0008273		1219.36	1208.74	
Japan (Yen)	.007831	.007849		127.70	127.40	
30-Day Forward	.007822	.007839		127.85	127.56	
90-Day Forward	.007809	.007830		128.06	127.72	
180-Day Forward	.007801	.007809		128.20	128.07	
Jordan (Dinar)	1.4738	1.4738		.6785	.6785	
Kuwait (Dinar)	3.4358	3.4358		.2911	.2911	
Lebanon (Pound)	.001138	.001138		879.00	879.00	
Malaysia (Ringgit)	.3821	.3821		2.6170	2.6170	
Malta (Lira)	3.1949	3.1949		.3130	.3130	
Mexico (Peso)						
Floating rate	.0003267	.0003267		3061.01	3061.01	
Netherland (Guilder)	.5475	.5520		1.8264	1.8115	
New Zealand (Dollar)	.5415	.5400		1.8467	1.8519	
Norway (Krone)	.1572	.1586		6.3605	6.3033	
Pakistan (Rupee)	.0408	.0408		24.52	24.52	
Peru (New Sol)	1.0359	1.0521		.97	.95	
Philippines (Peso)	.03883	.03883		25.75	25.75	
Poland (Zloty)	.00009526	.00009526		10498.00	10498.00	
Portugal (Escudo)	.007288	.007280		137.21	137.36	
Saudi Arabia (Riyal) ..	.26667	.26667		3.7500	3.7500	
Singapore (Dollar)	.6101	.6124		1.6390	1.6330	
South Africa (Rand)						
Commercial rate	.3559	.3572		2.8098	2.7993	
Financial rate	.2762	.2832		3.6200	3.5310	
South Korea (Won)	.0013072	.0013072		765.00	765.00	
Spain (Peseta)	.009815	.009890		101.88	101.11	
Sweden (Krona)	.1697	.1712		5.8915	5.8395	
Switzerland (Franc) ..	.6859	.6942		1.4580	1.4405	
30-Day Forward	.6841	.6923		1.4619	1.4445	
90-Day Forward	.6806	.6885		1.4692	1.4523	
180-Day Forward	.6754	.6832		1.4805	1.4636	
Taiwan (Dollar)	.040469	.040404		24.71	24.75	
Thailand (Baht)	.03951	.03951		25.31	25.31	
Turkey (Lira)	.0001801	.0001817		5552.00	5505.00	
United Arab (Dirham)	.2723	.2723		3.6725	3.6725	
Uruguay (New Peso)						
Financial	.000395	.000395		2530.01	2530.01	
Venezuela (Bolivar)						
Floating rate	.01581	.01586		63.24	63.04	
SDR	1.39649	1.39655		.71608	.71605	
ECU	1.25950	1.27110		....	....	

Special Drawing Rights (SDR) are based on exchange rates for the U.S., German, British, French and Japanese currencies. Source: International Monetary Fund.

European Currency Unit (ECU) is based on a basket of community currencies.

Reprinted by permission of the *Wall Street Journal*, © 1993 Dow Jones & Company, Inc. All Rights Reserved Worldwide.

a diamond ring and a mink coat as essential imports in order for the purchaser to obtain a more favorable exchange rate. Multiple exchange rates are an administrative nightmare because a ruling is necessary for every transaction involving a foreign currency. Venezuela eventually abandoned all pretense of maintaining a fixed rate of exchange by letting the bolivar float against other currencies. The exchange rate quoted in the *Wall Street Journal* shows that the floating rate of exchange is 63.24 bolivars to the dollar. This means that the Venezuelan government does not support the exchange rate of the bolivar with other currencies by intervening in the currency exchange market. The value of the Venezuelan bolivar is determined by the relationship between the supply and the demand for the currency—an example of a clean float.

The Mexican peso was fixed at 8.65 pesos for one U.S. dollar for a generation. In April 1954, the peso was devalued to 12.5 pesos to the dollar, which held until 1971 when the central bank of Mexico ran out of dollars to maintain the official rate of exchange. The Mexican peso began to float against the U.S. dollar. The rate between the peso and the dollar floats "cleanly" in response to the laws of supply and demand at more than 3,000 pesos to the dollar. Both the Venezuelan bolivar and the Mexican peso are considered "soft" currencies, where people have little, or no, faith in the currency as a storehouse of value. Any currency left over from spending on goods and services is not placed in a bank savings account or kept in a drawer, but is either invested in tangibles (land, inventory) or exchanged for stronger currencies. In essence, these currencies have been repudiated by the people.

The U.S. dollar has undergone a significant revaluation with respect to the Venezuelan bolivar and the Mexican peso. Venezuelans and Mexicans who switched their holdings to U.S. dollars have done much better in maintaining the purchasing power of their cash reserves than those who steadfastly held on to bolivars and pesos. Although fleeing from a currency is understandable, it does not help the economic development of a nation because unspent currency, in the form of savings, is no longer available as a source of funds to support trade and commerce.

The currency of Chile is listed at the official rate of 336.73. The day before, the official rate was 337.22 pesos per dollar. Because it requires fewer pesos on the given day to buy one U.S. dollar than on the prior day, the official rate of the currency is being revalued. The real question is to what degree is the central bank of Chile permitting the exchange of its currency with dollars at the official rate. It is possible that the official rate may simply be a quoted rate without any underlying transactions. If that is the case, then the true exchange rate is being established in the back alleys of Chilean marketplace, where there is a clean float determined by the supply of, and the demand for, a currency.

Most rates are not listed as floating or official rates, such as the Austrian schilling at 11.42 per U.S. dollar. This implies that there is intervention by the central bank to maintain a predetermined relationship between the schilling, the dollar, and other currencies, a so-called dirty float. It is possible that the Austrian central bank is primarily concerned with the relationship between the schilling and the deutschemark. If so, then the exchange rate between the schilling and the U.S. dollar is established indirectly. The rate between the schilling and the deutschemark and the rate between the dollar and the deutschemark establishes the rate between the schilling and the dollar.

Lastly, the *Wall Street Journal* Currency Trading table publishes exchange rates for two "basket" currencies—Special Drawing Rights and the European Currency Unit. SDRs is a basket of U.S., German, British, French, and Japanese currencies, whereas ECUs, as previously mentioned, is a basket of European Community currencies. Since the currencies making up SDRs and ECUs are exchangeable for U.S. dollars at published rates, the value of an SDR and an

ECU can be calculated in terms of U.S. dollars. Once expressed in dollars, an SDR and an ECU can be valued in terms of other currencies. SDRs and ECUs are quoted in the financial press because some transactions are denominated in basket currencies. Companies have financed their operations with ECU-denominated bonds and ships passing through the Suez Canal pay tolls in SDRs.

The published quotes are for conversion of $1 million or more of one currency to another. The "retail" market handles currency exchanges for smaller amounts where the quotes may differ from those published in the financial press. Tourists rely on the retail market where exchange rates tend to be less favorable than the quoted rates, and may even be negotiable. Two rates are usually quoted to a prospective customer such as $1.80/$1.95 for a British pound. This means that the retail trader is willing to buy a British pound for $1.80 and sell a British pound for $1.95. The difference, or spread, in the rates is the retailer's profit margin.

CROSS RATES

The rates published by the financial press in this country are in terms of U.S. dollars. These can be used to develop "cross rates" between two currencies by removing the U.S. dollar from the equation. For instance, the German mark, or deutschemark (DM), is quoted at 1.623 per U.S. dollar and the Swiss franc (SF) is quoted at 1.458 per U.S. dollar. For dealings between German and Swiss companies, the appropriate German mark/Swiss franc exchange rate can be calculated by dividing 1.623 DM per U.S. dollar by 1.458 SF per U.S. dollar for a cross rate of 1.113 DM per SF. In European currency markets, cross rates are usually in terms of direct quotes, but sometimes the liquidity of the dollar market is such that it is easier to exchange two currencies in a two-step process where one currency is exchanged for dollars and the dollars are then exchanged for the other.

FORWARD RATES

The rates quoted in the *Wall Street Journal* are for delivery within 2 business days. A few nations have quotes for forward rates—Britain, Canada, France, Germany, Japan, and Switzerland. These are "hard" currencies, where individuals or banks are willing to quote a rate where the delivery is not in 2 days, but in 30, 90, or 180 days. The forward quotes are not the same as spot quotes, but represent the belief on the part of currency traders and investors as to what spot rates will be when the currency is "delivered" to the buyer in the future.

From the *Wall Street Journal* listing, the spot rate for the British pound is $1.7725 and the 180-day forward rate is $1.7216. Those quoting the 180-day forward rate are expecting the spot rate of the British pound to decline by $0.0509 over the next six months. The annualized rate of decline can be calculated from the following formula where N is the number of months of the forward contract.

$$\frac{\text{NEW RATE} - \text{OLD RATE}}{\text{OLD RATE}} \times \frac{12}{N} \times 100$$

$$\frac{1.7216 - 1.7725}{1.7725} \times \frac{12}{6} \times 100$$

$$\frac{-0.0509}{1.7725} \times 2 \times 100$$

$$-0.0287 \times 2 \times 100 = -5.743\%$$

The forward rate contains an implied forecast of an annualized decline of -5.7 percent in the exchange rate between the British pound and the U.S. dollar. Those quoting a forward rate between two currencies have implicitly considered the relative rates of inflation, trade imbalances and interest rate differentials, and central bank reserve positions. Past trends in the exchange rate between the two currencies play an important part in the process of setting forward rates. Facts can only provide guidance on what is the appropriate rate for forward delivery of a currency. Although there is data available for past and current inflation and interest rates, and on the past balance of trade and bank reserves, what is more pertinent are changes to these economic and financial measures and how they impact on the future relationship between two currencies. Moreover, one has to guess at how much of central bank reserves might be committed, and how eager the central bankers are in defending against a devaluation of a currency or in fending off a revaluation.

Internal events, such as the outcome of an election, can change currency exchange rates. External events also have a bearing on exchange rates. The United Kingdom and Norway are oil exporters from crude produced in the North Sea. The British pound and the Norwegian krona have at times been called petro-currencies because of shifts in the balance of payments in the United Kingdom and Norway induced by changes in oil prices. Currency relationships are also influenced by changing economic developments between nations. The value of a currency must ultimately be linked to the political and economic health of a nation and the relative growth of its industrial base with respect to other nations. Both Germany and Japan emerged shattered from World War II only to successfully challenge the industrial supremacy of Great Britain and the United States in succeeding decades. Switzerland exercises more fiscal restraint than Great Britain and the United States by running its government operations without enormous budget deficits. There are sound economic reasons why there has been a long-term trend of an appreciating deutschemark, yen, and Swiss franc in relation to the British pound and the U.S. dollar. Forecasting the future direction of one currency with respect to another is both an art and a science. It is an unavoidable exercise for those who are willing to commit themselves to a future delivery of currency in the form of a forward contract.

DEVELOPING FORWARD CONTRACT QUOTES

Although there is no organized forward market for the Brazilian cruziero, suppose, for purposes of illustration, that an individual, or some institution, felt that the Brazilian cruziero would depreciate by 20 percent over some period of time, and was willing to quote a contract for forward delivery. If such a person existed, his calculation to determine the forward rate, with a current spot rate of 1,392.44 to the U.S. dollar, would be as follows:

$$\frac{\text{OLD RATE} - \text{NEW RATE}}{\text{NEW RATE}} = \frac{1,392.44 - x}{x} = -0.20$$

$$1,392.44 - x = -.20x \quad \text{or} \quad 1392.44 = 0.80x \quad \text{or} \quad x = 1,740.55$$

If an individual, or a collection of individuals and companies making up a market, anticipated a 20 percent devaluation of the Brazilian cruziero in relation to the U.S. dollar over the period of a forward contract when the spot rate was 1,392.44 cruzieros to the U.S. dollar, they would quote a forward contract at 1,740.55 cruzieros to the U.S. dollar. As a counter example, if the Swiss franc was expected to be revalued by 5 percent over the period of a forward contract with respect to the U.S. dollar, and had a current spot rate of 1.4580 Swiss francs to the U.S. dollar, then the forward contract would be calculated as follows:

$$\frac{\text{OLD RATE} - \text{NEW RATE}}{\text{NEW RATE}} = \frac{1.4580 - x}{x} = 0.05$$

$$1.4580 - x = 0.05x \quad \text{or} \quad 1.4580 = 1.05x \quad \text{or} \quad x = 1.3886$$

The spot rate of 1.4580 Swiss francs to the U.S. dollar and the forward rate of 1.3886 Swiss francs to the U.S. dollar anticipates a 5 percent revaluation between the Swiss franc and the U.S. dollar over the contract period. Cross rates would be more applicable for direct dealings between firms in Brazil and in Switzerland. The cross rate for the spot market between the cruziero and the Swiss franc is 1,392.44 cruzieros to the dollar divided by 1.4580 Swiss francs to the dollar or 955.03 cruzieros to the Swiss franc. The cross rate for the forward contract between the two currencies is 1,740.55 cruzieros to the dollar divided by 1.3886 Swiss francs to the dollar or 1,253.5 cruzieros to the Swiss franc. The spot and forward cross rate quotes do not reference the U.S. dollar, although the dollar is the reference currency for measuring the relative degree of devaluation and revaluation between the two currencies.

ROLE OF ARBITRAGERS

The presence of various money centers gives rise to various quotes for different currencies depending on the balance between buyers and sellers at each money center. Suppose that there are active centers of currency exchange in New York, Frankfurt, and Zurich where the following exchange rates are being quoted.

	$/DM	$/SF	DM/SF
New York	0.6161	0.6859	—
Frankfurt	—	0.6932	1.1133
Zurich	0.6204	—	1.1202

The New York market has individuals willing to buy German marks and Swiss francs for dollars, but there are no individuals interested in exchanging francs for marks or marks for francs. Therefore, there is no quote for this transaction. Suppose, for purposes of illustration, that individuals in Frankfurt are not interested in exchanging German marks and dollars, but are willing to exchange Swiss francs for dollars and marks. There is no quote available for the former transaction, but there are quotes for the latter transactions. A comparable situation holds for Zurich. These quotes reflect an active market of those interested in buying and selling the respective currencies for commercial purposes. An individual with no commercial interest in dollars, marks, and francs can examine these rates and play a "what if" game. What if 1,000 marks are sold in Zurich for dollars and the dollars are then exchanged for marks in New York?

Step 1—sell marks in Zurich for dollars.

$$DM\ 1,000 \times 0.6204\ \$/DM = \$620.40$$

Step 2—sell dollars in New York for marks.

$$\$620.40 \times 1/0.6161\ \$/DM = DM\ 1,006.98$$

Ignoring fees associated with these transactions, an individual can set up a round robin of selling marks in Zurich for dollars and buying marks for dollars in New York and make a 0.7% return on every round. Before doing this, he might want to play another what if game. What if marks are sold for Swiss francs in Zurich and the Swiss francs are then sold in Frankfurt for marks?

Step 1—sell marks in Zurich for Swiss francs

$$DM\ 1,000\ divided\ by\ 1.1202\ DM/SF = SF\ 892.70$$

Step 2—sell SF in Frankfurt for DM

$$\text{SF } 892.70 \times 1.1133 \text{ DM/SF} = \text{DM } 993.84$$

The trader, in this instance, would not enter into this last transaction, because it generates a loss. A profit would result if the nature of the transaction was reversed. Be that as it may, the three markets afford a large number of alternatives to play what if, including those with a greater degree of complexity. The best alternative for making money by taking advantage of disparities in currency exchange quotes between markets can be identified by examining every combination of trades.

An arbitrager is an individual who examines the rates of exchange in various markets seeking out those combinations of trades on which he or she can earn a profit. His or her purpose in the market is not to trade currencies to complete a commercial transaction, but to profit from price disparities between markets. As there are many markets, and many currencies, computers can be programmed to monitor exchange rate quotes on a real time basis, to identify those combinations of currency exchange trades that can be profitably executed net of trading costs. Naturally, such a painless way of making a living is going to attract a number of eager participants. The presence of arbitragers continually seeking currency exchange rate disparities and taking advantage of these disparities is vital in ensuring that every market consistently prices its exchange rates with others. Whenever disparities appear, the "arbs" will place orders to take advantage of the situation and will continue to do so until the disparity disappears. Arbs keep currency markets "in sync" with one another.

ACCOUNTING ASPECTS OF MULTIPLE CURRENCIES

There are two separate issues regarding accounting associated with multiple currencies: transactions and translations. Transactions are associated with the buying and selling of goods involving multiple currencies. An international transaction that is denominated in terms of a domestic currency does not differ, from an accounting viewpoint, from a domestic transaction. If a U.S. firm sells an item to a consumer in France and receives U.S. dollars in payment, the accounting for the transaction does not differ from selling the item to a consumer in Kansas. A currency transaction would result if the French buyer paid for the goods in francs. Translations, on the other hand, are part of the consolidation process whereby balance sheets and income statements expressed in nondomestic currencies are consolidated into a single financial report in the domestic currency.

TRANSACTIONS

Three dates are important in accounting for transactions that involve a currency, or currencies, other than the domestic currency. One is the date that a transaction was initiated by the rendering of service or the shipping of goods. The second is the settlement date when payment is made. The third is any interim reporting date for accounting purposes. For example, a U.S. company buys goods valued at 1,000 Canadian dollars from a Canadian manufacturer on 15 December. The goods are received with payment due on 31 January. An interim financial reporting date is 31 December. Each of these three dates may have a different exchange rate between the U.S. and Canadian dollars. Suppose that the Canadian dollar was worth $0.84 on 15 December, $0.86 on 31 December, and $0.88 on 31 January. The initial transaction of 1,000 Canadian dollars was recorded at $840 on 15 December when the order was placed, $860 on 31 December for financial reporting purposes, and $880 on 31 January when the payment was made. Three different liabilities are now associated with a single transaction. There are two accounting methodologies for handling this situation—the one- and two-transactions views.

One-Transaction View

The one-transaction view takes the position that the financial impact of exchange rate changes should simply be charged or credited against the purchase price of the goods or the receipt of a sale. The initial accounting record is considered temporary because the ultimate exchange rate in effect on payment or receipt of funds is not known at the time the transaction was initiated. In this example of buying goods for 1,000 Canadian dollars, the initial entry on 15 December would be $840 both for goods purchased and for accounts payable. Both these accounts would be increased to $860 on 31 December, and to $880 on 31 January, reflecting changes in the exchange rate between the U.S. and Canadian dollar.

The initial accounting records are temporary in the one-transaction view. The entry made on 31 January finalizes the accounting treatment of this transaction. The ordering of the goods and the subsequent changes to the exchange rates are handled as a single item. Although the one-transaction view is simple in its administration, currency exchange gains or losses are not explicitly recognized, because they are hidden by making direct adjustments to accounts receivable or payable. Financial reports incorporating the one-transaction view do not permit the reader to judge the management of a company with regard to their handling of currency exchange risk.

Two-Transactions View

Whereas the one-transaction view hides currency exchange losses by direct adjustments to accounts receivable or payable, the two-transactions view separates the currency exchange portion of the transaction from the transaction itself and views both as separate events. The cost of goods purchased is locked into the accounting records at the exchange rate on the initial transaction date. Subsequent changes to the exchange rate are separately handled as currency exchange gains or losses. The appropriate journal entries for the previously described transaction follow. Note that "foreign" exchange is used rather than "currency" exchange in the captions in agreement with Financial Accounting Standards Board (FASB) terminology. The desired goal of global business is to eliminate the words "domestic" and "foreign," but it is not clear what words would differentiate between "domestic" and "nondomestic" or "foreign" currencies when such differentiation is necessary.

15 December	Purchase of goods	$840	
	Accounts payable		$840
	1000 Can $ at $0.84		

31 December	Loss on Foreign Exchange	20	
	Accounts Payable		20
	1000 Can $ at ($0.86-0.84)		

31 January	Loss on Foreign Exchange	20	
	Accounts Payable	860	
	Cash		880
	1000 Can $ at $0.88		

The purchased goods remain at $840 in the two transaction view regardless of subsequent changes in currency exchange rates. In this case, the $40 increase in the cost of these goods is recorded as a currency exchange loss apportioned over two accounting periods. The first is at the end of the current accounting period on 31 December where the actual currency exchange loss is $20. The second reported loss, coincidentally another $20, is reported at the end of the succeeding accounting period. An alternative accounting treatment when the amounts are immaterial, which is less frequently employed, is to defer transaction gains or losses from one accounting period to the next until they are finally determined.

Had the Canadian dollar lost value in relation to the U.S. dollar with a value of $0.81 on 31 December and $0.77 on 31 January, the accounting for the transaction would have resulted in the following currency exchange gain.

15 December	Purchase of goods	$840	
	Accounts payable		$840
	1000 Can $ at $0.84		

31 December	Accounts Payable	30	
	Gain on Foreign Exchange		30
	1000 Can $ at ($0.84-0.81)		

31 January	Accounts Payable	810	
	Gain on Foreign Exchange		40
	Cash		770
	1000 Can $ at $0.77		

Transaction Aspects of FASB 8 and 52

The United States has long been a leader in accounting for currency exchange gains or losses. Most nations, in adopting such standards, look to the United States for its handling of currency exchange gains and losses as a reference point in their deliberations on setting accounting standards. Prior to 1975, U.S. accountants could choose between the one- or two-transaction views when dealing with currency exchange fluctuations. In 1975, FASB 8, "Accounting for the Translation of Foreign Currency Transactions and Foreign Currency Financial Statements," required the use of the two-transactions view. FASB 8 stipulates international transactions denominated in a foreign currency be translated into dollars at the exchange rate prevailing on the transaction date. Thereafter, foreign currency receivables and payables are "marked to the market" at the end of subsequent accounting periods with currency exchange gains or losses flowing through net income.

In 1981, FASB 52 introduced changes in accounting for foreign currency translations, but the aforementioned FASB 8 provisions for accounting for foreign currency transactions were not changed. However, FASB 52 permitted currency gains and losses for transactions denominated in foreign currencies to be deferred if the company insulates itself from the risk of exchange fluctuations by entering into a forward or futures contract. The forward or futures contract must be tailored to satisfy a specific commercial transaction in order to avoid currency exchange gains and losses flowing through income.

A forward or futures contract is an agreement between two parties who wish to exchange a certain amount of one currency for another at a prescribed date in the future. The words "forwards" and "futures" are frequently used interchangeably. Technically, two parties tailor the details of the forward contract to suit their needs. A futures contract differs from a forward contract in that a futures contract has standardized terms, requires margin deposits, and is traded on organized exchanges. The principal difference between the two is that a futures contract can be more readily traded or liquidated, whereas a forward contract has less liquidity because it is usually tailored to fit a given situation. Regardless of the semantic differences between forwards and futures, the accounting treatment is the same.

ACCOUNTING FOR FORWARD CONTRACTS IN HEDGING

Forward contracts have proven to be very useful in hedging against currency exchange risks. The effective cost of goods increased from $840 to $880 in the previous case of purchasing goods with Canadian dollars because of an adverse change in currency exchange rates when the Canadian dollar appreciated in value with respect to the U.S. dollar. Forward contracts can fix the value of an outstanding receivable or payable whose date of receipt, or payment, is in the future and neutralize the risk of loss from an adverse change in currency exchange rates.

The following illustrates both the use and the accounting treatment of forward contracts to fix the value of an outstanding payable. Suppose that the U.S. buyer of the Canadian goods also purchased a forward contract for 1,000 Canadian dollars on the day of buying the goods (15 December). Suppose that the spot rate on 15 December was $0.84 for a Canadian dollar and the forward contract rate for delivery on 31 January was $0.85. The purchase of the forward contract for the amount of 1,000 Canadian dollars satisfies the criteria associated with FASB 52 that the foreign currency commitment be firm and that the forward contract be specifically designated to a particular foreign currency transaction.

The following journal entries of 15 December are associated with a straight purchase of goods for 1,000 Canadian dollars and with the hedge associated with the forward contract.

```
      PURCHASE OF GOODS                    HEDGE

12/15 Purchases        $840   12/15 Can $ Receivable    $840
        Accounts Payable $840         Premium on Forward    10
      (Can $ @ 0.84)                    Accounts Payable      $850
                                       (Spot .84, Fwd .85)
```

These entries record the purchase of the goods, the resulting liability to the supplier, and the company entering into a hedge agreement to receive $1,000 Canadian dollars on 31 January.

```
12/31 Loss on Foreign         12/31 Premium Expense  $3.40
        Exchange      $20            Premium on
        Accounts Payable  $20          Forward            $3.40
      (Spot .84 to .86)
                                    Canadian $
                                      receivable      20
                                      Gain on
                                        Foreign Exchange  20
                                      (Spot .84 to .86)
```

The Canadian dollar appreciated in value to $0.86 and the company records the resulting loss of $20 and increases the amount owed to the supplier by $20. The company also amortizes the premium based the number of days that have elapsed. The premium of $10 represents the difference between the spot and futures rate on 15 December. There are sixteen days left in December and thirty-one days in January for a total of forty-seven days. The sixteen days of December represents 34 percent of the total time, which supports amortizing 34 percent of the premium, or $3.40. The gain in the value of the Canadian dollar receivable of $20 is also recognized. The hedge is working because the loss on currency exchange of the liability to the manufacturer is exactly offset by the gain on currency exchange related to the hedge.

On 31 January, the following journal entries close out the transaction.

```
1/31 (a) Loss on Foreign              1/31 (b) Canadian $
         Exchange (FX)    20                   Receivable      20
         Accounts Payable 860                  Gain on Foreign
         Cash                  880             Exchange              20
                                           (Spot .86 to .88)

                                      (c) Premium Expense    6.60
                                             Premium on
                                                Forward            6.60

                                      (d) Accounts Payable 850
                                             Cash                  850


                                      (e) Investment in
                                             Canadian $     880
                                             Canadian $
                                                Receivable         880

                                      (f) Cash            880
                                             Investment in
                                                Canadian $         880
```

(a) The company pays the manufacturer 1,000 Canadian dollars, which are trading at a spot rate of $0.88 on 31 January, resulting in an additional loss of $20.

(b) The company records a gain of $20 on the Canadian dollar receivable because the spot rate has risen to $0.88.

(c) The remaining premium on the contract is amortized as it has matured.

(d) The company pays $850 to the other party of the forward contract as agreed on 15 December.

(e) In exchange, the company receives 1,000 Canadian dollars from the other party of the forward contract and records the proceeds at $0.88, the spot rate on 31 January.

(f) Finally, the company sells the 1,000 Canadian dollars at the current spot rate of $0.88.

The overall effect of the hedge follows.

	PURCHASE OF GOODS	HEDGE		COMBINED
Asset Purchase	$840			$840
FX Loss	40	FX Gain	($40)	–
		Prem Expense	10	10
Cash Paid	880		(30)	850

The foreign exchange (FX) loss has been neutralized for a cost of $10, which preserved the purchase price of $840. If the forward contract had not been purchased, or if the conditions surrounding the purchase of a forward contract set forth in FASB 52 were not satisfied, the foreign exchange loss would have flowed through income. Foreign exchange gains and losses affecting the income of a company are not looked on with favor by financial managers. Currency exchange gains and losses become ''wild cards'' that can upset a financial forecast and influence corporate planning activities.

In the above example, the hedge provided protection against a currency loss that would have occurred because the Canadian dollar appreciated, or increased, in value. Had the hedge been in effect and had the Canadian dollar depreciated in value to $0.81 on 31 December and to $0.79 on 31 January, the outcome would have been as follows.

```
12/15 Purchases      $840        12/15 Can $ Receivable   $840
      Accounts Payable  $840           Premium on Forward    10
      (Can $ @ 0.84)                     Accounts Payable        $850
                                        (Spot .84, Fwd .85)
```

These entries record the purchase of the goods, the liability to the supplier, and the fact that the company has entered into a hedging agreement to receive 1,000 Canadian dollars on 31 January.

```
12/31 Accounts                  12/31 Premium Expense      3.40

      Payable        30               Premium on Forward      3.40
      Gain on                         Loss on Foreign
      Foreign                         Exchange          30
      Exchange          30             Canadian $
      (Spot 0.84 to 0.81)              Receivable              30
```

The Canadian dollar has depreciated to $0.81 and the company records the resulting gain of $30 and decreases the amount due to the supplier by $30. The company amortizes the cost of the premium based on the number of days that have elapsed as previously described. The value of the Canadian dollar receivable has decreased by $30, and the loss is recognized. The gain on foreign exchange relating to the liability of the manufacturer is exactly offset by the loss on foreign exchange related to the hedge.

```
1/31 (a)Accounts Payable 810    1/31 (b) Loss on Foreign
        Cash             790             Exchange      20
        Gain on Foreign                   Canadian $
        Exchange          20               Receivable        20
                                         (Spot .81 to .79)

                                    (c) Premium Expense   6.60
                                         Premium on
                                          Forward             6.60

                                    (d) Accounts Payable 850
                                          Cash               850

                                    (e) Investment in
                                          Canadian $      790
                                          Canadian $
                                          Receivable         790

                                    (f) Cash            790
                                          Investment in
                                          Canadian $         790
```

(a) The company pays the manufacturer 1,000 Canadian dollars, which are trading at a spot rate of $0.79 on 31 January, resulting in an additional gain of $20.

(b) The company records a loss of $20 on the Canadian dollar receivable because the spot rate has fallen to $0.79.

(c) The remaining premium on the contract is amortized.

(d) The company pays $850 to the other party of the forward contract as agreed on 15 December.

(e) In exchange, the company receives 1,000 Canadian dollars from the other party to the forward contract and records the proceeds at $0.79, the spot rate on 31 January.

(f) Finally, the company sells the 1,000 Canadian dollars at the current spot rate of $0.79.

The overall effect of the hedge follows.

	PURCHASE OF GOODS	HEDGE		COMBINED
Asset Purchase	$840			$840
FX Gain	(50)	FX Loss	$50	–
		Prem Expense	10	10
Cash Paid	790		60	850

In this case, where the Canadian dollar depreciated, the cost of goods remains at $840, but the purchase of the forward contract for $10 prevents the company from enjoying a foreign exchange gain of $50. This would have reduced the liability to the manufacturer to $790. The hedge worked in the sense of fixing the cost of goods at $840, but at the cost of giving up the currency exchange gain.

To recap the first example, on December 15 a liability of 1,000 Canadian dollars was booked at the current spot rate of $0.84 resulting in a total liability of $840. At that time, management believed that the Canadian dollar was likely to appreciate in value during the next six weeks. This would have caused the liability to the manufacturer to increase from a currency exchange fluctuation. To guard against this, management entered into a hedge, agreeing to purchase Canadian dollars at $0.85 on 31 January. This resulted in a cost to the company of $10 (0.01 × $1,000). This limited the company's downside exposure to $10 if there were an adverse change in currency exchange rates, which, in this case, would occur if the Canadian dollar appreciated in value during the six-week life of the contract. The hedge worked when the Canadian dollar appreciated because the company was protected from a currency exchange loss.

In the second example, when the Canadian dollar depreciated, the company did not enjoy the gain associated with a lessening liability because the gain was offset by a currency exchange loss related to the hedge. The company had, in effect, foregone a currency exchange profit to protect itself from a currency exchange loss. One might maintain that the true cost of the hedge to protect against an adverse change in currency exchange rates is the premium for the hedge plus the opportunity foregone for a currency exchange gain.

ACCOUNTING FOR SPECULATIVE FORWARD CONTRACTS

In the foregoing example, a forward contract was purchased for the purpose of hedging a specific commercial transaction. If the conditions surrounding the purchase of a forward contract do not meet the stipulations contained in FASB 52 for being considered a hedge, then the purchase of the forward contract is treated as a speculation. According to FASB 52, a speculative position is taken when the forward or futures contract is not associated with a specified commercial transaction. The rules that now apply stipulate that the premium or discount associated with the forward contract be ignored when initially recording the contract. At the end of each succeeding accounting period, the value of the contract is "marked to market" by reference to the applicable forward rate, and any resulting gain or loss flows through income.

Suppose that the deutschemark has the spot and forward values on the indicated dates shown in Table 6.2. Only those forward contracts for delivery at the end of October have been included in the table. Note that 29 October is exactly ninety days from 1 August.

Table 6.2
Deutschemark Spot and Forward Values

	SPOT RATE	90 DAY F'WARD	60 DAY F'WARD	30 DAY F'WARD
August 1	$0.6161	$0.6078		
August 31	0.6197		$0.6211	
September 30	0.6210			$0.6217
October 29	0.6155			

The financial market expects the DM to appreciate in value, which can be seen by comparing the forward rate with the spot rate. The financial officer, for any number of reasons, feels that it is in the company's interest to purchase a forward contract. However, he does not have a specific commercial transaction in mind when purchasing the forward contract. In accordance with FASB 52, the currency exchange position is treated as speculative in nature. On August 1, a 90-day forward contract is purchased to buy one million DM for $0.6078 per DM for a total contract cost of $607,800. The initial journal entry follows.

August 1 Contract Receivable (DM)	$607,800	
Contract Payable ($)		$607,800

Thirty days later at the end of August, the next monthly accounting period, the forward contract is examined for any gains or losses, which must be immediately applied to income. The applicable forward contract to judge the original 90-day contract is a 60-day contract that expires at the same time. The 60-day forward contract is quoted at $0.6211 per DM.

```
August 31 Contract Receivable (DM)              13,300
          Gain on contract                                  13,300
          (0.6211-0.6078) X DM 1 MM
```

At the end of September, the original futures contract can now be best matched with a 30-day futures contract, which is quoted at $0.6217 per DM.

```
Sept 30 Contract Receivable (DM)                 600
         Gain on contract                                    600
         (0.6217-0.6211) X DM 1 MM
```

On October 29, the forward contract is delivered, and the transaction is wrapped up with the following journal entries.

```
Oct 29  Contract payable                        607,800
        Cash                                               607,800

        Dollar Value of DM                      615,500
        (spot on 10/29)
        Loss on Contract                          6,200
        Contract receivable                                621,700
```

On October 29, the dollar value of the receipt of DM 1 million is determined by the current spot rate and is recorded as $615,500. The contract receivable was originally recorded on August 1 as $607,800, then was increased by $13,300 on August 31 and again by $600 on September 30 as forward rates changed. These gains were added to the company's income at these times. At the maturity date of the contract, a loss of $6,200 was generated and was recognized as such in the company's monthly income.

Summing up, if a forward or futures commitment does not meet the requirements of a hedge, both the forward or futures contract exchange rate and the amounts due to the broker are initially recorded at the forward rate. Neither the premium nor the discount is separately reported. Transaction gains and losses are measured by the difference between the forward rate in the contract and the forward rate for a comparable forward for the period remaining until settlement. Any resulting currency gains or losses flow immediately through income.

This accounting treatment of "marking to market" differs radically from that accorded to hedges. Forward exchange contracts that are classified as hedges are initially recorded using the current spot rate and the premium or discount is amortized over the life of the forward contract. Transaction gains or losses are keyed to changes in the spot rate with no currency gain or loss flowing through income. The same forward contract classified as a speculation is initially recorded using the forward rate, and is marked to market using comparable forwards with regard to time to maturity. Transaction gains and losses flow through income because, unlike a hedge, there is no offsetting change in valuation of an associated asset or liability.

In the United States, the Financial Accounting Standards Board requires that currency exchange gains and losses that are not hedged be treated as normal operating items for inclusion in income. In many other countries, gains and losses from foreign currency receivables and payables are not recognized until the transactions are finalized. There are no interim mark-to-market currency exchange gains and losses affecting income. Even then, there are a number of countries that do not require the explicit recording of such gains or losses in the income statement. Adjustments are made directly to the related asset or liability accounts as described under the one transaction view. Therefore, readers of the financial statements do not "see" currency exchange gains and losses because they are embedded in line items in a balance sheet, nor can they judge management performance in handling currency exchange risk.

TRANSLATION

Translation is the process whereby a financial report of a branch, affiliate, or subsidiary in one country is expressed in the currency of the parent company for financial reporting purposes. Three translations may be required for financial statements prepared by local accountants whose language, accounting practice, and currency are different from the nation of domicile of the parent company. The language translation is relatively straightforward. The accounting standard translation is handled line by line with suitable adjustments to take into consideration differences in accounting practices between the two nations.

Several issues must first be resolved before the third, or the currency, translation can be performed. They are the selection of the appropriate currency exchange rates, the choice of which exchange rate applies in the translation of each line item of a financial report, and the accounting treatment for translation gains and losses arising from using different exchange rates.

Three currency exchange rates are common in the translation process: the current, historic, and average rates. The current rate is the currency exchange rate at the end of the accounting period. The historic rate is the currency exchange rate in effect when a transaction took place. The average currency exchange rate is a single rate that applies for the accounting period, which may be a month, a quarter, or a year.

Suppose that a factory was built when the exchange rate between the U.S. dollar and the British pound was $1.90 and the exchange rate at the beginning of the accounting year was $1.50 and $1.60 at the end. The current exchange rate is $1.60, the historic exchange rate associated with the fixed asset is $1.90, and the average exchange rate for the year $1.55. The average exchange rate may not be exactly $1.55 if the averaging process is performed on a quarterly, monthly, or some other basis.

A number of methods, briefly summarized below, have been associated with currency translation of financial statements.

Current-Noncurrent Method

The essence of the current-noncurrent method is that all items that are easily convertible to cash, or are to be paid out or be paid within a year, are translated at the current exchange rate. Balance sheet items classified as current assets and liabilities are translated at the current rate and the remaining items are translated at the appropriate historic exchange rate. This method was widely employed until 1975.

Monetary-Nonmonetary Method

This method examines the nature of each element of a financial statement to be translated into the reporting currency. Monetary items are those financial assets and liabilities that can be expressed in currency units such as cash, receivables, and payables. Any item on a balance sheet not given a monetary classification is then considered nonmonetary. The principal nonmonetary items are inventories and fixed assets. One major difference between this model and the current-noncurrent model is the treatment of inventories.

Inventories can be divided into three categories. One is raw materials and components inventory that is first transformed into semifinished goods, or in-process inventory, by a manufacturing process before becoming finished goods inventory. Generally speaking, cost of goods sold is translated at the current rate under the current-noncurrent method and at the historic rate under the monetary-nonmonetary method. The former method translates the cost of raw materials and components consumed in the manufacturing process at the exchange rate applicable when they were transformed into finished goods. The latter method translates the cost of raw materials and components consumed in the manufacturing process when they were acquired.

Temporal Method and FASB 8

During the 1950s and early 1960s, neither the level of international trade nor the ownership of operating affiliates in other nations was a major factor in corporate America. The method of translation was not a significant accounting issue, particularly when most currency exchange rates were fixed and changes in exchange rates were infrequent. The issue of standardization of the methodology of translating financial reports for consolidation purposes for American-based multinational corporations was addressed in 1965 when the Accounting Principles Board suggested that the monetary-nonmonetary method be preferred for translating financial statements. However, companies were free to select their preferred methodology. The most common choice was the current-noncurrent method, but it was not the dominant methodology. Some companies selected the modified current-noncurrent method where long-term receivables and payables were translated at the current, rather than the historic, rate. Other companies used the monetary-nonmonetary approach in its pure form or in a modified form where inventories were translated at the current rather than the historic rate. A few companies preferred the temporal method, which, with some minor differences, is the same as the monetary-nonmonetary method, and others relied on the current rate method.

There was a striking lack of consistency in translating financial statements after the suggestion of a preferred method by the Accounting Principles Board. In 1975, the issuance of FASB 8, "Accounting for the Translation of Foreign Currency Transactions and Foreign Currency Financial Statements," was the first comprehensive accounting standard dealing with nondomestic operations of American companies including importing, exporting, foreign borrowing and lending, forward contracts, and translations of foreign affiliate financial statements for the equity and full methods of consolidation. FASB 8 stipulated that the foreign financial statements must first be recast to conform to American generally accepted accounting principles (GAAP) and then be translated into U.S. dollars using the temporal method. Any currency gains and losses from translation flowed through income.

FASB 8 was a contentious accounting document. American firms were restricted to one particular model for translating financial reports to U.S. dollars. The requirement that inventory be translated at historic, rather than current, rates, which was the prevalent choice, meant that record-keeping activities had to be expanded to keep track of the currency exchange rate at the time of each inventory purchase. Many objected to the fact that accounts payable, which often arose from the acquisition of inventory, was to be translated at the current rate, whereas the items that gave rise to the accounts payable, additions to inventory, were being translated at the historic rate. In theory, accounts payable is a natural hedge against currency exchange gains or losses associated with inventory. Others objected to the requirement that cost of goods sold be translated at the appropriate historic rate, while revenue was being translated at the average rate. Different exchange rates being applied to revenue and costs distorted the measurement of gross margin of an operating affiliate. The gross margin of an operating affiliate was not the same before and after translation. In addition, there was widespread opposition to translation gains and losses flowing through income.

The dollar was losing value during the years following the issuance of FASB 8. Profits made in non-U.S. affiliates in nations whose currencies were appreciating with respect to the dollar were diminished when translated in accordance with FASB 8. There were instances of local profits being transformed to losses by the translation process. As such, FASB 8 was not "directionally sympathetic" to changes in currency exchange rates. One would expect that an operating affiliate in a nation whose currency was appreciating with respect to the U.S.

dollar should be gaining economic value. Its profits should be enhanced, not reduced, by the translation process. American executives found themselves in a position of having to explain to their shareholders why a profitable enterprise in Germany was showing a loss, or to be more accurate, why a loss on the financial reports was really a profit.

The loss, of course, was a noncash translation loss arising from the use of multiple currency exchange rates in the translation of a financial statement from German marks to U.S. dollars. A translation loss could have been a gain had the mark weakened against the dollar. The earnings of American corporations were being buoyed up and driven down by shifting exchange rates and these swings were opposite to what one might logically expect. Reported earnings became more volatile as translation gains and losses flowed through income. Management had difficulty explaining the added volatility of earnings to the shareholders; particularly when a reported noncash translation loss was actually a real cash profit. Some firms made economic decisions to reduce the volatility of earnings based on the method of translation stipulated in FASB 8, by selling profitable operating affiliates to avoid translation losses. This is the tail wagging the dog. The purpose of accounting is to fairly represent the happenings of a company in the form of a financial report. FASB 8 created a situation where avoidance of translation losses on the financial report, and not the economics of the situation, were sometimes driving business decisions.

Current Rate Method and FASB 52

Efforts were underway to correct the situation soon after the publication of FASB 8. In 1981, FASB 52 "Foreign Currency Translation" was issued with a three year "window," giving corporations time to convert to the new rules on currency translation. The thrust behind FASB 52 was to ensure that the process of currency translation was directionally sympathetic to the real economic effects of changes in currency exchange rates and to ensure that the translation process would preserve financial relationships or ratios, such as the gross margin or liquidity ratio. Currency gains and losses from the translation process were no longer to be charged to income, but to a new component of stockholders' equity called Translation Adjustments.

FASB 52 stipulates that all assets and liabilities be translated at the current rate, with equity accounts translated at historic rates. Financial relationships, such as the liquidity ratio, are preserved in the translation process because the same currency exchange rate is applied to current assets and liabilities. The gross margin is preserved in the translation process because revenues and expenses are translated at the same currency exchange rate. Another advantage of FASB 52 is that the translation process is directionally sympathetic with regards to changes in exchange rates. If a U.S. company has an "asset exposure" in an operating affiliate where assets exceed liabilities, then such an operating affiliate's value is enhanced as its currency of operations appreciates against the dollar.

FASB 8 eliminates the "roller coaster" impact on income from changing currency exchange rates because gains and losses in the translation process no longer flow through the income statement but are recorded as a separate component of equity on the balance sheet. The methodology of translation set forth in FASB 52 is inherently simple and in harmony with translation practices in many other nations. One disadvantage of FASB 52 is the "disappearing asset" problem that results from applying the requirements of FASB 52 in hyperinflationary economies, which will be discussed in Chapter 8.

After the financial statements of a foreign subsidiary are recast in accordance with U.S. GAAP, the next step is currency translation. FASB 52 defines various categories of currencies for translation purposes. The "functional" currency is the currency of prime economic environment in which a company operates. A "foreign" currency is any currency other than the functional currency. The "local" currency is that of the country in which a subsidiary operates and the "reporting" currency is the currency of a company's financial reports. The functional currency of an entity is the currency of the primary economic environment in which the entity operates and generates cash flows. It may be either the local currency of the foreign entity or a different foreign currency or the currency of the parent, assumed to be the U.S. dollar. The choice depends on many considerations. No single consideration determines the selection of the functional currency as the final choice encompasses all of the following:

1. If cash flows are principally in the foreign currency, the usual situation, and do not have a direct bearing on the parent company's cash flow, the functional currency would probably be the local currency. If the subsidiary's cash flow is readily available for remittance to the parent company, the functional currency would probably be the U.S. dollar.

2. If the market for the entity's goods is primarily local, the functional currency would be the local currency. If the market for its goods is principally in the parent's country, and/or the sales contracts are principally denominated in the parent's currency, then the functional currency would be the U.S. dollar.

3. If the selling prices are mainly driven by local competition, or possibly by government regulation, and not by short-term fluctuations in exchange rates, then the functional currency would be the local currency. If sales prices are driven by international prices and competition, and also fluctuate with the dollar exchange rate, then the functional currency would be the U.S. dollar.

4. If costs and expenses for labor, raw materials, and other items primarily represent local costs, then the local currency would be the functional currency. If costs and expenses primarily represent items obtained from the parent company, then the functional currency would be the U.S. dollar.

5. If financing for the local company is mainly raised locally and denominated in the

local currency, and if debt service is expected to be covered by cash flows generated in the local currency, then the local currency would be the functional currency. If financing, including debt service, is provided by the parent, or is denominated in the currency of the parent, then the functional currency would be the U.S. dollar.

In summary, a foreign entity whose operations are integrated within its country and who is relatively self-sustaining would normally use the local currency as its functional currency. A foreign entity whose operations are essentially an extension of the U.S. parent would normally use the U.S. dollar as its functional currency. A foreign entity whose operations are essentially conducted in another foreign country would normally use the currency of the other foreign country as its functional currency. If an operation is located in a "highly inflationary economy," defined as cumulative inflation of 100 percent or more over a three-year period, the functional currency is the U.S. dollar.

The reporting company must examine all these aspects for each foreign branch, affiliate, or subsidiary to decide on the functional currency. Once this decision is made, it may only be changed if the underlying economic circumstances clearly show that a change can be justified. After foreign financial statements have been adjusted to conform to U.S. GAAP, assets and liabilities are translated from the functional currency to the reporting currency (in this example, U.S. dollars) at the current exchange rate. Revenue, expenses, and other gains and losses such as asset disposition of the foreign entity are translated from the functional currency to the reporting currency at the weighted average exchange rate for the period. Transaction gains and losses, unless associated with a hedge, are recognized as a part of income statement currently. Transaction gains and losses associated with hedges are not included in income.

Dividends remitted to the parent are translated at the exchange rate on the day of declaration. Shareholders' capital accounts, including Stock and Paid in Surplus, are translated at historic rates of exchange. Retained earnings are determined by a calculation, not by translation. The translated amount of retained earnings at the beginning of the period is added to the translated amount of income or loss during the current period less the translated value of dividend payments. Differences arising from translating financial statements using various exchange rates are recorded in a separate shareholders' equity account called Translation Adjustments. This is deferred as a separate component of shareholders' equity until the foreign entity is sold or otherwise liquidated. When it is sold or liquidated, the deferred translation adjustment associated with the entity is included in the net gain or loss of the disposition of the foreign entity.

If the cumulative inflation in a country is 100 percent or more over a three-year period, the currency of that country is unsuitable for a functional currency. In this case, financial statements of the foreign subsidiary must be remeasured into the functional currency of the parent. If the foreign entity's records are not maintained in its functional currency, they must first be remeasured into the functional currency before translation. Gains or losses resulting from the re-measurement are included in the income statement of the foreign entity.

The following example illustrates the current rate method of translating the financial statements of a foreign subsidiary for consolidation in a U.S. parent corporation financial report (see Table 6.3). The local currency is the functional currency, which is the usual situation. In this example, Global Corporation, a U.S. multinational enterprise, acquired all the outstanding common stock of Small Company, which is located in a country where the currency is the LC (local currency), on 2 January 1991. The LC is the functional currency of Small. For 1991, the exchange rates for the LC were as follows:

2 January	$0.20
31 December	0.40
Average	0.30

The average exchange rate for the year is used to translate the income statement, resulting in net income of $15,000. Retained earnings at the beginning of the year are translated at the historic rate of $0.20, the rate in effect when Global acquired Small. Net income in U.S. dollars ($15,000) is then added to retained earnings at the beginning of the year ($14,000). A dividend was declared and paid during the year and is translated at the actual spot rate on the day of declaration ($7,600). Retained earnings at the end of the year are calculated in dollars amounting to $21,400. This is not the result of translating the LC retained earnings, but represents the dollar equivalent of retained earnings at the start of the year plus the dollar equivalent of net income, less the dollar equivalent of dividends. Retained earnings on the books of the subsidiary at the beginning of the next year will be LC 100,000 and will be reflected in the U.S. dollar consolidated financial statements of Global as $21,400.

All assets and liabilities are translated at the end-of-year exchange rate ($0.40). The shareholders' capital accounts, consisting of Common Stock and Paid-in Capital, are translated at historic rates. In this case, the historic rate is that of 2 January 1991, when Global acquired all the outstanding shares of Small. These translated dollar amounts will not change in the future.

The dollar amount of Retained Earnings ($21,400) is determined in the Statement of Retained Earnings and then appears in the equity section of the balance sheet. The Translation Adjustment in U.S. dollars ($84,600) is derived by subtracting the dollar amount of liabilities and equity from the dollar amount of total assets ($408,000 less $323,400, or $84,600). The gain of $84,600, which occurred from the revaluation of the LC from $0.20 to $0.40 during the year, is deferred.

This discussion is based on the acquisition of Small Company at the beginning of the year. In succeeding years, the process of calculating the Translation Adjustment is repeated and added if a gain, and subtracted if a loss, from the start-of-year value of the Translation Adjustment. All else being equal, an ap-

Table 6.3

```
                              SMALL COMPANY
              Translation of Financial Statements to U.S. Dollars
                       For Year Ended December 31, 1991


     Income Statement           LC   X   Exchange Rate    =    U.S. $

Net Sales                  LC 200,000      $0.30  (A)      $     60,000
Costs and Expenses            150,000       0.30  (A)           45,000

Net Income                 LC  50,000                     $     15,000


Statement of Retained Earnings

Retained Earnings
    Start of Year          LC  70,000       0.20  (H)      $     14,000
Net Income                     50,000                           15,000

Subtotal                   LC 120,000                     $     29,000
Dividends                      20,000       0.38  (D)            7,600
Retained Earnings
    End of Year            LC 100,000                     $     21,400


    Balance Sheet
      Assets

Current Assets             LC  300,000      0.40  (E)      $    120,000
Net plant Assets               720,000      0.40  (E)          288,000

Total Assets               LC 1,020,000                   $    408,000

      Liabilities &
      Stockholders' Equity

Current Liabilities        LC  170,000      0.40  (E)      $     68,000
Long Term Debt                 420,000      0.40  (E)          168,000
Common Stock                   240,000      0.20  (H)           48,000
Paid-in Capital                 90,000      0.20  (H)           18,000
Retained Earnings              100,000                          21,400

Subtotal                                                       323,400

Translation Adjustment                                         84,600

Total Liabilities &
    Stockholders'
      Equity               LC 1,020,000                   $    408,000
```

(A)—Average exchange rate for year.

(H)—Historical exchange rate.

(D)—Spot rate when declared and paid.

(E)—End-of-year exchange rate.

preciating LC will increase the Translation Adjustment, whereas an LC undergoing devaluation will reduce the Translation Adjustment. If the devaluation is large enough, the Translation Adjustment may become negative.

TRANSLATION PRACTICES OUTSIDE THE UNITED STATES

Despite, or because of, the disputes associated with the development of translation practices within the United States, the United States is considered a leader in addressing translation issues. Some nations use the current method of translation and others use either the monetary-nonmonetary or the temporal methods. In the European Community, the Fourth and Seventh Directives merely require disclosure of the translation methodology incorporated in the consolidation process. There are no specific directions in Germany as to which translation method should be employed, however, the selected method should be disclosed and it should not affect net income. This latter requirement is necessary because financial reports in Germany may also serve as tax reports. There is no specified methodology in the Netherlands other than its identification and that it should have no impact on the profit and loss statement. Switzerland has no legal requirement to prepare consolidated financial reports. If a company desires to do so, it is free to select any translation method. Japan has no specific guidelines as to the appropriate method of currency translations. Canada has accounting requirements similar to FASB 52, except that deferred taxes are translated at the historic rate. In July 1983, the International Accounting Standards Committee required the use of the current rate method for translation purposes (IAS 21).

QUESTIONS PERTAINING TO TRANSLATION

Is a single translation methodology applicable for all situations? Should a company's financial statements be translated? Suppose that a company has no intent of repatriating cash from a foreign entity, and the foreign entity's bank accounts are all in the local currency. Is it appropriate for the parent to continually increase and decrease the reported U.S. dollar value of the cash holding in the foreign entity as exchange rates change? This, of course, is just one aspect of the problem. Every line item on the balance sheet of a foreign entity changes in response to changing currency exchange rates. Yet, in the final analysis, little or none of these assets and liabilities will ever be converted into U.S. dollars.

Is translation appropriate between stable and unstable currencies? If a currency is "soft," and essentially unconvertible to U.S. dollars because of currency exchange restrictions, should the entity be consolidated at all? Would it be preferable to "deconsolidate" these entities from those located in countries with more stable currencies that are convertible to U.S. dollars? In extreme cases of a soft currency nation, earnings must remain within a nation because they cannot be repatriated. Moreover, earnings cannot remain as cash without rapidly losing value. Usually, profits from operations are invested in tangibles to preserve purchasing power. Would it be preferable to "deconsolidate" such entities and reflect income in the financial statements of the parent only when actual cash is received from the foreign entity?

FASB 52 permits translation adjustments to be made directly to equity. What effect does this have on reported income and on price/earnings ratios? These gains and losses, which may be substantial, are excluded from the determination of income and may escape the notice of readers of the financial reports.

CHAPTER 7

TRANSFER PRICING AND TAXATION

A small operation managed by a few individuals was the typical beginning of a large corporation with a hundred operating affiliates dispersed around the world. Decision making was highly centralized and lines of communication were short. As the company grew, the founding management team found it more difficult to keep matters under control. This problem was greatly exacerbated when operations within the company became physically separated. Centers of activity in different locations called for a different style of management. Funneling of all decisions from diverse locations through a small group of individuals, who no longer possess the necessary intimate awareness of the circumstances surrounding each decision, is a surefire prescription for stifling growth.

Growth is the name of the game for modern corporations. Growth entails individual operating affiliates taking appropriate action to enhance productivity, market share, and the scope of a company's product line. It has been found that operating affiliates physically separated from the parent organization can best achieve these objectives under a decentralized style of management. Responsibility now falls on the shoulders of the manager of an operating affiliate to make the necessary decisions that will lead to improved financial results, the universal measure of performance. The parent organization takes on a new role as coordinator and monitor of activities now that responsibility for operations has been transferred to the operating units.

Far from playing a passive role, the parent organization focuses its attention on optimizing the performance of its semiautonomous operating affiliates. To do this, the parent organization must establish, and articulate, a set of strategic goals and allocate limited corporate resources to the various operating affiliates to best achieve these goals. It must ensure that the short-term action plans of the operating affiliates are in accord with its long-term plans. Top management positions in the operating affiliates must be filled with individuals capable of leading their affiliates in the right direction and an incentive system must be set up to induce managers to orient their thinking to the goals of the company. Finally, the parent organization must set up a financial reporting and control system to monitor its global operations, to provide necessary information for the making of decisions and to evaluate the performance of the affiliate managers.

Although operating affiliates appear to be semiautonomous units in that they are given a wide spectrum of decision-making responsibility in managing their local operations, they are not independent centers of corporate activity. They are often united in manufacturing and marketing a common product line, in the course of which they routinely buy and sell finished goods, components, or raw materials from one another. These intracompany exchanges of goods, components, and raw materials require a transfer price. The parent organization sets the transfer price after considering various factors with an eye on optimizing corporate performance as a whole.

Transfer prices are often not negotiated and agreed on by the actual buyers and sellers of the goods and components being shipped between operating affiliates. Yet transfer prices directly affect the revenue and cost of goods sold, and therefore, the profitability of the operating affiliates. Because the affiliate managers are monitored by a financial reporting and control system that scrutinizes their financial results, one can expect that affiliate managers have an entirely different perspective on transfer pricing than the executives of the parent organization. Transfer pricing can easily embroil executives of the parent organization and the managers of operating affiliates in endless disputes. Some firms have even established an administrative panel for reviewing transfer prices to resolve sharp differences of opinion between those responsible for managing operating affiliates and those responsible for setting transfer prices.

TRANSFER PRICES AND TAXES

A global company with operations in many nations must deal with a new dimension of complexity in establishing transfer prices, which is not present when a company operates solely within the confines of a single nation. A company whose operations are within a single nation pays the same taxes on profits regardless of the transfer pricing policy. The consolidation process, whether for financial or tax accounting purposes, eliminates intracompany transactions to arrive at either a book profit or a before-tax profit. When a company transacts business through affiliate companies in different nations, however, transfer pricing provides a mechanism for shifting taxable profits between tax jurisdictions.

Tax authorities in various nations are concerned with the notion that transfer pricing, often set by parent organizations outside their jurisdiction, is based on minimizing taxes paid in their jurisdictions. There certainly is an element of truth in this contention, but there are other considerations in administering transfer prices than minimizing taxes. The setting of transfer prices provides a way of moving funds internationally for a variety of purposes, of circumventing currency exchange controls that threaten to choke the operations of a company, of minimizing the deleterious impact of other artificial barriers to trade such as duties and tariffs, and of reducing currency risk exposure.

A transfer pricing policy attempts to satisfy a multiple set of objectives. Some of these objectives call for high transfer prices, whereas others require low transfer prices. A company must select what it considers to be an optimal transfer price, which is a compromise price for best achieving divergent objectives. This optimal transfer price may not be the one that minimizes taxes on profits. The selected transfer price may not be satisfactory both to the local tax authority and to the manager of an affiliate if it reduces the reported profitability of the affiliate. However, setting the transfer price is critical to optimizing the financial performance of the corporation as a whole, given the conditions that prevail at a point in time.

Minimizing Taxes

Tax authorities of most countries have guidelines or controls that are expected to be complied with in setting transfer prices. Management is not free to arbitrarily select transfer prices without having to substantiate their transfer price decisions. Nevertheless, there is still an element of choice where a selected transfer price may reduce the tax burden of a company.

Suppose that a company consists of a parent organization and two operating affiliates—one in nation A, where the tax rate on profits is 30 percent, and one in nation B, where the tax rate on profits is 40 percent. The tax is applied to each affiliate's gross margin for illustrative purposes. The affiliate in nation A makes a product that is entirely sold through the affiliate in nation B. Two cases are considered—a low and a high transfer price. The low-transfer price case is illustrated in Table 7.1.

Table 7.1
Case I—Low Transfer Price

	NATION A TAX 30%	NATION B TAX 40%	CONSOLIDATED
Sales	$2000	$3200	$3200
Cost of Goods Sold	1500	2000	1500
Gross Margin	500	1200	1700
Tax	150	480	630
Net Income	$350	$720	$1070

Everything made in a factory in nation A is sold through a marketing organization in nation B. Therefore, total sales in nation A, calculated on the basis of an administered transfer price, is also the cost of goods sold in nation B. Sales in nation B of $3,200 is the net consolidated sales for the company, because

all goods produced in nation A are sold in nation B. The actual cost of manufacturing the goods in nation A is $1,500. Because nation B does not add value
to the goods, the consolidated cost of goods sold for the company is also $1,500.
The consolidated tax is the sum of the $150 and the $480 paid to the tax authorities
of nations A and B, respectively. The consolidated net income is $1,070, the
sum of the net incomes of the two affiliates.

Suppose that the transfer price is increased from $2,000 to $2,500 for goods
shipped between the two affiliates (see Table 7.2).

Table 7.2
Case II—High Transfer Price

	NATION A TAX 30%	NATION B TAX 40%	CONSOLIDATED
Sales	$2500	$3200	$3200
Cost of Goods Sold	1500	2500	1500
Gross Margin	1000	700	1700
Tax	300	280	580
Net Income	$700	$420	$1120

Consolidated sales, cost of goods sold, and gross margin are unaffected by
the change in the transfer price, because it is netted out in the consolidation
process. Taxes paid in each nation are no longer the same because of the change
in the transfer price. In case II, the increase in the transfer price shifts the profit
to Nation A, which has the lower tax rate. The affiliate in nation A earns more
taxable income and pays more in taxes than in case I. The affiliate in nation B
earns less taxable income and pays less in taxes in case II than in case I. The
net effect, as seen by comparing case II with case I, is that the company as a
whole is paying less in taxes, which increases its consolidated net income.

It is true that had the two nations the same tax rate, the total taxes paid by
the company, and the consolidated net income, would not be affected by changes
in the transfer price. Even so, transfer prices determine what portion of total
taxes are to be paid to the tax authority in nation A and to the tax authority in
Nation B. Although the parent organization may be relatively insensitive concerning to whom it pays taxes, needless to say, the tax authorities are very much
concerned as to which is collecting taxes. The problem is compounded, from
the point of view of a tax authority, because the transfer price is probably set
by a parent organization not under its jurisdiction. The importance of transfer
pricing to both managers and tax authorities can be appreciated when it is realized
that between 40 percent and 60 percent of international trade involves goods
moving between affiliates of the same company. Corporate decisions on transfer
prices do have a meaningful impact on what a tax jurisdiction collects.

There are nations, islands, and localities where tax authorities exhibit little
interest in transfer prices. Ireland, Puerto Rico, and other nations or areas designated as free trade zones or having special tax privileges may not tax corporate
profits, or have a very low tax rate. These nations or locales are interested in
companies building plants on their soil for the social benefits that accrue from

employment of individuals who might otherwise be unemployed. Companies operating in such nations or locales can substantially decrease their overall tax rate. The effective reduction in tax rates depends on the transfer prices of imported components and semifinished goods and the transfer prices of exported finished goods.

Granting tax concessions is one way for a nation to attract companies. At this time, eastern European nations offer tax incentives but do not have a prescribed accounting methodology to calculate profits, which makes it impossible to quantify the tax benefit. More than one company has set up an operation in eastern Europe to later discover that the government had a much different version in mind of the nature of the tax benefits than the investors anticipated. Such shortsightedness by government officials has a deleterious impact on attracting other companies.

Many nations are discovering that viewing business solely as a way to fill the public coffers may not be in their long-term best interests. Within the United States, states with high corporate tax rates have experienced companies moving to states with low corporate tax rates. The higher they raise their corporate tax rates, the less they collect in taxes. As once companies moved from one state to another, now they move from one nation to another. In selecting a potential site, a businessman considers many factors, of which taxes are but one. Some of these are social and political stability; a system of commercial law to resolve disputes; a set of acceptable accounting practices (both to assess tax liabilities and evaluate tax incentives); a labor force with the requisite skills and will to work; and an infrastructure of transportation, communication, and utility and social (education, medical care) services.

There are more locations that offer good potential sites for factories than before. Managers no longer feel that their factories must be anchored to one nation and have learned to manage far-flung operations. Nations must now compete for factories. Tax authorities in developed nations are beginning to realize that they may end up collecting less tax revenue in their eagerness to collect more tax revenue by raising tax rates. The United States was forced to repeal a luxury tax on pleasure boats because pleasure boat construction virtually ceased with the passage of the new tax. New Jersey was forced to repeal a sales tax on trucks when truck selling companies moved their operations to nearby Pennsylvania. In both cases, tax revenues fell when tax rates were raised, and the tax authorities were forced to rescind tax increases. In a global economy, companies are mobile and will relocate to avoid especially burdensome taxes.

INTERNATIONAL FUNDING

Businesses operating in hard currency nations have the advantage of being able to transfer and convert currencies as necessary. Many nations, however, have currencies that lack convertibility, the so-called soft currencies. Transfer pricing provides a means of moving funds from one country to another, when direct currency convertibility is not possible. If a nation has an affiliate that completes the manufacturing process and sells its output within that nation, funds can be moved out of that nation by increasing the transfer price for goods imported by the affiliate. The same objective can be accomplished by increasing the charges for services rendered by the parent organization to the affiliate, such as selling and administrative (S&A) fees, research and development (R&D) expenses, financial charges on transferred assets, and royalties for rights to patents and dividends.

Sometimes currency exchange controls focus on the amount of dividends that can be paid by an affiliate to its parent. A quasi-dividend can be paid by raising the transfer price of goods moving into the nation or by increasing corporate fees, financial charges, and royalty payments. Some nations with severe restrictions on dividend outflows will permit increases in transfer prices and service fees. These quasi-dividend payments are allowed because the local government recognizes that few companies can afford the luxury of investing in a nation that prohibits the company from earning a return on its investment. However, actions such as these that drain funds out of a soft currency nation eventually result in some sort of currency exchange restriction. This often results in affiliate profits accumulating in a currency that may not be particularly desirable. Sometimes currency exchange restrictions can be bypassed by the affiliate making an investment, or lending funds, to an affiliate in another nation.

CONTROLLING REPORTED PROFITS

Shifts in transfer prices, corporate administrative fees, and other parent company charges to an affiliate are means of managing the affiliate's reported profitability. It may be in the interest of a parent organization to lower the reported profitability of an affiliate for reasons other than tax minimization. These include deflecting union demands for higher wages, reducing political pressure to nationalize or expropriate a profitable affiliate, and dissuading potential competitors from entering the market. Lowering profitability is also a way to counter price controls that limit profitability. If a government has set price controls based on the cost of production plus a limited markup for profits, increases in the transfer price of goods sent to the affiliate lowers the profit margin of goods sold in that nation. This may permit goods to be sold at government decreed profit margins with the company as a whole still able to earn its normal profits.

A few nations have tax rates that are linked to profitability. The greater the profitability, the higher the tax rate. The logic behind this taxation policy is that there is a level of profits on investment that seems "excessive" to the government. Such excessive profitability should be punished by the government, and there is no greater punishment than taking away the excess profits through a higher tax rate. By increasing the transfer price of goods being imported into the nation, the degree of profitability is decreased, lowering the tax rate and, presumably, restoring respectability in the eyes of the government.

Alternatively, it may be in the interests of the parent organization to enhance the profitability of an affiliate. This may be done by lowering the transfer price of imported goods. One reason for enhancing the profitability of an affiliate is to provide sufficient financial resources to the affiliate for it to withstand price cutting by competitive companies. Improving an affiliate's profitability, even at the cost of paying more in taxes, may allow the affiliate to borrow needed funds for operation from local banks and other financial institutions, to improve its credit rating to qualify for lower interest loans and to fund capital outlays from its own resources.

CIRCUMVENTING EXCHANGE CONTROLS

Governments with soft currencies often limit the amount of their currency that companies operating in their nations can exchange for other currencies. Their motivation is to discourage the selling of the domestic soft currency and the buying of a hard currency, which would exert downward pressure on the value of the local currency. In other words, exchange controls are set up to keep a soft currency from becoming softer. From the point of view of a parent organization, restricting hard currency outflows inhibits an affiliate's ability to pay for imported components or other items necessary for its operations. Transfer prices for the needed components can be kept artificially low to expand the volume of goods that are being imported into a soft currency nation. This sustains an affiliate's manufacturing operation without exceeding government decreed restrictions on converting soft currency to hard currency.

But there is an adverse consequence because such a course of action results in a parent corporation accumulating even larger amounts of soft currency. These holdings of soft currency are constantly losing purchasing power through inflation. The soft currency cannot be converted to a more desirable currency because of currency exchange restrictions and the soft currency, which has little value within the nation, has no value outside the nation. One of the knottiest problems associated with an operating affiliate in a soft currency nation is funding of hard currency imports necessary for its operation and obtaining a hard currency return on a hard currency investment.

Some companies will not set up an operation in a soft currency nation unless there is a prearranged means to earn hard currency to pay for hard currency imports and to provide a hard currency return on a hard currency investment. Pepsi Cola struck a barter deal for producing its soft drink in the former Soviet Union. Its soft ruble revenue, net of soft ruble expenses, is exchanged for Russian built tankers, which are then sold for hard currencies. Oil companies will not set up operations in the Commonwealth of Independent States, and other soft currency nations, unless they receive a share of the output, which is shipped out of the nation and sold for hard currency.

The easiest way for a company to earn hard currency in a soft currency nation would be to export a portion of its output to hard currency nations. However, most soft currency nations do not permit the hard currency revenue to remain with the company. The hard currency revenue is exchanged for an equivalent amount of soft currency, which is then credited to the exporter's bank account. In essence, the national government receives the hard currency revenue from exports and pays soft currency to the exporter. Sometimes international banks are at fault for imposing this condition on a nation as a means to guarantee repayment of international debt. Regardless of whether the nation or the international banks impose this condition, it is self-defeating because the economic development of a developing nation is held back by the inability of companies to earn sufficient hard currency to justify their investments.

MINIMIZING DUTIES AND TARIFFS

Duties and tariffs imposed on goods imported into a nation can be reduced by lowering the transfer price. This is the exact opposite of reducing taxes on profits by increasing the transfer price. Because the tariff rate is usually less than the tax rate on profits, lowering transfer prices to reduce import tariffs often results in a higher tax on profits.

In some nations, however, tariffs on certain imported goods and commodities are not set by a corporate-determined transfer price but by an internationally posted price. This can be done only for generic goods (steel) or commodities (oil), where there is an active market with published and verifiable prices. Sometimes tax authorities will reference costs not to a "transfer price" cost but to an internationally agreed standard. One example of this is tanker rates in the oil business. An oil company can manage the profitability, and therefore, the tax liability, of a refinery by the transfer price associated with international tanker transportation for moving oil to and from a refinery. The tax authorities of many nations and the oil companies have agreed to a panel of experts determining a fair and representative tanker rate that is used for the computation of taxes independent of the transfer price, or internal cost, that oil companies charge for shipping oil among their affiliates. This eliminates arguments between tax authorities and oil companies concerning the appropriate shipping charge.

Determining the optimal transfer-pricing policy is further complicated when a nation in which an affiliate operates has an export subsidy program or provides a tax credit on the value of exports. It may be advantageous to lower transfer prices to an affiliate whose output is exported to third parties or other affiliates in other nations to take advantage of these tax incentives. The optimal transfer price depends on the nature of the export subsidy or tax credit, the volume of the affiliate's output that is exported from the nation, the relationship between taxes on profits and the generation of tax credits and on the capacity of the affiliate to utilize the tax credit or export subsidy.

The nature of the taxes paid in a nation in the form of income taxes, duties and tariffs on imported goods, and export subsidies or tax credits on exported goods influence the setting of transfer prices. There is no hard and fast rule on whether a high or a low transfer-pricing policy is best for a company. The particular circumstances of a company's operations in a nation and the nature of taxes and subsidies determine the best transfer-pricing policy. A transfer-pricing system integrated into a financial reporting and control system should be capable of analyzing "what" if scenarios to evaluate the effect of different transfer-pricing policies.

REDUCING CURRENCY EXCHANGE RISK

Changes in currency exchange rates result in transaction and translation gains and losses. More importantly, they affect the competitive position of an affiliate. If an affiliate manufactures and markets its goods in a nation, and imports components from another nation, a revaluation of the currency where the finished goods are being sold relative to the currency of its purchased components reduces manufacturing costs. This makes the affiliate more competitive and profitable. A devaluation, on the other hand, increases the cost of imported components, making the affiliate less competitive and less profitable. Reality is much more complex than this simple example because affiliates may export and import components and finished goods to and from a variety of nations. Changes in exchange rates benefit some affiliates and hurt others, and it may not be obvious because of the nature of buying and selling of goods and services. It is possible that a change in currency exchange rates that is adverse to a particular affiliate may be beneficial to the company as a whole because of the nature of the net exposure of the company to the affected currencies. Adjustments to transfer prices may affect currency holdings before an anticipated change in exchange rates takes place and may be able to restore a company's competitive position after the change has taken place. Therefore, a financial reporting and control system should have the capacity to assess changes to both transfer prices and currency exchange rates to enable the parent organization to respond both to anticipated changes in currency exchange rates and to subsequent shifts in its competitive position.

TRANSFER PRICING AND JOINT VENTURES

A joint venture partner, a local partner owning a portion of an affiliate, and a minority shareholder are going to be as interested in transfer pricing as the local tax authority. Less often, a partnership is structured on the basis of a claim, or royalty, on revenue. More often, it is a claim on profits. If one party to a venture or partnership can influence revenue, costs, and profitability through transfer pricing, then the other party or partner, or a minority shareholder, will be deservedly concerned. One way to manage transfer pricing with regard to having partners or minority shareholders is to formalize the setting of transfer prices in some verifiable manner such as a set markup above costs, another is to reference transfer prices to an observable market transaction. Either way minimizes the opportunity for one party to a partnership or joint venture to manipulate transfer prices to its advantage. If the partners, participants, and minority shareholders feel that their interests are vulnerable by virtue of the other party to a business venture controlling transfer prices, then they may not contribute to the venture that which was expected of them.

Avoiding these problems can be more easily said than done. Some years ago, Ford Motor Company purchased the minority shares of its partially owned subsidiaries because the company felt that it could not administer transfer pricing in a way that was fair to all concerned. Some managements have made the strategic decision not to enter into joint ventures, or have local partners or minority shareholdings in corporate affiliates, where they can manage the profitability of the venture through transfer prices. Sometimes, the solution for a problem is to avoid the problem.

TRANSFER PRICING AND MANAGERIAL PERFORMANCE EVALUATION

It may be in the interest of the corporation as a whole to transfer in components that are more highly priced than those an affiliate can purchase from other sources. It may be in the interest of the corporation as a whole to transfer goods made in one affiliate to another affiliate for less than what the affiliate can sell them for to third parties. Although the corporation may gain by such a set of transfer prices for goods moving among affiliates, it does not serve the interests of the affiliate managers if they are subsequently judged on profitability.

This dichotomy of purpose in establishing a transfer-pricing policy for the good of the whole company, yet holding managers of affiliates accountable for profits that are contaminated, so to speak, by transfer prices has not been successfully addressed when transfer prices are different from market prices. In fact, this is one potent argument in favor of companies having transfer pricing policies based on the market price for comparable goods. If transfer prices are set at the price for goods exchanged between unrelated parties, then there is no dichotomy of purpose in setting transfer prices and measuring performance. Managers of affiliates can be judged in an unbiased fashion on the profitability of their operations because they are buying and selling at market prices—the same prices that would prevail if they were independent companies. The disadvantage of letting the market set transfer prices is that the parent corporation can no longer utilize transfer pricing as a means to pursue the overall optimization of the financial performance of the corporation. One possible approach to the dysfunctional aspects of setting transfer prices at other than market prices and measuring management performance of affiliates is to isolate and separately state the amount of intercompany "profit" or "loss" that each affiliate is experiencing in its transactions with other affiliates. This approach provides the parent organization with information on whether an affiliate is suffering from unwarranted decreased profitability or enjoying unwarranted increased profitability because of transfer pricing.

SETTING TRANSFER PRICES BY COST OF PRODUCTION

There are two general approaches for setting transfer prices: the cost of production and market prices associated with third party, or unrelated, transactions. The cost-of-production approach bases the price of goods to be transferred between affiliates on the variable cost of production, an allowance for fixed costs that are general in nature and are apportioned over the entire product line, and an allowance for fixed costs that can be apportioned among the individual products. This latter category usually includes research and development costs and selling and administrative costs. The remaining components may include financial fees and royalties associated with tangible and intangible assets to be apportioned to individual products and the selection of an appropriate profit margin.

The variable cost of production includes labor, material, and other direct costs that are consumed in the production of an item. If the policy of the company is to hire and fire (lay off) factory workers as production rises and falls, then labor is a variable cost. If a company is reluctant to let go of their workers when sales decline, then factory labor should be considered part of fixed costs. Factory labor costs are usually part variable and part fixed. Other variable costs can be the unit financing and utility costs associated with machinery and processes used in the manufacture of a particular product and unit shipping costs. These costs can also be treated as fixed costs depending on how the company's cost accounting system is set up.

Fixed costs are all costs not included in variable costs. Fixed costs are the financing or depreciation costs of the factory; the overhead costs of marketing, accounting, and supervision; the cost of inventories, warehouses, insurance, utilities, communication, property taxes, and other nonvariable cost items. Fixed costs may not be entirely fixed in that there is some variation as production levels change. For instance, bonuses, which would be considered part of the fixed costs of having an executive suite, rise and fall with profits, which are related to production levels. The number of staff personnel in marketing, accounting, engineering, and other overhead functions can vary with the production level.

Some elements of fixed costs are allocated in the transfer price setting mechanism in a way that fairly apportions the fixed cost burden among the various products. Other elements of fixed costs can be apportioned more on the basis of the benefit derived by an individual product. One of these is research and development, where the allocation can be made over a product line in proportion to the degree of R&D expenditures associated with the development of an individual product.

Although there is general agreement that this is a fair way to apportion R&D expenses of successful undertakings, there is lack of agreement on how to apportion R&D expenses for failed projects. Some maintain that the allocation of expenses associated with failed R&D projects should be apportioned to all products on the basis that every product should bear the risk of failed R&D efforts. Others object on the grounds that had the R&D effort succeeded, a particular product might not have benefited. Therefore, it makes no sense for the transfer price to contain the cost of a failed R&D effort, which, had it succeeded, would not be part of the transfer price of the product.

The question as to the proper treatment of failed R&D projects is not an internal accounting matter. Tax authorities are interested in who takes the write-off of a failed R&D project. In the United States, the Internal Revenue Service (IRS) is concerned whether a transfer price contains a provision for failed R&D expenditures. If a transfer price contains only that portion of R&D expenditures that were successful with regard to a particular product, then failed R&D projects of a U.S. corporation are being written off solely against U.S. income. A portion of the tax loss write-off is passed on to the tax authority of another nation by including an element of failed R&D expenditures in the transfer price.

Another fixed cost element that can be separated and apportioned in a different manner than general fixed costs are services provided to an individual product. These may be coordination and control expenses associated with a product; costs for enhancing the efficiency of operations for manufacturing the product or expanding the scope of its market; and the costs of recruiting and training of management and operations personnel associated with manufacturing, marketing, and repairing or servicing the product. The allocation of these service costs to individual products provides another element in deriving their transfer prices.

The derivation of the transfer price also includes elements for tangibles and intangibles associated with a product. Tangibles are the plant, equipment, and other physical assets dedicated to the manufacture of the product. Part of the transfer price provides a financial return for tangibles based on their value. Intangibles represent the technical knowledge and expertise and applicable patents that can be allocated to a particular product. The transfer price also contains an element that provides a company with a return on intangibles.

Intangible costs within a transfer price cannot be capriciously determined by management because intangible costs affect taxable profits. For this reason, the IRS has established guidelines for determining the intangible cost element in a transfer price. An intangible cost element must be present if there are intangible costs associated with the manufacture or marketing of a product and must be so identified. Intangible costs can be proportioned in relation to the income attributable to the intangibles by units of production, sales, net or gross profits, or other reasonable methods. The fee for intangible property incorporated in a transfer price must be similar to what would have been arranged with an independent third party.

The last part of the cost approach in setting transfer prices is determining the proper profit margin on the goods made by one affiliate and shipped to another. This may be the average profit margin for the company as a whole or a profit margin associated with a specific product line. Regardless, the stipulated profit margin must be reconciled in some manner with the profitability of the company or a product line to satisfy the tax authorities. The need for reconciliation of the profit and the various cost elements of the transfer price with the tax authorities sometimes results in the tax group within the finance department of a company being responsible for administering transfer prices. However, this choice may hinder general management from using transfer prices as a means to achieve corporate objectives.

The chief advantage of the cost of production approach for setting transfer prices is that the costs are available and are subject to quantification. For this reason, the production cost approach has been more common in the past than the market price approach. The chief disadvantage is that there is no real incentive for an affiliate to improve its manufacturing process, to enhance its efficiency, or to take steps to lower costs. Mistakes, errors, inefficiencies in manning or machinery, management inattention to detail, worker carelessness, and excessive remuneration of white and blue collar workers alike may all be incorporated in the determination of costs and passed on to the affiliates in the transfer price. Another disadvantage is that both the tax authority and the affiliates may object to the nature of the apportionment of R&D, S&A, tangibles, and intangibles among the various products and the assigned profit margin.

SETTING TRANSFER PRICES BY MARKET PRICES

The disadvantages associated with the cost-of-production method of setting transfer prices can be mostly avoided by referencing transfer prices to third party transactions for identical, or nearly identical, products. If an affiliate can obtain the item being purchased from a third party for a certain price, then that price can be the basis for setting the transfer price. The proponents of market-oriented transfer prices maintain that letting the market set the transfer price is inherently more fair than a production-cost-based system because one affiliate is not supporting the inefficiencies of another. If an affiliate receives only the global competitive price for its products, then there is an incentive for it to take whatever actions are needed to correct the inefficiencies in its operations that are resulting in higher costs.

In a truly decentralized operation, managers are expected to make their decisions on an independent basis, and unrelated companies are permitted to compete for the business of an affiliate, along with other affiliates. The parent organization does not set transfer prices and has little or no influence over the decisions made by the managers of the affiliates. No favor or special consideration is shown to fellow affiliates in the competitive process of selecting suppliers for components and goods. The hope, of course, is that everyone is kept on his or her competitive toes to produce salable goods at the lowest possible cost.

This managerial philosophy, where each affiliate is treated as an independent company, is sometimes referred to as the small business unit (SBU) management philosophy. The disadvantage is that, although each affiliate is focused on optimizing its operations, the end result may be suboptimal performance of the corporation as a whole. Suppose that affiliate X produces all of a component (part X) for a number of widget manufacturing affiliates. Total demand for part

X is 2 million per year. Affiliate X has $10 million in fixed annual costs, which include a profit margin on the investment in manufacturing facilities plus a return on the R&D investment for the development of part X. The variable costs for manufacturing part X is $5. The transfer price based on the fixed and variable costs of affiliate X supplying all other affiliates with part X is $10.

VOLUME OF SALES: 2,000,000

Fixed Costs	$10,000,000
Variable Costs at $5 per Unit	10,000,000
Total Costs	$20,000,000
Transfer Price Based on Cost of Making 2,000,000	$10.00

Affiliate A is free to cut its best deal and obtains a quote of $9.50 from another company. Affiliate A does what is best for maximizing its profits and purchases 200,000 part X's from a third party for $9.50 rather than pay $10 to affiliate X. Affiliate X has lost a contract for 200,000 part X's and now operates on a basis of a sales volume of 1,800,000 per year.

VOLUME OF SALES: 1,800,000

Fixed Costs	$10,000,000
Variable Costs at $5 per Unit	9,000,000
Total Costs	$19,000,000
Transfer Price Based on Cost of Making 1,800,000	$10.56

The remaining affiliates must pay a higher price because there is less sales volume to cover the fixed costs of affiliate X. The increase in transfer price to cover the fixed and variable costs is essentially equivalent to treating fixed costs as a component of variable costs, which it is not. Nevertheless, affiliate X must cover all its costs. When affiliate X announces the increase in price, affiliate B concludes a deal with a third party at $9.75 causing another loss of 200,000 for affiliate X.

VOLUME OF SALES: 1,600,000

Fixed Costs	$10,000,000
Variable Costs at $5 per Unit	8,000,000
Total Costs	$18,000,000
Transfer Price Based on Cost of Making 1,600,000	$11.25

Now it's time for affiliate C to say goodbye to affiliate X, as it maximizes its profit by reducing the cost of part X by paying $10.50 to another outside source. This is higher than the $10 price that applied when all the affiliates received part X from affiliate X. It is clear from the continuation of this exercise that, as each affiliate maximizes its profits by cutting costs, the corporation as a whole is being suboptimized. Even if the various affiliates do not pay more than an average price of $10 per unit for part X in purchasing all part X's from outside sources, the global company is stuck with an affiliate with no sales and a fixed annual cost of $10 million that represents, in large measure, financing costs on plant and equipment.

It is highly likely that the fixed costs in affiliate X contain an allowance for R&D expenses and product development that have to be recouped in the operation of a company, but do not have to be recouped by another company if it is essentially manufacturing a copy of part X. Copying is fairly common in global commerce because patent protection is limited to the nation issuing the patent. Global companies often obtain patents in a number of nations, but this may not be possible for all nations. A company may manufacture a copy of a product in one of these nations. Although it is true that affiliate X is free to pursue patent infringement action against sales in a particular nation where it has patent protection, the time involved in enforcement proceedings and the legal expenses may make such protection prohibitively expensive. Furthermore, there is no internationally recognized legal structure to handle patent infringements. In addition to R&D expenses, the fixed costs of affiliate X may also contain a service element for the benefit of the affiliates purchasing its output that may not be provided by third parties. By each affiliate "doing its own thing," the R&D and service costs cannot be covered.

One principal problem associated with using market reference points for transfer pricing is that the affiliates may be shipping components and parts that are not readily available from other firms. Most components and parts are specifically designed for a company's product line and are not available from third parties unless contracted for by an affiliate. Market prices for similarly designed components that cannot be actually used in the company's product line may not be relevant. Moreover, the quality inherent in third-party quotes for similar parts may not be up to the standards imposed on products made within a global corporate family.

There is no easy answer as to which approach for determining transfer prices should be followed. Both have their adherents and detractors. Either approach restricts transfer prices to something related to third-party, or market, transactions or to the cost of manufacture. Surveys have shown that nations seem to exhibit cultural preferences as to which approach to follow and as to what motivates companies in setting transfer prices. Companies in some countries favor cost-based transfer prices, whereas companies in other nations favor market-based transfer prices. U.S. based corporations have historically preferred setting transfer prices by the cost approach because the necessary data is available, whereas the necessary data for setting transfer prices on the basis of market transactions may not be available. Oftentimes, market quotes for uniquely designed parts and components may have to be derived rather than observed because there are no market transactions for the precise item. Should General Motors set its transfer price on carburetors being shipped to Europe based on its cost of production or on what Toyota charges its U.S. transplants? The two carburetors are not the same and do not have the same cost of production. Furthermore, there may not be a data base available for prices for carburetors sold between related and unrelated parties from which to derive a market price.

Preferences change with time. Surveys done in the 1970s indicated that the preponderance of U.S. companies were motivated by tax minimization in setting transfer prices. More recent surveys indicate that companies are more interested in setting transfer prices on the basis of measuring the performance of affiliate managers and of providing reliable and unbiased information for the making of decisions. This change in attitude in U.S. companies may be the result of the United States becoming a relative tax haven compared to other nations. Its corporate tax rate of 34 percent, plus state taxes, is less than in many other industrialized nations, where tax rates range between 40 percent and 55 percent. A U.S. company's total tax bill may, in fact, be reduced by allocating more profits to the United States. Regardless of changes in attitudes as to what is important in setting transfer prices, the essential point is that there is no unanimity on which approach to use and on what motivates companies in setting transfer prices.

Up to this point, an important assumption has been that the parent company has real control over transfer prices to manage corporate cash flows and the profits reported by affiliates and to overcome artificial barriers to trade in the form of custom duties, currency exchange, and price controls. Some recent surveys suggest that competitive forces and market conditions within a nation seem to be more important in setting transfer prices than decisions made by a parent organization. If transfer prices are being set by exogenous commercial forces, then the presumption that a parent organization is able to achieve optimal financial performance of a global family of affiliates through the careful orchestration of transfer pricing is being challenged.

TAX CONSIDERATIONS

Taxation and transfer pricing are intimately entwined, because transfer pricing of goods, parts, and components moving in and out of a nation has a direct impact on taxes on profits and on the amount of duties and tariffs paid to the tax authority. The discussion on transfer pricing based on the cost-of-production approach shows an intimate involvement with the tax authority in the methodology for calculating various elements of the transfer price.

There is little uniformity on taxation among nations. Taxes range from taxation of a corporation's activities to the "water's edge" or on its global earnings, the so-called "unitary tax." The state of California invented the unitary tax in the

1930s when movie companies in California began moving out of the state to avoid state taxes. A unitary tax was applied against the global earnings of a company and the tax was determined by the proportion of a company's sales, property, and payroll within the state to its global sales, property, and payroll. The resulting tax had no relation to the degree of profitability of a company's operation in California. A company could operate at a loss in California and still pay a tax based on its global profits.

Needless to say, both foreign governments and multinational companies have vigorously fought the unitary tax. A number of court decisions confirmed or restricted unitary taxation over the years. Ultimately, opposition to the unitary tax succeeded. In November 1991, Alaska was the last state to abandon having a company's state tax liability based on the global earnings of the company. The unitary tax still exists in a truncated form, where earnings are restricted to the "water's edge." The state tax is calculated on the portion of a company's activities within a state as compared to its activities within the United States.

Although most other countries limit their assessment on what is to be taxed to the operations of a company within their jurisdiction, there is no universal agreement as to what constitutes revenue and expenses in the calculation of taxable income and no uniformity on tax rates. Every nation decides what is subject to taxation and the applicable tax rates. The complexity of tax regulations, in general, and the diversity of tax laws among nations are such that it is necessary for an affiliate to retain the technical expertise necessary to understand and comply with local tax regulations. The parent organization must retain the technical knowledge for its own tax jurisdiction and have sufficient knowledge of tax matters elsewhere to coordinate tax planning among the various affiliates.

The vigor with which tax payments are enforced varies among nations. Some countries with seemingly high tax rates permit an underground economy to flourish without much in the way of enforcing tax payments. The other side of the coin is the willingness of companies to adhere to tax laws. In some nations, a businessman who scrupulously follows the tax laws and pays what is owed to the tax authority will find himself at a competitive disadvantage.

NATURE OF TAXES

Taxes can be direct or indirect. The United States relies more on direct taxation, which is applied to each taxable entity. A U.S. corporation is taxed at 34 percent on its profits. If a corporation pays a dividend to its shareholders, then the next taxable entity, the individual, pays a tax, which may be 28 percent or more. This is double taxation. Some nations, such as Germany, have two corporate tax rates on profits—one for retained profits and the other for distributed profits in the form of dividends. A lesser tax rate applies to profits that are distributed to shareholders to reduce the degree of double taxation.

Europe relies more on indirect taxes—particularly, the value added tax (VAT). The VAT is basically a tax applied to each stage of the production process and is not directly associated with the degree of profitability. Indeed, only a small portion of a VAT is associated with profits. Suppose that a company's manufacturing operations has the following financial results.

Wages, rents, interest, profit	$400,000
Outside purchases of goods and services for which VAT has already been paid	600,000
Total sales	$1,000,000

The additive method is to apply the VAT rate, say 10 percent, to all costs associated with the production of goods, including profit and excluding purchases of goods and services from third parties for which the VAT has already been paid. In this case, $400,000 of a company's activities falls into this category resulting in a VAT of $40,000. A simpler method of calculation is to take the gross sales of the company ($1,000,000), subtract all purchases of goods and services for which VAT has already been paid ($600,000), and apply the VAT rate to the balance ($400,000). Either method yields the same result. The VAT is essentially equivalent to a national sales tax, because every company associated with the production and marketing of goods and providing services pays a tax on whatever value it adds to the goods or services. The value added tax, like a sales tax, is a tax on consumption, whereas U.S. taxes are on income and profits.

Value added tax rates vary widely from country to country and according to the nature of the business. Certain European countries have low VAT rates (5 percent) for business transactions associated with food and high VAT rates (40 percent) for luxury products. Others attempt to have one rate that applies to most forms of commerce. Because the VAT is not paid on items that have already been exposed to a value added tax, and with the European economy becoming more integrated, there is a powerful incentive for the European Community to harmonize VAT rates and coordinate the handling of VAT payments for products or components shipped between members of the European Community.

The amounts of value added by a company are frequently disclosed in European financial statements. In the excerpt from the British company Bass shown in Table 7.3, the company had gross revenues of 3,213 million pounds in 1987 of which 919.1 million pounds represents added value by the company. Of the total of 919.1 million pounds of added value, 496.8 million pounds was paid to the company's employees, 157.1 million pounds was paid in taxes to government tax authorities, and the remainder was paid to the internal and external providers of capital.

U.S. TAXATION OF GLOBAL COMPANIES

Nations have different ways of taxing global companies domiciled within their jurisdiction. If a parent corporation is domiciled in the United States, it does

Table 7.3
Excerpt from Bass Financial Statement

	1987 £m	1986 £m	1985 £m	1984† £m	1983 £m
ADDED VALUE					
Turnover	3,213·4	2,709·7	2,410·8	2,252·3	1,988·4
Surplus on disposal of fixed assets	15·3	17·4	8·8	10·3	14·7
	3,228·7	2,727·1	2,419·6	2,262·6	2,003·1
Bought-in materials, services and depreciation	(1,681·2)	(1,299·4)	(1,116·6)	(1,049·4)	(910·6)
Excise duty	(628·4)	(627·4)	(618·5)	(576·2)	(517·5)
	919·1	800·3	684·5	637·0	575·0
DISTRIBUTION					
For employees					
Salaries, wages and pension contributions	484·7	430·8	379·6	365·3	345·9
Employee profit share scheme	12·1	10·8	8·7	7·7	6·2
	496·8	441·6	388·3	373·0	352·1
To governments					
Corporation tax	121·2	111·5	90·3	74·7	61·7
Social security contributions	35·9	31·1	27·8	28·7	25·7
	157·1	142·6	118·1	103·4	87·4
To providers of capital					
Cost of borrowing	21·4	17·2	13·3	16·9	22·2
Shareholders	72·4	59·8	48·5	43·1	37·6
	93·8	77·0	61·8	60·0	59·8
For reinvestment in the business					
Retained profits	195·6	85·6	116·3	91·4	75·7
Extraordinary items	(24·2)	53·5	—	9·2	—
	919·1	800·3	684·5	637·0	575·0

†53 weeks

not pay taxes in the United States on profits earned by incorporated affiliates in other nations, unless the nation is considered a tax haven. This, in the United States, is known as Subpart F income, which will be discussed later under reinvoicing centers. Unlike an incorporated affiliate, a branch of a U.S. company located in a foreign nation is taxed directly on its earnings regardless of whether the earnings are remitted to the home office or not. The taxes paid on remitted and unremitted earnings are not the same, in that unremitted earnings have to be translated to U.S. dollars before a tax liability can be assessed, and therefore, are influenced by changes in currency exchange rates. Taxes can also be calculated on the basis of the increase in the net worth of the branch, which can also be affected by changes in currency exchange rates. Sometimes a U.S. company will first open a branch operation in another country to permit startup losses to flow back to the parent organization. When the branch becomes profitable, it may be reorganized as a wholly owned subsidiary, reducing the company's overall tax liability.

U.S. based companies usually operate in the global market through operating affiliates whose stock is owned by the parent corporation. The parent corporation pays U.S. taxes only on the profits generated from dividends, royalties, and other service payments and fees paid by a non-U.S. domiciled affiliate to the parent organization. Taxes paid on profits by affiliates in their nations of domicile can be treated either as a tax credit or a tax deduction by the parent organization in the calculation of its U.S. taxes. To the degree that a tax paid on profits to a foreign government is treated as a tax credit, the net effect of a company paying taxes on its profits in a foreign country is that these taxes are essentially paid for by the U.S. government foregoing an equivalent amount of U.S. source-based tax revenue.

Obviously, taxes paid to foreign governments must pass certain criteria set forth by the Internal Revenue Service to be considered for a tax credit. Foreign tax credits apply to taxes paid on foreign source profits calculated in a conventional way as U.S. source profits. Tax credits are also available for foreign government withholding taxes on dividends, interest payments, and royalties paid by a foreign-based affiliate to a U.S. parent company. There is a maximum permissible limit on tax credits linked to the ratio of foreign source income to total worldwide income multiplied by the tax liability of U.S. operations. This effectively limits the foreign tax credit to the U.S., not the foreign, tax rate. A company doing business in a nation with a higher tax rate on profits than in the United States does not receive a tax credit equal to the taxes paid to the foreign government. The tax credit is based on the U.S. tax rate. With U.S. tax rates being lower than in most other industrialized nations, U.S. based global companies are not being fully compensated by tax credits on foreign income taxes. This may provide an incentive to shift taxable income back to the United States through changes in transfer prices.

The U.S. tax authorities permit a credit for taxes paid on profits to other nations under the notion of tax equity and tax neutrality. The principle of tax equity implies that a U.S. taxpaying entity with an operation in another nation should not pay more in taxes than having the operation domiciled in the United States. Were the equity principle absolutely true, a U.S. taxpaying entity would be indifferent, or neutral, to whether the operation was located in another nation or in the United States. Some maintain that the U.S. tax code does not adhere to the tax neutrality principle because a company doing business in New York City does not obtain a tax credit on its federal taxes for taxes paid to the state and city of New York on profits made in their jurisdiction.

A company with an affiliate in another nation not only receives a tax credit, which neutralizes its foreign and U.S. income taxes, but does not have to pay U.S. taxes on its foreign source earnings until those earnings are remitted to the parent in the form of a dividend, a royalty payment, or an equivalent thereof. As long as foreign source profits remain in the coffers of the affiliate, no taxes are due to the U.S. government, even though, under special circumstances, the affiliate may lend these funds to the parent company. Deferral of dividend payments is essentially an interest-free loan made by the U.S. government to the foreign affiliate of a U.S. parent company on the amount of U.S. taxes due if, and when, these funds are repatriated to the U.S. parent.

The principles of equity and neutrality built into the U.S. tax code were designed to provide an incentive for U.S. firms to invest overseas as part of the national policy of rebuilding war-torn nations. U.S. companies would be better off confining their activities within the United States, and would not invest in foreign affiliates, if the profits of these foreign affiliates were exposed to double taxation.

Qualified foreign taxes, which cannot be utilized as tax credits, may be used as a tax deduction. A tax deduction is not as valuable as a tax credit. Tax deductions apply when there is not sufficient U.S. taxes to be shielded by tax credits, or where the overall limitation on tax credits has been exceeded. Tax deductions can be carried back or carried forward, whichever is more useful.

REINVOICING CENTERS

Some companies have set up reinvoicing centers to manage all intracompany trading of products. A reinvoicing center is at a single location, buying the output of the manufacturing affiliates and selling it to the marketing affiliates. Each affiliate receives or pays in its own currency, thus concentrating all intracompany transaction currency exposure at the reinvoicing center. The center possesses the necessary data to assess the net currency exposure of intracompany transactions and can enter into appropriate currency hedges. The center may also receive better quotes from currency exchange dealers because all intracompany currency exchange transactions are done at one location.

The reinvoicing center can mark up the price of all products flowing through the center to cover its administrative expenses. If there is little or no profitability associated with the operations of a reinvoicing center, it does not matter where the reinvoicing center is located from a tax viewpoint. However, it is possible to increase the markup to the point where corporate profit can be diverted from the nations where the goods are manufactured and marketed to the nation where the reinvoicing center is located. Now the location of the reinvoicing center is critical from a tax viewpoint.

In the 1960s, the U.S. government became concerned with the accumulation of profits in reinvoicing centers located in tax havens. Tax havens were characterized as nations imposing no, or a very low, tax on profits, having a high degree of bank secrecy, and little or no currency controls. These nations consider financial activities of importance to their economy, provide modern communication facilities, and promote themselves as offshore financial centers. Bahamas, Bermuda, Cayman Islands, Liberia, Panama, and Vanuatu have been identified as tax havens.

It is possible to "run" a reinvoicing center through these nations without a physical presence of personnel or products. Profits can be easily diverted to tax havens by increasing the markup on selling prices, thus reducing tax liabilities to the nations where the products are manufactured and marketed. If the criteria for determining a tax haven is satisfied, then the income earned by a reinvoicing center, or any corporate entity in the declared tax haven, is deemed Subpart F income. This income flows directly to the U.S. parent corporation and is taxed as though the income was earned in the United States.

TAXATION IMPACT ON TRANSFER PRICING

Companies operating in the United States are guided by Section 482 of the Internal Revenue Code when setting transfer prices. Specifically, the IRS, through the Secretary of the Treasury, has the right to "distribute, apportion, or allocate gross income, deductions, credits, or allowances . . . between or among . . . businesses, if he determines that such distribution, apportionment, or allocation is necessary in order to prevent evasion of taxes. . . . " The IRS has been granted wide latitude to do whatever it wants if the IRS deems that dealings between a U.S. parent and its affiliates do not meet its standards. For instance, the IRS can reallocate income and deductions if loans have been made between a parent corporation and an affiliate at an unrealistic interest rate. Unrealistic interest rates are those that would not occur for similar transactions between unrelated third parties. This also applies to charging for services and use of property, and transfers of tangible and intangible property including lease payments and royalties. A reference to IRS guidelines has already been made in discussing R&D and intangible costs in setting transfer prices by the production cost approach. Basing transfer pricing on published data rather than corporate-derived prices is another example of the close working relationship, voluntary or not, between tax authorities and managers responsible for transfer prices.

In general, the IRS standard for determining transfer pricing, and other dealings between a parent and its affiliates, is whether it is an "arm's-length" transaction—one that would occur between a company and a third party having no affiliation other than the commercial transaction under consideration. This is independent of whether the transfer price is based on the cost of production or on market prices. If the transfer price between affiliates is seemingly out of line with a price that would have been charged to an unrelated party, then the IRS has the right to reallocate income or deductions according to what it feels to be the appropriate transfer price.

The IRS specifies various methods for establishing an appropriate transfer price. The preferred one is the comparable uncontrolled price method where prices are the same for goods sold to affiliated and to nonaffiliated companies. The price for goods sold to an unrelated third party establishes the transfer price for goods transferred to an affiliate. This method does not work when goods are not sold to third parties, but are totally transferred between affiliates. Under these circumstances, the second method for setting the transfer price is the resale price method. This is the price for which the company would sell the item to an unspecified third party. The third party would add the same comparable value as the affiliate and sell the completed product with an appropriate markup. By netting the market price of the appropriate markup and the value added to the product by an affiliate, one can "back into" an appropriate transfer price from the point of view of the tax authority. The third method is the "cost plus" method, where the IRS permits three different ways of allocating costs (full absorption, direct cost, and incremental cost). All these methods leave some margin of discretion as to what is the appropriate transfer price.

If all these fail, as they frequently do for high-technology products, customized components, or subassemblies, then so-called fourth methods are permitted, such as determining transfer pricing on the basis of a predetermined profit for the foreign firm's operations and, through a netting process of accounting for applicable costs, establishing an appropriate transfer price. Regardless of the methodology, the burden of proof in supporting a transfer price is with the taxpayer, not the IRS. To confuse matters more, there have been occasions when the tax courts have rejected the notion of arm's-length transfer pricing in settling tax disputes between corporations and the IRS.

OTHER NATIONS' POLICIES CONCERNING TRANSFER PRICING

The tax authority in Canada views transfer pricing of goods similar to the way the United States does. Transfer pricing for services differs in that it is based on a pro rata sharing of actual incurred costs between the parent corporation and its affiliate, and not necessarily at an arm's-length price. Tax authorities in Japan follow a system comparable to that of the United States. German tax code provisions permit the reallocation of domestic source income if revenue or income has been shifted to another nation through a transaction that is different from those that would have been entered into by unrelated parties. In other words, transfer pricing should be arm's-length, although the code is not specific in defining arm's-length pricing. The United Kingdom is similar to Germany in not specifically defining arm's-length pricing. The Inland Revenue may adjust taxable income based on fairness and arm's-length criteria. Disputes between corporations and Inland Revenue agents are frequently settled by negotiation, resulting in some sort of compromise between the two parties. This is unlike in Germany, where the adjustments made by the tax authorities are considered final, and unlike in the United States, where adjustments are litigated in tax courts.

Tax authorities in many nations are currently taking a much closer look at transfer pricing practices. Recently, the U.K. Inland Revenue recast the accounts of one non-British company operating in the United Kingdom and assessed back taxes of nearly 2 billion pounds. In the United States, there is growing political pressure for the IRS to take more vigorous action against foreign-owned companies operating through U.S. based affiliates. This pressure stems from the realization that the aggregate expenses for foreign-owned businesses operating in the United States exceed aggregate revenues. This means that, in the aggregate, foreign-owned subsidiaries are claiming to operate at a loss, although individual foreign-owned subsidiaries may be paying taxes on profits. Some foreign-owned affiliates operating in the United States have a twenty-year string of consecutive losses. This is not considered a realistic appraisal of performance because there are few profit-motivated foreign-based parent companies that would support twenty years of successive losses were they real.

Poor or nonexistent profits for foreign-based affiliates operating in the United States are blamed on transfer pricing. Transfer price manipulation is felt to have resulted in tax underpayments of between $12 and $50 billion. Legislation was passed in 1989 to require foreign-owned businesses in the United States to keep records, in English, of transactions with foreign related parties. Much of this legislation has to do with substantiating transfer pricing on either a cost or arm's-length transaction with an unrelated third party. All of this illustrates a growing risk associated with manipulating transfer prices for the purpose of tax minimization. The risk is that the tax authorities will recast the company's statements with their own version of the proper transfer price, thus exposing a company to the risk of double taxation.

Most nations have entered into tax treaties with various other nations with regard to taxing of affiliates of parent organizations domiciled in the treaty nations. These treaties determine withholding taxes on dividends, interest, and royalties; relief from double taxation; and the types of taxes and organizations covered by the treaty. Overall exposure to taxation can be reduced by judicious structuring of the legal corporate entities of a parent company and its affiliates in accordance with the provisions of these treaties.

Some of these treaties contain formal agreements for the mutual examination of the tax returns of affiliates of a parent company. The tax returns of affiliates and parent organizations are exchanged and examined by the tax authorities to determine correct tax liabilities, detect tax avoidance maneuvers, scrutinize transfer pricing practices, and exchange information useful to the tax authorities. These treaties also provide a forum for one tax authority to complain about the actions taken by another, when these actions are deemed detrimental to its interests.

Recent developments in international cooperation of tax authorities include the establishment of a formal agreement on transfer prices. The mutual agreement of various nations to reference a published source for tanker rates in determining oil company tax liabilities is an example of this. Australia and the United States are attempting to grant "advance determinations" of the proper transfer price for Australian companies dealings with their U.S. affiliates. A recent survey has shown that about half of IRS tax examinations of multinational companies involve transfer prices. If a mutually agreeable methodology could be arranged between a company and the IRS, many of these tax examinations could be eliminated.

The IRS is attempting to develop a procedure whereby a company and the IRS would mutually agree to a transfer-pricing agreement covering the distribution of finished goods, sales of raw materials and components, general and administrative expenses, and managerial and technical services. If the taxpayer develops an acceptable transfer-pricing methodology, then the taxpayer and the IRS would enter into an advance-pricing agreement. The IRS would limit its examinations to an audit to ensure that the taxpayer has complied with the agreement.

However, the taxpayer is obliged to submit pricing data of independent transactions, or an adequate substitute, to show that the transfer price possesses the necessary attributes of an arm's-length transaction. The taxpayer is also responsible to show that the agreed transfer-pricing methodology is generating acceptable transfer prices from an arm's-length perspective. The preference of tax authorities in many nations for arm's-length transfer pricing may act as an inducement to switch from the cost-of-production to the market price approach in setting transfer prices because, presumably, they are one and the same.

Questions associated with international taxation and transfer pricing are too numerous and complex to be dealt with in this chapter. Both are so intertwined that they cannot be separately treated. Yet the financial and taxation departments of multinational, or global, companies must deal daily with what are considered to be the most pressing issues in international accounting today. Those involved with transfer pricing must measure the consequences of their transfer-pricing decisions both on corporate profits and on current and potential tax liabilities. Potential tax liabilities, stemming from tax authorities rejecting management's transfer price decisions, and substituting their own, are enormous. This must weigh heavily on the shoulders of those responsible for setting transfer prices.

CHAPTER 8

ACCOUNTING FOR INFLATION

All currencies are heading down the road to worthlessness, some more rapidly than others. Many businessmen, however, have been commercially successful in highly inflationary environments. As long as increases in corporate revenue compensate for the ravages of inflation, one can prosper where others may not survive. Businessmen can more easily manage cash flow and monetary assets when inflation rates are low and interest rates substantially compensate for the loss of purchasing power. Cash can be held as cash. Games do not have to be played with inventories, receivables, payables, bank loans, and currency conversions to protect a company from erosion of the purchasing power of its monetary assets.

The simple reaction to avoid doing business in highly inflationary environments is understandable. A special financial acumen is necessary to stay ahead of inflation surging at several hundred percent per year. A company that decides to avoid the pitfalls of operating in highly inflationary economies restricts its activities to those areas where business is conducted in relatively stable currencies. There is a much larger market, in terms of population, called the third world. It is obvious by the size of third world economies that many businessmen and companies have learned to cope, and apparently to thrive, in less than desirable monetary environments.

INFLATION VARIES WITH TIME AND PLACE

A cursory examination of consumer price indices listed in the *International Financial Statistics*, published by the International Monetary Fund, shows that the rate of inflation is unique to a nation and varies with the times. Inflation was more subdued among the industrialized nations in the 1980s than it was in the

Table 8.1
Annual Inflation Rates of Low Inflation Nations

	JAPAN	GERMANY	NETHERLANDS	UNITED STATES
1975	11.9%	5.9%	10.5%	9.2%
1976	9.3	4.5	8.8	5.8
1977	8.1	3.9	6.4	6.5
1978	3.8	2.8	4.1	7.5
1979	3.6	4.1	4.2	11.3
1980	8.0	5.5	6.5	13.5
1981	4.9	6.3	6.8	10.4
1982	2.6	5.3	5.9	6.2
1983	1.9	3.3	2.8	3.2
1984	2.3	2.4	3.3	4.3
1985	2.0	2.2	2.2	3.6
1986	0.6	-0.1	0.1	1.9
1987	0.0	0.2	-0.7	3.7
1988	0.7	1.3	0.7	4.0
1989	2.3	2.8	1.1	4.8
1990	3.1	2.7	2.5	5.4
1991	3.3	3.5	3.9	4.2

1970s. It is possible to group nations in terms of low, medium, and high rates of inflation, although nations can shift their position among these broad classifications over time. Generally speaking, low inflation nations (Table 8.1) are the leading industrialized nations. They also exhibit social and political stability, which suggests that inflation of a nation's currency is not just a consequence of a government's fiscal and monetary policies.

The medium inflation nations listed in Table 8.2 have inflation rates more closely akin to low inflation nations than high inflation nations. Although France is listed as a nation with a medium rate of inflation, which was true for the 1970s, it should be listed among the low inflation nations in the 1980s. Both Italy and the United Kingdom have cut their inflation rates substantially during the 1980s. Two conditions, among others, for the European Currency Unit (ECU) becoming a common European currency are that interest and inflation rates be at comparable levels among the European Community nations, to permit the simultaneous conversion of all European currencies into a single currency.

The considerable reduction in inflation rates during the 1980s suggests that inflation can be controlled if nations have the will to do so. It is apparent in examining the disparity in inflation rates between the medium inflation nations in Table 8.2 and the high inflation nations in Table 8.3 that there appears to be a point where citizens and businessmen abandon a currency as a storehouse of value. This occurs when the inflation rate exceeds the interest rate on financial instruments by a sufficient margin to convince all that holding the currency, even in the form of an interest-bearing bank deposit, is a losing proposition. Once money has lost its attribute as a storehouse of value through a succession of rapid losses in purchasing power, the currency is essentially repudiated. Money

Table 8.2
Annual Inflation Rates of Medium Inflation Nations

	FRANCE	ITALY	NEW ZEALAND	UNITED KINGDOM
1975	11.7%	17.0%	14.5%	24.2%
1976	9.6	16.8	16.9	16.5
1977	9.5	17.0	14.5	15.9
1978	9.2	12.1	11.9	8.3
1979	10.8	14.7	13.8	13.4
1980	13.8	21.2	17.2	18.0
1981	13.4	17.8	15.4	11.9
1982	11.8	16.5	16.2	8.6
1983	9.6	14.7	7.3	4.6
1984	7.4	10.8	6.2	5.0
1985	5.8	9.2	15.4	6.1
1986	2.5	5.9	13.2	1.9
1987	3.3	4.7	15.7	3.7
1988	2.7	5.1	6.4	4.0
1989	3.5	6.3	5.7	4.8
1990	3.4	6.5	6.1	5.4
1991	3.1	6.4	2.6	4.2

Table 8.3
Annual Inflation Rates of High Inflation Nations

	ARGENTINA	BRAZIL	TURKEY	ZAIRE
1975	182.5%	28.9%	19.2%	30.7%
1976	443.2	42.0	17.3	88.2
1977	176.1	43.7	27.1	63.1
1978	175.5	38.7	45.3	58.4
1979	159.5	52.7	58.7	108.6
1980	100.8	82.8	110.2	42.1
1981	104.5	105.5	36.6	34.9
1982	164.8	98.0	30.8	37.2
1983	343.8	142.2	29.1	75.9
1984	626.7	197.0	48.4	52.2
1985	672.1	226.9	45.0	23.8
1986	90.1	145.2	34.6	46.7
1987	131.0	229.7	38.8	90.4
1988	343.0	682.3	75.4	82.7
1989	3,079.8	1,287.0	69.6	104.1
1990	2,314.0	2,937.8	63.6	81.3
1991	NA	440.8	NA	NA

NA: Not available

is spent on receipt. Excess cash is exchanged for tangible assets to preserve purchasing power. This increases the velocity of money, or the number of transactions per period of time, which adds to the inflation rate and brings a nation to a point of hyperinflation.

An inflation rate of 100 percent means that prices are doubling every year, 1,200 percent means, neglecting compounding, doubling every month, such as occurred in Brazil in 1989. Inflation of 2,400 percent means doubling of prices every two weeks, such as in Argentina and Brazil in 1990. In 1989, prices were doubling in Argentina in less than two weeks' time, posing quite a challenge for financial managers and accountants.

CUMULATIVE LOSSES IN PURCHASING POWER

Not apparent from these numbers is the cumulative loss of purchasing power over a period of time. In 1915, Henry Ford doubled the salary of his work force to $5 per day, which meant that workers at that time could survive (feed, house, and clothe their families) on $2.50 per day, or about $750 per year. When Ford doubled their pay to $5 per day, or $1,500 per year, the workers not only could increase their standard of living but they had enough money to buy a Model T automobile. Today, the poverty level for a family in the United States is around $15,000 per year, which is not adequate to purchase a new automobile. Viewed in this light, the cumulative loss in purchasing power of the U.S. dollar over the course of this century is on the order of 95 percent.

Cumulative loss of purchasing power is more severe in other nations. For highly inflationary nations such as Brazil, which, by the way, does not have the worst inflationary record, money is called in from time to time and exchanged for new money with a new name, the cruzerio or the cruzado. The exchange of 1,000 cruzerios for 1 cruzado to be followed some time later by the exchange of 1,000 cruzados for 1 cruzerio avoids confusion among Brazilians as to which currency is in vogue. The lopping off of three zeroes reduces the expense of having to print a wheelbarrowful of money to buy a quart of milk and of having to expand numerical data fields in the banks' computer systems.

The record for the highest cumulative loss in the shortest time by an industrialized nation is probably held by Germany. During the Weimar Republic, a mark, which was worth about $0.25 at the end of World War I, was reduced in value to 1 trillion marks per postage stamp over the course of about four years. When new money was issued, the conversion rate was several trillion old marks per new mark—the lopping off of twelve zeroes in one blow.

GENERAL VERSUS SPECIFIC INFLATION

Tables 8.1 through 8.3 express inflation in terms of the consumer price index, which is a general indicator of inflation of the aggregate weighted price of consumer purchases of goods and services. The wholesale price index is a general indicator of inflation of the aggregate weighted price of manufacturers' purchases. Specific items within the index have their unique inflation rates. As an example, the wholesale price index in the United States rose by 5.8 percent between 1987 and 1988. This does not mean that every component within this index rose by 5.8 percent. On the contrary, prices for machinery and equipment climbed by 16.3 percent and metals by 1.7 percent, whereas prices for pulp and paper fell by 16.4 percent and energy by 3.2 percent. However, the weighted average of these, and the other components to the index, caused the wholesale price index to increase by 5.8 percent.

Labor costs are usually tied to the general consumer price index because wage earners want to maintain their purchasing power for consumer goods and services. But a company's other costs are affected by specific price indices associated with material costs (e.g., steel, copper, and plastic) and transportation costs (vehicle acquisition, maintenance, and fuel costs). If a company produces a variety of consumer products, its revenue may track the general consumer price index, but this may not be true if it makes a single consumer item or industrial goods. Consequently, price hikes in the product line may under- or overcompensate for cost escalations caused by inflation. The general consumer price index, although of interest in the conduct of business in a highly inflationary environment, is only one of many possible indices of inflation and may not be relevant for a particular company.

MANAGEMENT'S REACTION TO INFLATION

Inflation is linked to government fiscal and monetary policies and to the productivity of a nation's industries and its people. Most blame inflation on government deficit spending, which is papered over by printing more currency or expanding of bank credit, rather than by raising taxes. This lack of fiscal responsibility to balance the budget usually ends up with a monetary policy that creates excess amounts of currency and bank credit by which the government pays or borrows to cover its deficits. Managers view inflation as something beyond their control. On an individual basis, this is true. Yet the growth in the productive capacity of a nation's industrial base is a consequence of decisions made by business interests, which are, in turn, influenced by government policies toward business. Presumably, productivity gains by businesses and corporations equal to the speed of the government monetary printing presses can keep inflation under control. If incremental output of goods and services were equal to incremental growth of the money supply, prices might not go up—the definition of inflation. Tables 8.1 through 8.3 show that it is far easier for a government to add currency and credit than it is for industry to add productive capacity.

OBJECTIVITY IN HISTORIC COST ACCOUNTING

Businessmen and accountants obviously prefer a stable currency for all sorts of good sound reasons, one of which is historic cost accounting. Historic cost accounting depends on a stable currency because transactions are recorded at actual cost with no further adjustments as the value of money changes. This allows for objectivity in accounting, in that no "guesstimates" are made with regard to what an item might have cost. The original $1 million cost of a factory remains on the books at $1 million.

There have been instances when historic cost accounting did not fulfill the dictum to present the true and fair view of a company's financial state. Several U.S. airlines have showed profits right up to the moment of financial oblivion. These airlines originally acquired their fleets at cheap prices. Their financial reports, based on historic cost accounting, showed a profit on the original investment. They provided no hint that the airlines were in danger of ceasing to be ongoing concerns. Yet this occurred because the accumulated profits fell far short of enabling the companies to preserve themselves as ongoing concerns when the time arrived to replace the aircraft. In one instance, the cost of the door on the new airplane was equal to the acquisition cost of the original aircraft. The revenue generation of these airlines provided a margin of profitability on the historic cost of their aircraft, but fell far short in servicing the financing charges of the replacement aircraft.

In extreme cases, financial reports can show profits up to the moment of a company's demise and do not present a true and fair view of its financial state. This problem becomes particularly acute in an inflationary environment. Historic cost accounting in an inflationary environment leads to an overstatement of earnings because depreciation is based on the historic cost of the productive assets, whereas their replacement is based on much higher current costs. Insufficient depreciation also may result in the overpayment of taxes, which takes away from the capacity to accumulate sufficient funds to replace productive assets. In addition, a manager operating a company in a highly inflationary environment must deal with continual demands for increases in wages and dividends. Workers need more money to feed their families. Investors need more money to provide a real return on their original investment. Governments in highly inflationary nations are apt to take actions to deal with the rapid loss of purchasing power of their currencies that are inimical to the interests of business. An obvious solution is to balance the budget. But this requires that government officials cut spending, which may be politically painful. Less painful moves are price controls and excess profits taxes, both of which hinder the accumulation of funds for replacement of productive assets.

SUBJECTIVITY IN INFLATION ACCOUNTING

There are several ways to measure inflation and to adjust the financial accounts for inflation. The choice of a measure of inflation and the choice of a methodology to recast financial statements to reflect inflation introduce an element of subjectivity that is not present in historic cost accounting. Some argue against this introduction of subjectivity in the preparation of financial reports because of the consequential loss of objectivity. However, in a highly inflationary environment, there is a greater degree of fairness in financial reports that attempt to take into consideration the impact of inflation, which admittedly introduces subjectivity, than in financial reports that rely on the objectivity inherent in historic cost accounting.

GENERAL APPROACHES

Financial reports consist of both monetary and nonmonetary items. Receivables and payables are monetary items, expressed in fixed amounts of money. Inventories and fixed assets are nonmonetary items, expressed in monetary terms. A general guideline for inflation accounting is that all items in financial reports should disclose the net effect of inflation on a company's accounts. The two principal approaches are general price level accounting and current cost accounting.

General price level accounting changes the values of all assets and liabilities to reflect the loss of the underlying purchasing power of the currency. Historic costs are adjusted to a new number of currency units representing the present equivalent amount of purchasing power. The conversions are based on a general price index of inflation, such as the consumer price index. Current cost accounting differs in that historic costs are recast in terms of replacement costs. Replacement costs usually escalate at a different rate than a general price level indicator. Current cost accounting, which applies to both assets and expenses, is tied to specific indices of inflation, not to a general index of inflation.

Examination of how various nations deal with currency inflation shows that there is a variety of approaches to this accounting challenge and that these approaches generally depend on whether a nation is experiencing a low, medium, or high inflation rate. Moreover, accounting practices within a single nation change in response to changes in that nation's underlying inflation rate. As the inflation rate climbs, there is a call for adjusting financial statements to reflect inflation despite the introduction of subjectivity. As the inflation rate falls, there is a call to return to the objectivity inherent in historic cost accounting.

UNITED STATES

U.S. generally accepted accounting principles (GAAP) and U.S. tax law require the exclusive use of historic cost accounting both for financial reports and calculation of tax liabilities. In the 1930s, the problem of accounting in an inflationary economy was first debated, but was really of no great concern in the midst of the nation's worst depression, where price and wage deflation, not inflation, was the worry of the day. The subject became relevant in the 1970s. In 1974, the Financial Accounting Standards Board (FASB) issued an exposure draft on the subject of "Financial Reporting in Units of General Purchasing Power." This was followed in 1976 with the Securities and Exchange Commission issuance of Accounting Series Release No. 190 (ASR 190) "Notice of Adoption . . . Requiring Disclosure of Certain Replacement Cost Data." This required footnote disclosure of replacement costs on the basis of "the lowest amount that would have to be paid in the normal course of business to obtain an asset of equivalent operating or productive capacity."

About one thousand of the nation's largest companes had to comply with footnote disclosure of replacement costs. ASR 190 was rescinded with the issuance in 1979 of FASB 33, "Financial Reporting and Changing Prices." Exhibit 8.1 shows the footnote disclosure requirements of FASB 33 in the 1985 annual report of GTE, a large, partially regulated communications company and manufacturer of communications equipment and electrical products.

GTE suffered a loss in operations of $198 million (MM) in 1985. This was an audited loss based on historic cost accounting. In accordance with FASB 33, GTE made an unaudited assessment that regulated communication rates were not recovering $377 MM in depreciation charges based on accounting in terms of replacement rather than historic costs. In addition, $124 MM was not being recovered in its unregulated business lines, and $3 MM in the company's cost of sales. There was another $349 MM in nonrecovery of investment in shifting from an index based on general prices to one that was industry-specific.

Interestingly, GTE felt that investors in GTE debt and preferred stock offerings were suffering $505 MM in capital losses—the loss of purchasing power between making the investment and receiving interest and dividends plus repayment of the principal of debt and the preferred stock. Their loss was the company's gain. This is a footnote disclosure of management's assessment of the foolishness of investors buying the company's fixed income securities in an inflationary environment. This also shows one way for companies to pass the ravages of inflation on to others. If the interest rate is less than the inflation rate, then a company can borrow funds, invest in tangible assets, and reduce its monetary exposure to the ravages of inflation at the investors' expense.

GTE lost $198 MM in operations and $348 MM in erosion of the equity of the company from inadequate depreciation associated with historic cost accounting practices, resulting in a total loss of $546 MM after inflation was taken into consideration. The 1980s became a period of more subdued inflation. At the end of 1984, FASB 82, "Financial Reporting and Changing Prices: Elimination of Certain Disclosures," made footnote disclosures on inflationary losses voluntary. As inflation waned, so did investors' interest in reading, and companies' desire to calculate, disclosures on inflationary losses. Inflation accounting in the United States ended, at least for the time being, with FASB 82.

JAPAN

Japan is a low inflation country. Accounting rules, set forth by the Ministry of Finance, call for historic cost accounting, as shown in Exhibit 8.2, a footnote from the 1990 annual report of Sumitomo Chemical. As an aside, note that the entire annual report from which Exhibit 8.2 is drawn is an English translation of the Japanese annual report, which is prepared in accordance with Japanese GAAP. Certain modifications have been made in presenting the financial reports

Exhibit 8.1
Portion of GTE 1985 Annual Report

15. Inflation Data (Unaudited)

The following tables show the effects of inflation on GTE for 1985 and over the past five years, as calculated using current costs as a measurement. This method restates historical costs in terms of current dollars using direct pricing or price indices. The calculations show the erosion of shareholders' equity as a result of the effects of price changes, including adjustments to write down telephone plant restated in current dollars to historical costs since only historical costs are recoverable in rates as depreciation under current regulatory practices.

The calculations are not precise and do not consider the effects of normal replacement of fixed assets with state-of-the-art technology or the effects of income taxes on increases in costs associated with replacement of assets at higher costs. However, the computations do indicate the general impact of inflation on the company's results.

Year Ended December 31, 1985	Current Cost
	(Millions of Dollars)
Loss from continuing operations applicable to common stock, as reported	$(198)
Cost in excess of original cost of telephone plant not recoverable in rates, including depreciation*	377
Depreciation-nonregulated companies	124
Cost of sales	3
	504
Excess of the increase in the general level of prices ($1.1 billion) over the increase in specific prices ($.8 billion)	349
Offsetting effects of debt and preferred stock financing	(505)
Net erosion of common shareholders' equity	348
Loss from continuing operations applicable to common stock, as adjusted for inflation	$(546)

*The additional provision for depreciation of telephone plant computed on a current cost basis was $766 million, but was reduced to the amount shown above because the higher amount would have reduced property, plant and equipment below recoverable amount. At December 31, 1985, the current cost of net property, plant and equipment and inventory at recoverable amounts was $21.8 billion and $1.5 billion, respectively.

Exhibit 8.2
Footnote from Sumitomo Chemical 1990 Annual Report

> *(f) Property, plant and equipment*
> Property, plant and equipment are carried at cost and
> depreciated by the declining balance method over the
> estimated useful lives.
>   Effective 1990, the Company and a consolidated
> subsidiary changed the methods of depreciation for
> plant machinery and equipment from the straight-line
> method to the declining balance method in order to
> reflect the effect of technological innovation on plant
> facilities. The effect of this change was to increase
> annual depreciation for 1990 by ¥5,718 million
> (US$42,481 thousand) and decrease income before
> income taxes by ¥5,532 million (US$41,100 thousand).

to "facilitate understanding by non-Japanese readers," without changing the accounting practices. The report also translates yen entries to U.S. dollars and is fully consolidated, reflecting another recent change in Japanese financial reporting practices. A company wishing to attract the attention of the global investment community is under pressure to issue fully consolidated financial reports, expressed in both the language and the currency convenient for potential investors.

The footnote in Exhibit 8.2 mentions that a more rapid declining balance method of depreciation is being substituted for straight line depreciation. This increases depreciation expense and reduces reported income. It is an admission by management that straight line depreciation is "too slow" in writing off productive assets. Changes in the characteristics of products, and in manufacturing processes, are occurring at a faster pace in today's world. Depreciation, which is usually based on the physical life of productive assets, may not adequately reflect their economic life. A manufacturing process may be technologically obsolete long before it has to be physically replaced. The decision to "speed up" the depreciation probably reflects management's assessment of the anticipated economic, rather than the physical, life of the assets.

NETHERLANDS

Accounting practices and business economics are closely allied in the Netherlands. The Dutch philosophy on accounting for profit is based on the concept of a company remaining in business as a going concern far into the future. Profit is measured on the basis that an ongoing concern should be as well off at the end of a period of time as it was in the beginning. A profitable concern is one that can accumulate sufficient funds to replace its existing productive assets at current replacement costs. From the Dutch viewpoint, replacement value accounting makes more sense than historic cost accounting. Dutch accounting practices require that profit determination and valuation methods be acceptable to business interests. Current cost accounting is preferred because the inflation rate is keyed to a specific index that best reflects the cost of replacing productive assets.

Exhibit 8.3 is taken from the 1983 annual report of the Royal Dutch Petroleum Company. The exhibit discusses the corporate view of current cost accounting practices and difficulties therewith, the nature of subjectivity inherent in inflation accounting.

Although it is common to adjust profits for the effects of inflation on land, buildings, equipment, machinery, and inventories, some companies have attempted to incorporate technological changes in their estimates of replacement value. Advocates of this approach argue that, as an example, a manufacturing plant is hardly ever replaced with a replica. In time, technological advances change the characteristics and design features of a new plant. Generally speaking, technological progress tends to increase the capital cost of a replacement plant for the benefit of producing goods at less unit cost. The obvious hindrance in taking this approach is that management may not be able to foresee the direction of technological progress in determining replacement cost, or for that matter, changes in the market for its product line that call for an entirely different investment in productive assets. Mention of this is made in Exhibit 8.3, where management expresses doubt whether productive assets, primarily in the form of oil and gas reserves, would be "replaced in their present form."

The Netherlands experienced less inflation in the 1980s than in the 1970s, which reduced the incentive to account for inflation and to surmount the difficulties associated with current cost accounting as discussed in Exhibit 8.3. As seen in Exhibit 8.4, Royal Dutch Petroleum had virtually abandoned supplementary current cost accounting by 1990, because of difficulties in estimating the replacement costs of its productive assets, namely, oil reserves.

As seen in Exhibit 8.4, earnings were adjusted to reflect the current cost of supplies rather than using the first in, first out method of inventory accounting. This adjustment is easily made because inventory supplies are primarily oil, for which the current market price is a reliable measure of replacement cost.

AG-AMEV/VSB is a Dutch financial services company whose business is concentrated in the Netherlands, Belgium, and the United States. Its auditors' report, signed by a Dutch accounting firm and the Belgian office of a U.S. accounting firm, states that the generally accepted accounting principles with regard to valuation and profit determination are in accordance with "international usage and developments," without reference to any particular GAAP. The annual report states the principles by which the financial statements are prepared, illustrating the practical business orientation of Dutch accounting practices. Assets (real estate and stock holdings) are written up or down as their values change. Unrealized gains or losses for assets above historic cost are added to shareholders' equity. If below historic cost, they are applied to unrealized capital gains/losses. The financial statements for this company are presented in three currencies: Dutch guilders, Belgian francs, and ECUs.

Exhibit 8.3
Excerpt from Royal Dutch Petroleum Company 1983 Annual Report

Supplementary information
—current cost accounting

The assessment of trends in profit and net assets measured under the historical cost accounting convention is complicated by changing prices, since current revenues are matched with out of date costs and net assets are stated on the basis of an unspecified mixture of historical costs. Current cost accounting (CCA) attempts to portray the profit which would have been achieved had both inventories and property, plant and equipment consumed been charged to income at their current prices and to present net assets on a current cost basis. Departure from the basis on which historical cost accounts are compiled inevitably introduces a considerable degree of subjectivity and imprecision due to the approximations and assumptions involved. The difficulties are compounded when account has to be taken of whether, in fact,

the revalued assets would be replaced in their present form. There is a particular problem in presenting in current cost statements the capitalized cost of oil and gas exploration and development activities. The cost of replacing oil and gas reserves is dependent on the location in which new reserves are found and the conditions under which they are developed. As these are not known, the capitalized costs are represented in current cost accounts only by the equivalent value of past expenditures at today's prices. For this reason and because of the approximations and assumptions referred to above, caution should be exercised in drawing conclusions from the current cost data. It is considered that at the present stage of development of current cost accounting there is no adequate alternative

to the historical cost accounting convention for the oil industry and that this convention should therefore continue as the basis for the primary financial statements.

The present experimental nature of CCA is manifested in differing accounting practice in the Netherlands, the United Kingdom and the United States over the items which should be reflected in current cost accounts. The accounting standard setting bodies of each of these countries are considering or reviewing alternative methods of calculating and presenting price change data, but the inherent difficulty of the subject makes it unlikely that effective and fully compatible solutions will be developed in the near future. Existing differences between the three countries relate to the treatment of monetary items and taxation. The information shown in the table on this page has been presented to reflect the current cost adjustments common to the three countries. In addition, a gearing adjustment has been included to recognize the offsetting effect of borrowing on cost increases arising from changing prices. The basis of restatement for this purpose is set out below. Further details are provided under the heading 'Additional information' to facilitate the appreciation of the Group current cost data in the light of Netherlands, United Kingdom and United States practice.

Basis of restatement
The accounting policies used are the same as those applied in the Group financial statements except as modified below.

Property, plant and equipment of Group companies has been restated to year-end current cost by applying appropriate indices to historical local currency acquisition costs or by estimating the current cost of acquiring assets of approximately equivalent productive potential where technological change renders the use of an index inappropriate. Property, plant and equipment of associated companies has been restated on a basis as far as possible consistent with that of Group companies.

Inventories have been restated to their approximate year-end current cost.

Historical cost operating expenses have been adjusted to reflect the current cost of sales as at the date of sale.

Depreciation, depletion and amortization charges have been calculated as an appropriate proportion of the restated

Current cost data

	1981	1982	1983 £ million
Summarized income data			
Historical cost net income	1.989	1.993	**2,754**
deduct Current cost adjustments:			
Depreciation, depletion and amortization	1.105	1.319	**1,296**
Cost of sales	1.033	211	**(51)**
Earnings of associated companies	164	79	**54**
Income applicable to minority interests	(162)	(222)	**(208)**
Income (loss) from continuing operations	(151)	606	**1,663**
Gearing adjustment	555	307	**215**
Current cost net income	404	913	**1,878**
Summarized statement of assets and liabilities			
Property, plant and equipment – net	28.326	33.449	**37,405**
Investments in associated companies	2.564	3.382	**3,958**
Inventories	7.994	8.263	**7,747**
Other assets, less liabilities (other than long-term debt)	(4,757)	(5,923)	**(5,645)**
Capital employed	34.127	39.171	**43,465**
deduct:			
Long-term debt and capitalized lease obligations	5.518	6.858	**6,825**
Minority interests	3.815	4.361	**4,942**
Current cost net assets	24.794	27.952	**31,698**

Exhibit 8.3 (continued)

property, plant and equipment at current cost, on the basis of the same asset lives as those used for historical cost accounting.

Income tax and provisions for deferred tax included in the income statement are the same as those included in the historical cost financial statements.

A gearing adjustment has been made to quantify the proportion of the depreciation and cost of sales adjustments which relates to assets financed by borrowing.

The proportion is calculated by reference to the ratio of average net borrowing to the average net operating assets over the year, taken at their current cost values. For this purpose net monetary working capital, which is not otherwise recognized in the current cost income statement, is included in the calculation of average net borrowing.

All figures are expressed in pounds of the years to which they relate.

Additional information

The following additional information is provided to assist in appraising the current cost data in the light of CCA practice in the Netherlands, United Kingdom and United States.

	1981	1982	**1983**
			£ million
Netherlands			
If the provision for deferred taxation were to include the potential tax effects of current cost revaluations, current cost net assets would become	19.600	22.600	**25,800**
If the historical tax charge were reduced to recognize tax effects related to the CCA additional depreciation and cost of sales adjustments in addition the gearing adjustment (for which there is no standard practice in the Netherlands) were excluded, current cost net income would become	900	1,300	**2,200**
United Kingdom			
If the Group current cost data were to include only provisions for those taxes that are likely to be paid within the foreseeable future in conformity with the UK accounting practice, current cost net income would become	700	1,400	**2,500**
United States			
Were the Group to adopt the LIFO basis of inventory accounting, which is common in the USA and which, after excluding any inventory drawdown profits, charges cost of sales on a current cost basis, the tax charge would be reduced in 1981 and 1982 and increased in 1983. In the USA adjustments for monetary items in the form of gearing are not recognized, but companies disclose the gain on net monetary items arising from changes in purchasing power. If the gain on net monetary items is included instead of the gearing adjustment and the above tax effects of valuing inventory on a LIFO basis are recognized, current cost net income would become	1,100	1,200	**2,300**

Report of the Auditors

on the supplementary information – current cost data

To Royal Dutch Petroleum Company and The "Shell" Transport and Trading Company, p.l.c.

We have reviewed the supplementary information – current cost data – of the Royal Dutch/Shell Group of Companies set out on pages 45 and 46.

In our opinion, the summarized data set out in the table on page 45 has been properly prepared in accordance with the basis of restatement described on pages 45 and 46.

Klynveld Kraayenhof & Co., The Hague

Ernst & Whinney, London

Price Waterhouse, New York

March 15, 1984

Exhibit 8.4
Excerpt from Royal Dutch Petroleum Company 1990 Annual Report

▣ Accounting policies

The annual accounts on pages 26 to 30
have been prepared under the historical
cost convention.

The determination of Royal Dutch's share
in the net income of the Royal Dutch/Shell
Group of Companies is explained in Note 3.
The valuation of Investments in companies of
the Royal Dutch/Shell Group is explained in
Note 4. The assets and liabilities are stated
at the amounts at which they were acquired
or incurred, unless indicated otherwise.

Administrative expenses, Interest income
and Taxation are stated at the amounts
attributable to the financial years.

Amounts in foreign currency relating to
the Balance sheet have been expressed in
guilders at appropriate rates ruling at the
balance sheet date, and those relating to the
Profit and loss account at average rates.

Supplementary current cost information is
not disclosed by the Royal Dutch/Shell Group
of Companies because of the impossibility of
satisfactorily determining current costs that
reflect the cost of replacing existing oil and
gas reserves. In explaining the results from
operations of the Royal Dutch/Shell Group
of Companies, however, use is also made of
information on the estimated current cost
of supplies, as this information does not
involve the uncertainties associated with
the replacement of oil and gas reserves.

UNITED KINGDOM

The United Kingdom experienced a higher degree of inflation than the United
States, Japan, Germany, and the Netherlands. The Institute of Chartered Accountants in England and Wales issued the Provisional Statement of Standard Accounting Practice (SSAP) No. 7 in 1974, entitled "Accounting for Changes in the
Purchasing Power of Money." Several interim reports and recommendations
were made leading up to SSAP 16, "Current Cost Accounting." In 1983, SSAP
16 was declared to be effective for a three-year experiment in dealing with inflation. In 1985, SSAP 16 became voluntary and continues to be so.

Exhibit 8.5, taken from the 1987 annual report of Bass, shows the impact of
writing up of assets. "Freehold" means owned property, whereas "leaseholds"
are leased properties, some for over a century of remaining time. These properties

Exhibit 8.5
Portion of Bass 1987 Annual Report

	Cost or valuation £m	Depreciation £m	Group total £m	Company total £m
b) At 30th September 1987				
Breweries and other industrial properties				
Freehold	180·9	(6·7)	174·2	—
Leasehold over 100 years	1·5	(—)	1·5	—
Leasehold 50 to 100 years	14·1	(·2)	13·9	—
Leasehold under 50 years	1·1	(·1)	1·0	·1
Licensed and unlicensed properties				
Freehold	1,638·1	(·8)	1,637·3	—
Leasehold over 100 years	83·3	(·1)	83·2	—
Leasehold 50 to 100 years	128·0	(2·0)	126·0	·4
Leasehold under 50 years	109·3	(9·8)	99·5	—
Total properties	2,156·3	(19·7)	2,136·6	·5
Plant and machinery at cost	401·5	(161·4)	240·1	—
Fixtures, fittings, tools and equipment				
at cost	503·0	(184·7)	318·3	10·2
	3,060·8	(365·8)	2,695·0	10·7
Cost or valuation of properties comprises				
1986 valuation	1,868·4			
Cost	287·9			
	2,156·3			
Comparable amounts for properties under the historical cost convention would be:				
at 30th September 1987	1,227·1	(149·2)	1,077·9	·4
at 30th September 1986	767·9	(73·2)	694·7	·4

A professional valuation of all properties (other than holiday centres) at 1st October 1986 was carried out by the Group's own professionally qualified staff in conjunction with Chesterton, Surveyors and Valuers.
The basis of the valuation in respect of breweries and maltings was depreciated replacement cost. However, after consideration of the available brewing capacity of the Group, these properties have been included in the accounts at directors valuation, being cost at 30th September 1986 and a lower value than that placed upon them by the valuers. In respect of the portfolio of licensed public houses, hotels, off-licensed properties, betting shops, bingo halls and depots together with non-trading properties, the basis was open market value for the existing use in the business of the Group.

are primarily public houses (pubs), which totaled 1,638.1 million pounds in 1987. Although there is virtually no depreciation (0.8 million pounds) associated with these properties, there is significant depreciation associated with plant and machinery and fixtures and fittings. Depreciation of these items infers the need for replacement, quite unlike the situation pertaining to pubs.

Management states that depreciating pubs on the basis of historic costs is not appropriate because they are gaining in value, mainly from inflation. Management also notes elsewhere in the report that the pubs are maintained in a condition such that there is no foreseeable end to their useful lives. Exhibit 8.5 states that the valuation of properties is based on an in-house appraisal of market values. The 1986 valuation of all properties was 1,868.4 million pounds, as compared to a 1987 valuation of 3,060.8 million pounds. The 1987 value of all properties under historic cost accounting would have been 1,227.1 million pounds. Therefore, the aggregate net write-up in the value of the pubs has been of the order of 1,833.7 million pounds. The low depreciation associated with properties is justified on the basis that it makes little sense to depreciate a tangible asset that is being written up in value.

Write-ups of properties do not flow through the income statement. Shareholders' equity is adjusted to reflect changes in valuation of assets under the line item "Revaluation Reserve," which increases the book value of the company. Depreciation, on the other hand, does flow through the income statement and the reduced depreciation associated with properties does affect reported profitability.

FRANCE

France experienced rampant inflation after World War II. This necessitated a departure from historic cost accounting, which was restored in 1959 with the issuance of a new currency. Changes in the Finance Acts in the 1970s mandated the use of current cost accounting. The financial statements of publicly traded companies were to report all assets on a current replacement cost basis. The prescribed methodology involved writing up the book value of the asset by an official coefficient. The applicable official coefficients, in turn, were based on price level changes of wholesale price indices of those commodities, including labor, which largely determine the cost of manufacturing fixed assets. This is a price-oriented adjustment system that does not take into account technological change.

Peugeot S.A. is a large French automobile manufacturer. The individual companies making up the Peugeot group prepare their financial statements in accordance with the GAAP of their respective nations. For those Peugeot companies located in France, financial reports are prepared in accordance with French GAAP, including any required write-up of assets. Exhibit 8.6 is the beginning of the notes to its 1990 consolidated financial statements. Since 1979, the company has presented the consolidated financial statements of its activities in forty-four nations in accordance with U.S. and IASC (International Accounting Standards Committee) GAAP, "which the group considers best adapted to the international context of its activities."

The principles of consolidation follow U.S. GAAP with specific references made to FASB 94 and 21 in paragraph (a). Paragraph (b) states that the legal revaluations required by French law, which are contained in the financial reports filed by the Peugeot companies in France, have been recast to historic costs in the consolidation process. Noted elsewhere in the report, a French company has the option to pay taxes based on the consolidated taxable income of its French activities, or on the results of each separate company within France. Peugeot elected to switch methods in 1990.

INFLATION ACCOUNTING IN HYPERINFLATIONARY NATIONS

Hyperinflation is defined in FASB 52 as occurring when any currency suffers from 100 percent cumulative inflation over three years. All the nations listed as

Exhibit 8.6
Portion of Peugeot S.A. 1990 Annual Report

NOTES TO THE CONSOLIDATED FINANCIAL STATEMENTS FOR THE YEARS ENDED DECEMBER 31, 1990 AND 1989

■

1) ACCOUNTING POLICIES

The financial statements of group companies, prepared in accordance with the accounting principles applicable in their respective countries, have been restated, for comparison purposes, in accordance with accounting principles generally accepted in the United States of America, which the group considers best adapted to the international context of its activities. These principles, which are essentially those described in note 1 (a) to (k) below, are in conformity with international accounting principles promulgated by the I.A.S.C. and the legal requirements for consolidation in France.

a) Consolidation

The financial statements of significant subsidiaries in which Peugeot S.A. holds directly or indirectly a majority interest are consolidated, with the exception of finance subsidiaries, which are included in the consolidated financial statements on an equity basis.

Companies in which Peugeot S.A. holds directly or indirectly an interest of 20 to 50 % and exercises significant influence over operating and financial policies, as well as finance subsidiaries, are included in the consolidated financial statements on an equity basis (note 4).

According to the "U.S. Financial Accounting Standard Board" (FASB) bulletin n° 94 banks and finance companies in which Peugeot S.A. holds directly or indirectly a majority interest should have been consolidated in the financial statements. Peugeot S.A. provides the presentation required by the FASB in note 21 and continues as in prior years to carry banks and finance subsidiaries on the equity basis in its main

financial statements. There is no difference between the financial statements presented in note 21 and the main financial statements in respect of consolidated net income and stockholders' equity.

Investments representing an interest of less than 20 % in the companies concerned are valued at cost except in the case of permanent decline in the value of the investment.

All significant intercompany transactions are eliminated.

b) Property

Land, plant and equipment are carried at cost, including capitalised interest expense since January 1, 1979. The French legal revaluations (laws of December 29, 1976 and December 30, 1977) and foreign revaluations are not reflected in the consolidated financial statements.

Maintenance and repair costs are expensed as incurred, except for those which enhance the productivity or prolong the useful life of an asset.

Depreciation is calculated on a straight-line basis over the estimated useful lives of the respective assets as follows:

	Useful lives, in number of years
Buildings	16 to 20
Material and equipment	6,66 to 16
Data processing equipment	3 to 4
Transport and handling equipment	4 to 7
Furniture and fixtures	10
Land improvements	25

high inflation nations in Table 8.3 qualify as hyperinflationary under FASB 52. Generally speaking, the conditions contained in FASB 52 result in the local currency (LC) being declared the functional currency and the selection of the current method of translation. Under the current method of translation, fixed assets are translated at the current conversion rate of a currency. Suppose that a factory is built for 10 MM LC and the local currency rate is 10 LC per U.S. dollar (/$). The initial translation of the fixed asset to U.S. dollars is $1 million. Neglecting depreciation, suppose that the LC devalues to 100 LC/$ over the subsequent year. The plant is translated at the current rate, or 100 LC/$, and the original 10 MM LC plant, costing $1 MM, is now shown on the balance sheet for $100,000. If the conversion rate falls to 1,000 LC/$ in the following year, the original $1 million plant has a translated value of $10,000 on the balance sheet. The plant, which physically exists and is in production, is literally disappearing from the financial statements.

To counter this disappearing plant phenomenon, FASB 52 requires that an affiliate operating in a hyperinflationary environment must declare the U.S. dollar as the functional currency and translate its financial statements in accordance with FASB 8. FASB 8 calls for the temporal method of translation, which uses the current rate of translation for cash, receivables, payables, and long-term debt and the historic rate for inventories, fixed assets, intangible assets, and contributed capital. The plant is now translated at the historic rate of exchange. The translation of the original value of the plant is at the conversion rate that was in effect when the plant was built, or 10 LC/$. Neglecting depreciation, the 10 MM LC investment in the plant is always translated at the historic rate of 10 LC/$, and the plant remains on the balance sheet at $1 million. Under the temporal method, translation gains or losses are reported in the income statement, not in the equity section of the balance sheet.

In contrast to U.S. practice, the International Accounting Standards Committee permits a company with a subsidiary in a hyperinflationary nation to adjust the financial statements for inflation before translation to the currency of the parent company, or to use a variation of the temporal method.

BRAZIL

For Brazilian companies operating in Brazil, there is no FASB 52, no U.S. dollar as a functional currency, and all accounting is done in accordance with Brazilian GAAP. Brazil recognized that high inflation rates destroy the validity of historic cost accounting and was the first nation to officially introduce indexing in the preparation of financial statements. It was also the first nation to have indexing apply to the calculation of taxes. This reduced government revenue from corporate taxes, but permitted corporations to more easily accumulate the funds necessary for replacement of their productive assets to continue as going concerns. This, by the way, is atypical behavior on the part of tax authorities. Most governments consider inflation their ally in revenue collection, neglecting, naturally, the impact of inflation on government spending.

The Corporation Law of 1976 requires that all companies adjust owners' equity and "permanent assets" to a government compiled price index. Permanent assets are property, plant, equipment, long-term investments, plus deferred charges and associated amortization. The difference between the adjusted owners' equity and the permanent assets is called the net monetary correction. This may be applied to a capital account entitled "Reserve for Unrealized Profit" or may be charged to income depending on the circumstances.

Indexing permeates the financial life of Brazil. It applies to the face value of bonds and mortgages, to salaries and wages, to savings, and to calculation of taxes. Indexing is a series of calculations that follow a prescribed set of procedures. An illustration of the complexity associated with indexing is shown for Mexico.

MEXICO

The Mexican peso was a stable currency until the explosion in oil prices made Mexico, an oil exporter, rich. For reasons that perhaps defy the imagination of economists, the floodtide of oil money pouring into Mexico transformed a once stable peso to a currency of dubious value.

Mexican accounting practices are closely allied to U.S. GAAP and the standards set forth by the International Accounting Standards Committee, with one glaring exception. Whereas U.S. GAAP is based on historic cost accounting, Mexico practices inflation accounting. All monetary assets and liabilities (cash, receivables, and payables) are restated in pesos of constant purchasing power as calculated from the National Consumer Price Index (NCPI). The NCPI is a general index of inflation published quarterly by the Bank of Mexico. Any gain or loss on the net monetary position is recorded in the income statement as the line item ''Monetary Gain (Loss).''

For nonmonetary items such as inventory and fixed assets, Mexican companies are given a choice of revaluation methods. Inventory can be adjusted on the basis of replacement cost, last production purchase price, the NCPI, or a specific price index. Fixed assets can also be revalued on the basis of appraisals, in addition to the aforementioned methods. The net effect of revaluing inventory and fixed assets is an adjustment to the line item ''Accumulated Gain (Loss) on Nonmonetary Assets'' in the stockholders' equity section of the balance sheet.

The National Consumer Price Index at the end of 1988 was 16,147.3 and 19,327.9 at the end of 1989. On the last day of 1990, the NCPI had a published value of 25,112.7, and at the end of 1991, 29,832.5. Suppose that a company was formed at the end of 1990, and had the following balance sheet at that time.

```
                        BALANCE SHEET
                       31 December 1990
                     (Figures in 1990 pesos)

  Cash           240              Payables        96
  Receivables      0
  Inventory       96
  Fixed assets   240              Equity         480

  Total          576              Total          576
```

At year-end 1991, the first step is to restate the opening (prior year's) balance sheet, and the prior year's cash flow and income statements using the end-of-current-year (1991) purchasing power of the peso. The year-end 1991 NCPI was 29,832.5, whereas the year-end 1990 NCPI was 25,112.7. The factor to be applied to the 1990 balance sheet to adjust it for year-end 1991 peso purchasing power is 1.188 (29,832.5 divided by 25,112.7).

```
┌─────────────────────────────────────────────────────────────────┐
│                        BALANCE SHEET                              │
│                      31 December 1990                             │
│                   (Figures in 1991 pesos)                         │
│                                                                   │
│   Cash             285           Payables         114             │
│   Receivables        0                                            │
│   Inventory        114                                            │
│   Fixed assets     285           Equity           570             │
│                                                                   │
│   Total            684           Total            684             │
└─────────────────────────────────────────────────────────────────┘
```

The balance sheet in pesos at year-end 1991 is shown in the next table.

```
┌─────────────────────────────────────────────────────────────────┐
│                        BALANCE SHEET                              │
│                      31 December 1991                             │
│                        (Unadjusted)                               │
│                                                                   │
│   Cash             180           Payables          62             │
│   Receivables       74                                            │
│   Inventory        120           Equity           480             │
│   Fixed assets     230           Retained                         │
│                                  Earnings          62             │
│                                                                   │
│   Total            604           Total            604             │
└─────────────────────────────────────────────────────────────────┘
```

The unadjusted 1991 balance sheet must take into consideration the changing value of the peso during the course of the year in order to state the balance sheet strictly in terms of the value of the peso on 31 December 1991. Inventory is recalculated using either first in, first out or replacement cost on the last day of the year or by applying a specific price index or the NCPI to historic costs. These adjustments are done quarterly using the appropriately adjusted conversion factors and/or replacement costs. Suppose that the adjusted inventory is 125 pesos. The unadjusted income statement in pesos for 1991 is as shown.

```
┌───────────────────────────────────┐
│         INCOME STATEMENT          │
│        31 December 1991           │
│          (Unadjusted)             │
│                                   │
│   Sales                   274     │
│   Cost of sales           202     │
│   Gross margin             72     │
│   Depreciation             10     │
│   Income from                     │
│      operations            62     │
└───────────────────────────────────┘
```

Table 8.4
Income Statement—31 December 1991

(Unadjusted)		(Adjusted)	
Sales	274	Sales	293
Cost of sales	202	Cost of sales	240
Gross margin	72	Gross margin	53
Depreciation	10	Depreciation	12
Income from operations	62	Income from operations	41

Having readjusted inventory, cost of goods sold must now be recalculated using last in, first out, using the last purchase price paid, or by applying specific indices. Obviously, the choice of methodology determines the outcome, and ultimately, the profitability of the company. An accountant, in selecting the methodology, is also selecting the final version of the reported profits. This is an example of the subjectivity introduced into accounting in attempting to recast the financial statements to reflect the impact of inflation on the operations of a company.

This adjustment is done quarterly to express cost of goods sold throughout 1991 in terms of the value of the peso on the last day of the year. Suppose that the adjusted cost of sales is 240. The fixed assets are next to be revalued to current cost either by independent appraisal or by applying a specific price index or the NCPI. There are limits in writing up assets—they cannot exceed "net realizable value," which is a measure of future aggregate earnings. Depreciation expense is recalculated on the adjusted value of individual fixed assets and their respective remaining useful lives. Suppose that the result of this calculation is a value of 300 pesos for fixed assets and a depreciation charge of 12 pesos.

After cost of goods sold and depreciation have been adjusted, the remaining item to be adjusted on the income statement is revenue. Again, using quarterly NCPI figures, adjustments are made to transform sales in pesos throughout the year into the purchasing value of year-end pesos. Suppose that the adjusted sales are 293 pesos. The unadjusted and adjusted income statements for 1991 are as shown in Table 8.4.

The line item "Monetary Gain (Loss)" is in the section of the income statement containing interest expense and foreign exchange gains or losses. The restated 1990 balance sheet has cash of 285 and payables of 114, less payables (none), for a net monetary asset position of 71 pesos. The 1991 balance sheet has cash of 180 plus receivables of 74 less payables of 62 for a net positive monetary position of 192 pesos. Inflation adversely impacts the purchasing power of net monetary assets resulting in a monetary loss. Had the company a net monetary liability, inflation would have created a monetary gain.

Starting with the net monetary asset at year-end 1990, adding in quarterly sales less quarterly purchases of inventory, adjusted to reflect the end 1991 value of the peso, and netting the year-end net monetary asset position of 192 pesos, results in the calculation of the net monetary loss. Suppose that this is 31 pesos, thereby reducing reported profit to 10 pesos. After adjusting the original capital contribution by 1.188 to reflect the change in value of the peso during 1991, the balance sheet and income statements can be cast in their final form. The item "Holding Gain on Nonmonetary Assets," or "HGNA" herein, is simply a derived figure that balances the balance sheet.

```
                        BALANCE SHEET
                      31 December 1991
                         (Adjusted)

       Cash             180          Payables          62
       Receivables       74
       Inventory        125          Equity           570
       Fixed assets     288          Retained
                                       Earnings        10
                                     HGNA              26
                        ___                           ___
       Total            668          Total            668
```

The amounts shown in these examples are illustrative in nature. The actual calculations for a real company are quite cumbersome and more complex than indicated in the discussion. Perhaps one lesson to be learned is that accounting is much more straightforward in a nation with a stable currency.

OPERATING IN A HYPERINFLATIONARY ENVIRONMENT

Many businessmen naturally shun operating in an environment where annual inflation may be 100 percent, 1,000 percent, or more. One factor to realize is that inflation is relative to the beholder. Brazil, with its high inflation rate, may be considered a citadel of financial stability to someone from Argentina. The Canadian inflation rate may be considered low by an Italian businessman and high by a businessman from Germany or Japan.

Another factor to keep in mind is that the usual assumption that inflation, once entrenched in an economy, will only get worse, is not necessarily true. Although government officials are usually not eager to give the economy the necessary medicine to treat the disease of inflation, there are exceptions. In the late 1980s, Bolivia was able to commit itself to a fiscal austerity program that reined in inflation from 20,000 percent per year to 10 percent per year. During the 1980s, the industrialized nations in Europe and North America have intentionally pursued policies, such as high interest rates, that slowed their economic growth and subdued the high inflation rates of the 1970s.

Another difficulty in running a business in a hyperinflationary environment is the matter of measuring success. How does one know if he or she is ahead in making an investment in a hyperinflationary environment? The fact that there is a positive return of, say, 10 percent on the original investment doesn't mean success if the currency has lost half its purchasing power in the interim. There-fore, the accounting data of a company must be adjusted, because, left unad-justed, the information is useless, misleading, or wrong.

Ultimately, only net cash flows can be used to reinvest in a firm and provide a return to equity holders through the payment of dividends. In hyperinflationary nations, cash flows must be managed on a daily basis to protect against the rapid decline in purchasing power. During the German inflation after World War I, workers were paid twice a day to allow them to spend the money immediately. A company operating in this type of inflationary environment manages its cash flow on an hourly basis.

A manager in a highly inflationary nation needs an effective cash management control system. Cash is not an asset in a hyperinflationary nation—in some ways it can be considered a liability that generates losses just by holding it. Greater demands are placed on the financial acumen of managers in dealing with a company's pricing policy and its inventory and cost containment strategies. Deviations from projected cash flows must be more carefully attended to because the repercussions can be devastating. For instance, the slow collection of re-ceivables in a nation with a stable currency may result a higher financing charge on borrowings to supply the company with necessary cash until the receivables are collected. In a hyperinflationary nation, the same slow collection of receiv-ables may bankrupt the company. Money received two months later than antic-ipated for payment of a given quantity of product may no longer be sufficient to purchase the material and components necessary to manufacture the same quantity of product. The loss in purchasing power caused by a delayed payment of a receivable does not allow the company to replace the sales represented by the receivable, thereby jeopardizing the company as a going concern.

In a hyperinflationary environment, the accounting system must be modified to reflect the ravages of inflation on the income statement and balance sheet. Only then can financial reports perform their intended function of measuring the performance of a company. If some means of accounting for inflation is not incorporated in adjusting the financial reports, then the owners of the company have no way of knowing whether they have made a successful investment. This is one reason why Brazil, and later Mexico, introduced a formal system of indexation.

Highly inflationary environments make classic return-on-investment (ROI) analysis very difficult. Assumptions regarding future inflation rates, as applied to sales prices and cost of goods sold, can dramatically impact the calculated ROI of the investment. In fact, the analyst is in a position to select those rates that make a project either economically attractive or not, according to some preconceived notion in the analyst's mind. As noted in the tables on inflation rates, there is no constancy in inflation rates from one year to the next. This makes selection of the appropriate inflation rate to be incorporated in an ROI analysis of a multiyear project more difficult, because there is no single inflation rate that is suitable for a multiyear project. ROI models, which have been devised in stable currency nations, have little validity in nations with high inflation rates.

However, something has to be used to determine the desirability of a project. Often, an ROI model assumes that present prices and costs are also the projected prices and costs without taking inflation into account. The analysis is done in units of "constant" local currency or equivalent dollars. The discounted cash flow is measured against the amount of the investment to judge its rate of return. The basic assumption in this approach is that escalation of costs from inflation can be passed on to the consumer in terms of price hikes. But this is inadequate. Price increases have to be greater than increases in costs to provide a real return in terms of net cash flow to the company, or dividends to the investors. Even this may not be adequate. Price hikes have to be sufficient to accumulate sufficient funds for replacing productive assets at some point in the future. This is the Dutch approach for measuring success. This is no easy task to accomplish in a hyperinflationary environment, but realization of its necessity is the first step to understanding business practices in these nations.

The financial earnings from a business venture in a hyperinflationary environment cannot be kept as a monetary asset, because it is unlikely that bank interest rates will compensate for the loss of purchasing power of the currency. This presents another challenge to operating a firm in a highly inflationary nation. Managers of companies, along with private citizens, avoid holding currency for any length of time. Individuals and businesses become adept at preserving purchasing power by spending cash immediately for needed items to run a home or a business and converting any remaining cash to a more desirable currency, if possible.

For soft currency nations, the latter alternative is usually hampered by local currency exchange restrictions. Aside from a black market to accommodate those fleeing from a currency, the alternative is to purchase tangible assets with excess currency holdings. When currency is needed, a portion of these assets are sold. Tangible assets tend to preserve the purchasing value of a currency, a characteristic lacking in the currency itself.

Businesses operating in highly inflationary countries tend to have large inventories and small amounts of cash on hand. Businesses operating in low inflationary countries tend to minimize inventory holdings because they represent a cost in terms of storage, insurance, spoilage, obsolescence, and pilferage, besides generating financial charges. Because inventory is widely recognized as a cost of doing business in nations with stable currencies, excess inventory holdings must be viewed as another cost of doing business in hyperinflationary nations. This is a means of preserving purchasing power, not a means of providing for the smooth operation of a company.

Cash management is a critical function in high inflation nations. Often inventory is the likely investment for excess holdings of cash, but one has to select whether raw material or finished goods inventory should be the chosen investment medium. Another consideration in managing cash is borrowing money in order to reduce the net monetary asset exposure of a company. The borrowings are usually invested in inventory, which can transform a company from an exposure to net monetary assets to net monetary liabilities.

A company with net monetary liabilities is thought to be better positioned to deal with inflation than one with net monetary assets. In theory, the company stands to win in an inflationary climate. This strategy depends, of course, on interest rates charged by banks. There have been times when bank interest rates on corporate borrowings were so high that there was serious doubt as to the efficacy of borrowing to enhance inventory holdings as a successful strategy for dealing with inflation. In other words, the real financing costs associated with having a net monetary liability exposure may not have been matched by un-realized inventory profits.

There is a risk in holding excessive inventory. If a company makes shoes and borrows money to put more shoes into inventory as a means of protecting itself from inflation, what happens to the value of the inventory when shoe fashions change? Or if raw material inventory holdings are performing this function, what happens to the value of inventory when degradation of the leather occurs from sitting too long in a warehouse? The purchasing power of currency invested in inventories of out-of-style shoes and rotting leather will not be preserved.

And, of course, even if the adjusted soft currency income is adequate to provide a return on a hard currency investment, the question of how to convert the soft currency back into a hard currency still exists. Selling a portion of the goods for hard currency, transfer pricing, and management fees for services and for transfer of tangible and intangible assets are means by which a company can obtain a hard currency return on a hard currency investment. But local currency restrictions may bar the way.

Inflation sometimes indicates underlying political and social problems in ad-dition to government fiscal and monetary problems. Companies operating under the threat of nationalization, changing government regulations, and the arbitrary administration of regulations and rules by those in power without means of appeal, or social and political instability react to the situation by changing the criteria associated with making investments. The greater the political, economic, or social risks, the shorter the desired time horizon in recouping an investment, and consequently, the higher the required ROI. Businessmen become reluctant to invest if the higher ROI cannot be achieved. This impedes the ability of a nation to raise the standard of living of its people, which is often the underlying reason for the political and social unrest.

MANAGERIAL GUIDELINES

Some of the guidelines for managing a company in a highly inflationary environment, which are not present, or are present in a subdued way in nations with stable currencies, follow.

1. Management of prices and costs has to be conducted in a manner to ensure

a cash flow sufficient to provide a real return on investment. This involves daily attention to cash flow and quick reaction to deviations in the projected cash flow.

2. Management of monetary assets and liabilities is necessary to avoid losses from currency devaluations. This sometimes leads a company to assume a net monetary liability position by borrowing from banks and investing the proceeds in tangible assets such as inventories. But, this may lead to a liquidity crisis if the tangible assets cannot be sold. This course of action can also be nonproductive if interest rates on bank loans become extremely high and are not compensated by gains in inventory values.

3. Accounting for inflation should be done in a fashion that permits the appraisal of the success of a company in terms of a real return on investment and the accumulation of sufficient funds to remain a going concern. This means that there has to be a correct choice of accounting methods and indices of inflation to take into consideration losses in the purchasing power of the currency and the concomitant increases in the replacement cost of productive assets.

4. Classic ROI models for evaluating new projects must, at the least, be viewed with suspicion. Such models cannot be dismissed out of hand because some methodology is needed to assess whether an investment, or which of a choice of investments, should be made. Performing the analysis in constant units of the local currency, or equivalent units of a hard currency, is common, but this does not address the ramifications of different rates of inflation affecting prices and various elements of cost.

5. In making new investments that require hard currency either in the form of the investment itself, or in importing parts and components to sustain an investment, some means of transferring goods or monetary assets, or of paying fees, should be arranged before these investments are made. This is necessary to amortize the hard currency investment, along with providing a return on the investment and/or paying for hard currency imports.

6. A realistic assessment of political risk and arbitrary action taken against a company by what may be a hostile government has to be made. The latter is sometimes influenced by those managing a company. One of the potential strengths of local management is their knowledge of both the regulatory and administrative requirements and those who are in charge of such matters. Local management can often deal more effectively with problems than managers from the parent company organization, who often lack the cultural appreciation of the way things are done in a different nation.

7. There has to be careful selection of personnel to ensure that an operation is well managed under the trying circumstances of buying and selling in a hyperinflationary currency. Here, again, local management, who have been raised in a hyperinflationary environment and have learned to cope with the system since childhood, may have an advantage over a manager brought up in a hard currency nation. The management evaluation system should be designed to ensure that managerial motivations and corporate objectives are more or less in harmony. Such a measuring system goes beyond conventional measuring of

performance by financial results commonly found in nations with relatively stable currencies. The measuring system should also include an evaluation of the effectiveness of management to protect the company against the continual erosion of the purchasing power of its monetary assets.

SUMMARY

Many people shun investing in hyperinflationary nations for what seem to be good reasons on a superficial level. However, instinctive shunning of operating in these environments may be shortsighted. Some of these economies offer unique opportunities as long as the investor, or businessman, knows how to operate in a nation with a high inflation rate. Real profits can be made in these nations. The existence of functioning economies in Latin America, Africa, Eastern Europe, and the non-Pacific-rim nations in Asia, which, in the aggregate, may represent over three quarters of the world's population, attests to humanity's capacity to adapt to almost anything. These economies have investment values equivalent to untold billions of real dollars, and must be providing, in the aggregate, returns equivalent to billions of real dollars to their investors. Otherwise, there would be no investments. This suggests that some of those who did invest in commercial enterprises in highly inflationary nations, where the currency lacks convertibility and suffers daily losses in purchasing power, must have succeeded. What appear to be insurmountable obstacles in the conduct of business, which are not present in doing business in more stable parts of the world, must be surmountable.

CHAPTER 9

RISK MANAGEMENT

In a world of stable currency exchange rates, there is no need for risk management. In a world of limited volatility and infrequent changes in a system of fixed exchange rates, there may be some interest in risk management. In a world of wide swings in currency exchange rates, risk management becomes a necessity.

This is a world of increasing volatility in currency exchange rates. Volatility, in general, is associated with instability. This, in itself, is a testament to our seemingly growing incapacity to control our created economic and financial systems. We first declared gold and silver to be deemed money. Currencies, which were convertible into gold and silver, eventually gave way to another man-made system of infrequently adjusted fixed rates of exchange among the leading currencies where one currency, the U.S. dollar, was convertible into gold. Then this system gave way to another predominantly "dirty" managed system of floating exchange rates, where a currency is convertible only into another currency.

Many of the world currencies have limited convertibility to other currencies. Companies doing business in these nations have to adapt their financial affairs to fit the situation. That is to say, the conduct of business is guided, among other things, with an eye on how much currency is being accumulated. Even for convertible currencies associated with industrialized nations, the conduct of business is influenced by which currencies are being accumulated and which are being liquidated. As shown in Chapter 6, changes in currency exchange rates since the early 1970s have been significant. Therefore, these changes have significantly impacted the reported profitability of subsidiaries and affiliates when their financial reports were translated to the standard currency of the parent company.

CONTROLLABLE AND UNCONTROLLABLE LOSSES

Running a business has its inherent risks. Many of these risks cannot be managed—that is, they are beyond the control of management. These include the risk of a general downturn in business activity that reduces the volume of sales and the risk of competitors slashing prices to aggressively expand their market share. A company must face the risk of competitors transforming the nature of the market by introducing an improved, or a new, version of a product that makes a company's product dated or obsolete. There is the risk of adverse government legislation, regulatory requirements, barriers to trade, and product liability suits. The list goes on, but added to this list is volatility in currency exchange rates. A receivable due in ninety days may not have the anticipated value in the domestic currency of a company that was envisioned when the transaction was consummated.

The risk of a currency exchange loss is a risk that has been dealt with by financial managers since the early 1970s. One might consider this potential loss of value in a financial transaction as uncontrollable in the sense that management cannot influence future currency exchange rates. Indeed, this is not so. Unlike a downward step in general business activity, an industry-wide price war, or a new product introduced by a competitor, there are ways for a company to protect itself against potential adverse changes in currency exchange rates. The availability of financial instruments to deal with this risk makes it controllable and gives meaning to the phrase "risk management."

PRICE VOLATILITY AS A MARK OF THE TIMES

Increased volatility transcends currency exchange rates. Prices of certain commodities that once were stable are now volatile. For example, the price of gold was constant from 1934, when President Franklin Roosevelt set the price of gold at $35 per ounce, until President Nixon shut the gold window in 1971. Although gold is not a commodity that affects the operations of most companies, its shift from a stable-priced commodity to one subject to wide swings in prices is instructive as to the nature of the problem of price volatility facing modern managers.

The purchasing managers of gold-consuming companies experienced a nearly forty-year history of paying $35 per ounce. During this time, the demands on the financial acumen of the purchasers to minimize the acquisition cost of gold were not overwhelming. Little thought had to be given to inventory valuations and the potential of an inventory loss. Since 1971, the purchasing managers have had to endure the transition from purchasing gold at a fixed price to a price that is influenced by the supply and demand balance of gold and market perceptions of changes in that relationship. Table 9.1 illustrates the volatility of a commodity that previously had nearly forty years of no volatility. The percentage change,

Table 9.1
High/Low Price of Gold (Nearest Dollar per Troy Ounce)

	HIGH	LOW	ANNUAL PRICE SWING	MEASURE OF VOLATILITY
1972	$ 67	$ 46	$ 21	37%
1973	121	66	55	59
1974	184	130	54	34
1975	180	143	37	23
1976	134	111	23	19
1977	163	133	30	20
1978	228	174	54	27
1979	463	228	235	68
1980	676	514	162	27
1981	557	409	148	31
1982	445	315	130	34
1983	490	388	102	23
1984	395	320	75	21
1985	330	299	31	10
1986	424	340	84	22
1987	488	403	85	19
1988	478	408	70	16
1989	409	362	47	12
1990	419	354	65	17
1991	385	342	43	12

a measure of volatility, is the annual price swing divided by the mid-price for gold for the indicated year.

Table 9.1 is based on monthly averages for New York quotes of gold, compiled by the *Wall Street Journal*. Daily quotes can be higher or lower than indicated. In 1980, spot gold spiked at over $800 per ounce for a short period of time. This is hidden in calculating monthly averages. Monthly or annual averages tend to mask the true nature of the volatility that is present in the daily, or spot, market. Purchasing managers focus on the current, or daily, market and must react to volatility on a daily, not on a monthly or annual, basis.

Volatility is better expressed as a percentage change from a base value than as an absolute difference between high and low quotes. The 1983 swing in prices of $102 per ounce appears to have greater volatility, or change, than the 1975 swing in prices of $37. Yet the volatility, as measured by the degree of change from the mid-value, is the same for both years. The $102 swing in prices in 1983, when compared to the mid-price of $439, is a measure of volatility of 23 percent. This is the same measure of volatility in 1975 when the $37 swing is compared to the mid-price of $162. Examining the indicated volatility in Table 9.1, it is apparent that volatility itself is not consistent on a year-to-year basis.

VOLATILITY IMPACTS PROFITABILITY

Nevertheless, the volatility of gold prices is going to affect the profitability of a company that consumes gold in its operations in two ways. Gold purchased in 1980 at an average price of $600 per ounce generated either operating losses or inventory write-downs when gold subsequently fell to $400 per ounce. Therefore, the task of management takes on a new dimension of meaning compared to what it was when the price of gold was fixed by government fiat. Poorly timed purchases of gold as a raw material with respect to the selling of the gold product can lead to substantial operating or inventory valuation losses, a risk not present when the price of gold was stable.

Loss from operations caused by a severe downturn in general business activity might be considered by managers to be beyond their control. An inventory loss may or may not fall into this category. Inventory is necessary for the smooth operations of a company and inventory requires management attention in terms of its quantity and safekeeping. So while a manager is focusing his or her attention on what he or she considers to be more important matters concerning marketing, production and financing, a loss may suddenly emanate from the warehouse. In his or her mind, this should not occur because one would not expect that something safely stored in a well-operated warehouse could generate a loss. Yet it can, if the price of whatever is stored in the warehouse declines substantially. Obviously, this uncontrollable loss becomes a controllable loss when managers accept the responsibility to minimize potential inventory losses and have some means of preventing the loss from occurring. For most inventories, management's tools may be limited to managing the quantity of inventory and, perhaps, terms of sales. But for other types of inventories, including inventories of currencies, there are means of insuring against such a loss. For generic forms of inventories such as metals, foodstuffs, energy, and currencies, there are a variety of risk management products available to reduce or contain the magnitude of a potential loss in the carrying value of an inventory.

VOLATILITY IMPACTS INVESTMENT DECISIONS

The discussion so far has been primarily from the buyer's perspective, where volatility introduces the potential for operating and inventory valuation losses. The other perspective is that of the seller, in this case, a gold mining company. Another complication arising from volatile gold prices is loss of confidence in the financial analysis associated with the decision-making process leading to a capital investment. When prices are constant, the projected revenue of a financial analysis of making a major capital investment in mining capacity can be viewed with a fair degree of confidence. As long as costs are reasonably accurate, and most companies have a fairly good handle on costs, a financial analysis with constancy of prices is reasonably reliable as long as the volume of output is realizable.

Instability in prices affects the confidence that management has in the validity of investment decision models. In 1940, one would confidently project a continued price of $35 per ounce in the decision-making process on making an investment in a gold mine. What price would one assume in 1980 to hold for the next ten to twenty years in order to justify the capital investment in expanding mining capacity? Five hundred dollars per ounce might have been considered reasonable at that time, but one would lack confidence in that price holding for the next decade or so because of past price volatility. In subsequent years, an average projected value of $500 per ounce turned out to be wrong. A capital project whose financing costs depended on an average price of $500 per ounce would certainly have impacted negatively on a company's earnings, and conceivably could have led to its bankruptcy. Therefore, volatility detracts from the confidence management can place in the underlying financial analysis of the investment decision process.

VOLATILITY COMMON IN TODAY'S WORLD

Increasing volatility is not restricted to currency exchange rates or gold. The cost of energy, as reflected in the cost for oil, was essentially constant at close to $2 per barrel from the 1930s until 1972. Interest rates were also stable up to this time. As Table 9.2 shows, volatility, not stability, is the common mark of the modern era. Yet by reviewing this table, one can see that there are times of general calm, and other times of tumult, in price volatility. The degree of volatility from year to year is itself volatile and unpredictable. This is an important point that adds to the challenge of risk management—hedging generally should be put in place before tumult in prices strikes the market. However, hedging during times of relative calm is sure to raise some questions as to its cost and need.

The sources of data in Table 9.2 are the *Statistical Abstracts of the United States* and the *British Petroleum Statistical Review*. In viewing the table, islands of stability in a sea of volatility can be seen for interest rates from 1975 to 1978 and from 1985 to 1988. The price of oil was relatively stable from 1974 to 1978 and from 1982 to 1985. Other periods exhibited enormous volatility. It was no fun being a corporate borrower from 1977 to 1981 or purchasing oil from 1973 to 1974, or from 1978 to 1979. But there is always the other side of the coin. Those with savings seeking interest income would not consider 1982 to 1985 memorable times nor do oil producers have fond memories of 1985 to 1986, or 1987 to 1988. Viewing price changes from the two perspectives of buyers and sellers creates a potential market for risk management products. The seller is interested in fixing the sales price so that he or she does not have to worry about falling prices eroding profit. A buyer is interested in fixing cost so that he or she does not have to worry about rising costs eroding profit. What appears to be an adverse change in price for one party is considered by the other to be an opportunity. This makes it possible for those involved as middlemen or market makers in risk management products to put a deal together, because each party has a different view of the consequences of the same price change.

The airlines have historically flown on thin profit margins because of competitive pressures within this industry. Airline executives learned about the impact

Table 9.2
Prime Rate versus Crude Oil Prices

	AVERAGE U.S. PRIME RATE	AVERAGE PRICE $ PER BARREL MIDDLE EAST CRUDE OIL
1961	4.5%	$ 2
1962	4.5	2
1963	4.5	2
1964	4.5	2
1965	4.5	2
1966	5.6	2
1967	5.6	2
1968	6.3	2
1969	7.9	2
1970	7.9	2
1971	5.7	2
1972	5.3	2
1973	8.0	3
1974	10.8	10
1975	7.9	11
1976	6.8	12
1977	6.8	12
1978	9.1	13
1979	12.7	30
1980	15.3	36
1981	18.9	34
1982	14.9	32
1983	10.8	29
1984	12.9	28
1985	9.9	27
1986	8.3	13
1987	8.2	17
1988	9.3	13
1989	10.9	16
1990	10.0	21
1991	8.5	17

of price volatility on profits the hard way. Both the cost of money and jet fuel are important in an airline's operations. With thin profit margins, 25 percent jumps in interest rates (10 percent to 12.5 percent) or jet fuel costs (60 to 75 cents per gallon) are sufficient to obliterate profit margins. During the 1970s, both jet fuel prices and short-term interest rates spiked at three times, or 300 percent, their levels at the start of the 1970s.

The normal "knee-jerk" response to higher prices is to jack up the airfares. Airline executives learned that such enormous increases in the costs of money and fuel could not be entirely passed on to the consumer in the form of hikes in airline fares. Although the business traveler may be relatively indifferent to the cost of airfare, the vacationing public is not. The vacationing public makes up a sizable portion of airline traffic and is, in general, sensitive to the price of a ticket. As airlines raised ticket prices to compensate for these unheard of swings in the cost of money and fuel, the vacationing public stopped buying airline tickets. The vacation in Europe gave way to a vacation on the Jersey shore. The reduced number of passengers made it impossible for the airlines to recoup the incremental costs. The volatility in the cost of money and fuel on air fares and the ensuing loss of passenger volume was more than sufficient to destroy the profitability of the industry and to drive certain airlines into bankruptcy. Airlines that did protect themselves partially from these changes in costs through shrewd management of the risks that they faced found themselves at a competitive advantage. They number among the survivors.

Yet during those times of relative stability in prices for gold, interest, and currency exchange rates prior to the 1970s, managers of certain industries had to deal in a world of price instability. Lumber, copper, and foodstuffs were, and still are, exposed to the vagaries of sharp price swings. Managers of firms that bought or sold these commodities were keen to protect themselves from adverse price changes through risk management. Financial instruments have been around for over a century to address this need. These financial instruments were expanded in scope, and modified as necessary, as price volatility spread to precious metals, energy, and interest and currency exchange rates.

A discussion on risk management can be easily adapted from one commodity to another. Risk management techniques can be applied to tangibles (grain, lumber, oil, and metals) and to intangibles (interest rates, stock prices, and currency exchange rates). A proposed risk management product can be tailored to anything that exhibits sufficient price volatility to create a need for individuals as normal buyers or sellers of the tangible or intangible item to seek protection from such price swings. In addition, a proposed risk management product should be attractive enough for speculators to assume risk in their quest for personal gain. A proposed risk management product requires an acceptable means of settlement and a large number of actively trading participants. Their trading activity in hedging or speculating provides the revenue to cover the cost of operations and the requisite liquidity for the buying and selling of the risk management product.

Both hedgers and speculators are required for the successful laying off of risk among the participants. The presence of speculators adds depth to the market, by their volume of buying and selling. They are said to bring information to the market by taking positions based on their analysis of available data, which, in turn, influences prices. They often are the mainstay of balancing orders when the "legitimate" hedgers are primarily on one side of the market. For instance, when gold was $800 per ounce, mining companies may have been eager to fix their future production at a price around $800. Consumers of gold may not have been so eager to fix their costs at $800. There is now a mismatch between the number of buyers and sellers. The transference of risk, which is the purpose of risk management products, cannot be accomplished because the market has become one-sided. However, the presence of speculators provides the mining companies with the opportunity to enter into financial transactions that would stabilize their future revenue by transferring the opportunity of further gain in prices to the speculators.

In this example, gold mining companies who entered into futures contracts to fix the price of future production at $800 per ounce turned out to have made the right decision. Consumers of gold and speculators who represented the other side of the transaction lived to regret their decision. Risk management products are a means by which the risk of a rise or fall in a price, or the opportunity associated therewith, is passed from one party to another. Risk management products do not obviate the risk; no more than fire insurance stops fires.

CURRENCY RISK MANAGEMENT

Currency risk management has to do with taking action to avert the risk of loss because of the nature of the currency held by a company and because of the nature of future commercial transactions that lead to an exposure to a currency. Currency risk management is more complex than risk management of a commodity such as copper. A global company must think about its exposure in a hundred currencies, whereas a company dealing in copper has one commodity to worry about. Management views of a currency as favorable or unfavorable depend on whether it is strengthening or weakening in relation to other currencies and on whether a company is long (held in reserves) or short (owed to others). A copper mining company with inventory to be sold and a copper using company with copper in a warehouse to be consumed do not as readily shift between a long or short position as does a global company with a hundred affiliates dealing in a hundred currencies.

A copper-consuming company can easily quantify its exposure. Copper on hand, plus anticipated receipts and commitments less planned shipments, pretty much measures the exposure. Besides dealing in many currencies, a global company has two types of currency exposures: transactions and translations. Although transaction exposure is more easily understood, as payables and receivables in various currencies, translation exposure involves other aspects of the balance sheet. Moreover, the nature of the consolidation process affects the magnitude of translation risk.

Management usually tries to simplify the confusion over currencies by referencing all currencies to one currency—the currency of the nation of domicile. An American-based company's management thinks of all currencies in terms of a dollar equivalent. British, German, and Japanese managers view currencies in their pound, deutschemark, or yen equivalents. There is also a tendency to reduce excess holdings in various currencies to the currency of the company's nation of domicile. Although understandable, it is possible that holding cash reserves in the nation of domicile may not be the optimal course of action. If the pound or dollar is weakening with respect to the deutschemark and yen, is it wise to convert all deutschemark and yen holdings to pounds or dollars as quickly as possible just because management happens to be British or American? One aspect of the transition from a multinational company to a truly global company may be in the way the company thinks of currencies. A global company may not think in terms of a single dominating currency, but in terms of several major currencies with changing attitudes on which to hold. Perhaps its financial records and earnings reports may not be in a single currency.

But for now, it is easier to discuss currency risk management in terms of a single currency in relation to others. The discussion that follows is based on a U.S. domiciled company, but the principles are similar to those of companies domiciled in other nations.

TRANSACTION EXPOSURE

A common practice for affiliates operating in various countries is to receive payment for goods sold in the currency of its nation of domicile. Suppose that a company consists of three affiliates operating in the United States, Germany, and France. These affiliates buy and sell among themselves and normally, but not always, expect payment in their currency of domicile. Normally, when the American affiliate (A) purchases goods from the German affiliate (G), it generates a deutschemark (DM) payable. When it purchases goods from the French affiliate (F), the American affiliate generates a French franc (FF) payable. Similarly when the German or the French affiliates purchase goods from the American affiliate, the American affiliate has dollar receivables.

Although this is common practice, it is possible for an affiliate to buy goods from another affiliate and pay for it in its own currency, and to sell goods to another affiliate and receive payment in the affiliate's currency of domicile. It is also possible that a third currency not related to either of the affiliates may be used as a means of settlement. Suppose, at a point in time, the intercompany receivables and payables are as in Table 9.3.

Managers of a U.S. domiciled company would view these currency transactions in terms of dollar equivalents. Translating these payables and receivables in terms of a deutschemark being worth about \$0.60 and a French franc about

Table 9.3
Intercompany Receivables and Payables

	A		G		F	
CURRENCY	REC	PAY	REC	PAY	REC	PAY
DM	–	100	300	80	–	30
FF	200	3000	300	2000	3000	–
$	–	–	150	40	–	70

Table 9.4
U.S. Dollar Equivalent of Intercompany Receivables and Payables

	A		G		F	
CURRENCY	REC	PAY	REC	PAY	REC	PAY
$0.60/DM	–	$60	$180	$48	–	$18
$0.20/FF	$40	$600	$60	$400	$600	–
$	–	–	$150	$40	–	$70

Table 9.4A

	RECEIVABLES	PAYABLES	COMBINED
$ VALUE OF DM	$180	$126	+$54
$ VALUE OF FF	$700	$1000	–$300
$	$150	$110	+$40

$0.20, the dollar equivalents of these transactions are approximately as in Table 9.4.

These receivables and payables can be combined as in Table 9.4A to obtain the net exposure to each currency.

Receivables and payables in the same currency are natural hedges. Thousands of individual receivables and payables can be combined to obtain the actual exposure of a company to a particular currency. In this example, the actual exposure of the company consisting of three affiliates in terms of intercompany buying and selling is a long position of $54 worth of deutschemarks (90 DM), a short position of $300 of French francs (1,500 FF), and a long position of $40 (U.S.). Once the natural hedges within, and without, a company have been combined, management is in a position to evaluate its actual exposure to various currencies and to decide on a course of action to reduce potential currency exchange losses.

Some commercial banks offer a "netting" or payment-clearing service to companies with global operations. All the affiliates of a company enter their intercompany receivables and payables, in terms of the actual currencies to be received or paid, through a telecommunications system into a common computer data bank. On a periodic basis, and under management control, all intercompany receivables and payables are netted and an affiliate receives, or owes, one payment. As an example, a Belgian affiliate may have dealings with a hundred different affiliates in as many nations. Generally speaking, most payables are in the currency of the nation of domicile of the affiliate and most receivables are in Belgian francs, but this may not be true for all transactions. At specified periods such as a month, and assuming that there are more in receivables than in payables in these intercompany transactions, the Belgian affiliate receives one payment in Belgian francs. All associated intercompany receivables and payables contained within the computer data base, which could number in the tens, the hundreds, or even the thousands, are thereby liquidated with the issuance of a single payment. If the Belgian affiliate has more payables than receivables, then it makes one payment in Belgian francs, and again all associated receivables and payables are liquidated. The bank makes all spot conversions of currencies necessary for the affiliates to receive or pay in their respective currencies of domicile.

Management can incorporate projected payables and receivables into the system in addition to actual payables and receivables in order to improve its measurement of exposure to various currencies from intercompany transfers. The netting service provides management with a full range of reports such as currency exposure, cash balance, transaction, consolidation, and working capital reports. These reports are used for control purposes, for cash management, and for measuring a company's current and projected exposure to various currencies from intercompany transfers. A full measurement of exposure also requires projected payables and receivables to other companies outside the netting system.

It is also conceivable that several global companies could join together in such a system, further reducing the administrative processing costs of making individual payments to affiliates in the same global company and to affiliates in other global companies. Conceptually, this is not unlike credit cards where individuals make one monthly payment, which covers a multitude of individual purchases from many merchants, and where merchants receive one monthly payment from the credit card company, which represents the purchases of many individuals.

TRANSLATION EXPOSURE

Currency translation exposure applies to balance sheets and income statements denominated in a different currency than the company's nation of domicile. Translation exposure is determined by applying the appropriate exchange rate to the various items of the balance sheet and income statements. The rules regarding which exchange rate is to be applied to individual line items of a

Table 9.5

Risk of Translation Loss—20 Percent Devaluation of LC (Figures in Thousands)

DEVALUATION:		BEFORE	AFTER	
METHOD OF CONSOLIDATION:			FASB 52	FASB 8
COLUMN:	1	2	3	4
	LC	U.S. $ EQUIVALENT AT LC=$.10	U.S. $ EQUIVALENT AT LC=$.08	U.S. $ EQUIVALENT AT LC=$.08
Assets				
Cash	LC 300,000	$ 30,000	$ 24,000	$ 24,000
Receivables	1,600,000	160,000	128,000	128,000
Inventories	700,000	70,000	56,000	70,000
Fixed Assets	2,200,000	220,000	176,000	220,000
Total	LC4,800,000	$480,000	$384,000	$442,000
Liabilities & Equity				
Payables	LC 700,000	$ 70,000	$ 56,000	$ 56,000
L.T. Debt	2,500,000	250,000	200,000	200,000
Equity	1,600,000	160,000	128,000	186,000
Total	LC4,800,000	$480,000	$384,000	$442,000

balance sheet and income statement differ with the consolidation method. Therefore, the amount and treatment of translation gains or losses vary with the method of consolidation.

As an example of the possibility of obtaining different measures of exposure to translation gains or losses, suppose that a company has an affiliate in country X and management is fearful of a 20 percent devaluation of the local currency (LC). For a U.S. company, however, there are two possible methods of consolidation as discussed in Chapter 6. One is the current rate method (Financial Accounting Standards Board [FASB] 52) and the other is the temporal method (FASB 8). Table 9.5 is a comparison of the magnitude of the potential exposure to translation risk for both methods of consolidation for a possible 20 percent devaluation of the LC.

The calculation for the potential risk of translation gain or loss for the two consolidation methods is shown in Table 9.6. The local currency balance sheet in column 1 of Table 9.5 has 4.8 billion LC in assets and in liabilities and equity. Column 2 of Table 9.5 contains the translated balance sheet at the current translation rate of 1 LC being worth $0.10. If management had previously decided that the LC was the functional currency, after having considered such things as sources of financing, determinants of local prices, and other matters as discussed in Chapter 6, the balance sheet would be translated using the current rate method

Table 9.6
Calculation of Potential Risk

METHOD OF CONSOLIDATION:	FASB 52	FASB 8
Cash	LC 300,000	LC 300,000
Receivables	1,600,000	1,600,000
Inventories	700,000	-
Fixed Assets	2,200,000	-
Total	LC4,800,000	LC1,900,000
Payables	LC 700,000	LC 700,000
L.T. Debt	2,500,000	2,500,000
Accounting Exposure	LC(1,600,000)	LC1,300,000
Translation (Loss)/Gain at LC=$0.08	$(32,000)	$26,000

in accordance with FASB 52 (column 3 of Table 9.5). All LC assets and LC liabilities are exposed, resulting in a positive exposure, or long position, of 1.6 billion LC. This exposure is calculated by assets less liabilities and would result in a writedown of $32 million (1.6 billion LC × 0.02 LC/$ change in the currency exchange rate), which will be recorded by the company as a separate component of stockholders' equity (cumulative translation adjustment). This write-down does not flow through reported income.

If, on the other hand, management had determined that the functional currency was the U.S. dollar, the temporal method of translation would be applicable as prescribed by FASB 8 (column 4 of Table 9.5). The temporal method must also be selected as the method of consolidation if the affiliate is operating in a hyperinflationary economy, which is defined as one where the currency has a three-year cumulative inflation exceeding 100 percent, as discussed in Chapter 8. Cash and accounts receivable total 1.9 billion LC and liabilities total 3.2 billion LC, resulting in a negative exposure, or short position, of 1.3 billion LC. Under FASB 8, inventories and fixed assets are recorded at historical values and are not exposed to changes in currency exchange rates. This short position, or negative exposure, of 1.3 billion LC will result in a translation gain of $26 million (1.3 billion LC × $0.02 LC/dollar change in the currency exchange rate). This gain is reflected in the income statement, not directly in the equity portion of the balance sheet.

Under FASB 8, the inventory is still recorded at the historic rate of $0.10. This means that in subsequent periods of operation, sales will be translated at 1 LC equal to $0.08, but cost of sales, as goods are withdrawn from the "old" inventory, will be translated at a rate of 1 LC being equal to $0.10 until the "old" inventory is depleted. New additions to the inventory will be translated at 1 LC equal to $0.08. The existence of the "old" inventory has a negative impact on future translated profit until it is depleted. In addition, depreciation expense on existing fixed assets at the time of the devaluation is translated at the rate of $0.10 to the LC after the devaluation, further depressing translated profitability.

Both the exposure to translation gain or loss and the accounting treatment of gain or loss differ widely between FASB 8 and FASB 52. The course of action pursued by management in its anticipation of a devaluation of the LC is, in this example, dramatically different as a consequence of the method of consolidation. In one case, there is a risk to translation loss that impacts the equity portion of the balance sheet. In the other, there is a translation gain with negative ramifications on future income.

FURTHER COMPLICATIONS

All assets and liabilities in the previous discussion are denominated in LC. The reason for this is that management is referring to the income statement and balance sheet as presented by the affiliate to the parent. The affiliate has translated all currencies contained in its financial statements to LC before presenting them to the parent organization. However, in today's global business environment, an affiliate usually deals in many currencies. Suppose that the affiliate in country X sells to local, Japanese, Thai, and U.S. markets and that the temporal method of consolidation (FASB 8) applies. Accordingly, cash, receivables, and liabilities are exposed to the risk of a revaluation or devaluation. In Table 9.7 the right-hand column is the U.S. dollar equivalent of the LC exposure on the books of the affiliate as presented to the parent company. However, the affiliate itself had multiple currency holdings as shown in their U.S. dollar equivalents.

Table 9.7
Multiple Currency Translation Exposure (Currencies Translated to Thousand U.S. Dollars before Devaluation)

BEFORE DEVALUATION

	LOCAL CURRENCY	JAPANESE YEN	THAI BAHT	U.S. DOLLARS	TOTAL
Exposed Assets					
Cash	$ 30,000	–	–	$ –	$ 30,000
Receivables	95,000	$10,000	$35,000	20,000	160,000
Total	$125,000	$10,000	$35,000	$20,000	$190,000
Exposed Liabilities					
Payables	$ 31,000	$ 4,000	$29,000	$ 6,000	$ 70,000
L.T. Debt	210,000	–	–	40,000	250,000
Total	$241,000	$ 4,000	$29,000	$46,000	$320,000
Net Exposure	$(116,000)	$ 6,000	$ 6,000		

There is no net exposure to the U.S. dollar because assets and liabilities already denominated in U.S. dollars do not require further attention. However, Table 9.7 still does not represent a company's complete exposure. Certain non-balance-sheet adjustments have to be made for management to realize the actual exposure to various currencies. One adjustment is the omission of cash on hand, because cash on hand is usually the minimum necessary to operate the business on a day-to-day basis. That being the case, management does not have to take action to protect these minimal, and necessary, holdings. Other adjustments involve the effect of known future transactions, which are not yet reflected on the balance sheet, such as future sales contracts, firm commitments, and operating lease payments. The previous exposure analysis is amended in Table 9.8 to include these items.

Table 9.8
Amended Multiple Currency Translation Exposure (Currencies Translated to Thousand U.S. dollars before Devaluation)

BEFORE DEVALUATION

	LOCAL CURRENCY	JAPANESE YEN	THAI BAHT	U.S. DOLLARS	TOTAL
Exposed Assets					
Receivables	$95,000	$10,000	$35,000	$20,000	$160,000
Future Sales & Commitments	-	10,000	-	-	10,000
Total	$95,000	$20,000	$35,000	$20,000	$170,000
Exposed Liabilities					
Payables	$ 31,000	$ 4,000	$29,000	$ 6,000	$ 70,000
L.T. Debt	210,000	-	-	40,000	250,000
Future Purchase Commitments	-	-	3,000	-	3,000
Leases	-	7,000	-	-	7,000
Total	$241,000	$11,000	$32,000	$46,000	$330,000
Net Exposure	$(146,000)	$ 9,000	$ 3,000		

If it happens that the long exposure in one currency equals the short exposure in another, the two cannot be offset against each other. They both must be dealt with separately because it is unlikely that any two currencies will move in tandem. Exposures are expressed in dollars because it is assumed that the company is U.S. domiciled. Managers of a corporation can more readily grasp the magnitude of the exposures if they are expressed in the common currency of the company.

The analysis of exposure performed by British management would be in pounds and the risk of translation exposure would take into consideration the U.K. method of consolidation. This would hold for all nations of domicile.

Including non-balance-sheet items such as future sales, purchase commitments, and leases changes the exposure to various currencies. In this example, the long position in Japanese yen has increased, the long position in Thai baht has decreased, and the short position in LC has increased. The data base is now complete for management to take an overview of the situation and consider what actions, if any, are necessary to protect the company with regard to its exposure to various currencies.

Measuring the exposure to transaction and translation risk requires a centralized information system in order for management to determine its exposure to various currencies. Without this information, managers involved in risk management are not able to act effectively. This information must be presented on a timely basis because it is possible for a company's exposure to a particular currency to swing from a long to short, or from a short to long, position in a brief period of time. Usually, monthly reports from all affiliates are consolidated and analyzed on a global basis for management to have a continual measure of the actual exposure of a company to all currencies.

Affiliates may report their exposure to various currencies by telecommunications means using a specified electronic spreadsheet format. Once the parent has the spreadsheet reports from the affiliates, they can then be combined into one master spreadsheet that calculates the company's global exposure to all currencies. Besides timeliness of data and ease of display for measurement of exposure, such an information system places the management of the parent in a position to exercise control over the financial decisions being made by the affiliates to prevent them from taking actions that would make managing exposure to transaction and translation risk more difficult.

MANAGEMENT MEANS TO DEAL WITH CURRENCY EXPOSURE

Management may feel comfortable being exposed to certain currencies that it feels will maintain or increase in value with respect to the currency of domicile of the company. For those currencies where management fears a loss of purchasing power, various methods can be employed to reduce the exposure to these currencies, which are briefly described below.

1. Local cash balances should be kept to a minimum level consistent with cash needs necessary for the operation of the business. Excess cash and profits should be remitted as quickly as possible from the subsidiary or affiliate to the parent by increasing the frequency or size of dividends, royalties, and licensing and management fees, remaining cognizant, of course, of tax considerations and local currency exchange controls.

2. If management believes that a devaluation is imminent, one possible course

of action may be to raise selling prices. In a competitive pricing environment, this will depress the sales volume, reduce receivables, and increase inventory. This, of course, is against the natural inclination of local management because raising prices to this extent also depresses profits. But this course of action is not intended to depress profits, but to reduce the potential of loss from an imminent devaluation.

Investment in inventory, as a nonmonetary asset, is a means of protection against the financial loss of a devaluation associated with cash balances and receivables. Transforming cash and receivables into tangible assets reduces the extent of write-downs of liquid assets. If FASB 8 applies, inventories are not written down because they are carried at historic cost. In addition, tangible assets tend to preserve their value as a currency loses purchasing power because they can be sold for a higher price after the devaluation. Once the impact of the devaluation on the local economy is over, selling prices can be reduced to competitive levels to enhance sales and reduce inventory. Of course, these price hikes have to take into account any local price control regulations that may be in effect.

3. Speeding up collection of receivables, and for that matter, slowing down payment of payables, would result in higher cash balances, which might then be invested, along with any other excess cash, in increased inventory or other tangible assets. However, as everyone's receivable is someone else's payable, the net result of this course of action might be a nationwide stalemate on paying bills until after the devaluation. Excess cash holdings can also be invested in a strong currency foreign asset, such as an investment in a related affiliate or in a new subsidiary. Local government regulations on currency exchange may constrain or eliminate this latter option.

4. Sometimes companies engage in "back-to-back" loans as a means of trying to reduce the impact of a devaluation, or a series of anticipated devaluations. Suppose that parent A has affiliate A operating in a nation where the local currency cannot be exchanged for a more desirable currency. One way to reduce the exposure to the local currency is to engage in back-to-back loans by lending surplus local currency to an affiliate (affiliate B) of a nonrelated company (parent B) that needs the local currency for its own purposes. Simultaneously, parent B makes a hard currency loan to parent A. In a typical arrangement, both of these loans are paid off at a stipulated future date in their respective currencies. This exchange of cash for a receivable in a local currency at least has the benefit of making hard currency available to parent A at a negotiated interest rate that is usually advantageous to parent A. This gives parent A some slight benefit in its holdings of a local currency. The problem of what to do with excess holdings of the local currency has been deferred, but not solved.

5. Leads or lags are timing differences in the payment or settlement of payables and receivables. This technique has two purposes. One is the funding of affiliates. Suppose that a Korean company sells $100,000 worth of goods to a Spanish company monthly. If these goods are sold on 60-day terms, the Spanish company

owes the Korean company $200,000 on a permanent basis. If the Spanish company requires more funds, this can be accomplished by changing the terms to 120 days, that is, increasing the lag. This will increase the amount payable to the Korean company to $400,000 on a permanent basis. If the Korean company requires funds, then the Spanish company can pay currently, or, perhaps, in advance, which is known as a lead.

The other purpose of leads and lags is to shift the currency exposure between two nations. Suppose that management believes that the Spanish peseta will devalue in the near future. The Spanish affiliate could be instructed to speed up intercompany payments; that is increase the lead, and obtain whatever financing is required from local lenders to make this possible. This reduces the exposure of the company in pesetas, before the devaluation occurs, by reducing its cash reserves of pesetas and increasing its payables in pesetas in the form of bank loans. The caveat here is that if all companies are making bank loans for the purpose of converting the proceeds to a different currency, then interest rates for these loans can become quite high, negating some of the benefit of reducing the exposure to currency exchange losses. Moreover, if everyone is joining in the rush to get out of pesetas, the devaluation becomes a self-fulfilling prophecy.

FINANCIAL ENGINEERING AND RISK MANAGEMENT PRODUCTS

The techniques just described can seldom accomplish all of management's objectives. To add to management's arsenal of tools to manage the risk associated with adverse changes in currency exchange rates, interest rates, and commodity prices, a host of risk management products have been devised by financial engineers. J. D. Finnerty, a professor at Fordham University, in an article titled "Financial Engineering in Corporate Finance: An Overview," appearing in the Winter 1988 issue of *Financial Management*, defined "financial engineering" as follows:

Financial engineering involves the design, the development, and the implementation of innovative financial instruments and processes, and the formulation of creative solutions to problems in finance.

Financial engineers work closely with a client firm to first identify and measure the potential exposure to risk and then create a solution to obtain a desired outcome. Some financial engineers specialize in the quantitative analysis of determining the exposure to risk. Others are responsible for coming up with what may be an innovative and creative solution. Still others are involved with the practical aspects of implementing the solution. Financial engineering usually requires the services of accountants, lawyers, tax specialists, analysts, modeling professionals, programmers, and information specialists.

Financial engineering is a sign of the times—as volatility of prices and interest and currency exchange rates increases, so does the risk of potential loss faced by corporations, and, therefore, the need for outside expertise to manage the risk of potential loss. The efficacy of financial engineering depends on modern methods of communication and the interfacing of communications and computers for the dissemination of information on various financial and commodity markets. Modern technology in the networking of computers allows multiple users to tap the same data base and use the same spreadsheet financial models for rapid analysis in preparing timely and effective recommendations to clients, both internal and external.

One interesting example of the technological impact of computers and telecommunications on financial markets is "program trading." Stock market index futures are used by portfolio managers as insurance, or protection, against a falling market. Suppose that a mutual fund manager is worried about a falloff in the stock market. By shorting the index futures, any falloff in the stock market, which creates portfolio losses, is compensated by profits made in the index futures. Program trading is the exploitation of discrepancies between the price of stock market index futures and the underlying market value of the stocks represented by these futures. Speed of execution of orders, computerized matching of buy and sell orders, buying and selling of "baskets" of securities, and rapid analysis of the complex mathematics associated with identifying pricing discrepancies are necessary technological preconditions for the existence of program trading.

Stock market index futures can be viewed as a financial tool, devised by financial engineers for stock portfolio managers to protect themselves against volatility in stock prices. But financial engineers are also hard at work devising innovative and creative ways for individuals and firms to increase their yield on investments. By examining the spread between index futures and the underlying value of the basket of securities, financial engineers can provide the necessary information and the means to buy one and short the other, locking in a superior return over investing in other securities such as Treasury bills. This particular financial tool, created by financial engineers to protect portfolio managers against adverse changes in stock prices, is also exploited by financial engineers to enhance the return on investment for investors. The irony of the situation is that the exploitation of a financial instrument to enhance yield may also be responsible for increasing the volatility of stock prices. If this is the case, then the medicine is both treating and contributing to the disease.

The ability to gather information promptly and accurately, and disseminate the information immediately throughout the world can be considered a risk management tool. This, too, may be responsible for increased volatility. A manager of a chocolate factory who first learned about a cocoa crop failure in West Africa in the nineteenth century from a captain of a sailing vessel probably had sufficient time to act on this information to protect his company's interest in cocoa beans before his competitors learned about it. His individual buying of cocoa beans would probably not affect the market to any great degree. The slow dissemination of the information about the crop failure allows for an orderly adjustment of prices.

Nathan Rothschild supposedly learned of the defeat of Napoleon at Waterloo by homing pigeon. This allowed him to buy depressed stocks in London before anyone else knew of the allied victory and sell them when everyone else knew. Leaving aside the moral implications of having sole access to vital information, the buying and selling by Rothschild probably reduced the volatility in the London stock market because his buying occurred when everyone was selling and his selling occurred when everyone was buying. In today's world, all those who deal in cocoa beans and stocks and everything else are tapped into the same source of news. No one has a timing advantage, which means that all act in unison, and by so doing, increase the volatility of prices.

CONNECTION BETWEEN CURRENCY EXCHANGE AND INTEREST RATES

There is a connection between futures in currency exchange rates and interest rates. This connection ties these two markets, which allows financial engineers to devise ways of hedging in interest rates by means of hedges in currencies and vice versa. Suppose that an American has $1,000,000 to invest and six-month (180-day) U.S. Treasury bills offer an annual yield of 4.0 percent. If the investor completes this transaction, he would have approximately $1,020,000 at the end of the 180-day period. Suppose, however, that the investor notes that a French government security is yielding 4.5 percent in 180 days. If he converts his dollars to francs, he will earn more interest, but will be faced with a currency exchange risk at the maturity of the French security. Suppose that the current spot rate for francs is 5.527 francs to the dollar and the 180-day forward contract is 5.538 francs to the dollar. The investor could convert his dollars to francs, receiving 5,527,000 francs, which when invested in the French 180-day note, yields 5,651,358 francs (5,527,000 × 4.5 percent × 180/360). Simultaneously with the conversion of dollars into francs, the investor also sells a 5,651,358 forward contract at the 180-day forward rate of 5.538 francs to the dollar. Upon receipt of the 5,651,358 francs in 180 days with the maturing of the French debt security, the investor fulfills his obligation under the forward contract by converting 5,651,358 francs to $1,020,469. This is in excess of the $1,020,000 he would have received had he invested in the U.S. Treasury 180-day bill.

The forward or futures rate for a currency is set not by the market impact of investors attempting to maximize their return as much as by arbitragers seeking a riskless return. An arbitrager enters into a riskless covered interest arbitrage by borrowing funds in one country, converting to another currency, investing the funds in another country, and selling a forward contract to cover the conversion back into the original currency to repay the loan. An arbitrager would continue entering into such transactions until the difference between the currency exchange spot and forward rates narrows sufficiently to remove the riskless profit of entering into such transactions. This is accomplished by the continual buying of spot contracts and selling of forward contracts, which causes the price of the former to rise and the price of the latter to fall until the riskless profit differential disappears. The role of investors in maximizing returns on their assets and arbitragers in seeking riskless profit opportunities establishes a link between interest rates and the spread between spot and forward currency exchange rates. This makes it possible for financial engineers to devise ingenuous solutions to interest rate exposure by entering into a currency exchange contract or to manage a currency exchange risk through an interest rate contract.

It also makes it possible for financial engineers to reduce interest costs by having a company borrow from financial institutions in other countries without exposing the company to a currency exchange loss. For instance, a Canadian company was able to borrow in yen from a Japanese financial institution at a favorable interest rate, which exposed the company to the possibility of an adverse change in the Japanese yen/Canadian dollar exchange rate. Financial engineers addressed that risk by having the company enter into a long-term currency exchange contract. The net effect of these two transactions was a lower effective interest rate to the company by borrowing in Japan and hedging the currency exchange risk rather than by borrowing directly in the Canadian capital market.

FUTURES AND FORWARDS

The terms "futures" and "forwards" are oftentimes used interchangeably for contracts between two parties that require a specific action to be taken at some later date. As these contracts generally take the form of a delivery of an underlying asset such as a certain amount of currency or a quantity of a physical asset, they are sometimes referred to as contracts for deferred delivery. There are, however, important differences between futures and forwards. A futures contract is traded on public exchanges with highly standardized terms other than the price of the contract, which is set by the market. A forward contract is traded in "over-the-counter" dealer markets where all terms, including price, must be negotiated between the buyer and seller. Over the counter means that a formal exchange or clearing house is not involved in a forward contract—deals are done on an individual basis with a dealer playing the role of a middleman or broker.

A clearing house or association stands between the parties of a futures contract, which removes the necessity of identifying the parties involved in the futures contract. This is similar to the trading of stock on a stock exchange—it is done between brokerage houses with the brokerage houses responsible for making the final settlement between the ultimate buyer and seller of the shares of stock. In a forward contract, each party is directly responsible for the fulfillment of the agreed terms and, therefore, their identity is a critical factor in the negotiation process leading up to the mutual agreement of contractual terms and conditions.

Futures markets, like the stock markets, are government regulated, whereas forward markets are not. The financial integrity of the futures market is ensured by each party to a futures contract maintaining the required margin, which can be likened to a performance bond. No such mechanism exists in the forward market. This is another reason why the identity of the parties, and their reputation, is a critical part of a forward contract.

In addition, the active market in futures contracts makes it easy to terminate a transaction by buying back the futures or entering into another that offsets the original transaction. In a forward contract where terms and conditions are uniquely defined for each contract, such ease of termination is not only difficult but may be impossible. There is liquidity in the continual buying and selling of futures in the futures market, whereas there is virtually no liquidity in the forwards market.

On the surface, one would wonder why anyone would enter into a forward contract rather than a futures contract. The primary reason is that the futures contract, being a highly standardized contract, may not fit the particular needs of an individual or company. Suppose that an importer must pay 20 million Japanese yen in forty-nine days. A futures contract is in units of 12.5 million yen to be settled thirty, sixty, and ninety days in the future. The futures contract does not meet the importer's specific needs. Rather than over or under hedge either in the amount of yen and the duration of time, by taking a position in futures on the futures exchange, the importer might negotiate a deal that meets his or her precise requirements with a forward contract arranged in the over-the-counter market.

SWAPS

Swaps are financial products originated by financial engineers in response to the growing instability in prices and in interest and currency exchange rates during the 1980s. Started in 1979, swaps became a popular financial instrument in 1981 because of the publicity associated with a currency swap arranged by Salomon Brothers between the World Bank and IBM. Currency swaps rapidly spread to swaps in interest rates and commodities. Swaps are built around the same basic structure as forwards and have been described as a series of forward contracts. Two parties, called counterparties, agree to one or more exchange(s) of specified quantities of underlying tangibles or intangibles, sometimes called notionals if there is a cash rather than a physical exchange of the underlying asset. Cash payments are the usual means of settlements between the counterparties of a swap.

A swap is usually arranged by a financial intermediary that negotiates a final deal between two counterparties entering into a swap. The intermediary, known as a swap dealer or market maker, receives his or her remuneration in the bid-asked spread between the two counterparties. Three illustrations are provided to explain the principal "plain vanilla" swaps.

Interest Rate Swap

Counterparty A is a company that requires $10 million to construct a factory. The creditworthiness of the company is not sufficient for an issue of fixed rate interest debt, but a bank is willing to lend the company $10 million on a floating rate basis. Counterparty A worries about the floating rate interest rate increasing over the next ten years and wants to hedge, or protect itself, against this risk. Counterparty A is willing to sacrifice the opportunity of having to pay less in interest expense if floating rates fall in order to safeguard itself from the risk of having to pay higher than the fixed rate that can be arranged through a swap.

Counterparty B is a company, or a financial institution, whose creditworthiness is sufficient for it to issue fixed interest rate debt. Suppose that counterparty B borrows on the basis of its own creditworthiness $10 million at a fixed interest rate of 10 percent. It could lend the money to counterparty A, but then counterparty B assumes the credit risk of counterparty A repaying the loan. Instead of lending the money to counterparty A, counterparty B deposits the funds in a floating rate account. Suppose that the floating rate is currently 8 percent. Counterparty B transfers the interest income of 8 percent on its $10 million deposit to the swap dealer in return for a fixed rate of 10.3 percent.

Counterparty B neither makes nor loses money on the floating rate deposit and makes a 0.3 percent spread on its capacity to issue fixed rate debt. Counterparty B has no credit risk in borrowing the $10 million in that the proceeds of the loan have been placed in a floating rate deposit that is sufficient to pay off the principal of the fixed rate debt.

The swap dealer passes the floating rate interest payment received from counterparty B to counterparty A. In return, counterparty A pays the swap dealer 10.4 percent fixed rate of interest. The difference between receiving 10.4 percent interest from counterparty A and paying 10.3 percent interest to counterparty B is the swap dealer's remuneration. Counterparty A takes the floating rate interest of 8 percent and pays the floating rate interest plus any applicable spread to its lending institution. If the interest rate on counterparty A's loan is the floating rate plus a spread of 0.75 percent, then counterparty A is actually paying 8.75 percent on its loan. Therefore, the net cost of interest to counterparty A is the 0.75 percent differential to be paid on the floating rate loan plus the fixed 10.4 percent to the swap dealer.

There is no point in counterparty A paying 10.4 percent to the swap dealer and receiving the floating rate of 8 percent from the swap dealer. It is easier to net the difference and pay that to the swap dealer. Under the circumstances, counterparty A pays the difference between 10.4 percent and 8 percent to the swap dealer, or 2.4 percent applied against the notional amount of the interest rate swap, in this case, $10 million. Counterparty A pays less if the floating interest rate rises. If the floating rate goes above the fixed rate, counterparty A will receive money from the swap dealer. This extra money will be used to pay the higher interest charge associated with counterparty A's floating rate loan.

Therefore, counterparty A has accomplished his purpose of swapping a floating rate for a fixed rate loan. His cost of interest is the fixed rate of 10.4% plus the spread of 0.75% on the floating rate loan. He is no longer at risk in having floating rates rise to a level that may imperil his financial survivability. For this, he has foregone any opportunity to benefit from floating interest rates being less than the arranged fixed rate.

A single payment is also made between counterparty B, representing the difference between the 10.3 percent to be received from the swap dealer and the floating rate to be paid to the swap dealer. The swap dealer simply passes the payment between the two counterparties extracting his piece of the action. The swap dealer is making 0.1 percent interest spread between counterparty B receiving 10.3 percent and counterparty A paying 10.4 percent on the notional amount of the principal. He has accomplished his objective in arranging the swap.

Counterparty B has borrowed funds at 10 percent and has lent them out at 10.3 percent with the difference being remuneration for entering into the transaction. This fulfills counterparty B's objective in entering into the swap. However, in entering this swap, counterparty B has given up any benefit from rising interest rates. He has deposited the funds from a fixed rate loan in a floating rate account and turns the interest earnings over to the swap dealer. If the floating rate were to go to 20 percent on funds borrowed at 10 percent, counterparty B would have been better off not entering into the swap.

Counterparty B can undo the transaction by purchasing an interest rate futures, but from the point of view of the swap, he has given up the benefit of rising floating interest rates. Therefore, he might have been reluctant to enter into the swap if he had strong feelings that floating interest rates would rise. However, by counterparty B depositing the funds from the fixed rate loan in a floating rate account, whether floating rates rise or fall, counterparty B has locked in his return. This is the spread between the fixed rate paid by the swap dealer and the fixed rate being paid on the incurred debt.

It is possible that counterparty B does not borrow the funds at a fixed rate of interest. Counterparty B may be a financial institution that feels that interest rates are going to fall and may delay arranging its fixed debt financing. It is possible that it does not intend to arrange any borrowings, but to cover itself through the purchase of interest rate futures should interest rates begin to rise. If counterparty B perceives this to be a desired course of action, then the swap dealer would definitely find it easier to put the swap together if both counterparties have opposite viewpoints on the future direction of floating interest rates.

The swap can be considered as a series of forward contracts in which the termination of each individual contract occurs at the time of payment of the interest rate differential, say, every six months. Collectively, in this example, the swap represents a series of twenty forward contracts that cover ten years of interest payments. Credit risk is not transferred in a swap. Both counterparties A and B have arranged their floating and fixed rate loans based on their individual creditworthiness. Each is responsible for the repayment of the underlying principal of the loan. If, by change, counterparty B did not arrange a fixed rate loan, then its creditworthiness must be sufficient to cover the differential in interest rates should its assessment on the future direction of rates be proven wrong. Even here, there are means for counterparty B to minimize, or avoid, losses.

The only connection between the two counterparties is the net payment representing the difference between the floating and fixed rates of interest. The bankruptcy of one of the counterparties affects only the interest rate differential payment between the two counterparties. In addition to the potential bankruptcy of a counterparty, swap dealers such as Drexel, Burnham, Lambert of junk bond fame, have gone bankrupt. The U.S. Bankruptcy Code has been amended to ensure that netting provisions of swaps be honored by the bankruptcy courts in the event of the bankruptcy of counterparties and swap dealers. Interest rate swaps have become so common that the plain vanilla variety are frequently arranged directly between banks without the services of a swap dealer.

Currency Swap

A currency swap can be arranged when one of the counterparties has more advantageous access to a financial market. Suppose that an American company desires to finance a factory to be built in Germany in deutschemarks at a fixed rate of interest. Further suppose that a German company has access to lower fixed rate interest financing in Germany than the American company. To complete the picture, suppose that the German company desires to borrow in U.S. dollars for its business purposes, at a floating rate of interest and the American company is in a position to borrow in the United States for less than a German-based company can do on its own. This situation of each party having access to lower cost loans than the other party permits the origination of a swap, where the German company borrows deutschemarks from a German financial institution at a lesser interest rate than what would be charged to the American company. The American company borrows a like amount of dollars for a lesser interest charge than what the German company could have negotiated.

A swap dealer then arranges a currency swap whereby the two companies can take advantage of borrowing at lesser cost in different markets. Each swaps the principal amounts of the loans, which are the same, and each makes interest payments to the swap dealer as agreed, with the American company making deutschemark payments that are sufficient for the German company to pay off its loan and the German company making dollar payments sufficient for the American company to pay off its loan. The swap dealer takes a little out of the middle.

A plain vanilla currency swap does not involve an exchange of a credit risk. Both companies borrow on the basis of their own creditworthiness. Each merely exchanges, or swaps, the payment of debt and interest such that the American company ends up paying a fixed rate German denominated debt, which it desired, and the German company ends up paying the type of dollar denominated debt, which it desired. Three exchanges are necessary. The first is the exchange of the principal of the loan, then the interest payments, and, at the end of the swap period, the final repayment of principal of the respective loans. Although currency swaps are usually floating/fixed rates of interest—that is, one counterparty paying a floating rate of interest and the other a fixed rate of interest—currency swaps can also be floating/floating and fixed/fixed.

This plain vanilla currency swap is also called an exchange of borrowings because that is exactly what it is. Its origin lies in each company's advantage in borrowing in its respective domestic market. However, the plain vanilla can easily become a more sophisticated variant because the exchange of borrowings may not exactly fit the desires of the two counterparties. An interest rate swap may have to be arranged along with the currency swap to change a floating rate loan to a desired fixed rate loan. The tenor, or the length of the repayment period, or the amount of the loan, may not entirely match the desires of each counterparty. The swap dealer may turn to a financial engineer to introduce a new level of complexity to transform an undesirable cash flow stream into one that is desired by the two counterparties to the currency swap. It is possible for the repayment of principal to be amortized with the regular payments of interest similar to a level payment type of financing common for home mortgages. By combining swaps with other swaps or with other financial instruments, all sorts of variants can be created, limited only to the imagination of the financial engineers and the needs of client firms.

Commodity Swap

Counterparty A is an oil producer who has financed his wells with loans. If oil falls below a certain price, he will not be able to generate the earnings necessary to pay the financing charges associated with drilling and developing the oil wells. This may force the oil producer into bankruptcy. Counterparty B is a refinery operator who sold a portion of his output at a fixed price and wants to stabilize the price of oil required to be purchased in the future in order to preserve the profit margin of these fixed priced contracts. Counterparty B worries about an increase in the price of oil that would destroy the economic worth of his fixed price contracts.

A swap dealer, being in touch with both individuals, can arrange a plain vanilla swap. The oil producer sells his actual output, called "actuals," into the spot oil market and receives the spot price, which may be higher or lower than the agreed fixed price of the swap. If higher, he must pay the difference between what he receives and the agreed fixed price to the swap dealer. If lower, the producer will receive the difference from the swap dealer. On the other side of the swap dealer's ledger is counterparty B, the refiner. Counterparty B buys his oil needs, or actuals, from the spot market and pays the spot price. If the spot price is higher than the agreed swap price, counterparty B receives what the producer has paid to the swap dealer. If the spot price for oil is lower than the swap price, then the refiner pays the difference to the swap dealer, which is passed on to the refiner. In order to avoid disagreements between the two counterparties as to what is the spot market price, the counterparties agree to base the spot price, not on actual purchases and sales, but on a spot price from a published source, such as the monthly average spot price for oil quoted in the financial press.

No matter in what direction the net payment is flowing, the swap dealer takes out a margin for his or her trouble, before passing the money to the other party. The swap dealer assumes no risk, which is why both the oil producer and the refinery operator must refer to the same published source for spot market quotes, such as a monthly average, to remove day-to-day price fluctuations, and other causes of price differences from becoming part of the calculation of what is to be paid between the two counterparties. Otherwise, the swap dealer would become embroiled in disputes over price differentials between what an oil producer receives when he sells and what a refinery operator pays when he buys. Although the producer is selling his output to the spot market and the refiner is buying his input from the spot market, the net effect is that they are essentially buying and selling from each other at the swap price. The swap can go on for as long as the two counterparties desire, again illustrating the point that a swap can be considered a series of forward contracts.

The question may arise as to why the producer and the refiner did not enter into a contract with one another directly, as is practiced by banks for plain vanilla interest rate swaps. First of all, the buyer and seller may not have known of each other's presence or needs—this is the classic role of the middleman. It is easier for a bank to canvass the market for interest rate swaps if there are relatively few banks providing the fixed rate portion of an interest rate swap. In the oil business, where there are hundreds of producers and refiners, a middleman or swap dealer, may be needed for the sorting out process of identifying and bringing together the two counterparties. Another reason for having a swap dealer involved in a transaction is that frequently the needs of the producer and refiner do not exactly match. The producer may want to fix the price of oil for a quantity and for a duration of time that does not exactly fit the refiner's needs. A deal cannot be directly negotiated between the two counterparties. However, a swap dealer can set up a swap that does match each of the two counterparties' needs. To do so, he or she may have to arrange another swap to take care of the differences in quantity and timing, or hedge the position for his or her own account.

Swap Variants

Swaps have grown from nothing in 1979 to a level of about several trillion in notional outstandings in the early 1990s. Notional outstandings do not necessarily mean actual deposits of funds in banks or assets in warehouses. Notionals are reference points from which the amount of payment between counterparties is calculated. In the previous case of a plain vanilla interest rate swap, the notional amount of the swap of $10 million was the reference point from which the interest rate differential payments between the counterparties were calculated. Plain vanilla swaps have given way to all sorts of variants that have been created to meet the specific needs of the counterparties to a swap. Variants to the plain vanilla swaps are as plentiful as mutations in a jar of fruit flies; a sampling follows.

An accreting swap is one where the notional principal increases, and an amortization swap is one where the notional principal decreases, over the life of the swap. An annuity swap transforms an irregular cash flow payment stream to a regular one. An asset swap is based on assets rather than liabilities. A basis swap deals with a mismatch between assets and liabilities. A blended interest rate swap combines two swaps to produce a more attractive overall rate. A callable and puttable swap gives one or the other counterparty the right to terminate the swap after a specified time. A capped swap is a swap with a cap, or a maximum limit, on the floating payment side of a swap. A cross currency swap is an exchange of cash flows of one currency for another that reverses at some point during the swap period. A debt-equity swap isn't even a swap, but a substitution of equity in local companies in lieu of interest or principal payments of a heavily indebted nation.

A deferred swap is one where the payments are deferred for a specified period, whereas a delayed LIBOR reset swap is one where the floating payment is based on a future rather than the present London Interbank rate. A differential swap is the swapping of floating interest rate payments referenced to different currencies. A discount swap has a large balloon payment at the end of the swap period to take into account the discount on the regular payments as opposed to a high-coupon swap where the fixed payments are above the market rate with some sort of compensating adjustment at the end of the swap period. A dual currency swap contains rights to repay principal and interest in a choice of currencies at preset exchange rates. An escalating rate swap permits the fixed rate side of a swap to escalate with time. An extendable swap contains the right for the payer to extend the swap. A forward swap is one that is arranged at some point before the start date. A naked swap is one without a corresponding asset or liability, an interesting concept. A reversible swap gives one side the option to alter the payment basis after a certain period as compared to a reverse floating swap where the floating rate payments are inversely proportional to interest rates.

The roller coaster swap alternates the counterparties between paying fixed and floating rates. The seasonal swap is one where the notional amount varies with the time of the year to fit the needs of companies that borrow on a seasonal basis. A spreadlock swap has one payment stream referenced to a fixed spread over a benchmark rate. The tax-exempt swap has its fixed rate interest tied to tax-exempt bonds. The warrant-driven swap is a swap with a warrant allowing an issuer of a bond to extend a swap if it exercises a similar warrant on a bond. The yield curve swap is one where the two interest rates reflect different points on a mutually agreed yield curve. The zero-coupon swap is one where one or both counterparties make one payment at maturity.

Finally, there is the swaption. A swaption is an option on a swap. The swap is set up in all respects except for the starting date. One of the counterparties to the swap pays a swaption premium for the right to start the swap at any point during the swaption period, say, in six months. If he or she does not exercise the swaption, the swap terminates without execution at the end of the swaption period. Swaptions have their family of variants.

Swap dealers are not in business to accept risk, but to transfer the nature of risk between the two counterparties. Swap dealers work off their "swap book" to tailor a swap to meet the needs of the two counterparties. In so doing, they may introduce an element of risk into their swap books. Swap dealers then enter into other swaps or hedges to remove the element of risk that may be present in their swap books. Swap dealers usually wish to neutralize any risk in their swap books to protect their remuneration, which is in the bid-ask spread between the two counterparties of a swap. However, if the swap dealers are confident about the emergence or continuation of a price trend, they may accept a degree of risk in their swap books to profit thereby.

PUTS AND CALLS

Futures and forwards are contractually binding agreements. Swaps, as a continuing series of forwards, are also contractually binding. These contractually binding agreements mean that each party must transfer a specified underlying asset, or a cash equivalent thereof, at known points in time. Puts and calls are options where the purchaser of a put or call has the right, but not the obligation, to buy or sell an underlying asset. A buyer of a call has the right, but not the obligation, to purchase something at a stipulated price, whereas the buyer of a put has the right, but not the obligation, to sell something at a stipulated price. However, the seller of a call or a put does have an obligation to sell the underlying asset at the stipulated price when the call is exercised or to buy the underlying asset at the stipulated price when the put is exercised. An American option can be exercised from the time it is written until the time it expires. A European option differs in that its exercise period is limited to a short period of time before its expiration date.

Staying with American options, pricing of options depends on several factors. One is the exercise price in relation to the underlying value of the asset. If the exercise price is $20 and the underlying value of the asset is $22, then the option has an intrinsic value of $2 and is described as being "in the money." If the underlying value is $20, the same as the exercise price, the option is described as being "at the money." If the underlying value is $18, the call option has no intrinsic value, but still has extrinsic value. Extrinsic value depends on the difference between the market and exercise prices, the remaining time to expiration, and the volatility of the price of the underlying asset. The smaller the difference between market and exercise prices, the longer the time to expiration, and the greater the volatility of the price of the underlying asset, the greater the extrinsic value of the option even though it may have no intrinsic, or inherent, value. Another factor in the pricing of options is interest rates, because a grantor, or a writer, of an option is seeking income by writing calls. Generally speaking, an option writer grants options on an owned asset. As an alternative, he or she can sell the owned asset and invest the proceeds in a secure interest bearing financial instrument. Because the grantor has the choice to sell the asset and invest in interest-bearing financial instruments or underwrite options, option writing premium income must be attractively priced in relation to interest-bearing securities.

All of these factors are built into the first complete option pricing model developed by two professors, Fisher Black and Myron Scholes, in 1973. Options are generally priced based on models derived or adapted from the original Black-Scholes model. The model is a mathematical expression containing the difference between the current price of the underlying asset and the strike price, a measure of past volatility in the price of the underlying asset, time to expiration and the interest rate on a secure deposit. The purpose of the model is to determine a theoretical price for an option. Dealers sometimes use the Black-Scholes model to examine prices being quoted by grantors or writers of options, by reversing the model to obtain the implied volatility in the quote. Some dealers use the implied volatility to differentiate quotes on different options for the same asset. By being able to identify options with differently implied volatilities for the same underlying asset, dealers can use this information for putting deals together or in hedging their own portfolios. Moreover, implied volatility can be charted and analyzed as to what feelings participants in the option markets have toward volatility. A period of falling implied volatility can be interpreted to mean that participants in the market feel that prices are approaching an island of stability in a sea of volatility. Rising implied volatility means that participants see storm clouds on the horizon. This information is of value for market makers in options.

OPTIONS IN RISK MANAGEMENT

From the perspective of a company attempting to manage the risk of price volatility, options can be used to change the cost profile of an asset in a way that serves the interest of the company. Suppose that a company buys an asset that management feels can vary in price from $15 to $25 per unit and the current price is $20. The company does not want to find itself in a position of paying much over $20 per unit for the asset. It buys a call option for $1 per unit with an exercise price of $20. For that portion of its needs covered by the call option, the company has changed the cost profile as illustrated in Table 9.9.

A company wanting to contain its costs to $21 per unit for the asset has done so by purchasing the option. The profit from the call option compensates for the extra cost of purchasing the asset. This protects the company whenever the price

Table 9.9
Buy Call Option for $1 with Exercise Price of $20

MARKET VALUE OF ASSET	COST OF OPTION	INTRINSIC VALUE OF OPTION	NET COST OF ASSET TO COMPANY
$17	$1	$0	$18
18	1	0	19
19	1	0	20
20	1	0	21
21	1	1	21
22	1	2	21
23	1	3	21

of the asset moves above $20. If the asset does not move above $20 per unit, the company has added $1 to unit to its acquisition cost. This can be likened to the premium cost of an insurance policy to protect against paying a higher than desired price for the asset. A company must weigh the cost of protection against the benefit of having the protection.

Suppose that a company has acquired a large supply of inventory at $20 and wishes to insure itself against a loss in value. The company buys a put option with an exercise price of $20 for $1. If the market value of the asset declines, the intrinsic value of the put will increase. The net value of the asset in inventory covered by the put is illustrated in Table 9.10.

Table 9.10
Buy Put Option for $1 with Exercise Price of $20

MARKET VALUE OF ASSET IN INVENTORY	COST OF OPTION	INTRINSIC VALUE OF OPTION	NET VALUE OF BOTH TO COMPANY
$17	$1	$3	$19
18	1	2	19
19	1	1	19
20	1	0	19
21	1	0	20
22	1	0	21
23	1	0	22

The company, in wanting to protect itself against loss, has maintained the value of the inventory at $19 per unit regardless how low the market value of the asset may sink. The profit from the put option compensates for the loss in inventory value. The cost of this protection is $1 per unit, which one can view as an insurance premium if the value of the asset remains above $20 per unit.

The portion of the inventory that is protected by the put is said to be hedged against a price decline.

Suppose that the price of the commodity is $20 and the company buys a put and a call, called a straddle, for $1 per option. The value of the straddle to the company is shown in Table 9.11.

Table 9.11
Buy Put Option for $1 with Exercise Price of $20 and Buy Call Option for $1 with Exercise Price of $20

MARKET VALUE OF ASSET	COST OF OPTIONS	INTRINSIC VALUE OF CALL OPTION	INTRINSIC VALUE OF PUT OPTION	NET VALUE OF STRADDLE TO COMPANY
$16	$2	$0	$4	$ 2
17	2	0	3	1
18	2	0	2	0
19	2	0	1	-1
20	2	0	0	-2
21	2	1	0	-1
22	2	2	0	0
23	2	3	0	1
24	2	4	0	2

If the price of the asset falls below $18, the profit from the put can be used to hedge against a write-down of the inventory. If the price rises, the profit from the call can be used to hedge against paying above $22 per unit. If the price of the asset hovers between $18 and $22, the company would have been better off not purchasing the straddle. Straddles are useful when management expects increased volatility in the price of the asset but is unsure of the direction of change in price. The straddle offers double protection in limiting the maximum amount to be paid for the asset and in limiting the maximum amount of loss of holding the asset in inventory. In offering more protection, the insurance premium also costs more.

Suppose that the company decides to buy a call option with an exercise price of $20 for $1 and sells a call option with an exercise price of $22 for $0.50. The net cost of buying and selling the options is $0.50. What would be profit profile of this course of action? See Table 9.12.

The idea of selling the second call is to reduce the cost of the hedge by the amount of premium earned on the selling of the call. A company would employ such a strategy of buying and selling a call option at different strike, or exercise, prices if it was worried about a rise in price in the commodity, but was convinced that such a rise would not go over $23. If management were proven wrong and the price did exceed $23, it could buy its way out by purchasing another call option to compensate for the "loss" associated with the call that was sold. Once a company begins to protect itself against price rises or declines through some sort of hedging technique, there is a tendency to keep purchasing and selling options to "undo" those past hedging positions that are costing the company

Table 9.12
Buy Call Option for $1.00 with Exercise Price of $20 (Option I) and Sell Call
Option for $0.50 with Exercise Price of $22 (Option II)

MARKET VALUE	NET COST OF OPTIONS	INTRINSIC VALUE OF OPTION I	INTRINSIC VALUE OF OPTION II	NET VALUE OF OPTION POSITION	EFFECTIVE COST OF ACQUISITION
$16	$.50	$0	$0	$-.50	$16.50
17	.50	0	0	-.50	17.50
18	.50	0	0	-.50	18.50
19	.50	0	0	-.50	19.50
20	.50	0	0	-.50	20.50
21	.50	1	0	.50	20.50
22	.50	2	0	1.50	20.50
23	.50	3	-1	1.50	21.50
24	.50	4	-2	1.50	22.50
25	.50	5	-3	1.50	23.50

money. In time, a relatively simple hedging position can become quite complex.

If the two call options in the previous example expire at the same time, it is called a vertical bull spread. If the call with the lower strike price is sold and the one with the higher strike price is bought, there would be premium income and the strategy would be called a vertical bear spread. If the expiration dates are not the same, but the exercise price is the same for the two options, these strategies are called a horizontal bull or bear spread depending on the expiration dates of the purchased and sold options. If there is a mix of expiration dates and strike prices, the strategy is known as a diagonal spread. To show that there is virtually no limit to the imagination, a butterfly spread would involve four options. All have the same expiration date. Two options with the same strike price are sold, whereas one with a higher strike price is purchased along with one with a lower strike price. If the buying and selling of the options are reversed, this is called a reverse butterfly or a sandwich spread.

What risk does management fear the most? The financial engineers can dream up a solution. There are barrier options (four major types including knock-in and knock-out options), basket options, binary and digital options, call and put spreads, chooser options, compound options, condors, cylinders, difference options, embedded options, forward start options, hi-low options, lookback or path-dependent options, straddles and strangles, table tops, and tunnels, which are similar to cylinders. Someone in the company better have a firm understanding of where the company stands when the price of the underlying asset changes. Although there is no commitment undertaken by the company when options are purchased, there is certainly a commitment associated with sold options as there are with swaps, futures, and forwards. Therefore, there should also be someone in a company with a firm handle on what commitments have been undertaken by a company in its hedging program. This someone should not be the person directing the company's risk management program.

RISK MANAGEMENT FOR OPTION MARKET MAKERS

The role of market makers in options is to have a balanced position in options with little exposed risk. They are not in the options market to assume a risk. Their role is to be intermediaries in the exchange of risk between two parties. In this role, they may have to assume some risk in order to complete a deal. Then they take action to neutralize, or hedge, the risk assumed in putting the deal together. A hedged portfolio of options may no longer be fully hedged because the price of the underlying asset changes. Price changes in the underlying asset can transform out-of-the-money options to in-the-money ones and vice versa.

As a matter of interest, option market makers themselves have a risk management challenge in maintaining a neutral position and living off commissions and bid-ask spreads between buyers and sellers of options. To do this, they depend on a world of Greek letters. Delta is the price sensitivity of an option to price changes of the underlying asset. When an option is deeply out of the money, a move in the price of the underlying asset has little or no effect on its price (delta = 0). For an option deep in the money, there is an exact one-for-one relationship between its price and the price of the underlying asset. On a per unit basis, as the price goes up by one, the value of a call would also increase by one (delta = 1). For puts that are in the money, an increase in the underlying value of the asset reduces their value by one (delta = -1). The delta associated with a short call in the money would be -1 and the delta associated with a short put in the money would be $+1$. For options where the market price is approaching the exercise price, there is an intermediate, not a one-for-one, relationship between changes in underlying value and in the value of the option. Therefore, delta values vary between 0 and 1 for long calls and short puts, and between 0 and -1 for short calls and long puts.

The net risk of a dealer's exposure to options on the same underlying tangible or intangible asset can be quantified by totaling the deltas of all the options. A "delta neutral" portfolio of options would be one where the sum of all deltas is near zero. However, there are complications associated with maintaining a delta neutral portfolio of options because, as just discussed, the delta of an option varies with the underlying price of the asset. The rate of change of delta with respect to changes in the price of the underlying value is measured by gamma. Theta measures the erosion of an options premium as the expiration date nears. Theta can be positive or negative depending on whether there is a long and short position. Rho measures the sensitivity of the option's price to changes in interest rates, whereas kappa, or vega (not a Greek letter, but an old Chevy car model) measures the change in an option's price with respect to changes to the volatility of the price of the underlying asset. Needless to say, delta, gamma, theta, kappa or vega, and rho measures of a portfolio of options are not calculated by hand. In addition, there are other Greek letters in a dealer's lexicon—beta trading is used by option traders to take advantage of similar financial instruments having diverging volatility, whereas omega is the risk associated with a buyer or seller of an option where the accounting of the option will be in a different currency than the option.

OPTIONS IN FUTURES

In addition, financial engineers have originated futures options. Calls and puts can be exercised calling for the delivery or sale of the underlying asset. Futures options are puts and calls on futures. A review of the U.S. financial press shows that one can buy and sell puts and calls on futures of U.S. Treasury notes and bonds, various currencies with both American and European variants including a cross trade between German marks and Japanese yen, various agricultural products, metals, various stock indices, and crude oil and oil products. Settlement of futures options is in cash, not a delivery or acceptance of an underlying asset. A futures option out of the money at the time of expiration is worthless.

EXCHANGE FOR PHYSICALS

There should be a strong linkage between an expiring futures contract and the cash price of the physical asset for futures to be effective as a hedging tool. Very few expiring futures end up with an exchange of physical assets. Usually, a long position is liquidated by selling the futures and a short position is liquidated by buying futures. But the possibility of a long position ending up with the physical possession of the underlying asset ensures that expiring prices and cash prices are very close to one another. For instance, an expiring copper future could end up with a change in ownership as 25,000 pounds of copper. The copper futures market has an associated warehouse holding a sufficient quantity of copper of the specified purity to provide for a change of ownership between the owner of an expiring futures contract and its seller.

Oil is a much less "homogenous" market than copper. The cash market in crude oil is based on commonly traded types of oil such as Saudi Arabian Light, North Sea, and West Texas Intermediate. The futures in crude oil traded on the New York Mercantile Exchange calls for delivery "at any pipeline or storage facility with pipeline access to Arco, Cushing Storage, or Texaco Trading & Transportation Inc. . . . " In the world of oil, this is a rather limited transformation of "paper" barrels to "wet" barrels. To take into account the wide variety of grades of oil and time and place of delivery, the financial engineers devised exchange for physicals (EFPs). EFPs extend the circumstances surrounding delivery of futures by permitting buyers and sellers of futures to agree to the exact buyer and seller, the nature of the crude oil, and place, volume, time, and other details of delivery. Payment is made by exchanging long and short positions in expiring futures.

BACKWARDATION AND CONTANGO

The relationship between the futures and the cash markets determines whether a market is in backwardation or contango. When a futures contract is selling for less than the current cash price, the market is said to be in backwardation. Using oil as an example, a backwardation market permits an oil company to sell a part of its inventory that is to be refined in the future in the cash market and buy a, say, two-month future. In two month's time, the "paper" barrel is transformed to a "wet" barrel through an EFP, if necessary, to process the oil. This would only occur if the discount for the futures compared to the cash price is sufficient to make this a profitable transaction. In calculating this profitability, one must bear in mind that an oil company can invest the cash proceeds of selling oil in inventory in an interest-bearing security. There are also transfer, shipping, and other costs involved with the delivery of the futures, or the EFP, that have to be taken into account.

A contango market is one where there is a premium on the futures in relation to the cash price. If the premium on the futures contract is large enough, and if there is sufficient storage capacity at the oil company refinery, it may be to the oil company's advantage to buy extra oil in the cash market and short a futures contract. On the maturing of the futures contract, the oil company delivers the oil rather than making a cash settlement. The spread between the cash and futures market has to be sufficient to cover the storage costs and the interest costs of investing in what amounts to extra inventory.

CAPS, FLOORS, AND COLLARS

Calls and puts have a finite life usually measured in months. Rarely do their expiration times exceed one year. Another example of financial engineering creativity are multiperiod options. These were created to address the need for providing a maximum rate of interest on a loan, called an interest rate cap. Loans usually run for more than a year and, therefore, calls and puts with an expiration time of one year or less do not provide a solution for a company that desires to hedge against rising interest rates on a multiyear floating rate loan. The writer of an interest rate cap agrees to pay the holder of the cap the difference between a reference rate above the ceiling rate, applied against a notional principal, every six months during the two to five year tenor, or length of time, of the cap, or any other agreeable tenor. The reference rate is a published rate such as the London Interbank or U.S. Treasury bill rates.

The ceiling rate is the maximum rate the holder of the cap will pay on a loan covered by the notional principal of the cap. For this protection, the cap holder pays an upfront fee. The effective interest rate has the appearance of a multiperiod call. The amortization of the upfront premium over the life of the cap is analogous to the premium paid for a series of single period calls. If interest rates do not rise to the ceiling rate, the holder of the cap is simply paying a higher effective interest rate. This is analogous to the previous example of illustrating how a call limits the maximum amount to be paid for some underlying asset. If the price does not rise to this limit, the premium for the call increases the effective acquisition cost for the underlying asset.

If interest rates rise above the ceiling rate, the profit from the cap offsets the higher cost of interest effectively capping interest at the ceiling rate. Obviously, the closer the ceiling rate is to current interest rates, the higher its cost. This holds true for calls—the closer the exercise price is to the current price of the asset, the higher the premium. A buyer of a call, or a cap, must decide on the amount of premium and the protection afforded by that premium in covering his or her perceived risks. Interest rate caps are sometimes combined with interest rate swaps or with currency swaps to produce an interest or a currency rate-capped swap. Caps can be assignable with the owner's permission, much as a call can be sold when its protection is no longer needed.

An interest rate floor is similar to a cap except that the purchaser of a floor receives payment when the reference rate drops below the contract rate. The classic use of a floor is an insurance company borrowing fixed rate money to be loaned out at a floating rate. In so doing, the insurance company is betting on an upswing in interest rates. If interest rates fall, the insurance company may not earn enough to service its policy holders. An insurance company can protect against this risk by purchasing an interest rate floor, which guarantees a minimum interest rate should the floating rate fall below the contract, or floor, rate.

Caps and floors do not involve the exchange of a credit risk. They are cash settlements at prescribed times whereby a purchaser of a cap does not pay more than the ceiling rate and the purchaser of a floor does not earn less than the floor rate. Because the principal covered by a cap or floor is not exchanged, the cash payments are based on a notional amount of a loan. If a cap is 10 percent and the referenced floating rate is 12 percent, and the notional amount is $10 million (MM) and settlements are made every six months, then the purchaser of the cap will receive the difference (2 percent × $10 MM × six months/twelve months) or $100,000 from the market maker. He then applies this against his floating rate loan, reducing its net interest cost from 12 percent to 10 percent. If the floor is 8 percent and the referenced floating rate falls to 6 percent, then the seller of the floor has to pay the market maker $100,000. This raises his effective interest cost from 6 percent to 8 percent, thus fixing his minimum interest rate at 8 percent.

A financial engineer can create collars from caps and floors. A collar is the purchase of a cap coupled with the sale of a floor. The proceeds from the sale of the floor reduce the cost of the cap. What this effectively does is lock the interest rate between the floor and ceiling rates. If a company has a floating rate loan on a certain amount of principal, a collar on the same notional amount of the loan fixes both the maximum and minimum interest rates. If floating interest rates exceed the ceiling rate, the company will receive a cash payment that compensates it for the incremental interest expense that is above the ceiling rate, thus capping the interest rate on the loan at the ceiling rate. If floating rates fall below the floor rate, the company will not benefit from the lower interest costs because it is obligated to pay the difference between the floating rate and the floor rate, applied against the notional amount of the collar, to the market maker. If interest rates stay between the floor and ceiling rates, the lender has increased his effective interest rate in the amortization of the cost of acquisition of the collar.

The concept of the interest rate collar as a multiperiod option to set a ceiling and a floor rate for interest rates can be applied to currencies and commodities. A currency collar is a series of multiperiod cash settlements, where the holder of the collar limits his exchange rate within a prescribed band. This is accomplished by a cash settlement representing the differences in actual currency exchange transactions and the contractual upper and lower exchange rate limits— the ceiling and floor rates of conversion. For a premium, a company can collar, so to speak, the currency exchange rates on, say, Swiss franc to dollar conversion within a prescribed upper and lower rate of exchange based on a stipulated notional amount of currency. This is a powerful financial tool in managing the long-term exposure to a currency risk.

The collar is applied to commodities. For the payment of a premium, the holder of a collar, sometimes referred to as a range forward, can limit his purchases of a commodity, such as oil, to a prescribed band. Using a publicly available source of pricing for oil as a means of measuring spot purchases, a holder of a range forward receives money from the market maker when spot purchase prices exceed the upper limit or ceiling price. When spot purchase prices fall below the lower limit or floor price, the holder of the range forward must pay the difference to the market maker. When prices are between the floor and ceiling prices, the effective cost of oil is the spot price plus the premium paid for the collar, or range forward. The buyer of a collar or a range forward is obtaining protection against paying more than the ceiling price, but, in so doing, gives up the opportunity of buying for less than the floor price. He has, in effect, avoided a risk that he cannot endure by giving up an opportunity that he could enjoy.

RISK MANAGEMENT ACCOUNTING ISSUES

FASB 52 sets forth a series of conditions for accounting for currency exchange futures as hedges, avoiding having to "mark to market" the value of a futures on the last day of each accounting period. Mark-to-market gains and losses flow through the income statement, which adds to the volatility of earnings. Managers take a dim view of the mark-to-market accounting treatment of futures because of its unpredictable impact on earnings. Earnings, in the mind of many managers, should reflect the result of operations and not be distorted by the "snapshot" valuation of futures contracts. FASB 52 also accords the same accounting treatment to currency exchange forward contracts as to currency exchange futures contracts.

In 1984, FASB 80, ''Accounting for Futures Contracts,'' was issued to deal with futures contracts for other than currency such as stock index, commodities, and interest rates. FASB 80 defers the loss or gain of a futures contract if the company owns, or is liable for, the delivery of the underlying asset. The gain or loss of a futures contract can also be deferred if there is a legally enforceable obligation to make or accept delivery of the underlying asset. And the third criterion for deferring a gain or loss is entering into a futures or forward contract on the basis of an anticipated transaction. This transaction need not be legally enforceable. In other words, if in management's judgment, there is sufficient probability of some transaction occurring to warrant entering into a futures or forward contract, and even if there is nothing legally binding to enforce the consummation of the contract, the gains and losses of the associated futures or forward contract can be deferred.

Under FASB 52, deferral of gains and losses can occur only if the currency exchange forward or futures contract reduces the risk of loss of a specified transaction. FASB 80 has a much broader interpretation of the conditions permitting deferral of gains and losses associated with other forms of futures and forward contracts. In particular, hedging based on anticipated transactions, in addition to exposure to risk of existing conditions and firm commitments, is permitted deferral of gains and losses. Mark to market, or the immediate recognition of gains and losses associated with non-currency-exchange futures and forward contracts, is required only when the futures and forward contract cannot be related to any underlying or anticipated exposure to risk. In essence, FASB 52, which applies only to currency exchange futures and forward contracts, and FASB 80, which applies to all other futures and forward contracts, are inconsistent in the accounting treatment of futures and forward contracts. This, not surprisingly, has sparked a continuing controversy among accounting professionals.

Neither FASB 52 nor FASB 80 addresses options. In 1984, the American Institute of Certified Public Accountants (AICPA) began to study this issue, which led to the publication of the ''Options Issues Paper'' in 1986. The paper tends to apply the principles underlying FASB 80, rather than FASB 52, to options. That is, using options to hedge against anticipated happenings should be treated similar to the treatment of futures and forward contracts in FASB 80. The ''Options Issues Paper'' has neither been endorsed by the Securities and Exchange Commission nor has there been follow-up in the form of a published FASB statement. Therefore, the issue of accounting for options is essentially yet to be fully resolved. Hedge accounting frequently has the effect of shifting reported gains or losses from one period to another. Given that the rules of accounting for hedges involving options are still evolving, management must be accordingly cautious on their approach to accounting for hedges.

In 1990, FASB 105, ''Disclosure of Information about Financial Instruments with Off-Balance-Sheet Risk and Financial Instruments with Concentrations of Credit Risk,'' came into effect. Futures, options, and financial swaps fall within the definition of a financial instrument as set forth by FASB 105. The purpose of FASB 105 is not to specify accounting principles applicable to these financial instruments. Its purpose is footnote disclosure of the off-balance sheet risk associated with certain financial instruments and also concentrations of credit risk. Off-balance-sheet risk is the risk of an accounting loss that exceeds the amount recognized as an asset or liability on the balance sheet.

Prior to FASB 105, a company could have entered into a speculative futures contract that might have resulted in a potential loss far exceeding the amount of investment that would be recorded on the balance sheet. No further special accounting or disclosure was required. Normal accounting treatment would handle any gain or loss attributed to the futures contract. With the adoption of FASB 105, footnote disclosure is now required if a company takes a speculative position in a financial instrument that can result in a loss exceeding the acquisition or carrying cost of the financial instrument. FASB 105 describes the nature of the footnote disclosure and also requires disclosure of credit risk where financial instruments are concentrated by geographic regions, industries, or customer groups that have common exposure to adverse economic developments.

The 1990 annual report of the Coca-Cola Company contains these required footnote disclosures. Note 4, shown in Exhibit 9.1, discloses the company's exposure to credit risk of its associated bottlers and customers. Note the reference to outstanding interest rate swaps.

Exhibit 9.1
Note 4 to Coca-Cola 1990 Annual Report

4. Finance Subsidiary. Coca-Cola Financial Corporation (CCFC) provides loans and other forms of financing to Coca-Cola bottlers and customers for the acquisition of sales-related equipment and for other business purposes. The approximate contractual maturities of finance receivables for the five years succeeding December 31, 1990, are as follows (in thousands):

1991	$38,199
1992	30,609
1993	20,156
1994	11,290
1995	7,111

These amounts do not reflect possible prepayments or renewals. Finance receivables include amounts due from Johnston of $56 million and $59 million at December 31, 1990 and 1989, respectively.

At December 31, 1990, CCFC had outstanding interest rate swap agreements which effectively change CCFC's floating interest exposure on $60 million of commercial paper to a fixed rate of approximately 8.2 percent.

Note 7 of the same annual report, Exhibit 9.2, discloses non-U.S. dollar denominated debts, which are acting as hedges against the company's investments in these countries. Note 8 discloses that the company has entered into a substantial amount of foreign currency exchange and interest rate contracts, which are subject to the risk of loss if there is a change in rates. Because "such changes would generally be offset by opposite effects on the items being hedged," there is no speculative aspect associated with these financial instruments.

Exhibit 9.2
Notes 7 and 8 to Coca-Cola 1990 Annual Report

7. Long-Term Debt consists of the following amounts (in thousands):

December 31,	1990	1989
11 ⅜% notes due November 28, 1991	$ 85,675	$ 85,675
9⅞% series B notes due November 26, 1992	59,667	31,034
5¼% notes due April 24, 1996	222,977	212,623
5¼% notes due March 25, 1998	166,953	148,854
Other	97,861	83,380
	633,133	561,566
Less current portion	97,272	12,858
	$535,861	$548,708

Notes outstanding at December 31, 1990, were issued outside the United States and are redeemable at the Company's option under certain conditions related to U.S. and foreign tax laws. The 5¾ percent notes due April 24, 1996, are denominated in Japanese yen and the 5¾ percent notes due March 25, 1998, are denominated in German marks. Portions of such notes have been swapped for U.S. dollar, Swiss franc and Belgian franc denominated liabilities. The Company has designated such foreign currency borrowings as hedges against its net investments in those respective countries.

Other long-term debt consists of various mortgages and notes with maturity dates ranging from 1991 to 2013. Interest on a portion of this debt varies with the changes in the prime rate, and the weighted average interest rate applicable to the remainder is approximately 12.7 percent.

Maturities of long-term debt for the five years succeeding December 31, 1990, are as follows (in thousands):

1991	$97,272
1992	78,353
1993	24,750
1994	14,103
1995	8,009

The above notes include various restrictions, none of which are presently significant to the Company.

At December 31, 1990, the Company is contingently liable for guarantees of indebtedness owed by third parties of $139 million, of which $82 million is related to independent bottling licensees.

Interest paid was approximately $233 million, $319 million and $250 million in 1990, 1989 and 1988, respectively.

8. Financial Instruments. The Company has various financial instruments with off-balance-sheet risk for the primary purpose of reducing its exposure to fluctuations in foreign currency exchange rates and interest rates. While these financial instruments are subject to the risk that market rates may change subsequent to the acquisition of the financial instrument, such changes would generally be offset by opposite effects on the items being hedged. The Company's financial instruments typically mature within one year of origination and are transacted at rates which reflect the market rate at the date of contract.

At December 31, 1990, the Company had $1.3 billion of foreign currency financial instruments, substantially all of which were forward exchange contracts to purchase or sell foreign currency (primarily French francs, German marks and Japanese yen). These instruments were employed to hedge balance sheet and transactional exposure.

See Note 4 for discussion of interest rate swaps and Note 7 for discussion of foreign currency swaps and financial guarantees provided by the Company.

TAX ACCOUNTING

There is a question whether gains and losses associated with futures and options purchased for a business purpose ought to be treated, for tax purposes, as ordinary income or as capital gains. If treated as ordinary income, losses associated with futures and options reduce the company's overall tax liability. If treated as capital gains or losses, capital losses can only be netted against capital gains. Because most companies have little in capital gains, the effect is little, or no, tax loss benefit for net losses associated with futures and options. In other words, a gain associated with a futures or option would be taxed as a capital gain. A loss associated with futures or options can only be netted against a capital gain. If there are no offsetting capital gains, the loss remains on the books as a capital loss and cannot be used to reduce taxes currently. Basically, a company finds itself paying taxes on net gains of holding positions in futures and options, but not being able to shield income if there are net losses associated with futures and options. This is sometimes termed as "asymmetric" treatment of gains and losses.

The tax treatment of futures and options acquired for business purposes has traditionally been to match gains or losses against ordinary income. However, in 1988, the Supreme Court made a decision with regard to the *Arkansas Best* case, which has been interpreted by the Internal Revenue Service to mean that such gains or losses should be treated as capital gains or losses. This has opened up Pandora's box, as the IRS audits past corporate income tax returns and recasts the tax treatment of futures and options, as well as forwards and swaps. These tax adjustments have been estimated by one expert to be $2 billion. Congressional legislation is required to clear up the situation.

RISK MANAGEMENT STRATEGIC CONSIDERATIONS

A U.S. based company sells a product for a million British pounds, to be paid in six months, with a current exchange rate of $1.80 per pound. The financial advisors to the company feel that the pound is likely to fluctuate in a range of $1.70 to $1.90 per pound. A futures contract can be purchased to guarantee conversion at $1.78 per pound, indicating some negative feelings about the prospects for the pound by those selling futures. What should be done?

There are two pure strategies: do nothing or hedge everything. The do nothing approach is simple—do nothing. In six months, the pound might be worth $1.70, meaning that the company will receive $100,000 less than what it anticipated when the goods were sold for 1 million pounds. The hedge everything approach is just as simple. This would commit the company to honoring a futures contract that would, in effect, lock the proceeds from the sale of goods at $1,780,000. Many financial managers subscribe to the latter course of action because a fully hedged portfolio "let's them sleep peacefully at night." The cost of a futures contract is small, being the brokerage fee associated with buying the contract. So the peaceful sleep costs the company little, unless, of course, one wants to overlook the loss of opportunity gain associated with the pound moving up to $1.90. In this case, the true cost of the peaceful night's sleep could escalate from the small brokerage fee up to about $100,000. This is a very expensive tranquilizer.

A less expensive tranquilizer might be a futures option to establish a minimum exchange rate for a million pounds, while letting the company benefit if the British pound gains in value. This costs more in the form of an upfront premium than a futures contract, but there may be offsetting opportunity gains associated with a strengthening British pound that could justify the extra cost. Between these two extremes are all sorts of mixed strategies where the individual hedge does not cover the entire million pounds, or where the strike, or option price, does not match the current exchange rate.

The key question is which of these myriad of possibilities does one follow? Utility theory allows the mathematical modeling of risk aversion, or fear, on the part of managers. What kind of a disaster awaits the company if the pound should fall to $1.70? Suppose this sale has a profit element of $300,000 with the pound at $1.80. The worst that can happen is that the profit element is reduced to $200,000. That may be acceptable given that, by doing nothing, the profit element may grow as large as $400,000 if the pound rises in value to $1.90.

On the other hand, perhaps the profit element in the transaction is not the main concern to the manager. Perhaps, the receipt of the $1.8 million is crucial for the firm continuing as a going concern. Suppose that approximately $1.78 million must be dedicated to repaying a loan and bankruptcy looms if the company does not repay the loan in full. Now there is no question that the company had better lock in the $1.78 million through a futures contract; the financial officer has good reason to buy a futures contract to guarantee a peaceful night's slumber.

No manager actually knows the future price of a commodity or the exchange rate of a currency. If so, he or she would be better off giving up his or her position and taking a speculative position in the asset. But managers do know the consequences if the price of a commodity, the interest rate on a loan, or the exchange rate of a currency reaches certain levels. These thresholds of financial pain vary with the circumstances of every company, and with the perceptions of every executive.

As an example, a public bus company consumes an enormous quantity of diesel fuel oil. The last thing the bus depot manager wants is to have to go before the town budget committee and beg for more money because diesel fuel costs have gone beyond his budgetary allotment. Risk management provides the financial means, such as a range forward, to avoid this pain. The fact that he might end up paying more for fuel if it falls below the floor rate is not of any great concern; the manager is still within his budgetary limit. Pain is on the side of high prices, not low prices. He may forego the opportunity to enjoy lower prices in order to avoid the pain of paying higher prices.

A manager of the fuel purchases for an airline cannot afford to pay more for jet fuel than some stipulated amount. On the other hand, he has no authority for paying upfront premiums for protection. A market maker in the jet fuel offers the airline a participating forward where the airline will not pay more than a ceiling price on the purchase of jet fuel. However, when the price of jet fuel is less than the ceiling price, the airline pays some premium over the market price. For instance, the price of jet fuel may be adjusted upward by half the difference between the spot and ceiling prices. This, of course, is the hidden premium for this risk management product because, in the world of finance, there is no free lunch. In this case, there are two pains. One is the pain associated with jet fuel prices escalating above a certain level. Pain is also in requesting upfront premium fees to pay for this risk management product. The financial engineers created a remedy for both pains by devising the participating forward contract.

Financial engineers or market makers stand between the oil producers and the oil consumers. An oil producer has a large amount of debt. He cannot afford to have oil fall below a certain price because he will not generate the earnings necessary to repay his loans. He is an obvious candidate for entering into some sort of arrangement that fixes the price at which he can sell his oil. The bus company and the airline and a host of other companies want to fix their cost of oil products. A financial engineer has to devise hedging tools not just in crude oil but also in gasoline, heating oil, and other petroleum products. Once these financial tools are developed, a market maker can stand between the various parties making up the oil industry fixing revenue, fixing cost, to everyone's heart's content, even devising clever schemes to hide the premiums. With financial engineers creating futures in crude oil, gasoline, heating oil, and jet fuel, a market maker can now approach an oil refiner and induce him to sell futures in gasoline and heating oil and buy futures in crude oil and fix his margin. That is, the refinery operator can lock in his operational profit margin through risk management products. When risk management is used in ways that lock in profit margins, it is sometimes referred to as economic management.

An example of economic management is a copper mining company wanting to borrow funds to expand its capacity. Lenders are wary of the project because of the inherent volatility in copper prices. A falling copper price will jeopardize the repayment of the loans. To combat this risk, the copper mine operator can use a risk management product to enter into a swap that stabilizes the price he is going to receive for his copper production. Since the economic risk of a falling copper price is no longer of concern to the bankers, they offer a floating rate interest loan to finance the mine project.

Now it is the copper mine operator's turn to worry about the financial risk of a rising floating rate interest destroying his profitability, now that his revenue is fixed by virtue of the copper swap. To accommodate the mine operator's perception of risk, another risk management product, an interest rate swap, can be set up to fix the rate of interest. If by chance, different currencies were involved between the selling of the copper and the financing of the loan, a currency swap can also be part of the picture. With both the copper price and the interest rate, along with any possible currency exchanges involved with the project, fixed, the projected cash flow can be sufficiently stabilized to proceed with the development of the mine. The economic risks associated with the project were addressed by an assortment of risk management products. Once in place, they made the project financially viable.

Another example of economic management is a U.S. exporter competing in the global market. His non-U.S. based competitors quote in different currencies. The U.S. exporter quotes only in dollars. He perceives this to be a competitive disadvantage. One way to address the marketing risk of not satisfying the needs of customers is to enter into currency exchange rate swaptions, or other financial instruments, based on estimates of sales in these currencies. If these currency exchange risk management products can be properly designed, a company can quote in different currencies and not be exposed to a currency exchange loss.

SYNTHETICS

Finally, the financial engineers can set up synthetic instruments. Synthetics use risk management products not directly related to the underlying asset. The use of currency exchange futures to hedge interest rate positions and vice versa are examples of synthetic instruments. Suppose that there is no way to hedge against currency X. However, in tracking past movements of currency X, and comparing these movements with those of currency Y, it is noted that there is good correlation between the two. That is to say, the two currencies move more or less in tandem. If there is a market for risk management products in currency Y, then it is possible for financial engineers to devise a hedging vehicle for currency X using risk management products based on currency Y. The problem here is that future movements of currency X may not correlate, or be in tandem, with currency Y. In which case, the hedge may not only be ineffective, but may be a financial disaster.

One example of a synthetic instrument that failed to perform as intended was the use of heating oil futures as a synthetic hedge for jet fuel futures by airlines before the development of jet fuel futures. The synthetic instrument had previously shown a good degree of correlation between the prices of heating oil and jet fuel. Their respective prices more or less moved in tandem. Unfortunately, one day the two diverged. Jet fuel prices went up and heating oil futures went down. Not only did the heating oil futures fail to provide any protection against rising jet fuel prices, but the heating oil futures themselves were liquidated at a loss.

MODELING AND MANAGEMENT JUDGMENT

To manage risk, management must first have an assessment of its exposure to a particular risk. A financial reporting and control system could have a projection of the financial statement and balance sheet projection of a company set up using nominal values for those currency exchange rates, interest rates and commodity prices that are of importance in the operation of a company. This does not have to be an integral part of an financial reporting and control system per se. It could be done on a spreadsheet where a single change in the value of one of these key variables can be transmitted throughout the income statement and balance sheet in such a way that management can see the associated impact of a change on reported profitability and cash flow.

The company is now in a position to play what if scenarios for different values of the key variables whose volatility can be addressed by risk management products. By keeping all variables at their nominal value and adjusting one at a time for likely changes in value, exposure to risk can be quantified for each variable and ranked in importance. Such an analysis can also lead to determining those values of key variables that approach a threshold of financial pain. That is, if the floating interest rate rose to a certain level, if a particular currency exchange rate fell to some other level, if the price of an important commodity rose or fell to another level, then the earnings would not be sufficient to satisfy the cash needs of the company. This defines the threshold of financial pain. Presumably, management is willing to pay for some degree of coverage to avoid the threshold of financial pain.

If the spreadsheet is designed to handle futures and options, and this is no small task, then it would be possible for management to compare a futures with a call from the point of view of avoiding financial pain for a given cost. A sophisticated spreadsheet may be able to provide information for management on how much coverage, and what form of coverage, should be taken to financially safeguard the company. A simulation is a very large number of what if scenarios. This, too, can be used as a risk management tool in deciding on the requisite degree of coverage. Simulations have been used to sort out the efficacy of various hedging programs relying on historic price fluctuations. The problem with this approach is the underlying assumption that the past is a prelude to the future. The fact that a specific hedging program worked best in the last five years is no guarantee that it is the best choice for the coming year.

Several companies have developed an in-house capability to analyze their exposure to risk and measure the effectiveness of various hedging techniques. Other companies rely on outside vendors who sell systems that are adaptable to the particulars of a company. Some of these systems are dedicated to handling currency exchange risk, because this is a risk faced by all global companies. Others cover a broader range of currency, interest, and commodity risks. Some confine their output to exposure to risk and tracking of hedges in place. Others provide analysis of alternatives, and some are better described as decision support systems because their output offers suggested optimal risk management strategies. There are about thirty software companies offering risk management systems. In addition, certain banks offer tracking and analysis systems to their clients.

Regardless of the nature of the software systems, the simplicity or complexity of what if spreadsheet models, or the nature of other computer aids, their purpose is to provide quantitative data to decision makers. There is little question that a well-designed quantitative model improves the quality of decisions. The designing of such models enhances the understanding of the participants in the inner financial workings of a corporation. On the other hand, models cannot run companies unless human judgment can be reduced to a series of 0's and 1's, the language of computers.

Judgment is more than 0's and 1's. Judgment is required in "what if" analysis because there must be management inputs on the perceived direction rates or prices may take in orchestrating the what if scenarios. Judgment is necessary in assessing volatility. Volatility itself must be judged by people because volatility is not predictable. Periods of calm with relative stability in prices or rates follow and precede periods of tumult. Management judgment is required in deciding on what must be avoided; that is, what is the threshold of financial pain for a company. Judgment also comes into play in deciding the degree and cost of the risk management product coverage necessary to avoid this pain. The final decision on which risk management program to implement must be made by management. No computer program can perceive the world better than a human mind, which, after all, is also the programmer of the computer. Therefore, risk management, like all management functions, is ultimately as effective as the people making the decisions.

APPENDIX: LISTING OF INTERNATIONAL ACCOUNTING ORGANIZATIONS

INTERNATIONAL ACCOUNTANCY INSTITUTES

ARGENTINA

Federacion Argentina de Graduados en
  Ciencias Economicas
Viamonte 1592 Piso 3
Buenos Aires 1055

Federacion Argentina de Consejos
  Profesionales en Ciencias Economicas
Viamonte 1145, 3.A
Buenos Aires 1053

AUSTRALIA

Australian Society of Accountants
Accountants House
170 Queen Street
Melbourne 3000

Institute of Chartered Accountants in
  Australia
GPO Box 3921 NSW
37 York Street
Sydney 2001

AUSTRIA

Institut Osterreichischer Wirstchaftsprufer
Bennoplatz 4
A-1081 (Vienna)

BAHAMAS

Bahamas Institute of Chartered
  Accountants
P.O. Box N-7037
Nassau

BANGLADESH

The Institute of Chartered Accountants of
  Bangladesh
Chartered Accountants Bhaban
16-17 Kawran Bazar
Commercial Complex
Dhaka 8

Institute of Cost and Management
  Accountants of Bangladesh
ICMA Bhavan Nilkhet
Post Box 2629
Dhaka 1205

BELGIUM

College Nationale des Experts
  Comptables de Belgique
49 Rue de Congres
Brussels 1000

Institut des Reviseurs d'Enterprises
Avenue Marnix 22
Brussels 1050

Chambre Belge des Comptables
2 Galerie de la Reine
Brussels 1000

Institut des Reviseurs Agrees par la
  Commission Bancaire
Avenue Louise 99
Brussels 1050

BELIZE

Institute of Chartered Accountants of
  Belize
22 Regent Street
P.O. Box 1235
Belize City

BERMUDA

The Institute of Chartered Accountants of
  Bermuda
P.O. Box HM 1625
Hamilton HM GX

BOLIVIA

Colegio de Contadores de Bolivia
Edificio Litoral Piso 7 Of. 1
Av. Mariscal Santa Cruz esq. Calle
  Colon
Casilla No. 21414
La Paz

Colegio de Professionals de Ciencias
  Economicas de Bolivia
St. Velasco No. 655
Casilla de Correo No. 601
Santa Cruz

BOTSWANA

Association of Accountants in Botswana
P.O. Box 448
Gaberone

BRAZIL

Instituto Brasileiro de Contadores-Ibracon
Rua Barao de Itapetininga
151-11 Andar CJ 114
Sao Paulo 01042, SP

BURMA

Burma Society of Accountants
54 Latha Street
Rangoon

CANADA

The Canadian Institute of Chartered
  Accountants
150 Bloor Street West
Toronto M5S 2Y2

Certified General Accountants'
  Association of Canada
Suite 740 — 1176 West Georgia Street
Vancouver, B.C. V6E 4A2

The Society of Management Accountants
  of Canada
154 Main Street East
P.O. Box 176 M.P.O.
Hamilton, Ontario L8N 3C3

CHILE

Colegio de Contadores de Chile, A.C.
Dieciocho 121
Casilla 10201
Santiago

CHINA

Accounting Society of China
Ministray of Finance
San Li He — Beijing
People's Republic of China

National Federation of Certified Public
Accountants Associations of the
Republic of China
10th Floor
142 Chung-Hsiao E. Road
Sec. 4
Taipei, Taiwan
Republic of China

The Chinese Institute of Certified Public
Accountants
2 Nan Heng Jie, San Lie He, Xi Cheng
Qu, Beijing 100045

COLOMBIA

Instituto National de Contadores Publicos
de Colombia
Carrera 71, 27-52 piso 4o.
Apartado aereo 6275
Bogota, D.E.

COSTA RICA

Colegio de Contadores Publicos de Costa
Rica
Apartado 4368
San Jose

CUBA

Asociation de Contadores de Cuba en el
Exilio
4545 N.W. 7th Street, Suite 14
Miami, Florida 33126

CYPRUS

The Institute of Certified Public
Accountants of Cyprus
Charalambides Building
4th Floor
Grivas Dighenis Avenue
P.O. Box 1657
Nicosia

DENMARK

Foreningen af Registrerede Revisorer
Frr-Huset
Flintholm Alle 8
Postboks 90
DK 2000 Frederiksberg

Foreningen af Statsautoriserede Revisorer
Kronprinsessegade 8
2306 Copenhagen

DOMINICAN REPUBLIC

Instituto de Contadores Publicos de la
Republica Dominicana
Edificio Induca, 2da. planta
Ave. Jose Ortega y Gasset esq. Av.
San Martin
Apartado postal 1082
Santo Domingo

ECUADOR

Federacion Nacional de Contadores del
Ecuador
Calle Acuna 637 y Av. America
Casilla 2197
Quito

EGYPT

Egyptian Society of Accountants and
Auditors
P.O. Box 216
Cairo

EL SALVADOR

Asociacion de Contadores Publicos de el
Salvador
Villa Fontana Rosa
Calle la Reforma 133
Colonia San Benito
San Salvador

Corporacion de Contadores de el
Salvador
Villa Fontana Rosa
Calle la Reforma 133
Colonia San Benito
San Salvador

ENGLAND

Institute of Chartered Accountants in
England and Wales
Chartered Accountants' Hall
Moorgate Place
P.O. Box 433
London EC2P 2BJ

The Chartered Institute of Management
  Accountants
63 Portland Place
London WIN 4AB

The Chartered Institute of Public Finance
  and Accountancy
3 Robert Street
London WC2N 6BH

The Association of Cost and Executive
  Accountants
Tower House
141-149 Fonthill Road
London N4 3HF

The Association of International
  Accountants
2-10 St. John Street
Bedford, England MK42 ODW

The Chartered Association of Certified
  Accountants
29 Lincoln's Inn Field
London WC2A 3EE

ETHIOPIA

Ethiopian Professional Associations of
  Accountants and Auditors
P.O. Box 457
Addis Ababa

FIJI

Fiji Institute of Accountants
Fiji Professional Centre
  1 DesVouex Road
  P.O. Box 681
  Suva

FINLAND

KHT - Yhdistys Foreningen CGR
Fredrikinkatu 61A
00100 Helsinki 10

FRANCE

Ordre des Experts Comptables et des
  Comptables Agrees
109 Boulevard Malesherbes
75008 Paris

Compagnie Nationale des Commissaires
  aux Comptes
6 rue de l'Amiral-de-Coligny
75001 Paris

GERMANY

Institut der Wirtschaftsprufer in
  Deutschland
Tersteegenstrasse 14
Postfach 32 05 80
4000 Dusseldorf 30

GHANA

Institute of Chartered Accountants
P.O. Box 4268
Liberty Avenue
Swanmill, Accra

GREECE

Institute of Certified Public Accountants
  of Greece
28 Kapodistriou Street
Athens 147

The Institute of Incorporated Public
  Accountants
53, Patission Street
R-104 33 Athens

Association of Certified Accountants and
  Auditors of Greece
POB 11085, 103 10
Athens

GUATEMALA

Corporacion de Contadores de Guatemala
61, Avenida 9-50 Zona 1
Apartado Postal 441
Guatemala, C.A.

Instituto Guatemalteco de Contadores
  Publicos Auditores
Edificio PANAM 6to
6a. Ave. 11-43 Zona 1
Efs. 8-3 y 4 6to nivel
Guatemala, C.A.

Colegios de Economistas, Contadores
  Publicos y Auditores
Avenida Elena 14-45 Zona 1
Guatemala City

Asociation Nacional de Contadores
Apartado 488
Guatemala City

GUYANA

Institute of Chartered Accountants of
  Guyana
P.O. Box 786
Georgetown, Demerara

HAITI

Ordre des Comptables Professionnels
  Agrees D'Haiti
196, Angle Lalue et lere
Impasse Lavaud (Etage)
Port-Au-Prince

HONDURAS

Colegio de Peritos Mercantiles &
  Contadores Publicos de Honduras
Apartado Postal 588
Tegucigalpa, D.C.
Honduras, C.A.

HONG KONG

Hong Kong Society of Accountants
17th Floor, Belgian House
77-79 Gloucester Road
Wanchai

Association of Chartered Accountants in
  Hong Kong
P.O. Box 13428

ICELAND

Felag Loggiltra Endurskodenda
P.O. Box 945
Reykjavik

INDIA

Institute of Chartered Accountants of
  . India
P.O. Box 7100
Indraprastha Marg
New Delhi 110 002

The Institute of Cost and Works
  Accountants of India
12 Sudder Street
Calcutta 700 016

INDONESIA

Indonesian Institute of Accountants
Gatot Subroto St., KAV 54
Iisma Baja Bldg., 7th Floor
Jakarta 12790

IRELAND

Institute of Chartered Accountants in
  Ireland
87-89 Pembroke Road
Ballsbridge
Dublin 4

The Institute of Certified Public
  Accountants in Ireland
22 Upper Fitzwilliam Street
Dublin 2

ISRAEL

Institute of Certified Public Accountants
  in Israel
1 Montefiore Street
P.O. Box 29281
Tel-Aviv 61292

ITALY

Consiglio Nazionale dei Dottori
  Commercialisti
Via Poli 29
Rome 00187

Consiglio Nazionale dei Ragionieri e
  Periti Commerciali
Via F. Paisiello 24
Rome 00198

Federazione Nazionale del Collegi dei
  Ragionieri
Piazza Scuole Pie
7-9 Bis.
16123 Genoa

Instituto di Richerche Economico-
  Aziendali
Piazza Arbarello, 8
Turin

JAPAN

Japanese Institute of Certified Public
  Accountants
5-18-3, Hongo 5 chome
Bunkyo-ku
Tokyo 113

JORDAN

Arab Society of Certified Accountants
Housin Bank Center, 7th Floor
Near the Ministry of Interior
P.O. Box 921100
Amman, Hashemite

Arab Society of Certified Accountants
ASCA House
148 The Strand
London, England, WC2R IJA

KENYA

Association of Accountants in East Africa
P.O. Box 40716
Nairobi

Institute of Certified Public Accountants
  of Kenya
P.O. Box 59963
Nairobi

LIBERIA

Liberian Institute of CPAs
P.O. Box 4179
Monrovia

LUXEMBOURG

Ordre des Experts Comptables
  Luxembourgeois
7 rue Alcide de Gasperi
B.P. 1362
1013 Luxembourg — Kirchberg

MALAYSIA

Malaysian Association of Certified Public
  Accountants
15 Jalan Medan Tuanku
50300 Kuala Lumpur

Malaysian Institute of Accountants
111 Kompleks Antarabangsa
Jalan Sultan Ismail
50250 Kuala Lumpur

MALTA

The Institute of Accountants
1 Wilga Street
Paceville, St. Julians

MEXICO

Instituto Mexicano de Contadores
  Publicos
Tabachines 44
Bosques de las Lomas
Mexico 11700, D.F.

Colegio de Contadores Publicos de
  Mexico, A.C.
Dolores 17
40 Mexico, 1 D.F.

MIDDLE EAST

Middle East Society of Associated
  Accountants
P.O. Box 6972
Beirut, Lebanon

MONACO

Conseil de l'Ordre des Experts
  Comptables de Monaco
30 Boulevard Princesse Charlotte
Monte Carlo

NETHERLANDS

Nederlands Instituut van
  Registeraccountants
Mensinge 2
Postbus 7984
1008 AD Amsterdam

NEW ZEALAND

New Zealand Society of Accountants
Willbank House
57 Willis Street
P.O. Box 11342
Wellington

NICARAGUA

Colegio de Contadores de Nicaragua
Apartado 1172
Managua

NIGERIA

The Institute of Chartered Accountants of
  Nigeria
Idown Taylor Street
Victoria Island
P.O. Box 1580
Lagos

NORWAY

Norges Statsautoriserte Revisorers
  Forening
Hranienborg terrasse 9
Oslo 3

PAKISTAN

The Institute of Chartered Accountants of
  Pakistan
G-31/8, Kehkashan, Clifton
Karachi — 75600-11

Institute of Cost and Management
  Accountants of Pakistan
Hussain Shah Shaheed Road
Soldier Bazaar
P.O. Box 7284
Karachi — 3

PANAMA

Colegio de Contadores Autorizados de
  Panama
Calle 31 Este no. 32
Apartado 1101
Panama 1

Asociacion de Mujeres Contadores de
  Panama
Edificio Santa Monica
Urb. Campo Alegre Calle 52
y Ricardo Arias local 2-6
Apartado Postal 4103
Panama 5

Asociacion de Contadores Publicos
  Autorizados de Panama
Apartado 6-4835
El Dorado

PAPUA NEW GUINEA

Papua New Guinea Association of
  Accountants
P.O. Box 5831
Boroko, N.C.D.
Papua

PARAGUAY

Colegio de Contadores del Paraguay
Yegros 860
Casilla de Correo no. 2932
Asuncion

PERU

Federacion de Colegios de Contadores
  Publicos del Peru
Av. Arequipa no. 998
Apartado 140386
Lima 14

Instituto de Contadores del Peru
Carabaya 780
Lima

PHILIPPINES

Philippine Institute of Certified Public
Accountants
PICPA Building
700 Shaw Boulevard
Mandaluyong
P.O. Box 1440
Metro Manila

PORTUGAL

Sociedade Portuguesa de Contabilidade
Rua Barata Salgueiro 1, 2 E
1100 Lisbon 2

PUERTO RICO

Colegio de Contadores Publicos
Autorizados de Puerto Rico
Edificio Esquire 2do. piso
Calle Vela esq. Ponce de Leon
Hato Rey, PR 00918
Call Box 73152
San Juan, PR 00936

SAMOA

Western Samoa Society of Accountants
P.O. Box 146
Apia, Western Samoa

SCOTLAND

Institute of Chartered Accountants of
Scotland
27 Queen Street
Edinburgh EH2 1LA

SENEGAL

Amicale des Comptables Professionnels
du Senegal
Chambre de Commerce de Dakar
B.P. 118
Dakar

SINGAPORE

Institute of Certified Public Accountants
of Singapore
116 Middle Road #09-01/04
ICB Enterprise House
Singapore 0718

SOLOMON ISLANDS

Institute of Solomon Islands Accountants
(ISIA)
GPO Box 33
Honiara

SOUTH AFRICA

The South African Institute of Chartered
Accountants
7th Floor, Burlington House
22 Rissik Street
P.O. Box 964
Johannesburg 2000

SOUTH KOREA

Korean Institute of Certified Public
Accountants
KICPA Building
46-22 Soosong Dong Chongro-Ku
Seoul

SPAIN

Spanish Association of Accounting and
Tax Administration
Alberto Aguilera
31, 5 derecha
28015 Madrid

SRI LANKA

The Institute of Chartered Accountants of
Sri Lanka
30A Longden Place
Colombo 7

Institute of Cost and Management
Accountants
3 Havelock Road
Colombo 7

ST. LUCIA

Institute of Chartered Accountants of St.
Lucia
P.O. Box 195
Castries
St. Lucia

SWEDEN

Foreningen Auktoriserade Revisorer
Norrtullsgatan 6
box 6417
S-113-82 Stockholm

SWITZERLAND

Schweizerische Treuhand-und
  Revisionskammer
Limmatquai 120
8001 Zurich

TANZANIA

Tanzania Association of Accountants
P.O. Box 459
Dar es Salaam

The National Board of Accountants and
  Auditors
NIC Investment House
P.O. Box 5128
Dar es Salaam

THAILAND

Institute of Certified Accountants and
  Auditors of Thailand
60/31-3, 9th floor
ITF Silom Palace Building
Bangrug

TURKEY

Turkiye Muhasebe Uzmanlari Dernegi
P.O. Box 508
Karakoy, Istanbul

UNITED STATES OF AMERICA

American Institute of Certified Public
  Accountants
1211 Avenue of the Americas
New York, NY 10036

Institute of Management Accountants
10 Paragon Drive
Montvale, NJ 07645

American Accounting Association
5717 Bessie Drive
Sarasota, FL 34233

Institute of Internal Auditors
249 Maitland Avenue
P.O. Box 1119
Altamonte Springs, FL 32701

URUGUAY

Colegio de Doctores en Ciencias
  Economicas y Contadores del Uruguay
Colonial 981, piso 1
Montevideo

VENEZUELA

Asociacion de Contadores de Venezuela
Apartado del Este 61325
Caracas

Federacion de Colegios de Contadores
  Publicos de Venezuela
Apartado 61548
Caracas

Colegio Nacional de Tecnicos en
  Contabilidad
Apartado del Este 61325
Chacao - Caracas

WEST INDIES

The Institute of Chartered Accountants of
  Barbados
P.O. Box 111
Bridgetown, Barbados

Institute of Chartered Accountants of
  Jamaica
8 Ruthven Road
P.O. Box 333
Kingston 10
Jamaica

Institute of Chartered Accountants of
  Trinidad and Tobago
67 Independence Square
P.O. Box 864
Port of Spain, Trinidad

YUGOSLAVIA

Yugoslav Association of Accountants and
  Financial Experts
Njegoseva 19
11000 Belgrade

ZAMBIA

Zambia Association of Accountants
The Professional Centre of Zambia
P.O. Box 3730, Chadwick House
Chachacha Road, Lusaka

ZIMBABWE

The Institute of Chartered Accountants of
    Zimbabwe
52 Gordon Avenue
Fourth Street
P.O. Box 8197
Causeway, Harare

INTERNATIONAL
ORGANIZATIONS

AABWA

Association of Accountancy Bodies in
    West Africa
1 Dowu Taylor Street
Victoria Island
P.O. Box 1580, Lagos
Nigeria

AAC

African Accounting Council
B.P. 11.223 KIN1
Kinshasa
Zaire

IAA

Interamerican Accounting Association
Edificio Hache, John F. Kennedy Avenue
Apartado Postal 1467
Santo Domingo, Dominican Republic

IASC

International Accounting Standards
    Committee
167 Fleet Street
London EC4A 2ES
England

IFAC

International Federation of Accountants
540 Madison Avenue
New York, NY 10022

CAPA

Confederation of Asian and Pacific
    Accountants
P.O. Box 4516
Manila, Philippines 2800

FEE

Federation des Experts Comptables
    Europeans
83 rue de la loi
1040 Brussels
Belgium

NORDIC FEDERATION OF
ACCOUNTANTS

Norges Statautoriserte Revisorers
    Forening
Revisorenes Hus
Uranienborg Terrasse 9
0351 Oslo 3
Norway

SOUTHEAST ASIA FEDERATION
OF ACCOUNTANTS

Secretariat: The Institute of Cost and
    Management Accountants of
    Bangladesh
ICMA Bhaban
Nikhet
Dhaka - 1205
Bangladesh

BIBLIOGRAPHY

PERIODICALS

Abbott, Hilary. "Standardized Financial Reporting." *International Accounting Bulletin* 38 (September 1986): 6–9.

Abdallah, Wagdy M. "Changing the Environment or Change the System." *Management Accounting* 68 (October 1986): 33–36.

Abdallah, Wagdy M. "How to Motivate and Evaluate Managers with International Transfer Pricing Systems." *MIR* 29 (January 1989): 65–71.

"Accounting for International Operations." *CPA Journal* 59 (October 1989): 63–65.

"Are European Company Annual Accounts Comparable?" *Brussels: Kredietbank Monthly Bulletin* 46 (March 1991): 1–6.

Balbo, Anthony. "Uncooking the Books." *Financial World* 160 (March 5, 1991): 34–35.

Bartlett, Christopher A., and Sumantra Ghosbal. "Managing Across Borders: New Strategic Requirements." *Sloan Management Review* 29 (Summer 1987): 48–53.

Beresford, Dennis. "Commentary: Internationalization of Accounting Standards." *Accounting Horizons* 4 (March 1990): 99–107.

Blake, John. "Issues in International Transfer Pricing." *Company Accountant* 102 (June 1991): 22–24, 28.

Blake, John. "Problems in International Accounting Harmonization." *Management Accounting* 68 (February 1990): 28–31.

Bloom, Robert, and Araya Debessay. "A Comparative Analysis of Recent Pronouncements on Accounting for Changing Prices." *The International Journal of Accounting Research* 19 (Spring 1984): 119–138.

Bourguignon, J. C. "The 1990's: Wither Europe 1992." *CMA Magazine* 63 (December/January 1990): 30–31.

Bowes, Elena. "Top Of The Bloc: Ninety for The Nineties." *FW* 159 (March 6, 1990): 56–61.

Cairns, David. "AASC's Blueprint for the Future." *Accountancy* 104 (December 1989): 80–82.

Carey, Anthony. "Harmonisation, Europe Moves Forward." *Accountancy* 105 (March 1990): 92–93.

Cats-Baril, William, James F. Gatti, and D. Jacque Grinnell. "Transfer Pricing in a Dynamic Market." *Management Accounting* 69 (February 1988): 40–44.

Chandler, Roy. "IFAC: The Consensus-Seekers." *Accountancy U.K.* 106 (July 1990): 84–86.

"The Chase Guide to Risk Management Products." *Risk Magazine* (1992): 3–32.

Cheney, Glen Alan. "Soviet-American Financial Coexistence." *Journal of Accountancy* 169 (January 1990): 68–72.

Cheney, Glen Alan. "Western Accounting Arrives in Eastern Europe." *Journal of Accountancy* 170 (September 1990): 40–43.

Choi, Frederick D. S., and Vinod B. Bavishi. "Diversity in Multinational Accounting." *Financial Executive* 50 (August 1982): 46–49.

Cinnamon, Allan, and Zigurds Kronhergs. "EC Mergers Directive." *Accountancy U.K.* 107 (January 1991) 48.

Clarke, Pamela. "New Kids on the Bloc." *CA Magazine* 123 (July 1990): 17–22.

Cohen, Roger. "Argentine Roulette." *Wall Street Journal*, 23, September 1988, 13R.

Copeland, Tom, Tim Kolher, and Jack Murrin. "How to Value a Multinational Business." *Planning Review* 18 (May/June 1990): 16–24.

de Cerqueira Leite, E. "Transfer Pricing in Brazil." *1991 International Bureau of Fiscal Documentation* (February 1991): 76–79.

"Defective Accountants East & West." *Accountancy U.K.* 105 (February 1990).

Donleavy, G. D. "Aspects of Hungarian Accounting." *Advances in International Accounting* 1 (Fall 1987): 85–109.

Doost, Roger K., and Karen M. Ligon. "How U.S. and European Accounting Practices Differ." *Management Accounting* 68 (October 1986): 38–41.

Doupnik, Timothy S. "The Brazillian System of Monetary Correction." *Advances in International Accounting* 1 (Fall 1987): 111–135.

"Facts from IFAC." *CA Magazine* 123 (November 1990): 14.

Financial Accounting Standards Board. *Statement of Financial Accounting Standards No. 8.* "Accounting for the Translation of Foreign Currency Transactions and Foreign Currency Financial Statements." (FASB, 1975).

Financial Accounting Standards Board. *Statement of Financial Accounting Standards No. 52.* "Foreign Currency Translation." (FASB, 1981).

Financial Accounting Standards Board. *Statement of Financial Accounting Standards No. 80.* "Accounting for Futures Contracts." (FASB, 1984).

Financial Accounting Standards Board. *Statement of Financial Accounting Standards No. 105.* "Disclosure of Information About Financial Instruments with Off-Balance-Sheet Risk and Financial Instruments with Concentrations of Credit Risk." (FASB, 1990).

"Firms Gain Foothold Behind the Iron Curtain." *Accountancy U.K.* 107 (October 1992).

Fuhrman, Peter. "Esperanto for Accountants." *Forbes*, 18 March 1991, p. 72.

Genetelli, Richard W. "Significant Unitary Developments in California May Provide Refund Opportunities." *CPA Journal* 61 (August 1991): 65–66.

"Global Finance Rankings: The World's 100 Largest Public Companies." *Wall Street Journal* 23 September 1988, p. 20R.

Grey, Sarah, Elizabeth Fisher, and Flavia Hawksley. "Accountants Stand by as East Approaches West." *CPA Journal* 60 (October 1990): 103.

Grey, Sarah, Flavia Hawksley, Julia Irvine, and Elizabeth Fisher. "Getting Down to Business." *Accountancy U.K.* 106 (August 1990): 66–72.

Groot, Bert, and Peter Holgate. "Accounting in the Netherlands." *Accountancy UK* 108 (July 1991): 55.

Gupta, Parveen P. "International Reciprocity in Accounting." *Journal of Accountancy* 173 (January 1992): 46.

Heaston, Patrick H. "Qualification Requirements for Public Accounting in Select Foreign Countries: A Comparison with the United States." *International Journal of Accounting Education and Research* 20, no. 1 (Fall 1984): 77–94.

Hegarty, John. "Breaking Down The Barriers." *New Accountant* (December 1990) 23–26.

Horner, Larry. "Issues." *World*, November/December 1985, p. 4. International Accounting Standards Committee. *International Accounting Standard No. 21.* "Accounting for the Effects of Changes in Foreign Exchange Rates." (IASC, 1984).

International Accounting Standards Committee. *International Accounting Standard No. 29.* "Financial Reporting in Hyperinflationary Economies." (IASC, 1989).

Irvine, V. Bruce. "Setting Accounting Standards for the World." *CMA Magazine* 62 (April 1988): 13–17.

"Japanese Management Accounting: A Comparative Survey." *Management Accounting* 71 (November 1989): 20–23.

Jaruga, Alicja A. "The Evolution of Accounting in East European Nations." Paper unpublished 1989.

Jaruga, Alicja A. "Governmental Accounting, Auditing, and Financial Reporting in Eastern European Nations." Published paper Mossey University, Palmerston North, N.Z. 84 (1989).

Jayson, Susan. "IFAC's Traveling Salesmen." *Management Accounting* 68 (October 1986): 22–25.

Joseph, M. S. "Hedge Accounting Puzzle Clarified." *Corporate Risk Management* 3 (March 1991): 8–9.

Kanaga, Williams. "International Accounting: The Challenge and the Change." *Journal of Accountancy* 162 (November 1986): 55–60.

Karpen, Patrick N., and Robert N. Aginian. "European Community Finance Ministers Agree on Direct Tax Measures." *The Michigan CPA* 42 (Fall 1990): 80–81.

Keslar, L. "U.S. Accounting: Creating an Uneven Playing Field?" *Corporate Risk Management* (February 1991): 20–25. vol. 3

Kim, Il-Woon, and Ja Song. "U.S., Korea, and Japan: Accounting Practices in Three Countries." *Management Accounting* 72 (August 1990): 26–30.

Kinast, Andrew. "Pomoc Potrzebna, Come and Help Us." *Accountancy* 105 (February 1990): 21.

Kislyakov, M. "Oh, East is East and West is West and Never the Twain Shall Meet." *Internal Auditor* 47 (October 1990): 25–29.

Kleeschulte, Chuck. "To the Waters Edge: Repeal of the Worldwide Unitary Tax." *Alaska Business Monthly* 7 (November 1991): 42–46.

Kvint, Vladimir. "Moscow Learns the Language of Business." *Journal of Accountancy* 17 (November 1990): 104–118.

Latanich, Gary A., and John Kominarides. "Accountants In International Business."
    International Journal of Accounting Research 19 (Spring 1984): 157-164.
Lesser, Frederic E. "Does Your Transfer Pricing Make Cents?" *Management Accounting*
    69, no. 6 (December 1987): 43–47.
Levey, Marc M., and Russ O'Haven. "Transfer Pricing Guidance Offered by Sunstrand."
    The Journal of International Taxation (July-August 1991): 69–77.
Loeffelholz, Suzanne. "Dealing on the Danube." *Financial World* 159 (6 March 1990):
    38–42.
"London's Bubbling Market in International Shares." *The Economist* 303 (30 May 1987):
    73–74.
Lowe, Howard D. "Shortcomings of Japanese Consolidated Financial Statements." *Ac-
    counting Horizons* 4 (September 1990): 1–9.
"Major Change in Apportionment for Unitary Business." *The Tax Advisor* 22, no. 7
    (July 1991): 438(2).
McConnell, Pat. "Accounting Issues: Los Fundamentos De la Contabilidad en Mexico."
    Investment Research. Bear Stearns and Company, Inc. New York, October 11,
    1991.
McDowell, Angus. "The Uncharted Minefield of U.S. Company Tax." *Accountancy*
    106 (August 1990): 28–29.
McKie, A. B. "Open up that Golden Gate." *Canadian Banker* 98 (May-June 1991):
    56–57.
"Management: New Qualifications for the CFO of the 80's." *The Week In Review*, 4
    May 1984, p. 18.
Miller, Stephen H. "Special Report: The Post Coup Soviet Union: Greater Role for
    CPAs." *Journal of Accountancy* 172 (November 1991): 24.
Millman, Gregory. "Currency Risk Management At Monsanto." *Management Account-
    ing* 72 (April 1991): 43–48.
Millman, Gregory J. "The Trauma of Transfer Pricing." *CFO* 7 (November 1991): 30–
    34.
Millman, Gregory J. "Will Audits Spell Tax Disaster?" *Corporate Risk Management* 3
    (July 1991): 8–10.
Morais, Richard. "Invisible Ink: The Global Market Might Be Here, But the Accounting
    Standards To Go With It Are Not." *Forbes* (15 December 1986): 44.
Moravy, J., and A. Browning. "Before and After Statement 105." *Corporate Risk
    Management* 146 (November 1990): 38–39.
Morgese, Michael. "California Worldwide Unitary Taxation Held Unconstitutional."
    The Tax Advisor 22 (April 1992): 239(2).
Moulin, Donald J., and Morton B. Solomon. "Practical Means of Promoting Common
    International Standards." *CPA Journal* 59 (December 1989): 38-40, 45-46, 48.
Nobes, Christopher. "Setting Professional Standards." *International Accounting Bulletin*
    31 (January 1986): 13.
Nobes, Christopher. "The Importance of Thinking International." *International Ac-
    counting Bulletin* 33 (March 1986): 2
Nobes, Christopher. "Variations in Accounting Practices." *International Accounting
    Bulletin* 36 (June 1986):
Nobes, Christopher, and Sadayoshi Maeda. "Japanese Accounts: Interpreter's Needed."
    Accountancy U.K. 106 (September 1990): 82–84.

Nobes, Christopher, and Stefano Zambon. "Piano, Piano: Italy Implements the Directives." *Accountancy U.K.* 108 (July 1991): 84–85.

Nodar, Andrew L. "Coca-Cola Writes an Accounting Procedure Manual." *Management Accounting* 68 (October 1986): 52–53.

Norman, Peter. "Monetary Trade Off." *Wall Street Journal*, 23 September 1988, pp. 24R–25R

O'Connor, Walter F. "A Comparative Analysis of the Major Areas of Tax Controversy in Developed Countries." *Journal of International Accounting Auditing and Taxation* 1 (1992): 61–79.

Onak, M., and Lindrooth, B. "When Is a Hedge Not a Hedge?" *Corporate Risk Management* 3 (October 1991): 28–29.

"Pacioli: 1494!" *The CPA Journal* 61 (November 1991): 34.

Peavy, Dennis E., and Stuart K. Webster. "Is GAAP the GAP to International Markets?" *Management Accountancy* 72 (August 1990): 31.

Petzet, G. Alan. "Soviet Accounting Poses Problems." *Oil and Gas Journal* 88 (16 April 1990): 34–36.

Pfirman, Kathryn, and Dahli Gray. "International Affairs." *The Woman CPA* 51 (October 1989): 14–18.

Picker, Ida. "Indecent Exposure." *Institutional Investor* 25 (September 1991): 81 (3).

Pletka, Danielle. "Community's Goal: A State of Oneness." *Insight* (20 June 1988): 8–17.

Pryce, Vicky, and David Brown. "Economic Fundamentals in a State of Flux." *Accountancy U.K.* 106 (August 1990): 73–75.

Reier, Sharon. "Lessons of a Samba Dancer." *Financial World* 159 (6 March 1990): 66–67.

Rozvany, George. "Transfer Pricing: Nightmare on Elm Street." *Taxation in Australia* 25 (June 1991) 782–787.

Schmedel, Scott R. "Multinationals Must Chew Hard to Digest the Proposed Transfer Pricing Rules." *Wall Street Journal*, 29 January 1992, p. A1.

Schwarz, Jonathan S. "Transfer Pricing European Style." *The Journal of International Taxation* (July-August 1991): 120–123.

Slipkowski, John N. "IASC Chairman Kirkpatrick On International Standards." *Management Accounting* 68 (October 1986): 27–31.

Slipkowski, John N. "The Volvo Way of Financial Reporting." *Management Accounting* 70 (October 1988): 22–26.

Sutcliffe, Paul. "Towards An Australian Accounting Standard." *Australian Accountant* 60 (June 1990): 33–34.

Theunisse, Hilda. "Accounting and Reporting in Belgium." *Advances on International Accounting* 1 (Fall 1987): 191–248.

Van Hulle, Karen. "The EC Experience of Harmonisation: Part 1." *Accountancy U.K.* 104 (September 1989): 76–77.

Van Hulle, Karen. "The EC Experience of Harmonisation: Part 2." *Accountancy U.K.* 104 (October 1989): 96–99.

Viehe, Karl William. "Advance Pricing Agreements: Stability for Transfer Pricing." *The International Tax Journal* 18 (Winter 1991): 46–75.

Wallace, R. S. Olusegun. "Survival Strategies of a Global Organization." *Accounting Horizons* 4 (June 1990): 1–22.

Walsh, Mary Williams. "Riding the Golden Dragon." *Wall Street Journal*, 21 September 1988, pp. 5R–6R.

Weis, William, and David Tinius. "Luca Pacioli: Renaissance Accountant." *Journal of Accountancy* 172 (November 1991): pp. 95-102.

"Who's Where on the World Markets: How the Heavyweights Shape Up." *Euromoney* (May 1990): 56–66.

Wickham, Dale W. "The New U.S. Transfer Pricing Tax Penalty: A Solution, or a Symptom of the Causes, of the International Transfer Pricing Puzzle?" *The International Tax Journal* 18, no. 1 (Winter 1991): 1–45.

Yoshikawa, Takeo, John Innes and Falcones Mitchell. "Japanese Management Accounting: A Comparative Survey." *Management Accounting* 67 (November 1989): 20-23.

Vangermeersch, Richard. "The Route of the 7th Directive of The EEC on Consolidated Accounts—Slow, Steady, Studied and Successful." *International Journal of Accounting Education and Research* 20, no. 2 (1985): 103–118.

Zelenka, Ivan. "Czechoslovakia: The Curtain Rises on Joint Ventures." *Accountancy U.K.*, 106 (August 1990): 76-78.

BOOKS

Ahadiat, Nas. *Royal Apparel Company. A Case Study:* Carbondale, Illinois: Southern Illinois University, 1979.

Arpan, Jeffrey S., and Al Hashim. *International Dimensions of Accounting*. Boston, Mass.: Kent Publishing, 1984.

Arpan, Jeffrey S., and Lee H. Radebough. *International Accounting and Multinational Enterprises*. New York: John Wiley and Sons, 1985.

Belkaoui, Ahmed. *International Accounting: Issues and Situations*. Westport, Conn.: Quorum Books, 1985.

Business Guide To The Association Of South East Asia Nations. Washington, D.C.: U.S. Department of Commerce, International Trade Commission, 1980.

Choi, Frederick D. S. *Handbook of International Accounting*. New York: John Wiley and Sons, 1991.

Choi, Frederick D. S., and Gerhard G. Mueller. *International Accounting*. Englewood Cliffs, N.J.: Prentice-Hall, 1984.

Fox, Samuel, and Norling Rueschoff. *Principles of International Accounting*. Austin, Tex.: Austin Press, 1986.

The Future of Harmonization of Accounting Standards within the European Communities Conference. Brussels: Office of Official Publications of the European Communities, 1990.

Gray, S. J. *International Accounting and Transnational Decisions*. London: Butterworth, 1983.

Harris, Trevor. *Global Enterprises, Inc. A Case Study*. New York: Columbia University, 1988.

Holzer, H. Peter. *International Accounting*. New York, Harper and Row, 1984.

Marshall, John F., and Vipal K. Bonsal. *Financial Engineering*. Needham Heights, Mass.: Allyn and Bacon, 1992.

Naumes, William, ed. *Northeast DSI 1987 Proceedings of the 16th Annual Regional Conference*. Atlanta, Georgia: Decisions Science Institute. 2–3 April 1987.

Nobes, Christopher. *Accounting Harmonisation in Europe: Towards 1992*. London: Financial Times Business Information Ltd., 1990.

Nobes, Christopher. *The Baring Securities Guide to International Financial Reporting*. Oxford: Basil Blackwell Ltd., 1991.

Nobes, Christopher. *Interpreting European Financial Statements: Toward 1992*. London: Butterworths and Co., Ltd., 1989.

Nobes, Christopher, and Robert Parker. *Comparative International Accounting*. New York: St. Martin's Press, 1985.

Nobes, Christopher, and Robert Parker. *Issues in Multinational Accounting*. Oxford: Philip Allan Publishers, Ltd., 1988.

Palombra, H. *Multinational Corporations and Developing Countries*. New York: Conference Board, 23 January 1980.

Powell, Normat, and Frank Keller. *First Southwest Commerce Bancshares. A Case Study*. Clear Lake, Tex.: University of Houston, 1986.

Samuels, J. M., and A. G. Piper. *International Accounting: A Survey*. New York: St. Martin's Press, 1985.

Segmented Financial Information, Organization for Economic Cooperation and Development. Paris: OECD, 1990.

Shillinglaw, Gordon. *Strassli Holding, AG. A Case Study*. Lausanne, Switzerland: International Management Development Institute, 1965.

Spronck, Lambert H. *The Financial Executive's Handbook For Managing Multinational Corporations*. New York: John Wiley & Sons, 1980.

Sweeney, Allen, and Robert Rachlin. *Handbook of International Financial Management*. New York: McGraw Hill, 1984.

Treat, John Elting, ed. *Energy Futures: Trading Opportunities for the 1990s*. Tulsa, Okla.: Pennwell Publishing Co., 1990.

INDEX

About the Authors

JAMES A. HEELY is chair of the Accounting and Business Law Department at Monmouth College. He was Chief Financial Officer of J. J. Newberry Co., Vice President and Controller of the Sewing Products Group of the Singer Company, and Corporate Vice President and Controller of N. L. Industries. He is a Certified Public Accountant and maintains membership in the American Institute of Certified Public Accountants, the New York State Society of Certified Public Accountants, and the American Accounting Association and the Administrator of Accounting Programs Association.

ROY L. NERSESIAN is chair of the Management Department at Monmouth College. His previous books include *Ships and Shipping* (1981), *Computer Simulation in Business Decision Making (Quorum, 1989), Corporate Planning, Human Behavior, and Computer Simulation* (Quorum, 1990), and *Computer Simulation in Financial Risk Management* (Quorum, 1991).